The Civil Procedure Rules at 20

The Civil Procedure Rules at 20

Edited by
ANDREW HIGGINS
Associate Professor of Civil Procedure
University of Oxford and Mansfield College

OXFORD
UNIVERSITY PRESS

OXFORD
UNIVERSITY PRESS

Great Clarendon Street, Oxford, OX2 6DP,
United Kingdom

Oxford University Press is a department of the University of Oxford.
It furthers the University's objective of excellence in research, scholarship,
and education by publishing worldwide. Oxford is a registered trade mark of
Oxford University Press in the UK and in certain other countries

First Edition published in 2020

Impression: 2

Published in the United States of America by Oxford University Press
198 Madison Avenue, New York, NY 10016, United States of America

British Library Cataloguing in Publication Data

Data available

Library of Congress Control Number: 2020937904

ISBN 978–0–19–886318–2

Printed and bound by
CPI Group (UK) Ltd, Croydon, CR0 4YY

Foreword

It feels strange to be celebrating the anniversary of such a generally unloved young creature as the CPR. There are many, some in very high places, whose dearest wish is that it might be towed out to sea and sunk. Almost everyone laments its length, or at least the length of the White Book in which it is presented and explained to the world. Why should a modern rule book for the civil courts be longer than the King James Bible, they ask. How can the conventional view that everyone is expected to know the rules be reconciled with their almost complete inaccessibility to the increasing number of litigants in person using the courts after the virtual disappearance of civil Legal Aid? Why is almost everything laid down twice, once in a rule and then again in a practice direction? This ugly duckling is never going to transform itself into a swan, however large it grows.

And yet, and yet . . . there really is something, quite a lot in fact, worth celebrating. The CPR have been the medium for the introduction of a genuinely new and ground-breaking procedural *leitmotiv*: the Overriding Objective, which has at least started to introduce notions of proportionality, common sense and just a little discipline into civil litigation, even if the endless battle against excessive cost is still to be won. The CPR has somehow, due to the untiring work of the Rule Committee and its supporting staff, just about managed to retain procedural control over an unprecedented increase in the complexity of the civil law, and in the number of increasingly self-contained specialisations within it. It has been an extraordinary success as an export to numerous common law jurisdictions around the world, none of whom were compelled to choose it as a model to regulate their civil procedure. And by the imaginative and skilful use of pilot practice directions it is supervising and even contributing positively to the development and staged roll-out of the civil Online Court, due to the repeated failure of Parliament to pass the primary legislation needed to create a system of bespoke online rules.

One day maybe the Online Court will make procedure rules redundant, or at least liberate court users from having to read, learn or understand them. This is because the underlying thinking behind the design of the Online Court is that its users (lay as well as professional) will only have to obey one rule: do what it tells you to do on the screen. Mobile phone prompts will remind court users of time limits. There will still of course need to be statutory authority for the software writers to create the screens, probably in the form of rules, but they will be nothing remotely like the CPR. I hope that this will eventually come to pass, but it will be a long, hard journey. In the meantime, like the steam locomotive in the 1950s and 1960s, the CPR will continue to do its job, grimy, unloved, its eventual demise lamented only by a few eccentric enthusiasts, but still absolutely necessary for the rule of law.

This short collection of contributions, from the most authoritative sources, goes a long way to explain how the CPR has been designed and developed to meet the needs of civil court users. It justly celebrates the painstaking and usually unpaid hard work of those, on the Rule Committee and elsewhere, who have kept it up to date and relevant, something that I was privileged to witness during two sessions on the committee, latterly as its de facto (but strictly deputy) chair. These contributions come from a galaxy of those best qualified to tell this story, from judges, practitioners and academic scholars each with their own unique perspective. They were originally delivered orally to a celebratory conference at the Bonavero Institute of Human Rights at Mansfield College, Oxford last year, to which I was lucky enough to be invited. It is good now to have these contributions available in writing to a wider audience, in the form of a permanent record. I commend it to any serious student or user of the CPR, and to those, many yet to be chosen, who will have the responsibility of developing our civil procedure in an uncertain future.

Lord Briggs of Westbourne
Supreme Court

Preface

On the 10th June 2019 the Bonavero Institute of Human Rights, one of the Oxford Law Faculty's five research centres, and Mansfield College, jointly hosted 'The CPR at 20', a conference to mark the twentieth anniversary of the Civil Procedure Rules coming into force.

As conference organiser I deliberately used the word "mark" rather than "celebrate" the anniversary because I was aware that views on the success of the CPR vary widely, as Lord Briggs' foreword vividly demonstrates.

I set out my own tribute to Lord Woolf's vision and, in particular, the proportionality principle introduced into the new overriding objective, in my chapter in the book. Yet every judge, practitioner, and scholar, myself included, will have their gripes with aspects of the CPR that are overly complicated, unclear, or plainly unsatisfactory. Not all of these faults can be laid at Lord Woolf's door. Even the CPR in its original form departed in significant respects from Lord Woolf's recommendation in his landmark access to justice report.

Over the last twenty years the influence of politics and events has also played its part in the development of the CPR. This includes the introduction, and subsequent expansion, of special rules governing closed material proceedings (or 'secret courts') in which judges hear evidence in the absence of one or more parties, due to its sensitive nature and concerns that disclosure to even the parties might compromise national security. That these special and controversial procedures depart radically from Lord Woolf's vision is evident from the fact that in CPR 82 the overriding objective is expressly modified, and made subject to national security interests. Other notable changes to the CPR include government initiated reforms designed to restrict the scope of, and use of, judicial review and the regular if not constant tinkering with the disclosure and costs rules with the aim of trying to get a grip on the rising and often disproportionate costs of litigation. In other areas there have been reforms outside the scope of the CPR because lawmakers did not want to make certain procedural reforms generally applicable to all proceedings – such as the introduction of competition class actions before Competition Appeal Tribunal. This, and the expansion of other specialist Tribunals, has had some impact on the unitary and trans-substantive nature of the CPR which allows litigants to use one set of rules from small claims in the County Court to appeals before the Court of

Appeal. On the other hand, the success of Lord Woolf's reforms can be seen in their influence in the drafting of the Tribunals' procedural rules and the export of many key features of the CPR, especially the overriding objective, to other common law jurisdictions including my home country Australia.

It was because of these significant changes to the CPR and the civil justice system more broadly that I wanted the conference to go beyond the "standard fare" of procedure to include consideration of these major developments as well as the challenges and opportunities presented by the digitisation of the justice system, and possible use of machine learning in the court room.

We were extremely fortunate to have a long list of distinguished current and former judges, practitioners, and scholars working in this field to present on these topics and chair sessions. Lord Justice Peter Coulson opined it may be the first time in English legal history where we have had three Masters of the Rolls contributing to the same forum. I am deeply grateful to all the contributors of this book who have carefully edited their presentations, and in many cases substantially expanded them to create full papers, for the purposes of this edited collection.

There are a lot of other people to thank for making both the conference and this book possible. In no particular order, thank you to Herbert Smith Freehills for sponsoring the event; Professor Kate O'Regan of the Bonavero Institute of Human Rights and Helen Mountfield QC, Principal of Mansfield College for jointly hosting the conference; Jess Allen for providing me with valuable assistance in organising the conference and preparing transcripts; all the Mansfield Law student volunteers and the staff of the Bonavero Institute, the Oxford Law Faculty, and Mansfield College who helped the event run smoothly on the day; and to Jamie Berezin and the team at Oxford University Press for overseeing this book from start to end.

Who knows what the CPR, or any digital successor to it as predicted by Lord Briggs, will look like in 10 years or 20 years' time? As I write, England and the world are in the grip of the COVID-19 pandemic. Change to all aspects of life, including the justice system, are being forced upon us. While it is a miserable time for everyone, the old cliché that in every crisis there is opportunity is surely also true of the justice system. Judges are presently holding wall to wall skype meetings and hearings. 2020 could tell us a lot about the potential of a digital justice system: what works, what works better than the current system, and what needs further work.

The one thing we can say for sure about the next milestone anniversary of the CPR is that there will still be plenty to write about by those applying, using, and studying the rules, and some of what they write will come as a surprise to those working in the field now. We can, however, confidently assert that whatever the future court room looks like, and whatever the content of the rules regulating civil litigation, one constant will be the recognition that an accessible justice system is an indispensable pillar of a society governed by the rule of law. In the words of Lord Reed in the landmark Unison case [2017] UKSC 51:

> Courts exist in order to ensure that the laws made by Parliament, and the common law created by the courts themselves, are applied and enforced. That role includes ensuring that the executive branch of government carries out its functions in accordance with the law. In order for the courts to perform that role, people must in principle have unimpeded access to them. Without such access, laws are liable to become a dead letter, the work done by Parliament may be rendered nugatory, and the democratic election of Members of Parliament may become a meaningless charade.

That is a passage that deserves to be, and will surely be, recited for many decades to come.

Andrew Higgins
March 2020.

Table of Contents

PART III COLLECTIVE REDRESS

PART IV DISCLOSURE

PART V JUDICIAL REVIEW

PART VI COSTS AND FUNDING

PART VII NATIONAL SECURITY

PART VIII TECHNOLOGY

List of Contributors

Ruth Allen is a Professional Support Lawyer at Herbert Smith Freehills LLP.

Rabeea Assy is Associate Professor, Faculty of Law at the University of Haifa.

Lord Michael Briggs of Westbourne is a Justice of the Supreme Court.

Mr Justice Martin Chamberlain is a Judge in the Queen's Bench Division of the High Court.

Lord Justice Peter Coulson is Deputy Head of Civil Justice and Chair of the Civil Procedure Rule Committee.

Lord John Dyson is an Arbitrator at 39 Essex Chambers and former Master of the Rolls and Justice of the Supreme Court.

Sir Terence Etherton MR is the Master of the Rolls and Head of Civil Justice.

Richard Goodman is Change Director at HM Courts & Tribunals Service.

Andrew Higgins is Associate Professor of Civil Procedure, Faculty of Law and Fellow of Mansfield College, University of Oxford.

Damien Byrne Hill is Managing Partner, Disputes, at Herbert Smith Freehills LLP.

Charles Hollander QC is a Barrister in Brick Court Chambers London and Temple Chambers Hong Kong; Deputy High Court Judge.

Hayley J. Hooper is Associate Professor of Law at Harris Manchester College, University of Oxford.

Sir Rupert Jackson is an Arbitrator at New Square Chambers and Former Justice of the Court of Appeal for England & Wales.

Mrs Justice Nathalie Lieven is a Judge in the Family Division of the High Court.

Maura McIntosh is a Professional Support Consultant at Herbert Smith Freehills LLP.

Rachael Mulheron is Professor of Tort Law and Civil Justice, Department of Law, Queen Mary University of London, UK.

Lord David Neuberger of Abbotsbury is an Arbitrator at One Essex Court and former President of the Supreme Court and Master of the Rolls.

Professor Kate O'Regan is Director of Bonavero Institute of Human Rights, Faculty of Law, University of Oxford.

Alison Pickup is Legal Director at the Public Law Project.

Sir Ernest Ryder is the Senior President of Tribunals.

Professor Stuart Sime is BPTC Programme Director, Associate Dean and Head of Department of the academic programmes at The City Law School, City, University of London.

John Sorabji is a barrister and was previously the Principal Legal Adviser to the Lord Chief Justice and Master of the Rolls; Senior Teaching Fellow at University College London.

Maurice Sunkin QC (Hon) is Professor of Public Law and Socio Legal Studies, University of Essex.

Joe Tomlinson is Senior Lecturer in Public Law at the University of York and Research Director at the Public Law Project.

Stephen Wisking is Managing Partner of Competition, Regulation and Trade a Partner at Herbert Smith Freehills LLP.

Adrian Zuckerman is Emeritus Professor of Civil Procedure at the University of Oxford.

List of Abbreviations

ADR	alternative dispute resolution
AI	artificial intelligence
APIL	Association of Personal Injury Lawyers
ATE	after-the-event [insurance]
BTE	before-the-event [insurance]
CA98	Competition Act 1998
CAT	Competition Appeal Tribunal
CCO	cost capping order
CJC	Civil Justice Council
CLSA	Courts and Legal Services Act 1990
CMA	Competition and Markets Authority
CMP	closed material procedure
CPO	collective proceedings order
CPR	Court Procedure Rules
CPRC	Civil Procedure Rule Committee
ECHR	European Convention on Human Rights
ECtHR	European Court of Human Rights
GLO	group litigation order
HMCTS	HM Courts & Tribunals Service
IPEC	Intellectual Property and Enterprise Court
LEI	legal expenses insurance
LiP	litigant in person
MIFs	multi-lateral interchange fees
ML	machine learning
NPC	National Pensioners' Convention
OCMC	Online Civil Money Claims
OCS	one-way costs shifting
PCO	protective costs order
PD	Practice Direction
PII	public interest immunity
QOCS	qualified one-way costs shifting
RSC	Rules of the Supreme Court
SIAC	Special Immigration Appeals Commission
TFEU	Treaty on the Functioning of the European Union
TPIM	terrorism prevention and investigation measures

PART I
INTRODUCTION

1

The Civil Procedure Rules Twenty Years On

The Practitioners' Perspective

Damien Byrne Hill and Maura McIntosh

Introduction

Cost and delay have always been the two great challenges facing the civil justice system.

Lord Woolf sought to address these issues with his recommendations, which were largely implemented in the Civil Procedure Rules (CPR) twenty years ago. Lord Justice Jackson again took up the challenge in his Review of Civil Litigation Costs ten years later, leading to further significant reforms. But the reform process is far from over, with the rules on disclosure and witness statements currently in the spotlight.

This chapter considers how the CPR and the various reforms have worked in practice from the perspective of the commercial solicitor, and whether more needs to be done to address the challenges. In particular, it looks at the following:

1. Pre-action behaviour
2. Case management
3. Costs management
4. Disclosure
5. Witness statements
6. Expert evidence
7. Part 36 settlement offers
8. ADR
9. Overview and the future

In preparing this chapter we have canvassed views of partners at Herbert Smith Freehills, through a combination of an online survey and face-to-face interviews. Partners were asked for their reflections on how various aspects of the

Damien Byrne Hill and Maura McIntosh, *The Civil Procedure Rules Twenty Years On* In: *The Civil Procedure Rules at 20*. Edited by: Andrew Higgins, Oxford University Press (2020). © the several contributors.
DOI: 10.1093/oso/9780198863182.003.0001.

rules are working in practice in large-scale commercial litigation, which is the focus of our practice.[1]

The chapter builds to some extent on a similar exercise conducted at the ten-year anniversary of the CPR. The results of that exercise were published in an article entitled 'The Civil Procedure Rules Ten Years On: The Practitioner's Perspective' by Tim Parkes (who has since retired from the firm). Many of the issues considered in that article remain important today, though of course things have moved on in some areas, including as a result of changes introduced by the Jackson reforms.

Pre-action behaviour

Pre-action protocols were introduced by the CPR to encourage parties to settle their disputes without the need to issue proceedings, implementing Lord Woolf's view that litigation should be seen as a last resort. Specific protocols were introduced for various types of proceedings, as well as a general practice direction on pre-action protocols which sets out behaviours expected of parties where no specific protocol applies. The relevant practice direction has seen a few different iterations since it was first introduced under the CPR, but in general terms it requires parties to exchange correspondence and information sufficient to understand each other's positions, attempt to settle the dispute without the need for proceedings and reduce costs. The court was given the power under the CPR to take into account non-compliance with the pre-action protocols and practice direction when making orders for costs.

Partners generally see the pre-action protocols and related practice direction as a success, in that they help to narrow the issues and encourage early settlement, although they do lead to the frontloading of costs.

> I think they are worthwhile if complied with properly, in terms of concentrating minds on what the case is about: what issues are contested, what issues are agreed. The problem with them is that while the work is front-loaded, the costs sanctions are back-loaded.

Some comment that the benefit of pre-action protocols may be less significant where there are sophisticated commercial parties on both sides, as they would

[1] The survey and interviews were conducted in March, April and May 2019.

likely have made sensible efforts to resolve matters before issuing proceedings whether or not required to do so by the rules.

> By the time we are instructed to issue or defend proceedings, it is a fair bet that there has been a good commercial, and indeed legal, exchange of views between the parties. It's rare in big ticket commercial litigation that a failure to engage has given rise to the proceedings.

Partners say that there is often wrangling about whether parties have complied with pre-action requirements (over 80% have experienced such arguments being raised), with complaints typically made about delays in responding to pre-action correspondence, or whether claimants have set out their claims sufficiently, or whether defendants have engaged sufficiently in disclosing relevant documents. But it is very rare to see costs sanctions imposed for non-compliance (fewer than 10% have seen sanctions imposed).

That leads some partners to comment that pre-action protocols generate time-consuming and costly exchanges, but are ultimately fairly toothless as costs sanctions are unlikely to be imposed, or be very significant, and will only come at the end of the case in any event.

> Arguments are frequent but in reality there is no real sanction for non-compliance save some potential risk on costs but at the end of the case.
>
> I have often seen and taken part in arguments about compliance with the pre-action protocols but have never seen sanctions (in terms of costs recovery) applied.

The general view, however, is that the procedures have helped to bring about a culture change where there is much greater engagement between the parties than there used to be at a pre-action stage, which is seen as a good thing.

> Parties are keen to reach commercial resolutions, and the pre-action process gives them the opportunity that they might not otherwise have had if they felt the need to be seen to be taking an aggressive position.
>
> It gives people an excuse to engage in pre-action correspondence without looking weak.
>
> I think it has led to a change of behaviour. Twenty years ago people might have written a pre-action letter and said 'you've got 14 days to pay or else'. Now there is an understanding that you have to articulate a claim reasonably

well in correspondence and at least wait a reasonable period for a response before commencing proceedings.

Case management

The CPR introduced the new concept of an 'overriding objective', to which the court must seek to give effect whenever it exercises any power or interprets any rule. The overriding objective, as originally introduced, was to enable the court to deal with cases 'justly' (later amended as a result of the Jackson reforms to refer to dealing with cases 'justly and at proportionate cost'). The overriding objective of dealing with cases justly was said to include various elements such as ensuring the parties are on an equal footing, saving expense and dealing with the case in a way that is proportionate to the amount at stake as well as the importance of the case and complexity of the issues.

A key feature of the CPR was the new requirement for the court to further the overriding objective by actively managing cases. This effectively transferred responsibility for controlling litigation from the parties to the court. The CPR also introduced the summary assessment of costs for applications of a day or less, so that costs would not only be awarded to the successful party at the end of the hearing, but would be assessed on the spot and payable within a short period thereafter. The aim was to curtail the practice of parties making numerous interlocutory applications, often of a tactical nature.

These innovations are widely viewed as a success by partners, reducing costs and increasing cooperation between the parties. In fact, a number of partners commented that these reforms made such a fundamental change to how litigation was conducted that many people tend to forget how different the process was pre-CPR.

> I think people have simply forgotten that there was really no timetabling at all, which seems extraordinary now. You issued a writ and then, at every stage, you'd have to go down to the Bear Garden[2] and argue over how much time there should be.
>
> The introduction of the CMC and a timetable through to trial, combined with a reluctance to allow extensions that would affect the trial date, has been

[2] The Bear Garden is an area in the Royal Courts of Justice in which Masters would sit to hear short applications. It is no longer used for hearings.

fundamental. Indeed, the cause of delay is now largely the court's own inability to offer a trial window closer to the end of the timetable.

The days of cases meandering for years without case management are happily behind us—that is a major change.

Summary assessment of costs, particularly on short procedural applications, has had a very significant impact. The threat of an immediately payable adverse costs order ensures that the great majority of procedural matters are resolved between the parties, in circumstances where pre-1999 the parties would have frequently ended up in the Bear Garden.

The Woolf reforms have reduced the number of interlocutory applications substantially. The costs now incurred in interlocutory hearings are such that the disputed issue really has to be worth the time, effort and risk in contesting it.

Costs are front-loaded more than under the old RSC, but the reforms have cut down on the number of cases just drifting through the court system until shortly before trial.

The overriding objective has been a useful tool for parties and the courts to deploy to encourage sensible behaviour, and to avoid unnecessary costs.

Despite the dramatic nature of these changes, by the time Lord Justice Jackson conducted his Civil Litigation Costs Review some ten years later, there was a widespread perception that the courts had become overly tolerant of unjustified delays and breaches of court rules and orders. Lord Justice Jackson recommended that this should change. To bring about the change, the rules on applications for relief from sanctions under CPR 3.9 were amended from April 2013. A new element was also introduced into the overriding objecting, namely 'enforcing compliance with rules, practice directions and orders'.

Initially the courts took an overly strict approach in applying the new rules, following the high-profile *Mitchell*[3] decision in November 2013, and cases were struck out or draconian sanctions imposed for relatively minor failings. This was replaced by a more tempered approach, once the Court of Appeal 'clarified' the *Mitchell* guidance in its *Denton*[4] decision in July 2014. However, the extent to which the court's approach has been relaxed should not be overstated. The courts have been keen to emphasise that there can be no return to the old culture of non-compliance.

[3] *Andrew Mitchell MP v News Group Newspapers Limited* [2013] EWCA Civ 1537.

[4] *Denton v TH White Ltd, Decadent Vapours Ltd v Bevan, Utilise TDS Ltd v Davies* [2014] EWCA Civ 906.

Among partners surveyed, there is broad agreement that the tightening up of case management and the court's approach to granting relief from sanctions under the Jackson reforms was necessary, if initially painful for many parties who fell foul of the strict new regime. Although the partners questioned have had very little experience of an application for relief having been made post-Jackson, on either side of the argument (just over 10% have had such experience), there is a broad perception that the changes have made parties more likely to comply with rules and court orders (just over 80% believe that this has been the case to at least some extent).

> In the early years post-Woolf, if you opposed someone's request for an extension of time, you ended up getting rapped on the knuckles for being uncooperative, and that led to a culture of 'deadlines don't really matter, you always get more time'. So the balance needed to be corrected.
>
> It sort of goes in waves—every few years you need a shock which just enforces people's compliance with the rules.
>
> It has reinforced in people's minds the importance of hitting deadlines and, if they think they won't be able to, of doing something beforehand and not just trying to sort it out afterwards.

The key frustration among partners, in relation to case management, is the lack of effective judicial docketing. From a practitioner's perspective, high on the wish list is a system of docketing which is implemented consistently to ensure that, for major cases, there is a single judge who has a continuing grip on the case.

> Docketed judges are so much better—the judge making case management decisions understands the issues and has ownership because they are going to hear the trial.

At the moment, even where there is a designated judge, partners have experience of cases where case management conferences have been listed before another judge, or sometimes multiple judges, and the trial judge did not make an appearance until perhaps pre-trial review stage. This can cause frustration, as it can hamper effective case management, either because the case management judge is less familiar with the case and the issues, or because of the understandable fear of tying the trial judge's hands.

> My personal frustration from the experience I've had on one recent matter is the failure of the docketing system and the adverse impact that has. We had three CMCs with three different judges—none with the designated judge. That is really unhelpful in a big, complicated case.

There are of course challenges with docketing, not least in terms of judicial resourcing, but it is something that would make a significant difference in practice.

A related frustration is the lack of judicial reading time, which can have an adverse impact on the quality of case management, whether or not there is a docketed judge, as it can lead to case management decisions being made on a less than robust basis.

> Judges are still not given sufficient reading time to equip themselves to understand the issues in a case properly and this is hampering them from exercising proper case management and oversight.

Costs management

As noted above, the CPR introduced summary assessment of costs, particularly for applications of a day or less, in an effort to discourage parties from making numerous tactical applications during the course of the litigation. Otherwise, however, costs control was left to operate retrospectively, with the court determining at the end of the case the level of costs that should be recoverable.

Lord Justice Jackson took the view that the only way to control costs effectively was to do so in advance, with the court focusing upfront on how much should be spent (or at least recovered) in the litigation, rather than assessing costs after the event. To that end, he recommended the introduction of a regime of costs management, or costs budgeting, with a view to bringing certainty as to the parties' financial commitment—in so far as the liability to pay adverse costs is concerned—and bringing costs down to a proportionate level.

When the regime was first introduced, from April 2013, there were exceptions for the Commercial Court, and claims in the other courts for more than £2 million. From April 2014, however, the budgeting regime has applied to claims in all courts, including the Commercial Court, unless the amount claimed is more than £10 million.

Although the court has power to disapply budgeting in cases that fall within the automatic regime (ie claims under £10 million) partners surveyed have no experience of that power being exercised. In contrast, a number of partners have experience of the court exercising its discretion to apply the budgeting regime even though the case was valued at over £10 million.

> I have seen the court ordering budgets where the claim value exceeds £10 million because the judge feels it is the right thing to do and ultimately a financial institution can cope with the work involved.

There were mixed views among those partners who have experience of costs management as to its impact. A number of partners expressed scepticism as to the value of formal costs management procedures in large commercial cases.

> In large commercial cases, much more time is spent on costs management than whatever will be saved in the long run. Even without costs estimates from the other side, it is possible to guess roughly what their costs will be. In my view, the time and cost of costs management vastly exceeds its value.

One partner commented that costs management may make clients more willing to pursue or defend claims, as there is greater clarity as to the costs involved if unsuccessful. This may promote access to justice, but may also remove an incentive to settle.

> The costs budgeting process emboldened my client, the defendant, to roll the dice perhaps more than he would otherwise have done—since he knew the costs were essentially capped if he lost. There's nothing like being afraid of what the costs might be at the end of the day to encourage settlement.

Disclosure

Disclosure is widely recognised as a key driver of cost in English civil litigation. There is broad agreement among partners that the process has continued to be overly costly, despite various attempts over the past twenty years to get the process under control and reduce costs.

Pre-CPR, the 'discovery' obligation (as it was then called) was very wide-ranging. Parties to litigation were obliged to disclose any document which was broadly relevant, or which could lead to a train of inquiry that could produce relevant information. This is often referred to as the *Peruvian Guano*,[5] or train of enquiry, test.

Under the CPR, that very broad test was replaced with a presumption in favour of 'standard disclosure', which required a party to make a reasonable search for documents within its control, and to disclose those on which it relied and/or which supported or adversely affected any party's case.

But despite the introduction of this narrower test, the costs of disclosure continued to explode. This was in part because of the ever-increasing mass of electronic documents produced and stored by businesses, and in part because it was often seen as cheaper and easier to disclose documents that were broadly relevant than to apply consideration to whether each document was genuinely helpful or harmful under the standard disclosure test—particularly as a strict application of that test could lead to arguments later as parties followed up on apparent 'gaps' in the documentary record disclosed by their opponents.

The Jackson reforms, introduced from April 2013, again tried to rein in the process, replacing the presumption of standard disclosure with a 'menu' of disclosure options from which the court must choose 'having regard to the overriding objective and the need to limit disclosure to that which is necessary to deal with the case justly'. The intention was to instil a more focused approach, tailoring the disclosure order to the requirements of the case at hand, rather than simply defaulting to standard disclosure.

But for all its good intentions, the menu approach did not succeed in that aim. The general perception among practitioners and clients was that standard disclosure continued to be the default option in most commercial cases. That is borne out by the experience of our partners. Only a minority (around 25%) have experienced the court departing from standard disclosure. It is worth noting, however, that this does not mean the process is entirely unbridled in the majority of cases. In partners' experience, the orders made by the court are generally more sophisticated than a mere order to conduct standard disclosure. They will typically set parameters on the searches to be carried out, by specifying custodians, date ranges and key words, and may also mandate the use of technology assisted review procedures.

> I've never had an order for disclosure apart from standard disclosure, but always by reference to agreed custodians, key words, etc. Regardless of the pilot,

[5] So-called as it derived from *Compagnie Financiere du Pacifique v Peruvian Guano* (1882) 11 (QBD) 55.

> right from issue of the claim we engage with the other side on disclosure and that does bear fruit, because it gets people to focus earlier.

Nevertheless, in light of concerns expressed by practitioner and client representative bodies, a disclosure working group was set up in 2016, chaired by Lady Justice Gloster. The result was the introduction of a compulsory disclosure pilot scheme in the Business and Property Courts, which was launched at the beginning of 2019 and will run for two years.

As at the time of writing, it is too early to reach a firm view as to whether the disclosure pilot will save costs. It is fair to say, however, that there is a significant degree of scepticism among partners as to the potential impact on costs in large-scale commercial litigation. More than 90% consider that the changes introduced by the disclosure pilot will not result in a reduction in costs, or that it is too early to say. Some expressed concerns that the increased complexity and uncertainty will lead to more cost, not less, as well as increased front-loading (eg in the need to agree a list of issues for disclosure).

> I don't see the changes resulting in a reduction in costs in major commercial cases. If anything there will be more complication with overlapping issues and potentially differing disclosure regimes for each.
>
> The process is complicated and uncertain. That will only lead to increased costs.

Partners recognise that, as a result of the pilot, there is likely to be significant pressure to reduce the costs of the process, and therefore orders for disclosure may become more limited. However, a number of partners commented on a mismatch between the pre-trial phase, when judges are keen to reduce the numbers of documents disclosed, as compared to the position at trial, when judges may be critical of (ostensible) gaps in a party's disclosure, for example if a witness mentions a document which has not been disclosed—even though its significance may not have been apparent until a point emerged in cross-examination.

> There is a fundamental tension between the desire to reduce disclosure so that only the key documents have to be produced, as compared to when the case gets to trial and the judge says, 'What about all the emails?' Judges want something different at trial—they want the full narrative.
>
> You can have all these rules about how to reduce disclosure, but you get to trial and under cross-examination the witness refers to some note, and the

> advocate says, 'Where's this note? It hasn't been disclosed'—and suddenly the impression is given that documents are being withheld.

In general, partners do not see the problems with disclosure as a failure of the rules, but rather as a product of the explosion in electronic documents over the past twenty or more years. A number of partners expressed the view that while changes to the test for disclosure might reduce the numbers of documents that ultimately need to be disclosed, that won't always reduce the amount of work that needs to be done to find those documents. It may in some cases, if it's straightforward to map issues against custodians or document sets, but that will not always be the case.

So while changes to the rules may be of some help, there is a widely held view that the problems with disclosure are caused by IT and ultimately cry out for an IT solution.

> I have always thought the way to bring costs down in relation to disclosure is the use of technology, with judges exercising a soft touch approach—rather than introducing more paperwork and certificates. I'm not at all sure the new approach will make things any better.
>
> All of these changes to disclosure are just ways of trying to cope with the exponential growth in the availability of electronic documents, and they are all likely to be somewhat inadequate. In the end the answer is almost certainly going to be AI and the rest of it is just putting fingers in holes.
>
> One question is whether it will remain acceptable for parties not to use the technology that's available. So if a party says it's going to do key word searches and linear reviews, when predictive coding would have cut the costs of the exercise in half—maybe that should be allowed but the extra costs should not be recoverable.

Witness statements

The CPR did not change the basic principles regarding witness evidence. However, the court was given specific powers to control the evidence by giving directions as to: the issues on which it requires evidence; the nature of the evidence it requires; and the way in which evidence is to be put before the court.

At the time of Lord Justice Jackson's review, the perception was that these powers were used very rarely, at least outside the Commercial Court. New express powers were therefore brought in, from April 2013, under which the court can define and/or limit factual witness evidence by making directions: identifying or limiting the issues to which factual evidence may be directed; identifying the witnesses who may be called or whose evidence may be read; or limiting the length or format of witness statements.

Despite these reforms, however, concerns continued to be expressed, including in reported judgments, that many witness statements had become too long, too prone to reciting the documents, or too full of submissions and argument. In light of these concerns, a working group was set up in 2018 to review the current rules and practice and make recommendations for potential reform of the procedures for factual witness evidence.

Views among partners are mixed as to whether there is a need for reform to the rules and procedures governing witness evidence, and if so what changes are needed. The majority (around 75%) expressed scepticism as to the need for reform, as opposed to generally agreeing that more could be done to use current powers to enforce the rules more forcefully.

> The rules are fine—they could be applied more actively to ensure that the worst excesses are challenged.
>
> I don't think the rules generally need reform, though I would like to see tighter control in terms of identification of what issues witnesses will address and their statements will be directed to.
>
> The answer may be for judges to give comments in judgments to the effect that they are unimpressed with statements for particular reasons. If we get more of those sorts of judgments, the practice may change.

Although the general perception is that the current powers are rarely used, a sizeable minority of partners (around 30%) have experience of the court imposing some sort of limit on the factual witness evidence, including by limiting the numbers of witnesses or the issues they are to address or by striking out inadmissible evidence. Some partners also have experience of the court directing limited examination in chief, rather than solely cross-examination.

> In our case, the trial judge ordered both parties to delete various passages of the witness evidence on the basis that it was inadmissible opinion evidence.
>
> Our case centred on an oral contract alleged to have been agreed at a meeting. The judge heard evidence in chief for around half an hour from each of the two individuals involved, and it was very effective.

Some partners noted that, despite the concerns regarding over-citation of documents, a certain amount of commentary on the documents may be needed to put the documents into context—particularly where they are lengthy or numerous—and tell the story for the judge. And that some judges will in fact expect to see a witness deal with all the relevant documents, though clearly long recitations of passages from the documents are not helpful.

> I think witness statements do an important job in explaining the significance of documents, particularly as organisations, products, industries are all more complicated than they were. The documents can't necessarily speak for themselves without that context.
>
> I have seen judges criticise parties or witnesses where the witness statements don't comment on every document. So I can understand why the practice of regurgitating all the correspondence has emerged. There is also the question of how you tell a story where the witness won't be examined in chief.

The witness evidence working group's report was published in December 2019. It does not propose radical change but makes a number of recommendations to improve the quality of witness evidence. These include measures to reinforce compliance with current rules, such as developing an authoritative statement of best practice, beefing up the statement of truth, and introducing a solicitors' certificate of compliance, as well as greater use of costs sanctions and judicial criticism where there is non-compliance. There is also a recommendation aimed at encouraging the use of examination in chief on specific issues where appropriate, and a recommendation that individual courts within the Business and Property Courts should give further consideration to the introduction of a pre-trial statement of facts setting out a party's factual case, in addition to witness statements. The aim would be to give the parties an opportunity to advance their case on the facts and thereby encourage them to confine witness statements to their appropriate content.

Whatever changes may be made as a result of the working group's recommendations, there is a large degree of consensus among partners—and commercial clients generally appear to share this view—that the answer is not to jettison witness statements, which are an important part of the cards on the table approach to litigation that increases predictability and (associated with that) assists settlement. If that benefit were lost, more cases would be likely to go to trial, thereby negating any overall saving in costs. The working group's less radical approach to reform is therefore welcome.

Full witness statements help the parties evaluate the other side's case. If that is lost I anticipate more cases will go to trial leading to no overall saving in costs.

Certainly I think the evidence in chief should be supplied in writing in advance of the trial, even if it is supplemented at trial. Otherwise you lose the ability to analyse the evidence in a forensic way, at least in complex matters, and that is one of the things international parties value about the English courts.

Expert evidence

The CPR sought to address the cost of expert evidence by: restricting expert evidence to what is reasonably required to resolve the proceedings; requiring the parties to obtain permission by reference to a particular field of expertise (if not a particular named expert); introducing provisions regarding joint meetings between experts and joint statements to seek to narrow the issues in dispute; and encouraging the use of single joint experts.

The Jackson reforms did not introduce major changes but added requirements, from April 2013, that parties seeking permission for expert evidence must: identify the issues the evidence will address; and provide an estimate of the costs of that evidence. The rules also now specify that an order granting permission may specify the issues which the expert evidence should address.

The general view among partners is that procedures for expert evidence are working well. The introduction of joint meetings under the CPR is generally seen as helpful, as it can help to identify the real issues in dispute between the experts and potentially narrow those issues (over 80% of partners have experienced this). Some however describe the impact as limited, saying that while some genuinely bad points may be dropped as a result of this process, the narrowing of issues is not generally substantial.

I have seen expert meetings narrow the issues, though not usually substantially. They have also highlighted points where an opposing expert does not feel on secure ground, even if they are not formally conceded.

Their impact is limited but sometimes genuinely bad points get shed during this process.

This is a valuable tool, especially where solicitors help with expert agendas so that relevant issues are identified and discussed by experts.

I have experienced issues being narrowed, but the narrowing is often very limited and often counter-acted by the expansion of the points and arguments

> in the joint list produced following the meeting, which often appears heavily lawyered.

The requirement to identify issues the experts will address, rather than merely expert disciplines, is also generally welcome. Where the expert evidence is not sufficiently tied down to specific issues this can lead to a lack of efficiency and increased costs, particularly where there are large numbers of expert disciplines which may overlap.

> One of the practical difficulties is where you have multiple disciplines which are not neatly delineated. The parties should be able to give a clear indication of which expert is dealing with which issue, and the court needs to control that process.
>
> It is clearly sensible to identify the issues in broad terms but it can't really be pinned down to specific questions. I am a big fan of sequential expert reports, which are the norm in my cases—that avoids the risk of ships passing in the night.

One controversial change under the CPR was to remove privilege in instructions to experts, though the rules state that the court will not require disclosure of the instructions unless there are reasonable grounds to consider the expert's statement summarising his/her material instructions (which must be contained in the report) to be inaccurate or incomplete. At the time, there was some concern that, as a result, parties would not be able to speak freely with their experts.

In practice, partners have had very little experience of the court requiring disclosure of an expert's instructions, or allowing cross-examination on those instructions, despite the removal of privilege under the CPR. However, it has become quite common to use a silent or investigative expert in addition to the CPR expert (more than 70% of partners have done so). This is typically with a view to obtaining assistance in posing the right questions to the expert who is instructed to give evidence in the proceedings, and identifying the key issues for them, without giving the impression of trying to influence that expert inappropriately. Concerns regarding a loss of privilege are less of a driving force, but may also play a part in some cases.

> You want to be sure that you're asking the right questions and putting the right things to your experts. Having a second expert in the background means you can have a full and frank discussion with that expert, eg as to strong and weak

points, without any suggestion that you're trying to influence or manipulate your expert.

Part 36 settlement offers

The CPR introduced Part 36 offers as a new formal process for making settlement offers, replacing (or supplementing) the old system of *Calderbank* offers.[6] The latter are 'without prejudice save as to costs' offers which the courts will take into account in determining the parties' respective costs liabilities, and to that extent they are similar to Part 36 offers. However, *Calderbank* offers leave the courts with a broad discretion as to the extent to which the offer will be taken into account and the effect it will have. In contrast, where a party has made an effective Part 36 offer, the courts must apply the relevant Part 36 costs consequences unless it is unjust to do so. Their impact is therefore more predictable, if not entirely guaranteed.

In addition, and importantly, the potential for costs protection under a *Calderbank* offer was available only to defendants; if the defendant made an offer that the claimant failed to beat, the claimant would typically bear the costs liability from that point onwards, reversing to that extent the usual rule that a successful claimant will be awarded its costs. But conversely, where a claimant made an offer that the defendant failed to beat, it was unlikely to have any impact on costs. For the first time, Part 36 allowed claimants to make a formal settlement offer with potential costs consequences if it was not accepted and the claimant went on to obtain a judgment more favourable than its offer.

Most partners (around 75%) said that Part 36 offers are routinely made in their cases. Partners generally see Part 36 offers as helpful in allowing parties to put forward settlement offers in a way that looks strong rather than weak, and therefore helping to encourage settlement.

> One of the great things about Part 36 is that, where a client has a gut feeling that making offers looks weak, you can say actually a Part 36 offer is not a weak offer, in fact it's quite an aggressive offer—so that's powerful.

A number of partners commented, however, that the costs consequences under Part 36 are less significant in very large cases. That is particularly for

[6] The name derives from *Calderbank v Calderbank* [1976] Fam 93.

claimant offers where the potential benefits are indemnity costs and enhanced interest together with an additional amount capped at a relatively low level (£75,000) in the context of a large claim—in contrast to defendant offers which can effectively reverse the costs burden of the litigation, if made at a sufficiently early stage.

> Where there are tens or hundreds of millions of pounds at stake, the Part 36 sanctions are not significant—they don't really affect anyone's decision making.
>
> They are particularly powerful where the costs are high in the context of the principal sums at stake—particularly for a defendant, where you can look to shift quite a lot of that onto the other side.

In addition, Part 36 has generated huge amounts of case law and has been significantly amended, and indeed completely rewritten, on a number of occasions. The technical and prescriptive nature of Part 36 is seen by partners as a downside and a disincentive to its use. Most partners reported that non-Part 36, or *Calderbank*, offers are still commonly made as a result of the restrictions inherent in the use of Part 36 (more than 75% of partners have made or received such offers). They may be used, for example, where a party wishes to put forward a costs inclusive offer or a 'drop hands' offer (neither of which is permitted under Part 36), or to make a tightly time-limited offer (a Part 36 offer must be open for acceptance for at least twenty-one days and will not bear the Part 36 costs consequences if it is withdrawn—automatically or otherwise—after that period).

> The requirements of Part 36 stifle the ability to make creative offers, which need to be made as *Calderbanks* sometimes.

A number of partners also commented that, while Part 36 offers are commonly made, their cases only infrequently settle through the straightforward acceptance of an offer (only around half have experienced a case settling by means of acceptance of a Part 36 offer). Parties often seek to agree a more complex settlement agreement, with additional terms, even if the Part 36 offer may be acceptable in principle.

> I can't think of a case where a party has simply accepted the Part 36 offer. It is usually a step towards a more structured settlement process such as mediation.

> I think with Part 36 the focus is more on costs protection and tactics rather than necessarily putting forward the sort of offer you expect the opponent to accept.

So, overall, the Part 36 regime is seen as generally useful but perhaps not sufficiently flexible for large, complex cases.

Alternative Dispute Resolution

Alternative dispute resolution has become an integral part of the litigation process, so that it is now rare for a major commercial case to proceed to trial without at least one, and often more than one, mediation. There is general agreement that this culture change was largely brought about by the CPR and their encouragement of ADR at various stages of the process.

> There has been a sea-change in the approach to settlement. Rather than counsel haggling at the doors of the court when all the costs have been incurred, the pre-action protocols and the use of ADR have brought the resolution of disputes forward in many cases.
>
> In more or less every piece of civil litigation we are conducting in the English courts, we will mediate at least once and often twice.

The mechanisms used to encourage ADR include express statements in the pre-action protocols and practice direction that the parties should consider ADR, and provisions allowing the parties to request a stay of proceedings while they attempt ADR, or for the court to make such an order of its own initiative. The court's duty of active case management, as introduced by the CPR, includes encouraging the parties to use ADR, if appropriate, and facilitating the use of ADR. It is now common for the courts to make orders encouraging ADR, such as via the standard draft ADR order which appears in the Commercial Court guide and which includes provision that the parties 'shall take such serious steps as they may be advised to resolve their disputes by ADR procedures' by a particular date. And some partners have experienced more direct encouragement of ADR.

> Judges tend to lightly encourage mediation, noting as they do that the parties are well represented and will know when best to do so.

> The trial judge in our case took the unusual step during his 'reading in' time of emailing the parties and encouraging them to have commercial discussions before cross-examination commenced.
>
> Chancery Masters are very supportive. We had one once who offered to make a 'Daly's Order'. When Counsel expressed puzzlement, he explained it was an order to go over the road to Daly's wine bar on Fleet Street, to try to settle the matter over a bottle of wine.

Parties can be penalised in costs for an unreasonable failure to attempt ADR.[7] Very few partners (only around 10%) have had direct experience of this, but many commented that despite the relative rarity of such orders there is still a significant reluctance to refuse ADR. This is in part to the risk of costs sanctions, but perhaps equally important is the fear of looking unreasonable in the eyes of the court.

> I have seen the argument made, but cannot think of an example where cost penalties have actually been imposed.
>
> I think people are very reluctant to decline an offer of mediation. They might say it's too soon, push it off a little bit, but I can't think of a case where they've said, 'No, we aren't going to do it—it will be a total waste of time'.

A number of partners noted that, often, even if cases don't settle at a mediation, the mediation leads to a process of further discussion and negotiation that results in settlement perhaps a few weeks or months later. And even where ADR is unsuccessful, in that it does not lead to an overall resolution, it can help narrow and focus the issues in dispute.

> I've have cases where immediately coming out of the mediation you might think, 'Was that really worthwhile?' but then a settlement is achieved within two or three months and you realise that there was useful progress.

Overall, the integration of ADR into the litigation landscape is seen by partners as a success story of the CPR.

> The fact that ADR and mediation is now baked in to commercial litigation is one of the most profound impacts of the CPR.

[7] See in particular *Halsey v Milton Keynes General NHS Trust* [2004] 1 WLR 3002.

This influence of the Woolf reforms is borne out by research conducted via the Global Pound Conference (GPC) Series, which gathered views from more than 4,000 people at twenty-eight conferences in twenty-four countries across the globe in 2016 and 2017 as well as further data contributed online.[8]

In particular, when asked what role parties to commercial disputes typically want their (in-house or external) lawyers to take in the dispute resolution process, delegates in London were most likely to say they wanted lawyers to work collaboratively with parties to navigate the process, rather than (as elsewhere) viewing the lawyer's role as advocate for a party as being of broadly equal or greater significance. And when asked about the main obstacles or challenges parties face when seeking to resolve commercial disputes, delegates in London were much less likely than in other regions to refer to insufficient knowledge of the options available.[9] This data illustrates the sophistication of the London disputes market when it comes to knowledge of ADR procedures and attitudes towards ADR.

Overview and the future

When asked for views as to the extent to which the CPR and the various sets of subsequent reforms, taken as a whole, have addressed Lord Woolf's concerns regarding cost, delay, unpredictability and complexity, partners were generally positive. Particular areas where there is broad agreement that the rules are working well include:

- The introduction of active case management with a timetable through to trial, so as to remove the need for claimants constantly to go back to court to move the process along. That dramatically reduced cost and delay and meant cases weren't just allowed to go to sleep.
- The introduction of summary assessment of costs. That meant a huge reduction in the numbers of tactical applications that were brought, as parties realised they might have to pay costs straight away rather than it all coming out in the wash after trial or on settlement. That in turn reduced costs and encouraged cooperation.

[8] Seehttps://www.herbertsmithfreehills.com/latest-thinking/global-pound-conference-series-re-defining-dispute-resolution (accessed 21 June 2019).

[9] See *Global Pound Conference Series: Global Data Trends and Regional Differences*, pp 24–25.

- The expansion in the use of ADR. Although there is some debate about the extent to which it was a product of the Woolf reforms, many consider that this culture change was largely brought about by the CPR and their encouragement of ADR at various stages of the process.
- The pre-action protocols/practice direction are generally seen as a success, in that they help to narrow the issues and encourage early settlement, although they do lead to frontloading of costs and there is often lots of wrangling about whether parties have complied. But the procedures have helped bring about a culture change where parties engage pre-action to a much greater degree than previously, which is generally seen as a good thing.
- There is a general perception that procedures for expert evidence are working well, and the introduction of joint meetings and statements has generally been helpful as it can help to identify the real issues in dispute between the experts. The requirement to identify issues the experts will address, rather than broad disciplines, is also welcome.

Praise for the CPR is not, however, universal. Some take the view that the current rules and procedures are overly complex, leading to unnecessary costs being incurred.

> The Woolf reforms did away with the complex set of procedural rules under the RSC and ultimately ended up replacing them with a new set of even more detailed CPR rules. We have gone full circle. English litigation has actually become more expensive than ever before and can only really be justified economically in the larger commercial cases.
>
> I would be surprised if the CPR has improved things. The CPR has grown inordinately over the size of the RSC. Costs are now wasted on producing enormous costs schedules—and there is anecdotal evidence that that is driving commercial parties into arbitration.

Most partners, however, were more upbeat as to the impact of the CPR and the state of the current procedural framework.

> The current CPR are a good set of rules, if followed by the parties and enforced by the courts.
>
> Costs have grown in spite of the rule changes, largely due to the exponential growth in electronic documentation in the same period. BUT that does not mean the CPR weren't a success—litigation would have become twice

as costly, lengthy, unpredictable and complex than it was as a result of e-disclosure if the Woolf reforms hadn't happened.

There are, however, three areas where many agree that more needs to be done to reduce costs and increase efficiency:

Disclosure: This is perhaps the greatest challenge. There is broad agreement that disclosure has continued to be overly costly, despite the various attempts to get the process under control—though this is not generally seen as a failure of the rules in themselves. There are mixed views as to whether the disclosure pilot will improve matters. Overall, while changes to the rules may be of some help, there is a widely held view that the problems with disclosure are caused by IT and ultimately cry out for an IT solution.

Witness evidence: There is a general view that many witness statements have become too long, too prone to reciting the documents, or too argumentative, but there is little consensus as to what should be done about it. There is certainly quite a large degree of consensus that the answer is not to do away with witness statements, which play an important role in allowing parties to assess an opponent's case and thereby facilitate settlement.

Docketing: Partners agree that a key priority is to have a system of judicial docketing which is implemented effectively to ensure that, for major cases, there is a single judge who has a continuing grip on the case. There are of course challenges with docketing, not least in terms of judicial resourcing, but it is something that would make a significant difference in practice.

2

Keep Calm and Keep Litigating

Andrew Higgins[1]

Introduction

In my presentation to the CPR at 20 conference at the University of Oxford in June 2019, I gave a broad overview of some of the themes covered in the conference, and some of the key challenges facing those administering the civil justice system, from an academic perspective. This chapter adopts the same approach, and presents both normative arguments and empirical data about the functioning, and mal-functioning, of the English civil justice system. Given the scope of the subject, the chapter is necessarily marked by its breadth rather than depth of analysis. There are two main related points I wish to consider. The first is the English civil justice system's vexed relationship with proportionality and, in particular, the requirement to deliver justice at proportionate cost. The second is whether this vexed relationship can be partly attributable to any cultural wariness in England towards civil litigation.

The chapter outlines the case for defining proportionality in mathematical terms by reference to claim values in all cases except for those that may set a legal precedent. In so doing, it considers whether it is formally time to separate out the civil dispute resolution's dual functions: rule clarification on the one hand, and law enforcement and dispute resolution on the other. In relation to the social benefits and costs of litigation and English attitudes towards it, the chapter argues that there is nothing inherently divisive about litigation per se. There are sound reasons to avoid litigation if a dispute can be fairly resolved by other means. There is also a need to ensure substantive laws and rules of procedure do not unnecessarily antagonise and deepen divisions between the parties. At its core, however, litigation is merely a

[1] I want to thank Rory Gregson for his research assistance on the studies of media coverage of litigation, legal concepts and Supreme Court cases and the following persons for their assistance on identifying relevant sources for comparative rates of civil litigation: Xiaoli Li (China); Natalie Fricero (France); Johannes Kist (Germany); Chiara Besso Marcheis (Italy); Toru Takagi (Japan). All errors are, of course, mine. Email correspondence to Andrew.higgins@law.ox.ac.uk.

Andrew Higgins, *Keep Calm and Keep Litigating* In: *The Civil Procedure Rules at 20.* Edited by: Andrew Higgins, Oxford University Press (2020). © the several contributors. DOI: 10.1093/oso/9780198863182.003.0002.

form of protest directed towards the protection of one's legal rights and liberties. In a society based on the rule of law such protests should be welcomed, or at the very least, they ought not be actively discouraged through procedural rules. Using procedural rules to deter litigation is regressive, it breaches principles of equality that underpin civil procedure, and it tends to subvert the relationship between substantive law and procedure. The chapter concludes by presenting some basic quantitative data on civil claim numbers in different jurisdictions, and coverage of legal concepts and cases in the UK media. The data suggests that, empirically at least, the English do not appear to have an aversion to litigation and are actually more litigious than comparable European jurisdictions. According to one measure, it is even slightly more litigious than the United States. By contrast, media coverage of tort concepts and cases suggests a preoccupation with the possibility of a rise of a compensation culture in England relative to coverage of recognised legal principles, which the courts apply in practice. The data also reveals relatively limited coverage of leading Supreme Court cases that establish the legal principles that govern us all. As a consequence of this coverage, there is a risk that the public may develop a skewed picture of the law and the legal system.

The justice in proportionality

The insertion of an overriding objection into the new CPR was one of Lord Woolf's great achievements as Master of the Rolls. CPR 1 recognised that the rules could not provide for all eventualities, and there was a risk that courts could get lost in the detail of the rules to the detriment of fulfilling its overriding objective.[2]

In its original form the overriding objective expressly recognised that dealing with cases justly required dealing with cases in a way that was proportionate:

(i) to the amount of money involved;
(ii) to the importance of the case;
(iii) to the complexity of the issues; and
(iv) to the financial position of each party;[3]

[2] Lord Woolf MR, Access to Justice: Final Report (July 1996) p 274.
[3] CPR 1.1(2)(c).

It is widely acknowledged that the CPR failed to deliver on this aspect of the overriding objective. As Lord Jackson succinctly put it in his landmark review of the Costs of Civil Litigation in 2009: 'Despite the general success of the Woolf reforms, the costs of civil litigation continue to rise'[4] and '[i]n some areas of civil litigation costs are disproportionate and impede access to justice'.[5]

The CPR are not the only cause of disproportionate costs. This is evidenced by the range of disputes, that can incur disproportionate costs notwithstanding differences in the procedural rules governing them. This includes low value disputes in Tribunals or the small claims track, or complex commercial litigation in the multi-track.[6] It can also affect claims subject to cost shifting[7] and claims where costs are always or usually borne by the parties incurring them.[8]

However, a recurring problem in all litigation under the CPR is the open ended nature of the definition of proportionality itself. At the same time that Sir Rupert Jackson recommended an amendment to the overriding objective to stress the need to deal with cases at proportionate cost, he also recommended a definition of proportionate costs that was equally imprecise as the definition in the overriding objective. CPR 44.3(5), which is based on Lord Justice Jackson's recommendation, provides that:

[4] R Jackson, *Review of Civil Litigation Costs: Preliminary Report* (TSO May 2009) Chapter 1 [1.2].

[5] R Jackson, *Review of Civil Litigation Costs: Final Report* (TSO December 2009) Foreword.

[6] The near constant reform efforts to reduce excessive disclosure in multi-track litigation has led to the latest disclosure pilot in the Business & Property Courts, which has taken important steps towards an approach to disclosure more in keeping with that used in civil law countries. For details on the disclosure pilot see: https://www.judiciary.uk/you-and-the-judiciary/going-to-court/high-court/courts-of-the-chancery-division/cpr-guides-and-forms/disclosure-pilot-for-the-business-and-property-courts/.

[7] The moral hazard and perverse incentives built into a loser pays full cost shifting model is obvious. Allowing litigants to enter into fee agreements with their lawyers which can be shifted to a third party—specifically their opponent—depending on the outcome of the case gives litigants the power to dramatically 'ratchet up' the potential liability of their opponent. The only ways the opponent can avoid this additional liability are to settle or to invest even more in the dispute in an effort to avoid losing. A case can be quickly transformed from a dispute about the underlying legal claim into an attempt to avoid paying the costs incurred by an opponent, which often exceed the amount in dispute. The mass of litigation in England dedicated to the *costs of litigation* is testament to the distorting effects of full cost shifting. As Lord Justice Jackson put it, the 'inevitable result' of 'unrestrained costs shifting' is a system that is 'exorbitantly expensive': R Jackson, 'Fixed Costs—The Time Has Come' IPA Annual Lecture (28 January 2016). Where the risks involved in losing cases (as reflected in reasonable success premiums) can also be shifted to the other side, this ratchetting effect is turbo charged. For discussion of the viability of private funding models for civil justice see: A Higgins, 'The Costs of Civil Justice and Who Pays?' (2017) 37 *Oxford Journal of Legal Studies* 687–713.

[8] One alleged cause, which was a focus of Lord Justice Briggs' Civil Court Structure Review, is that the 'civil courts are, by their procedure, their culture and the complexity of the law which they administer, places designed by lawyers for use by lawyers': Lord Justice Briggs, *Civil Court Structure Review: Interim Report* (December 2015) [5.24]. Whether it is possible to design a civil justice system fit for purpose that can be navigated by litigants without legal assistance has been doubted by many scholars: R Assy, 'Revisiting the Right to Self-Representation in Civil Proceedings' (2011) 30 *CJQ* 267; A Zuckerman, 'No Justice Without Lawyers: The Myth of an Inquisitorial Solution' (2014) 33 *CJQ* 355.

> Costs incurred are proportionate if they bear a reasonable relationship to—
>
> (a) the sums in issue in the proceedings;
> (b) the value of any non-monetary relief in issue in the proceedings;
> (c) the complexity of the litigation;
> (d) any additional work generated by the conduct of the paying party; and
> (e) any wider factors involved in the proceedings, such as reputation or public importance.

These multi-factorial definitions of proportionality do not represent a correlation between known values; they are open ended and not capable of precise calculation. In the absence of a clear correlative standard, judges are not constrained to ensure that the dispute is resolved at what most people would regard as reasonable cost, for which most people, even most lawyers, would be willing to litigate if they were required to bear the cost—namely some percentage of the value of the rights at stake. The most damning indictments always come from those in the know, and the fact that Lord Briggs in his Civil Court Structure Review could find no one involved in the legal sector who would recommend litigation to a non-legal friend for low value disputes, except in the case of personal injuries (where we might observe disproportionate costs are shifted to insurers) underlines the dysfunctional nature of the present system.[9]

The risk of incurring disproportionate costs makes it economically irrational or futile to litigate, producing a de facto barrier to access to justice. As Lord Briggs explained in his Review:

> [T]he outlay and risk of disproportionate sums for the purpose of recovering or preserving money or value in civil litigation is just not sensible or rational conduct. Thus the barrier to justice constituted by this weakness affects not only those who, being unable to afford legal representation, are nonetheless forced to litigate in person at in the particular case grave disadvantage. It affects that large, silent class of persons with civil rights or disputes that deserve the attention of the courts who, even if they can afford to do so, rationally choose not to deplete or risk their resources in litigating at disproportionate cost and risk with an uncertain outcome. This leads both to civil rights not being vindicated by potential claimants, and to those with a good

[9] Lord Justice Briggs, *Civil Court Structure Review: Final Report* (July 2016) [5.15].

defence to a claim submitting to it rather than risk the disproportionate costs of contesting it.[10]

Despite widespread recognition of the 'evil' posed by disproportionate costs, reform proposals designed to ensure litigants are never liable for more than a fixed percentage of the value in dispute—an approach inspired by the German system of fixed recoverable costs—has historically met fierce resistance in England. There are both cultural and institutional reasons why English lawyers tend to define proportionality in ways that make it as straightforward to measure as a piece of string. There is an inherent tension between the functions of a civil justice system in common law jurisdictions. This was highlighted by Lord Reed when in the *Unison* case, his Lordship articulated the public value of access to civil justice: dispute resolution through final and peaceful determination of legal claims, and rule creation through development of the common law.[11] It should be stressed that *both* these functions are part of the court's constitutional role of law enforcement. As Zuckerman has argued, the principal function of civil legal process is law enforcement. This role may sometimes require the courts to clarify the law, or resolve factual disputes, but in every case its role is to uphold the law and enforce the civil rights and obligations of the parties before it.[12] It is a melancholy reality of our civil justice system that many cases before the courts do not involve factual disputes between the parties, or legal uncertainty requiring clarification by the courts, but instead constitute a 'dispute' only in the sense that one party is refusing to comply with their legal obligations without an order from the courts to do so, or in extreme cases, without a court order being enforced against them. The fact that such cases exist[13] is an indictment on the accessibility of the England justice system. The recalcitrant defendant, who consciously chooses not to voluntarily comply with their obligations, is making a calculation that the costs of enforcement through litigation are so high that the claimant might choose not to enforce them at all, and if they do, the time required to do so, means the defendant will obtain a financial advantage from the delay involved in enforcing the claim.

[10] Lord Justice Briggs, *Civil Court Structure Review: Interim Report* (December 2015) [5.40].

[11] *Unison v Lord Chancellor* [2017] UKSC 51 [69]–[71].

[12] A Zuckerman, *On Civil Procedure* (3rd edn, OUP 2013) [1.5]–[1.7].

[13] It is difficult to verify the numbers but the number of cases that are undefended is at least a useful starting point. According to Ministry of Justice Statistics in 2017 less than 15% of the cases filed in the County Court are actually defended (2048,446 cases filed, of which 297,936 were defended: Ministry of Justice Civil Justice Statistics Quarterly https://www.gov.uk/government/collections/civil-justice-statistics-quarterly).

Except for those cases that are artificially generated by the transaction costs of enforcement, all 'disputes', even those that concern facts only, could ultimately find their way to the Court of Appeal or Supreme Court. Recognising the potential significance of these disputes, combined with professional pride in preparing cases fully, and the economic incentives to over prepare cases, lawyers often invest more resources in a case than what, measured in financial terms, is at stake in the case. This may be justified in *some* cases; the challenge is identifying which cases.

Courts determining private disputes through public judgments that help clarify the law generate obvious public benefits. Not only do such judgments reinforce the rule of law, it helps parties conduct themselves in a way that avoids future disputes and/or provide information as to what would constitute a fair settlement of the dispute. All of these points were powerfully made by the UK Supreme Court in the *Unison* case.[14] This analysis has implications for the definition of proportionality. In cases where there is a real prospect that the courts will provide rule clarification, it will be generally be inappropriate to measure proportionate costs solely by reference to the financial value of the claim, and what the individual litigants, acting rationally, would be willing to bear. The mixed private and public benefits of court adjudication also raise distributive justice questions about the appropriate mix of public and private funding of a civil justice system. It is important to recognise, however, that what is a proportionate level of investment in a dispute is a logically distinct question from who should pay for that investment. Unfortunately, English law has conflated these two questions by using the source of funding to mask the disproportionate levels of investment in the dispute. I am always amazed by news stories where journalists report, without comment, that a party has received some modest damages award, but that their opponents must now also pay their legal costs which amount to many multiples of the compensation awarded. Historically, English law has sought to get around the problem of disproportionate cost by transferring the costs of vindicating rights to third parties, typically the losing party and their insurers or onto the taxpayer through legal aid (the availability of which has dramatically shrunk). While there are sound arguments for fairly (re)distributing the costs of access to justice, these are illusory solutions for tackling the problem of disproportionate costs. It would be unjustified to extract from those who seek court assistance a disproportionate price as a condition of determining a legal dispute whether they be claimant or defendant, or ultimately successful or not. Resolution of a dispute at disproportionate cost

[14] *Unison v Lord Chancellor* [2017] UKSC 51 [71].

is just as much a denial of justice to a losing defendant as it is to a winning claimant, and may even deny the defendant access to court altogether if the 'chilling effect' of the risk of disproportionate costs may force defendants into settling claims, irrespective of their merits.

Similarly, a lack of public funding is not a cause of *disproportionate* costs. Governments of all persuasions could reasonably ask why they should be funding parts of a justice system generating disproportionate cost rather than spending the money on other stretched public services. In other words, there is no greater moral case for publicly funding a disproportionately expensive justice system than there is a disproportionately expensive health care, education or transport system. This normative argument is only reinforced by the imperfect nature of legal systems where it is usually impossible to verify whether a court has delivered the correct outcome, and the real debate is how much we should invest in trying to get to the truth consistently with the other objectives of legal process, and other interests a society may wish to pursue.

For the purposes of defining how much to invest—ie the proportionality question—in disputes rather than *who* should pay, we need some form of mechanism to decide, ex ante, those legal disputes that may require rule clarification and/or will affect large numbers of people beyond the immediate parties, such that a larger investment of resources than the nominal value of the claim is warranted. This raises the difficult question of whether we should formally separate the system's rule creation and dispute resolution functions to more effectively triage cases warranting substantial investment because of their potential broader significance, and to deal with the rest in a more summary fashion. There would be a cost to doing this. A strength of the common law is its organic development, based on an almost evolutionary process of survival of the fittest judgment. But arguably we have already lost this organic development, or it has been seriously skewed, due to the inaccessibility of the system, and the capacity of well-resourced repeat players to choose which cases to settle and which to litigate. This phenomenon is famously described by Marc Galanter in his article speculating on the limits of legal change: 'Why the Haves Come out Ahead'.[15]

None of the above is intended to suggest that cases of public importance do not find their way to appellate courts in England. However, the treatment of these cases can be fortuitous in that they can depend on the ability to attract commercial funding, or crowd sourced funding, or public spirited hedge fund

[15] M Galanter, Why the Haves Come Out Ahead: Speculations on the Limits of Legal Change (1974) 9 *Law and Society Review* 1.

managers, or charities willing to employ their resources, or enough lawyers willing to donate their labour. Few could confidentially assert that there are not other cases raising issues of real significance to people's daily lives, which do not get ventilated in the appropriate fora. We need to explore whether there are fairer and more efficient ways of identifying and funding cases that warrant test case treatment. Linda Mulcahy has argued that this should not be mistaken for a mere call for more litigation: the focus ought to be on 'the mechanisms that exist to propel cases with precedent-setting potential to the appellate courts'.[16]

We also need a new approach for the overwhelming majority of cases which only concern the parties themselves. For these 'ordinary' cases, it is never defensible to require the parties to spend more money on their dispute than the value of the rights in question. As we have already seen, few parties, acting rationally, would choose to make such an investment if they were required to bear the costs. Yet many lawyers are resistant to using mathematical definitions of proportionality—to equate proportionality with rational litigant behaviour—because they fear it involves compromising justice. A recurring concern amongst English lawyers is that a more summary legal process would increase the risk of wrong outcomes, or lead to over- or under-compensation in some cases. As one lawyer observed in one of my seminars, defining proportionality by reference to claim values recognises the price of everything and the value of nothing.[17] The response of Adrian Zuckerman and I would be that lawyers can be reliably entrusted to uphold every value worthy of legal protection, provided *someone else* is paying them to do the upholding.

The flaw in the English approach to proportionality is the tendency to measure the quality of justice delivered by the court system independently of the costs incurred in delivering it. This enables many observers, including Lord Briggs in his Civil Court Structure Review, to maintain two contradictory claims: that the lack of accessibility of the civil courts is 'shocking'[18]

[16] L Mulcahy, 'The Collective Interest in Private Dispute Resolution' (2013) 33 *Oxford Journal of Legal Studies* 59, 62.

[17] Continued judicial resistance to measuring proportionality mathematically by reference to claim values, and concomitant reliance on the open textured concept of reasonableness, was evidenced in the Court of Appeal's recent guidance on the meaning of proportionate costs in *West v Stockport NHS Foundation Trust* [2019] EWCA Civ 1220. See, eg, the Court (at para [91]): '[A]ny reductions for proportionality should exclude those elements of costs which are properly regarded as unavoidable, such as court fees, the reasonable element of the ATE premium in clinical negligence cases, and the like. Specifically, therefore, if the ATE premium is assessed as reasonable, it will not fall to be reduced by any further assessment of proportionality.' In fairness to the Court of Appeal the rules themselves, notwithstanding the Jackson reforms, are not a model of clarity when it comes to explaining the relationship between proportionality and reasonableness.

[18] Lord Justice Briggs, *Civil Court Structure Review: Interim Report* (December 2015) [5.2]: 'It will no doubt be tempting for critics of the current civil court structure to treat parts of what follows, taken on their own and out of context, as confirmation from within that the civil courts are unfit for purpose.

and that those very same courts 'continue to justify their reputation as among the very best in the world'.[19] Even those who have publicly advocated for less intensive legal procedures have suggested the result would be a reduction in the quality of justice: more 'quick and dirty' justice for everyone, rather than perfect justice for the lucky few.[20] Although it is undeniable that summary legal processes will increase the risk of error, it would be wrong to characterise these processes as unjust or even second tier justice. Cost and time considerations are not separate from justice, but integral to it. The imperfect nature of legal systems means that we can never guarantee the 'correct' result, and to try to achieve it at disproportionate cost either destroys the value of the successful party's rights, or breaches the losing party's common law right of access to justice, and sometimes both. This principle was upheld by the UK Supreme Court in the *Unison* case. The Court declared that Employment Tribunal Fees that made litigation economically irrational or futile for those with reasonably arguable claims constituted a breach of the common law right of access to justice. Although the case concerned Tribunal (or Court) fees for claimants, the concept of rational litigant behaviour that underpinned the decision applies equally to defendants deciding whether to contest claims. Similarly, there is no reason in principle why the common law right of access to justice should be confined to court fees, and not extended to legal costs that a court may order litigants to pay.

The tendency to describe simplified, quicker procedures as dirty justice requires us to revisit the definition of justice. As Assy has observed:

> The longstanding failure to improve access to justice [in England] can in part be attributed to dogged adherence to accurate outcomes, while treating resources as external constraints over the achievement of justice, rather than as parts of the very definition of procedural justice. When justice is redefined in a thick and rich way, it is clear that changing the balance between accuracy and resources is not a matter of accepting 'second-class justice'. To give more weight to time and cost entails a change in the point of balance, but this is not

This would be both wholly wrong and irresponsible. Viewed as a whole the civil courts continue to justify their reputation as among the very best in the world. Viewed separately from the other courts, they cost the taxpayer nothing. Although in my view insufficiently well regarded, they continue to be a major and vital contributor to a law-abiding, fair and just society.'

[19] Lord Justice Briggs, *Civil Court Structure Review: Final Report* (July 2016) [5.14].

[20] Martin Bentham, 'Lord Neuberger: Quick and dirty justice is better than the risk of no justice at all', *The Evening Standard* 15 November 2013 (https://www.standard.co.uk/news/politics/lord-neuberger-quick-and-dirty-justice-is-better-than-the-risk-of-no-justice-at-all-8942341.html).

> to reduce the quality of justice—as more fully understood. This is a change in the ingredients of justice, not in its quality.[21]

It should be stressed that a justice system that separates out its rule creation and dispute resolution functions would not result in a two-tiered justice system: test case treatment on the one hand, and summary justice on the other. There are other mechanisms available to allow courts to dedicate more time and resources to disputes than the financial value of the rights in issue, even though they involve no question of law. In some cases there is, in reality, more to the dispute than the claim before the court, because there are many others who are in a similar *factual* predicament to the parties. A legal system could, and ordinarily should, utilise collective redress procedures to deal with these cases. Collective redress procedures have the distinct advantage of allowing the judge to get a better grasp of the scale of the dispute and accordingly work out what would be a proportionate level of resources to invest in its resolution. Historically, however, the English legal system has been extremely cautious in its use of collective redress procedures. Opt-out class actions are still only permitted in competition actions before the Competition Appeal Tribunal (CAT), and no collective action has been certified by the CAT to date. The now 30-year-old observation by the National Consumer Council, stating that the English legal system treats all disputes as essentially bi-polar disputes about individual rights, is still valid today:

> The legal system in this country has developed around the basis of individual rights. Today in a mass production society, its rules do not easily lend themselves to resolving problems which affect large numbers of consumers.[22]

In the case of *Merricks v Mastercard* the Competition Appeal Tribunal controversially denied certification in a price fixing competition on behalf of consumers affected by breaches of European competition law as determined by the European Commission.[23] The CAT held the case was not suitable for a collective proceedings order because it was not possible to make a reliable aggregated damages assessment of the loss suffered by the class. This was because the expert modelling put forward by the lead applicant did not attempt to measure the loss suffered by, and thus the compensation due to, each individual class

[21] Rabeea Assy, 'Briggs's Online Court and the Need for a Paradigm Shift' (2017) 36 *Civil Justice Quarterly* 70, 84.
[22] National Consumer Council, Group Actions: Learning from Open (October 1988) p 5.
[23] *Merricks v Mastercard* [2017] CAT 16.

member. The CAT denied certification even though it recognised that the effect of the decision was to deny victims of Mastercard's competition breaches any redress at all.[24] On appeal, the Court of Appeal held that the CAT had adopted an overly onerous approach to the certification requirements; that, provided there was a realistic prospect that a reliable aggregate damages assessment could be made, the adequacy of that assessment was ultimately a matter for trial. Moreover, the purpose of the class action regime introduced by the Consumer Rights Act 2015, which specifically included a power to assess damages on an aggregated basis so that it would be easier for victims of anti-competitive conduct to obtain redress, meant that damages need not be distributed on a compensatory basis where that was impracticable.[25] Mastercard has appealed the decision to the Supreme Court, and at the time of writing the Supreme Court's judgment was still pending. The Court of Appeal's decision in *Merricks* is surely right, not just on ordinary principles of statutory construction,[26] but also on first principles. Aggregated damages assessments may involve imprecision in the estimates of loss to the class as a whole and/or losses suffered by individual class members, but, unless there is an alternative method that could produce *more* precise determinations at proportionate cost and within a reasonable time, the use of such procedures is justified provided the risk of imprecision is borne equally as between the defendant and the class i.e. there is an equal risk of both over and under compensation.[27]

It is true that lawyers cannot always invoke the maxim that the perfect should not be the enemy of the good. Courts must sometimes decide, in absolute terms, what the law permits; whether a legal procedure is fair or not. For example, special advocates will candidly acknowledge that their involvement in closed material procedures—when one of the litigants is denied access to some of the evidence considered by the court—only gives the appearance of

[24] Ibid. The CAT stated at [91]: the '[Counsel for the claimant] argued eloquently that since it would be totally impractical for members in the class to bring claims on an individual basis, if the Tribunal declined to grant a [Collective Proceedings Order] a vast number of individuals who suffered loss would get no compensation. However, that is effectively the position in most cases of widespread consumer loss resulting from competition law infringements.'

[25] *Merricks v Mastercard* [2019] EWCA Civ 674.

[26] The CAT's analysis flies in the face of not just the second reading speech for the bill but the entire government consultation that led to the introduction of the new class action procedure: see Consumers Rights Bill, Second Reading Speech (The Secretary of State for Business, Innovation and Skills (Vince Cable)), 28 January 2014, Columns 768–777 and Department for Business Innovation and Skills (BIS), *Private Actions in Competition Law: A Consultation on Options for Reform: Government Response* (London: BIS, 2013).

[27] Deterrence based theories of tort law, by contrast, are more likely to hold that the risk of error should be borne by the tortfeasor.

due process, not the reality.[28] Sometimes we are forced to make hard choices between law and other interests like national security. But the lesson from Lord Woolf, and those who have followed him, is that there is never a need to choose between justice and proportionate cost. Justice requires proportionality.

Is there cultural resistance to a more accessible, and a more utilised, civil justice system?

Resistance to delivering a more proportionate—and affordable—justice system may not boil down only to theoretical conceptions of justice, or the economic interests of legal service providers. As an outsider I have also detected a degree of cultural ambivalence in England about what access to justice entails: what might happen if we actually delivered an accessible system. In particular, there is general scepticism about people going to courts to enforce their rights, and lawyers profiting from the process. These reservations can be seen in the arguments against expanding class actions,[29] the arguments made for restricting the scope of judicial review and increasing the costs of using it,[30] and even in consultations on the current HMCTS reform programme. I have heard civil servants, working in this very area say that we do not want to make it too easy to litigate. We have certainly achieved that aim.

[28] See eg M Chamberlain, 'Special Advocates and Amici Curiae in National Security Proceedings in the United Kingdom' (2018) 68 *University of Toronto Law Journal* 496–510, and further to this, Mr Justice Chamberlain's speech to the CPR at 20 conference, an extended version of which can be read in chapter 7.

[29] See eg the Government's response to the recommendations of the Civil Justice Council for the introduction of a generic class action procedure for all types of civil claims. The Government cited the potential for 'adverse economic and other impacts', including the risk of abuse, of an opt-out procedure: Ministry of Justice, The Government's Response to the Civil Justice Council's Report: 'Improving Access to Justice through Collective Actions', July 2009. Since that time governments of all persuasions have only contemplated collective redress on a sector by sector basis, and balanced the greater access provided by collective redress with the need for safeguards to prevent abuse: see eg Department for Business Innovation and Skills (BIS), *Private Actions in Competition Law: A Consultation on Options for Reform: Government Response* (January 2013) [5.12]–[5.13].

[30] Legislative reforms to judicial review (JR) were driven directly by government. See eg David Cameron, Speech to the CBI on 19 November 2012: '[JR] is a massive growth industry in Britain today. Back in 1998 there were four and a half thousand applications for review and that number almost tripled in a decade. Of course some are well-founded. But let's face it: so many are completely pointless. Last year, an application was around 5 times more likely to be refused than granted. We urgently needed to get a grip on this. So here's what we're going to do. Reduce the time limit when people can bring cases. Charge more for reviews so people think twice about time-wasting. And instead of giving hopeless cases up to four bites of the cherry to appeal a decision, we will halve that to two.' See also Anthony Grayling, 'No more using judicial review as a cheap delaying tactic' (Ministry of Justice Press Release, 23 April 2013) https://www.gov.uk/government/news/grayling-no-more-using-judicial-review-as-a-cheap-delaying-tactic. The majority of restrictions on the use of JR were introduced by the Criminal Justice and Courts Act 2015. For discussion see Maurice Sunkin's chapter in this collection at chapter 14.

A country whose motto, endorsed by the monarchy, indeed delivered by the monarchy, is to keep calm and carry on is going to look askance at anything that looks remotely divisive, even something as polite as asking a neutral adjudicator to resolve a dispute. But except where litigation is vexatious or brought for an improper purpose, litigation per se is no more, or less, divisive than the circumstances that give rise to it. This is no doubt a controversial proposition, especially to those who have observed the trauma of litigants having their lives raked over in forensic detail as part of the litigation process. Litigation is usually stressful and the process can, depending on the rules governing the litigation process, deepen conflicts between the parties. A legal system may have adversarial rules of procedure that have an antagonising effect—allowing parties to conduct mini-royal commissions into each other's lives with the hope of undermining their opponent's credibility. A system can also have antagonising substantive laws that exacerbate conflict within relationships. For example, family law rules could encourage parties in relationships to allege impropriety on the part of their spouse as a precondition to legally ending their relationship. But none of these circumstances are intrinsic to litigation per se. Thankfully they are also largely a relic of history.[31] The courts have broad powers to limit the scope of cross examination, and to limit the adducing of evidence, where it would be irrelevant or of marginal probative value and involve disproportionate time and expense. Barristers are also prohibited by their own code of conduct from asking questions with the aim of humiliating or causing distress to witnesses.[32]

Putting to one side legal rules that can deepen conflict, what about litigation per se? Is it inherently divisive? Litigation is a form of peaceful protest. Protests and examination of the grievances underpinning them can be divisive, but it is both empirically and normatively artificial to say that a protest is more divisive than the grievances to which it relates. To illustrate the point, let us take two examples: one mundane, the other extreme. Someone jumps a queue to get on a bus, and other passengers protest. In this case, the protest is simply a continuation of the division created by the queue jumping. It is true that the way a protest is carried out can have the effect of escalating a dispute. Hence passengers beating up a queue jumper as summary punishment would be a disproportionate response which escalates the dispute. But demanding the queue jumper go to the back of the queue would not be an escalation of the dispute because it

[31] Plans to introduce no fault divorce in England and Wales are currently before the Parliament: Divorce, Dissolution and Separation Bill 2017–19.

[32] Bar Standards Board Code of Conduct (Version 4.3, October 2019), Rule C 7.

is doing no more than reversing the wrong committed. The correcting part of corrective justice cannot, as a matter of logic, be as divisive as the commission of the primary wrong.[33] In some disputes there may be a disagreement about the facts; whether there was in fact any queue jumping. But disputes about what happened simply reflect the existence of an underlying dispute.

The continuation of disputes, including by litigating them through the courts, can have socially undesirable consequences. It takes time and energy, and can require the investment of resources, all of which might be more productively spent elsewhere. That is why a strong case can be made for encouraging, or even mandating alternative dispute resolution (ADR)—both before and after commencement of legal proceedings—as a complement to court adjudication. ADR has the distinctive benefit of allowing parties to identify any underlying, non-legal causes of their dispute and address them through creative solutions that are beyond the legal powers of the court to remedy.[34] But as several distinguished commentators and judges have noted, the use of ADR without an accessible legal system is like the sound of one hand clapping. Without the credible option of enforcement through court adjudication, there is no institutional pressure on the parties to comply with the law in the first place, or to agree fair settlements of their disputes which reflect their underlying rights and obligations.[35] This is why the possibility of legal compulsion is necessary to support the otherwise peaceful resolution of legal disputes. The State can compel parties to comply with their legal obligations, but can do so only in accordance with due process, and such compulsion only becomes necessary if a person refuses to voluntarily comply with their legal obligations. As Lord Reed observed in the Supreme Court's landmark judgment on the common law right of access to justice in *Unison*, the courts must be accessible to all because:

> People and businesses need to know, on the one hand, that they will be able to enforce their rights if they have to do so, and, on the other hand, that if they fail to meet their obligations, there is likely to be a remedy against them. It is that knowledge which underpins everyday economic and social relations.

[33] Of course, bus queue jumping does not constitute a legal wrong, but the point holds wherever a dispute relates to an alleged wrong.

[34] For detailed discussion of the social value of ADR, in light of the limitations of formal legal adjudication, see eg C Menkel-Meadow, 'From Legal Disputes to Conflict Resolution and Human Problem Solving: Legal Dispute Resolution in a Multidisciplinary Context' (2004) 54 *Journal of Legal Education* 7–29; J Sternlight, C Menkel-Meadow, L Love and A Schneider, *Dispute Resolution: Beyond the Adversarial Model* (Aspen, 2010)

[35] H Genn, *Judging Civil Justice* (CUP, 2009). 125.

> That is so, notwithstanding that judicial enforcement of the law is not usually necessary, and notwithstanding that the resolution of disputes by other methods is often desirable.[36]

One advantage that both ADR and court adjudication share as a means of dispute resolution is the ability to achieve some semblance of finality. Parties reaching an agreement to settle their dispute, or getting a court to finally determine the parties' respective rights and obligations, allows the parties to get on with their lives. By focusing the parties on the dispute at hand, and whether they can resolve it by agreement, or need an independent and impartial adjudicator to resolve it according to law, these complementary processes may help end, rather than continue, disputes.

Criticising litigation as inherently divisive also fails to acknowledge that there is a normative dimension involved in assessing whether a protest deepens disputes. This is best demonstrated by using an extreme example of conflict. Imagine a slave protesting their detention. Empirically there may be more peace if the slave does not protest their slavery, or what their captor/owner orders them to do, but could it seriously be contended that the slave deepens the conflict by protesting their slavery, and seeking their freedom and wages for the unpaid or underpaid work they perform?

Perhaps a more empirically accurate and normatively defensible explanation of wariness of civil litigation flows from concerns about unmeritorious or inappropriate litigation: some claims are totally without merit, and some disputes do not really belong in the courts and are better dealt with by other means. Both these propositions can be readily accepted but their implications for the design of a civil justice system is a more complex matter.

The definition of unmeritorious litigation, as opposed to the concept, is extremely difficult to pin down. While all lawyers can recognise, and have often come across, claims and defences based on hopeless points of law, the possibility of legal change means that what constitutes a 'weak' legal claim is contestable and subject to change over time. Today's established precedent was often yesterday's speculative or discredited legal proposition. As for factually unmeritorious claims and defences, all can agree that litigation rules should be designed to discourage manufactured allegations without, at the same time, discouraging meritorious actions. It is generally accepted that the legal system is quite good at weeding out fraudulent and vexatious claims; the greater challenge lies in avoiding situations where it is cheaper for defendants, and usually

36 *Unison v Lord Chancellor* [2017] UKSC 51 [71].

their insurers, to settle hopeless claims rather than to expose and defeat them.[37] There are a range of adverse orders and sanctions that can be imposed on those who bring dishonest actions.[38] No one asserts that these safeguards work perfectly, but there are no perfect safeguards against fraud in any domain and a balance has to be struck between accessibility and vulnerability of the system, taking into the account the importance of accessing the system and the costs of abuse. To take internet banking as an example, no one would seriously suggest that that we deliberately make internet based transactions incredibly burdensome to bona fide customers as a means of deterring those acting in bad faith. Beyond fraudulent and vexatious claims, and claims unknown to the law, how meritorious a claim or defence ought to be before it becomes worthy of court adjudication is a difficult question both in theory and practice. I am personally a strong proponent of robust summary judgment procedures, but the appropriate threshold that a case needs to pass to avoid summary adjudication is a matter upon which reasonable minds will often differ.[39] Moreover, even if there is agreement on the relevant standard, applying it to the facts of individual cases can be difficult. This is why even summary judgment applications can result in the smallest majority opinions reached by final appellate courts.[40]

Turning to the proposition that there are some disputes that are not really legal matters, and should not be resolved through litigation, this claim is axiomatically correct, but irrelevant to the design of a civil justice system which only exists to help resolve *legal* disputes. The idea that we might create a litigious society if litigation is cheap, quick and easy has an intuitive appeal. If legal assistance and litigation is so accessible that anyone can resort to it for anything with a legal dimension, there is a risk that lawyers could become involved in very small things. My favourite example is from an acquaintance who was doing their medical training in Switzerland. He received a letter from a lawyer acting for his neighbour which requested that he desist from committing the nuisance of flushing the toilet after 10pm at night, or litigation may ensue. Yet making litigation difficult is a not a sensible solution, either in principle or as a practical means of deterring the 'legalisation' of disputes. Debates and decisions as to

[37] Lord Sumption, 'Abolishing Personal Injuries Law—A Project' Personal Injuries Bar Association Annual Lecture, 16 November 2017, p 5; see also Lord Dyson MR, 'Compensation Culture and Magna Carta' The High Sheriff's Law Lecture, Oxford, 13 October 2015.

[38] This includes a power to award indemnity costs; exceptions to one way cost shifting under CPR 44.15 for claims that have no reasonable grounds, are an abuse of court, or would obstruct the just disposal of the proceedings; *Willers v Joyce* [2016] UKSC 43 (tort of malicious prosecution); and *Jet2Holidays v Hughes* [2019] EWCA Civ 1858 (contempt for false pre-action statements).

[39] Including in the context of class actions: see A Higgins, 'Driving with the handbrake on: competition class actions under the Consumer Rights Act 2015' (2016) 79 Modern Law Review 442.

[40] *Three Rivers DC v Bank of England (No 3)* (Summary Judgment) [2003] 2 AC 1.

what should and should not be a legal matter are best held in Parliament or by judges defining the substantive common law. To use civil procedure as a means of deterring disputes where we think the game is not worth the candle is poor legal policy, and risks subverting the relationship between substance and procedure. First, it is inherently regressive. If you are rich enough to litigate about a neighbour's untimely loo flushing you can still do it. Secondly, and most judges know this from painful experience, recalcitrant litigants or those simply up to no good are rarely deterred by procedural obstacles put in their way. By contrast procedural obstacles can easily dissuade those with legitimate grievances because they think the process is just too hard and too costly.

Equally importantly, the wariness of civil litigation overlooks one of its defining characteristics: that there is equivalence between the moral harm in a false positive (an outcome that wrongly favours the claimant) and the moral harm in a false negative (an outcome that wrongly favours the defendant). It is for this reason that the civil standard of proof favours neither party, and that the burden proof is used sparingly as a 'tiebreak' rule to determine who should lose when the court cannot be sure, on the balance of probabilities, who ought to succeed.[41]

I readily acknowledge that action between private parties and the state reviewing the legality of decisions by the state fall into a different category. Certainly, there is no equivalence in the harm that would be caused to the parties in the event of a wrong outcome.[42] But based on the principle of equality in 'ordinary' civil litigation, the suggestion that we should not make it too easy to litigate makes little sense because it ignores the equally strong imperative *not* to make it too easy to avoid litigation.

Comparative data on rates of civil litigation

The above arguments presuppose that there is a general cultural aversion to litigation in England. But is this true of the general populace? I conducted some basic empirical research on comparative rates of civil litigation in England & Wales and six of the other largest economies in the world: the United States, China, Japan, Germany, France and Italy (Figure 2.1).[43] I looked at levels of

41 See eg *Pickford v ICI* [1998] 3 All ER 462; *Rhesa Shipping Co SA v Edmund* (The Popi M) [1985] 1 WLR 948.

42 Though this difference between public litigation and private litigation, militates in favour of making judicial review proceedings more, not less accessible, than ordinary civil litigation.

43 A notable omission from this list is India. Unfortunately, there is no central repository of litigation statistics in India.

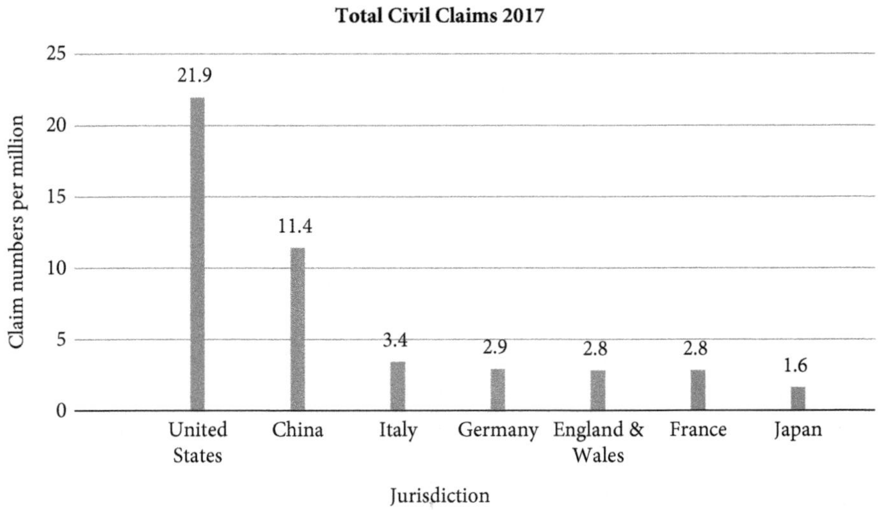

Figure 2.1 Total civil claims 2017

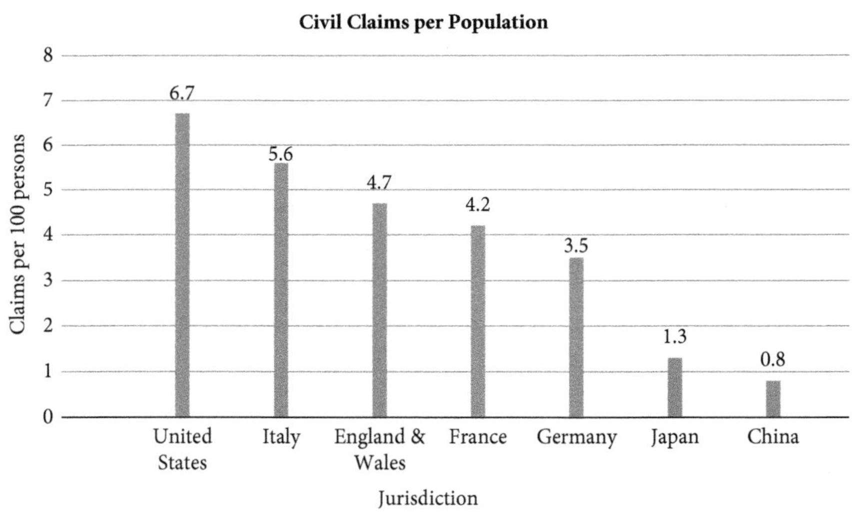

Figure 2.2 Civil claims per population

litigation per head of population (Figure 2.2) and national GDP (Figure 2.3), given that people and economic activity are two obvious drivers of litigation. Not surprisingly, the countries with the largest populations and GDP, the United States and China, also have the highest volumes of litigation. Yet in relative terms England & Wales can be considered one of the more 'litigious'

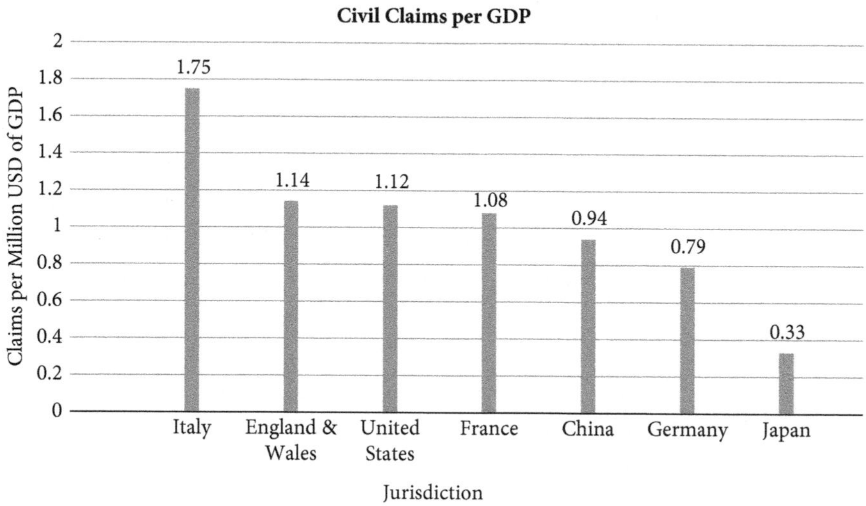

Figure 2.3 Civil claims per GDP

members of this group. Only the Italians rank more highly on both civil claims per capita and civil claims per GDP. When it comes to the amount of litigation as a share of GDP, England is slightly more litigious than the United States. By contrast the Germans and French are less litigious than the Italians, Americans and the English, and the Japanese are dramatically less litigious than the Western world. By population measures, China is even less litigious than the Japanese, but as a proportion of GDP rates of litigation in China come closer to those observed in the west, and even exceed that in Germany.

A range of important caveats need to be added to this research. Data is not reported uniformly across jurisdictions,[44] and in some countries there is

[44] Data on claim numbers was obtained from the following sources: China: Xiaomei Wu (Ed), *Law Yearbook of China 2018* (China Law Yearbook, October 2018); England & Wales: Ministry of Justice Civil Justice Statistics Quarterly https://www.gov.uk/government/collections/civil-justice-statistics-quarterly, and Tribunal Statistics Quarterly https://www.gov.uk/government/collections/tribunals-statistics#tribunal-statistics-quarterly; France: Les chiffres-cles de la Justice 2018 http://www.justice.gouv.fr/; Germany: Statistisches Bundesamt https://www.destatis.de/EN/Themes/Government/Justice/Tables/judicial-proceedings.html; Italy: Corte Suprema Di Cassaziona Relazione sull'amminstazione della giustizia nell'anno 2018 http://www.cortedicassazione.it/cassazione-resources/resources/cms/documents/20190125_RelazioneAG2018.pdf; Japan: Supreme Court of Japan Statistics http://www.courts.go.jp/english/publications/index.html;

United States: Administrative Office of U.S. Courts https://www.uscourts.gov/statistics-reports (For Federal Filings) and National Centre for State Courts Court Statistics Project: http://www.courtstatistics.org/ (State Filings). Note claim numbers have been rounded to the nearest 100,000. All population and GDP data, except for England & Wales, was taken from the World Bank: https://data.worldbank.org/indicator/SP.POP.TOTL, https://data.worldbank.org/indicator/NY.GDP.MKTP.CD. For England & Wales population data was taken from the Office of National Statistics https://www.ons.gov.uk/peoplepopulationandcommunity/populationandmigration/populationestimates and GDP

a possibility that total claims reported may include some appeals (ie not new claims) because it includes courts that exercise both first instance and appellate jurisdiction.[45] The fact that 'civil litigation' is not uniformly classified across jurisdictions is also a potential confounding factor. I have included civil, administrative and family claims in the claim numbers in Figures 2.1–2.3 above, but where possible excluded 'juvenile' matters. The attractiveness of different jurisdictions as a venue for transnational commercial litigation can also affect claim numbers, even though this litigation does not reflect any litigiousness of residents in the host jurisdiction. Similarly, substantive rules could also affect claim numbers where there is, in substance, no 'dispute' between the parties and hence a claim is not evidence of 'litigiousness'. Thus, for example where a married couple must file a claim to dissolve their marriage this is invariably going to affect the numbers of family law claims. Were family law claims to be removed from the data, this would not have a substantial impact on the relative litigiousness of different jurisdictions, with the notable exception of Japan. Once family law matters are removed from the Japanese data, the volume of civil litigation in that country becomes vanishingly small.[46] Claim numbers can also be affected by rules that facilitate or restrict collective redress. For example, in the United States one claim may incorporate thousands of class members who would otherwise have to file individual suits in other jurisdictions. As such some countries may be more litigious than the raw claim numbers might suggest.

Although the comparative litigiousness of these different countries is interesting, one cannot say that the differences between the *Western* nations measured is stark. Using the population measure, the difference between the most and least litigious nation (the United States and Germany respectively) is less than 2 to 1, and using the GDP measure the difference is less than 2.5 to 1 (Italy and Germany respectively). Nor can one readily conclude from this data that any nation, even the Italians, are objectively litigious. It is debatable whether the concept of litigiousness is even capable of objective measurement.[47] How

data was calculated using a combination of World Bank data and Scotland specific data: https://www.gov.scot/collections/economy-statistics/ (Note that while GDP for England & Wales excludes Scotland, it does not exclude Northern Ireland economic activity, hence claims per GDP of England & Wales is likely to be slightly higher than that represented in the table.) All data sources are published official statistics.

[45] Although in every jurisdiction the total case numbers for such mixed appellate and first instance courts was relatively low.

[46] Approximately two thirds of total civil claims in Japan in 2017 were family cases: http://www.courts.go.jp/english/publications/index.html.

[47] For discussion see Marc Galanter, 'The Vanishing Trial: An Examination of Trials and Related Matters in Federal and State Courts' (2004) 1 *Journal of Empirical Legal Studies* 459

much is too much, or too little, litigation must take account of the place of a legal system within the broader political and economic framework of a nation in terms of methods of dispute resolution, law enforcement and welfare provision, and that is even before one turns to more nebulous concepts such as cultural differences. Despite the different systems, traditions and cultures represented in this research, the total numbers of claims in all jurisdictions could fairly be described as modest by all measures.

That the English are on one measure (claims per GDP) slightly more litigious than their American cousins, who the English frequently deride for being 'litigation happy', would suggest that any English desire not to promote 'US style' litigation is a cultural aspiration, or reflects a degree of cultural anxiety about the current state of English society. A more significant finding, however, is that there is no necessary correlation between the accessibility of a legal system and the volume of litigation. The Germans do not use their courts just because they can. Comparative analyses of civil justice systems around the world have suggested that Germany has a much more accessible legal system than other advanced legal systems, principally because of their ability to keep costs proportionate to the value in dispute through a strict regime of fixed costs.[48] Yet the Germans litigate less than the English, despite the English system being less affordable and often disproportionately expensive to the value of the claim.[49] In short, the concern amongst some law and policy makers in England that making it 'too easy' to litigate would inevitably lead to undesirably higher rates of litigation appears not to be borne out by the statistics, at least as they relate to other jurisdictions.

Media coverage of litigation

The concern that the English would rush to the courts if it were easy to access them is not confined to law and policy makers. Fears about England becoming a litigious society can be seen in the media coverage and commentary

[48] A Zuckerman (ed), *Civil Justice in Crisis: Comparative Perspectives of Procedure* (OUP, 1999).

[49] One interesting difference between Germany and England is that rates of litigation not resolved through settlement in Germany appear to be much higher than they are in England. Approximately 25% of civil claims in local courts that were terminated in 2017 were resolved through a 'controversial decision' ('streitiges Urteil', ie a contested judicial determination following a hearing. See German data at n 45). By contrast, in England approximately 15% of claims only in the County Court were formally defended (see n 13). Germany does not keep statistics on the number of contested claims but that number is likely to be considerably higher than the number of claims that were resolved through a controversial decision as non-controversial claims also include claims resolved part way through the legal process including settled and withdrawn claims.

on litigation. In particular, the rise of the term 'compensation culture', which appears to have been first used in a newspaper article in 1994[50] to pejoratively describe the practice of people making legal claims for compensation, suggests deep sceptism about, if not outright hostility towards, litigation. The empirical soundness of claims of a *rise* in a compensation culture have been questioned by a number of commentators, who have reviewed claim statistics for certain categories of tortious litigation over a number of years.[51] What is beyond doubt, however, is that it has been a driver, indeed stated policy reason, for reforms to certain areas of tort law and the civil justice system.[52] And this policy agenda is likely in part a reaction to media coverage about the financial costs, or social undesirability, of a compensation culture.

With the help of a research assistant I conducted some simple quantitative research into media coverage of litigation and legal concepts in England & Wales newspapers between 2016 and 2018 to examine the balance of coverage between real legal concepts and cases and concerns about a compensation culture (See Figure 2.4).[53] We focused on tort related concepts given tortious litigation, and especially personal injuries litigation, is the predominant focus of those criticising a compensation culture.[54] Over a two-year period between

[50] Levin B, 'Addicted to Welfare' *The Times*, 17 December 1993.

[51] These have grown substantially in number since the 1960s but have been relatively stable for the past quarter of a century: K Patten, 'Compensation, Culture, and the Mythologising of Justice' (2020) 39 *CJQ* (forthcoming). See also Annette Morris, 'Spiralling or Stabilising? The Compensation Culture and Our Propensity to Claim Damages for Personal Injury' (2007) 70 *MLR* 349.

[52] Lord Sumption, 'Abolishing Personal Injuries Law—A Project' Personal Injuries Bar Association Annual Lecture, 16 November 2017, p 2. In his speech Lord Sumption pointed to measures to curtail the activities of claims management companies, including changes to the solicitors' conduct rules, costs rule changes that are largely unfavourable to claimants, proposals for requiring new forms of medical evidence in insurance claims can be settled, and a statutory scale of damages awards for whiplash claims. To this list can be added proposed reforms to clinical negligence claims due to concerns about the cost of claims against the National Health Service. See also n 55.

[53] The English & Welsh newspapers held in the Lexis database were Bath Chronicle; Belfast News Letter; Belfast Telegraph; Birmingham Evening Mail; Birmingham Post; Bristol Post; chroniclelive.co.uk; The Citizen Gloucester; Coventry Newspapers; coventrytelegraph.net; The Daily Mail and Mail on Sunday (London); Daily Post (North Wales); Daily Star Online; The Daily Telegraph (London); Derby Telegraph; East Anglian Daily Times; Eastern Daily Press; The European; Evening Gazette; Evening News (Norwich); The Evening Standard (London); Evening Star; Exeter Express and Echo; The Express; Gloucestershire Echo; Grimsby Telegraph; The Guardian (London); Hull Daily Mail; The Independent (United Kingdom); Johnston Press Plc; Leeds Weekly News; Leicester Mercury; Liverpool Echo; Manchester Evening News; The Mirror (The Daily Mirror and The Sunday Mirror); Northcliffe Newspapers; The Northern Echo (Newsquest Regional Press); Nottingham Post; The Observer (London); The People; The Plymouth Herald; Regional Independent Media; Scunthorpe Telegraph; South Wales Echo; South Wales Evening Post; Sports Argus; Stoke The Sentinel; The Sun (England); The Sunday Express; Sunday Mercury; The Sunday Telegraph (London); The Sunday Times (London); Sunderland Echo; TES; The Times (London); Times Higher Education; Torquay Herald Express; UK NewsQuest Regional Press; Wales on Sunday; Western Daily Press; The Western Mail; Western Morning News; Yorkshire Evening Post; Yorkshire Post.

[54] For example, Lord Young 'Common Sense, Common Safety' (London: Cabinet Office, October 2010) p 7; Ministry of Justice, 'Curbing Compensation Culture: Government to Ban Referral Fees', Press Release, 9 September 2011.

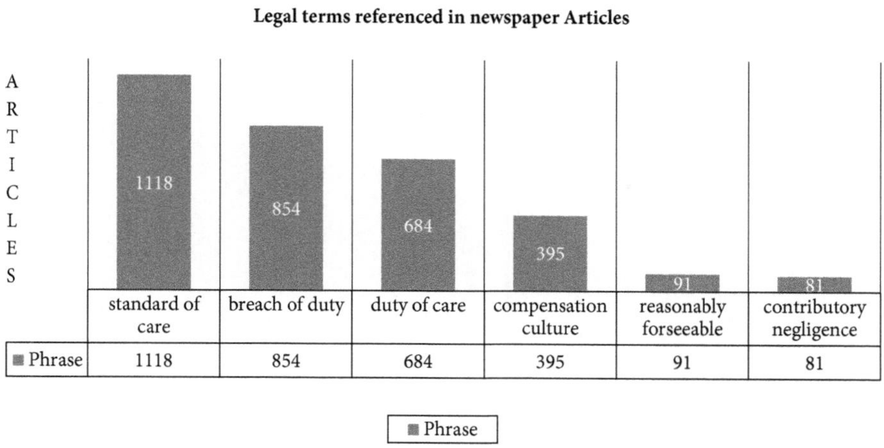

Figure 2.4 Legal terms referenced in newspaper articles

2016 and 2018 in newspapers in England & Wales, there was one article referring to 'compensation culture' for approximately every two articles that mentioned 'duty of care' or 'breach of duty'—common law legal terms dating back to *Donoghue v Stevenson* and beyond.[55]

As can be seen from Figure 2.4, the one term that was used well above all others was 'standard of care', although this result can be partly explained by the fact that it is not a law specific term, and was frequently used in public policy contexts; for example newspapers assessing, and politicians discussing, the standard of care in the National Health Service.

It is notable that there is considerable variation between newspapers in the level of usage of the term compensation culture, including the relative use of it and other legal concepts. Figure 2.5 sets out the five English-based publications that contained the most references to compensation culture over the relevant period. Worthy of particular mention is Rupert Murdoch's News Group Newspapers. *The Times* mentioned the term more than any other publication and almost as often as it did the term 'duty of care'. The Murdoch tabloid, the *Sun*, came third on the list and used the term more than both the terms 'duty of care' and 'breach of duty'. Although not appearing in Figure 2.5, another of Murdoch's English papers, the *Sunday Times*, came 6th on the list with 16 references, despite it being published only once a week. Like the *Sun* it also used the term more often than it did duty of care or breach of duty. The Mail group

[55] For discussion of the origins of the concept see J Plunkett, 'The Historical Foundations of the Duty of Care' [2015] *Monash University Law Review* 25

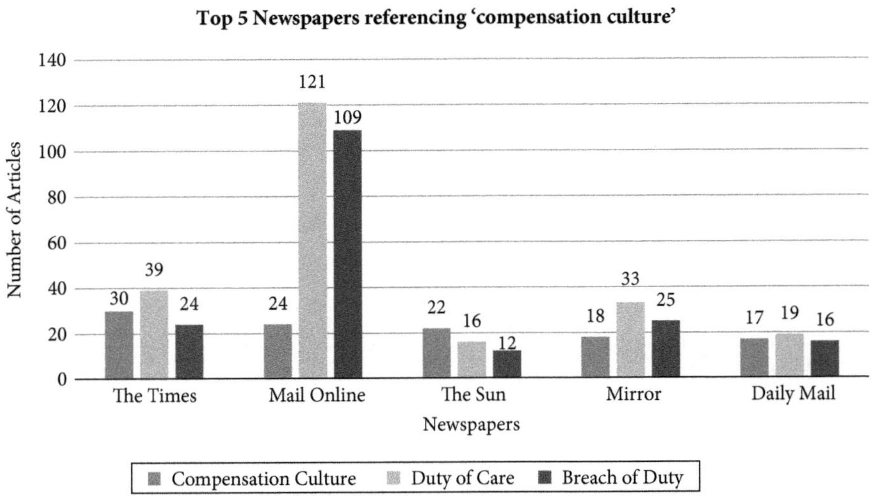

Figure 2.5 Top five newspapers referencing 'compensation culture'

also features prominently on this list but the *Mail Online* did have the most significant negative ratio between coverage of compensation culture and standard tort legal concepts.

It is important to acknowledge that these statistics are purely quantitative. They do not consider how the concepts were reported and whether they were treated negatively or positively. However, a qualitative review of these articles reveals that reporting of compensation culture was largely, although not universally, negative in nature. The *Times* coverage is again a good example. Some reports suggested that the compensation culture in Britain was not as 'bad' as in other countries but law reform was still needed,[56] however many reports from the same newspaper suggested compensation culture caused real damage to British society, from the NHS, to the costs of insurance, to intrusion by those soliciting claims. Headlines included:

> 'Many NHS victims should settle for an apology; As litigation costs soar and doctors quit, it's time to kick back against the compensation culture';[57]
> 'Compensation culture is 'fault of lawyers'; Top insurer urges action to tackle rising payouts for fraudulent claims and lump sums, writes Katherine Griffiths';[58]

[56] *The Times* (London) Editorial, 28 February 2017.
[57] *The Times* (London) Clare Foges, 5 February 2018.
[58] *The Times* (London) Katherine Griffiths, 12 June 2017.

'Public hit by 12m daily nuisance calls from ambulance chasers; Time to end scourge of nuisance calls'.[59]

Although preoccupation with a 'compensation culture' amongst certain media outlets is noteworthy, similar concerns have been expressed in other circles including legal academia. In his 2015 High Sheriff Lecture, Lord Dyson MR quoted the tort scholar Tony Weir who was bemoaning what he felt was an undesirable cultural shift towards more litigation:

> There is a view that as a society we have undergone a cultural shift. No longer is British Society characterised by a philosophical and accepting approach to life. On the contrary, the view is taken that we are becoming more American in our approach, more ready to rush into litigation. To borrow from Tony Weir we have become a 'wondrously unstoical and whingeing society with an endemic neurosis for litigation' and which rather than see us 'grin and bear it' sees us 'grit our teeth and sue'.[60]

By contrast the senior judiciary has appeared unfazed by concerns over the rise of compensation culture, which is not altogether unsurprising given that the term does not sound in any recognised legal principle.[61] Unfortunately however, there is limited media coverage of the leading cases in which the courts have developed the principles of tort law that apply to all of us. We examined media coverage of Supreme Court cases dealing with tort claims over a similar period for our study of media coverage of tort related legal concepts and 'compensation culture'[62] (see Figures 2.4 and 2.5). Indeed there were more articles

[59] *The Times* (London) Andrew Ellson, 21 March 2016.

[60] Lord Dyson MR, 'Magna Carta and Compensation Culture', The High Sheriff's Law Lecture, Oxford, 13 October 2015 [19] citing T Weir, 'Governmental Liability' [1989] *Public Law* 40, 76.

[61] As Lord Sumption stated in a speech considering the case for abolishing personal injuries law: compensation culture is 'a slogan, and not a carefully thought out position. It encompasses at least two complaints, which are very different although they share a common rhetoric. One is that too many fraudulent claims are being made: in other words, people are being too greedy. The other is that too many justified claims are being made: in other words, the law is being too generous.' In relation to fraud, Lord Sumption observed that the law does not countenance fraud and never has. As for legitimate claims, he stated: 'To those like me who believe that litigation is an evil, the active solicitation of claims can seem distasteful. But it is really not a matter of taste, and I find it impossible to say that it is wrong. If the law entitles the victim of an accident to compensation, it ill becomes us to criticise him for knowing it and claiming.' See Lord Sumption, 'Abolishing Personal Injuries Law—A Project', Personal Injuries Bar Association Annual Lecture, 16 November 2017, pp 5–6. See also Lord Dyson MR, 'Compensation Culture and Magna Carta', The High Sheriff's Law Lecture, Oxford, 13 October 2015.

[62] We looked at Supreme Court cases between January 2016 and March 2018. We conducted an Advanced Search for cases on Westlaw under the 'Subject/Keyword' field of '"animals" OR "defamation" OR "health and safety at work" OR "negligence" OR "nuisance" OR "personal Injury" OR "personal property" OR "torts"'. Cases from jurisdictions other than England and Wales—such as Scottish Supreme Court cases—were then removed from the list. In addition, cases were removed from the

referring to compensation culture then there were articles reporting on all tort related Supreme Court cases over the same period. A number of cases received no coverage at all, including the Supreme Court's decision in *Willers v Joyce* in which the Supreme Court held that bringing baseless litigation for a malicious purpose was itself an actionable tort.[63] The lack of coverage of this case is surprising, given that media outlets and commentators concerned about a compensation culture should welcome a decision by the Supreme Court providing remedies against those who launch litigation with improper motives. One of the leading cases on the law of negligence in the last 30 years, *Robinson v Chief Constable of West Yorkshire Police* [2018] UKSC 4, was covered in just two articles by regional newspapers where the unfortunate incident in that case—a public arrest in Huddersfield that led to a member of the public being injured by a police officer—occurred.[64] Other examples of the importance of regional media include coverage of *Cox v Ministry of Justice* [2016] UKSC 10, which is a leading decision on the relationships that can give rise to vicarious liability. This case was covered by just one national newspaper. There were three more articles on the case in regional and local newspapers from the area in which the prison where the accident in that case occurred. Another leading decision on vicarious liability, *Armes v Nottinghamshire County Council* [2017] UKSC 60, was reported in a few more media articles but the most in-depth coverage (three out of seven articles in total) was provided by the *Nottingham Post*. Figure 2.6 displays Supreme Court Tort cases reported by number of articles, and Table 2.1 lists the Supreme Court Tort cases that received no coverage according to our study.

Apart from underscoring the value of regional newspapers in reporting on cases of national significance,[65] the study also highlighted that no legal question attracts more media attention than what rights the media have to report

list if the substantive issues considered by the Court did not fall within the law of torts. An example was *Moreno v Motor Insurers' Bureau* [2016] UKSC 52. Sweet & Maxwell classified this case under the 'Subject/Keyword' 'personal injury', though the Court only considered the preliminary issue of the law applicable to the claimant's personal injury claim. We then gathered media coverage of our sample of cases. To do this, we conducted a search of UK Newspapers under the 'News' tab of LexisNexis. As search terms, we used the name(s) of each case in our sample. This search returned some false positives: articles which included the parties' names but were not about the case. These articles were removed from our results. We also removed results from the Times Law Reports, because their audience is not the general public.

63 *Willers v Joyce* [2016] UKSC 43.

64 *Robinson v Chief Constable of West Yorkshire Police* [2018] UKSC 4. The case was reported in the *Yorkshire Post* and the *Huddersfield Daily Examiner* only.

65 This is a worrying finding given the challenges faced by regional media to remain economically viable in the age of the internet.

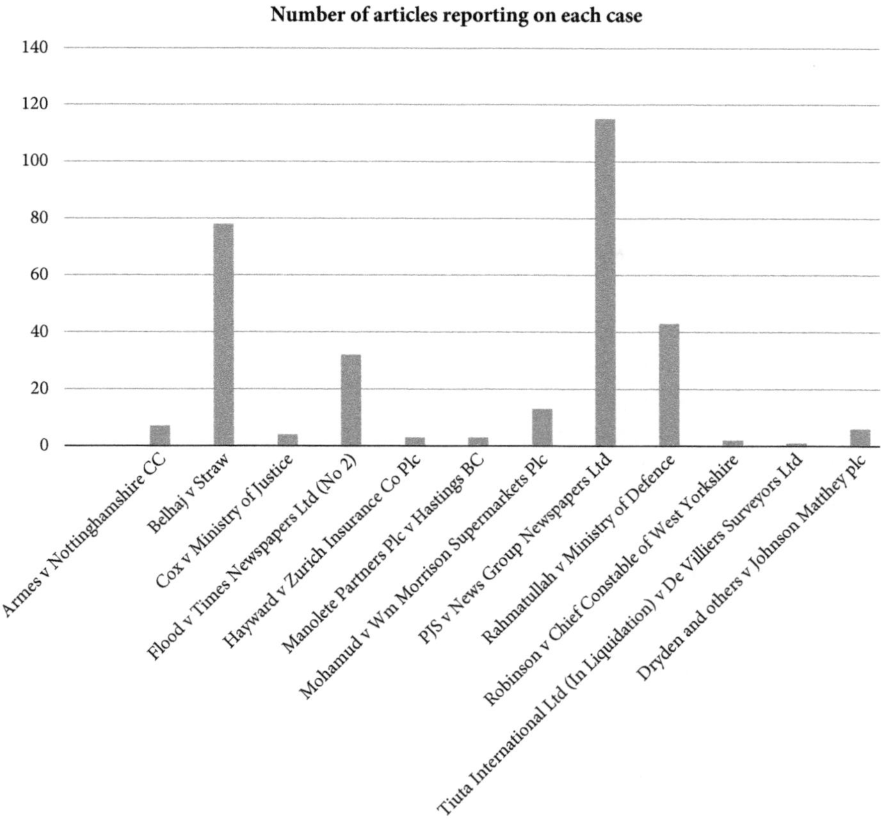

Figure 2.6 Number of articles reporting on each case

on legal cases. The case with the most newspaper coverage was *PJS v News Group Newspapers Limited*[66] a case considering the media's right to report on the details, and specifically the identities, of parties to litigation involving an alleged breach of privacy. The second most reported case was that of *Belhaj v Staw* which raised a number of important legal questions arising from the UK Government's involvement in the rendition of Mr Belhaj and his wife to Libya where they were imprisoned and tortured.[67] Thus while some important decisions are covered extensively by the media, it is a pity that the open justice principle that the media campaigns so vigorously to defend, is not more regularly

[66] *PJS v News Group Newspapers Ltd* [2016] UKSC 26.

[67] UK involvement in the war on terrorism and press freedom (and specifically the impact of English cost rules on the right to freedom of expression) were also the subjects of the third and fourth most reported cases: *Rahmatullah v Ministry of Defence* [2017] UKSC 1; *Times Newspapers Limited v Flood* [2017] UKSC 33.

Table 2.1 UKSC Tort Cases Reported in the Media

Supreme Court decision	Number of articles
Armes v Nottinghamshire CC	7
Belhaj v Straw	78
Cox v Ministry of Justice	4
Dryden and others v Johnson Matthey plc	6
Flood v Times Newspapers Ltd (No 2)	32
Hayward v Zurich Insurance Co Plc	3
Manolete Partners Plc v Hastings BC	3
Mohamud v Wm Morrison Supermarkets Plc	13
PJS v News Group Newspapers Ltd	115
Rahmatullah v Ministry of Defence	43
Robinson v Chief Constable of West Yorkshire	2
Tiuta International Ltd (In Liquidation) v De Villiers Surveyors Ltd	1
AIG Europe Ltd v OC320301 LLP	0
AMT Futures Ltd v Marzillier, Dr Meier & Dr Guntner Rechtsanwaltsgesellschaft mbH	0
Four Seasons Holdings Inc v Brownlie	0
Gabriel v Little	0
Knauer v Ministry of Justice	0
Impact Funding Solutions Ltd v Barrington Support Services Ltd (formerly Lawyers At Work Ltd)	0
Swynson Ltd v Lowick Rose LLP (In Liquidation) (formerly Hurst Morrison Thomson LLP)	0
Willers v Joyce	0

taken advantage of by the media to report on cases that determine the legal principles that govern us all.

Conclusion

This chapter has provided a brief and broad overview of some of the themes touched upon in the CPR at 20 conference, and some of the challenges facing the civil justice system today. There is a strong case for redefining the legal definition of proportionality. Notwithstanding Lord Woolf's introduction of a proportionality principle into the overriding objective, disproportionate costs are a common feature of the English civil justice system. English law has historically provided an open textured definition of proportionality which makes it possible for 'proportionate costs' to exceed the financial value of the claim in dispute. As the UK Supreme Court held in the *Unison* case, it cannot be proportionate to require anyone to engage in economically irrational behaviour to litigate reasonably arguable claims. Except where claims warrant test case treatment because they raise matters of general public importance, all cases should be resolved at costs that are mathematically proportional to the value of the rights in issue. Accordingly, it may be necessary to formally split the dual functions of the civil justice system—rule clarification on the one hand and dispute resolution on the other. More summary procedures should not, however, be dismissed as prefect justice for the few and rough justice for the many. English law's Achilles heel has been a tendency to measure justice independently of the time and cost involved in achieving the outcome; only once it is recognised that costs and time are integral to just outcomes is there any hope of Lord Woolf's proportionality being realised in practice.

The chapter also examined whether there is a deeper cultural objection in England to civil justice reform to make litigation quicker and cheaper, which lies in a general aversion to litigation as a divisive and often socially undesirable phenomenon. The chapter argues that litigation is a form of peaceful protest which is not divisive per se, and need not be more divisive than the underlying circumstances that give rise to it. The chapter presents some empirical data about civil claim numbers in England and other advanced legal systems, which suggests the English are more litigious than one would imagine based on 'stiff upper lip' and 'keep calm and carry on' stereotypes. By contrast, there is significant media preoccupation about the alleged rise of a compensation culture in England, and worryingly, comparatively less coverage of the key legal decisions handed down by the Supreme Court which articulate the legal principles that govern our everyday lives. As such the public may be receiving a distorted picture of the law and the legal system as it actually operates in practice.

PART II
JUDICIAL PRESENTATIONS

3

Rule-Making for a Digital Court Process

The Civil Procedure Rules—20th Anniversary Conference, 2019

Terence Etherton

I am delighted to be here today at this conference to mark the 20th Anniversary of the introduction of the Civil Procedure Rules. Reform of civil court processes has been and continues to be ongoing. The Woolf reforms were followed by the Jackson review, the Civil Courts Structure Review and now the HMCTS Reform Programme. The present reforms are, however, different. One aim of the Reform Programme is to deliver a more efficient, effective and high performing courts system through the use of new technology. Experience on the ground in developing a new digital civil justice process has made clear the need for a different way of approaching rule making.

I must dispel one myth at the very outset, a myth which is widespread. We do not have, nor are there any plans for, a single online court. The senior judiciary originally had a bold vision for a single common digital platform for Civil, Family and Tribunal claims, with, so far as possible, common forms and processes and without any formal jurisdictional divisions. That proposal was rejected by the Government in 2017. Accordingly, since that time the non-crime Reform Programme has proceeded on the basis of individual digital dispute resolution initiatives in each of the existing jurisdictions—Civil, Family and Tribunals. Each has its own rule-making procedures. Each has its own arrangements for consultation and for collaboration with HMCTS and the MoJ.

So far as civil is concerned, digitisation of dispute resolution is currently focused on the Online Civil Money Claims project (OCMC). This was established as part of the Reform Programme in August 2016. OCMC is currently limited to claims for a specified sum of less than £10,000, with a view to an increase in due course to claims of up to £25,000. In other words, these are the claims which are currently classified as small claims and fast track claims. The importance of these claims cannot be overstated. In 2018, of the total number of money claims issued, 173,432 were allocated to a track. 53% of those were

Terence Etherton, *Rule-Making for a Digital Court Process* In: *The Civil Procedure Rules at 20.* Edited by: Andrew Higgins, Oxford University Press (2020). © the several contributors. DOI: 10.1093/oso/9780198863182.003.0003.

allocated to the small claims track and 40% were allocated to the fast track. Accordingly, only 7% of money claims allocated to track in 2018 were over £25,000. Certain claims are excluded from OCMC, such as personal injury claims and certain consumer credit claims.

The development of OCMC has proceeded with contributions from a number of different bodies aside from HMCTS. The Civil Judicial Engagement Group provides a forum for liaison between staff working on the civil Reform Programme and members of the judiciary. Critically, a new sub-committee was established in October 2016 by the Civil Procedure Rule Committee (the CPRC) to address rule changes needed by the introduction of OCMC. The sub-committee has played a critical role in the review and approval of Practice Directions (PDs) for OCMC. Formally, a PD does not need to be approved by the CPRC. A PD is issued by the MR with the concurrence of the Lord Chancellor. Since the CPR were introduced, however, it has been the practice of MRs to refer intended PDs to the CPRC for comment and approval in order to ensure consistency between PDs and the CPR.

It is necessary to emphasise the importance of PDs in the development of OCMC, and in particular PDs made under CPR Part 51. Part 51 provides for Transitional Arrangements and Pilot Schemes. Rule 51.2 provides:

> Practice directions may modify or disapply any provision of these rules—
>
> (a) for specified periods; and
> (b) in relation to proceedings in specified courts, during the operation of pilot schemes for assessing the use of new practices and procedures in connection with proceedings.

This is a useful provision which allows PDs to override the CPR as part of a pilot scheme. Part of its utility is that PDs can be made and amended relatively simply whereas rule changes require a statutory instrument to be laid before Parliament. That normally occurs on a six-monthly cycle.

It was clear from the start that the work the sub-committee was going to do had never been done before. The drafting of the rules would go hand in hand with the construction of the computer system by the project team. I will come back to this theme in due course.

The new rules and procedures were to be designed in an incremental way, starting with the early part of the civil process, such as issuing and serving a Claim Form and Particulars of Claim. The system is intended to encourage settlement and facilitate mediation at an early stage. Later steps in the civil process would be added afterwards so that, if the dispute does not settle, the process would run all the way to trial and on to enforcement. In the same way the rules were also to be created step by step, in parallel with the system, again a theme to which I will return.

HMCTS' initial approach was to run focus groups with court users to investigate how best to design a digital court process. This work did not involve real cases. It allowed the team to design prototype screens and the like. These prototypes were called 'Alpha'. The next step would be to create a system to handle real cases—so called 'Beta'. The project would be initiated using so called 'Private Beta' and 'Public Beta' systems. The new IT system would begin as Private Beta. That would involve a small number of real cases brought by claimants on an invitation only basis. The claimants would be selected by HMCTS from a pool of people who contacted the courts about bringing a claim. Once the Private Beta IT system was working well, it would be ready to be released to Public Beta. The Public Beta system would be open to the public in general. The cases would still have to satisfy the eligibility criteria (e.g. a claim below a certain threshold value) but anyone could access the system and try to bring a claim.

Accordingly, a 'release' of the IT system, underpinned by suitable rules in a pilot PD, would be run first in the Private Beta. The cases would be closely monitored. The small numbers of invited litigants meant that if problems arose with the new release (or the new rules) then they could be addressed. Assuming this worked successfully, the IT would move into Public Beta.

By early 2017 the first drafts of the new rules for the Private Beta system were being considered by the sub-committee of the CPRC. The early version of the IT system was being considered at the same time. A number of rule-making issues were emerging. The rules needed to reflect the fact that a digital court process does not work in the same way as a paper-based process (taking the simplest example, a tick box rather than a signature for a statement of truth). Another emerging issue was whether characteristics of the court process should be stated in the rules or be left simply as characteristics of the computer system itself.

The process of drafting rules alongside the development of the IT is a difficult iterative process. The sub-committee spent considerable time working with the technical team and the drafting lawyers to produce the draft PD. The technical team had both financial and time constraints and it was difficult to match the programme for OCMC with the meetings of the CPRC. It was as a result of those considerations that Sir Peter Coulson, the acting chair of the CPRC, with the approval of the CPRC, and I agreed that the PD and future amendments would be considered for approval on the basis of the sub-committee's recommendations without recourse to the full CPRC. The sub-committee chair would continue to provide the full Committee with progress reports and revert to the full Committee if any particular matter arose which required their expertise. This new way of working has been in force ever since. It is plain that this is the only way the project could have been run given the amount of detailed work involved and the close liaison between the rule makers, HMCTS staff, MoJ drafters, and the IT programmers.

The first pilot PD for OCMC—PD51R—came into force and the IT system went live on 7 August 2017. That was Private Beta (i.e. by invitation only) for specified money claims under £10,000 brought by Litigants in Person (LiPs) to be filed online.

In the work which led to the approval of the Public Beta system in March 2018 for OCMC the question of governance again came into focus on the project because the sub-committee wanted to be satisfied not simply that the rules of the pilot PD made sense but that the IT system itself would work appropriately before it started.

OCMC went into Public Beta in March 2018. It has developed since then and as at today's date comprises the following features. LiPs can file claims online. As at 31 May 2019, 69,000 claims have been filed voluntarily by LiPs. A defence can be filed online. 16,000 defences have been filed voluntarily online. As from a couple of months ago, claims can be admitted in whole or in part. Where there is an admission but also a request for time for payment, the IT system will gather the evidence and calculate an appropriate repayment schedule. There have been 835 admissions online. Offers to settle can be made on line. 668 such offers have been made. A standard settlement agreement online can be reached. There have been 223.

The IT system will cater for a request for a stay to negotiate or mediate. The system also gives information to litigants as to facilities for mediation. There can be a request for judgment in default of defence. 44,000 such requests have been made. The online forms to be completed by the litigants enable them to articulate their case in a more straightforward and chronological way than might otherwise be the case.

It is necessary to explain where the IT currently begins and ends. If a claimant voluntarily completes a claim online, which includes a statement of truth and payment of the appropriate fee, the claim is issued. The claim form is printed in the Northampton Business Centre and posted, by way of service, to the defendant's address. If, in completing the claim online, the claimant has provided an email address for the defendant, the IT system instantaneously sends an email to the defendant informing them of the existence of the claim and giving them secure access to the IT system to be able to read the claim form online. Although that is not technically service, a number of defendants do immediately respond doing all the things that the IT system allows, and so there are cases where the claim is settled within minutes of the claim being completed online. If the case is defended and has not reached a settlement, it falls outside the pilot and the PD. It proceeds at Northampton. The litigants complete directions questionnaires and, on receipt of those, the papers are sent to the appropriate court where the case proceeds in the usual way. If the defendant has responded online, it is likely in practice that the case will be sent to the appropriate local court more speedily than with a pure paper process. Feedback from members of the judiciary suggests that there will also be less need to give further directions for greater particularity in the claim or defence.

When OCMC is in full operation, there will be an online end-to-end process. This means that, in addition to the filing online of claim and defence, the directions questionnaires will be completed online, the order giving management directions will be online, the parties will upload their evidence online in accordance with the timetable and deadline specified online, and, following a determination on the merits (which may be online or not according to circumstances to be determined), an order will be generated online.

It is currently contemplated that the end-to-end process in the Public Beta pilot will be completed by June 2020. In the meantime, the next steps will be directions questionnaires online, opt-out mediation, legal advisers giving case management directions in claims under £300 for 4 pilot courts (Manchester, Birmingham, Edmonton and Clerkenwell & Shoreditch). After that, the pilot will cater for online upload of evidence and for determination on the evidence online, without an oral hearing, for claims under £300 for the 4 pilot courts.

By way of clarification on opt-out mediation, which is a major aspect of the new digital process, this will be by way of referral to the existing small claims mediation service, which is a telephone service. My own hope is that this will be translated in due course into a full online mediation process.

It should also be mentioned that, as part of the general civil Reform Programme, there is a video pilot currently under way for a 'skype' type hearing for applications to set aside default judgments.

An end-to-end online process of this kind requires not only electronic filing but also a digital case file management facility. A digital case file management system is currently being extended from the Rolls Building to the rest of the High Court and the Civil Division of the Court of Appeal. Another digital file management system is currently being piloted in the family justice system.

With the unattractive name of Core Case Data, this is to be rolled out in county courts starting with the 4 pilot courts.

As I have said, the current Public Beta pilot for OCMC is a voluntary process limited to LiPs. It is intended that in due course an online money claim process will be extended to professional court users based on the same file management system as OCMC.

There is, of course, currently a digital filing process for money claims in the form of Money Claims Online—MCOL, which operates out of Northampton. This is limited to online filing, including bulk issuing by organisations such as HMRC, and to filing requests for judgment and warrants. It has a higher money limit than the current OCMC pilot. It does not have the other facilities currently in play or planned for OCMC and also has a character limit. In due course HMCTS has said it will be closed down.

What I have so far described is the factual setting for the practical and policy issues about rule making for a digital court system. There are several aspects to this. First, as I have already mentioned, the creation of a digital court process and additions or alterations to it involve an intense, ongoing, interaction between software writers or coders, those with a knowledge of litigation process and drafters. There is a continual trial, error and refinement of the steps by which the user is to be taken through the litigation process by responding to instructions and information on the screen and of the responses from the user which the IT system will accept or reject.

Second, that iterative process would be unworkable if there had to be formal approval by a rule-making body—whether the CPRC or some other body—of each such decision reached between the various groups building the system and each refinement of the IT system. The drafting process is being carried out at the same time as the digital system is being designed. There is no system specification which exists in advance and which can be given to a rule drafter.

Furthermore, the process requires a very considerable judicial resource to provide the coders and HMCTS with guidance on a proper court process. It was for that reason that I recently set up the Judicial Digital Steering Committee (JDSC), under the chairmanship of Birss J, with HHJ Chris Lethem as vice-chair. Both of them are also members of the CPRC digital sub-committee. There are 8 other civil judges—2 CJJ, a QB Master and 5 DJJ. I recognised that, in addition, it would be sensible to include representation from the Family and Tribunal jurisdictions so that all the jurisdictions can be aware of what is happening and learn from each other. The overall purpose of the JDSC is to provide judicial leadership for the digital aspects of the Reform Programme in the civil jurisdiction, including providing judicial leadership for the OCMC pilot, giving expert advice (including drafting guidance) on the procedure and rules aspects, providing assistance to HMCTS in relation to online projects, and contributing to HMCTS's understanding of the justice, lay advice, legal and tech professions' perspective when considering and designing digital systems.

Third, there needs to be a record of the way the IT system will work and will interact with the user at any one moment of time. Otherwise, it would be possible for the system and so the court process to be changed without any formality or oversight by a properly authorised body. An analogy can be drawn with court paper forms. They are designed by HMCTS, but neither HMCTS nor its designers have the power or authority to turn them into CPR Forms. That comes from CPR r.4.1 and PD 4. The paper form can only become a lawful one when annexed to the PD. In a similar fashion, reason dictates that the digital design for an online court process can only become a lawful procedure when approved in a rule or a PD.

These considerations nevertheless raise the issue as to whether a distinction is properly to be made in a digital court process between, on the one hand, what may be called the specifications of the IT system, a function of the software, and, on the other hand, rules as we currently understand them. Take, for example, the limitation in MCOL of a claimant to 1080 characters. That is currently encoded into the IT system but is also written into the relevant rules (PD7E.5.2). In an end-to-end digital OCMC there would be hundreds of such instances. In a properly constructed IT system, however, the litigant in person would not be concerned to look at the rules at all or only minimally. The IT itself would determine, and inform the LiP, what is permissible and what is not and what the next steps are in the process. Take, as an example, judgment in default. OCMC allows a claimant to seek default judgment in certain circumstances. They are coded into the IT system. If the request is well founded a default judgment is issued without human intervention. In OCMC a claimant cannot make a request in the IT system for default judgment until after the time for the defendant to defend has passed. That would be 19 days after issue (or with an extension 33 days). That must be recorded somewhere but would it be better and simpler to have it recorded in an approved specification of the system rather than as a formal rule? In a digital court process there is, perhaps, the opportunity to have two types of public document, each tailored to its proper function. First, a set of rules in the form of simple guidance, simply expressed for the benefit of litigants to guide them what to do. Second, and separately, an approved PD setting out detailed specifications of the IT system, to which litigants ought never need to refer, but which will still be subject to proper oversight.

At the present time, as I have said, these various considerations are being addressed by (1) providing the rules for the OCMC pilot in a PD, which can be added to and varied easily pursuant to my powers as Master of the Rolls, in concurrence with the Lord Chancellor, with review of the draft PD being undertaken by the digital sub-committee of the CPRC, and (2) the Judicial Digital Steering Committee providing detailed technical, legal and judicial advice to HMCTS and the technical operatives. What is as yet undetermined is the formulation of a policy and methodology for formal approval of the IT specifications and to distinguish between what needs only to be approved and formally recorded as the specification and what needs to be formulated as a rule.

Into this complex and fluid but workable and working scenario, the Courts and Tribunals (Online Procedure) Bill has recently been introduced into Parliament by the Government. The origins of this legislation lie sometime in the past, in the form of the Prison and Courts Bill which was introduced into Parliament in 2017. Although the Government had by that time rejected the idea of a single online court covering Civil, Family and Tribunals, it nevertheless considered that it would be desirable for there to be a mechanism by which simply expressed common rules and common processes could be applied across the different jurisdictions. That was, of course, before the development of the individual digital projects in the different jurisdictions and a full realisation of the difficulties and methodology of constructing a digital court process. That Bill fell with the dissolution of Parliament in 2017.

The aim carried over into the present Bill is that there will be a new Online Procedure Rule Committee comprising 2 judicial members, a barrister or solicitor or legal executive and two other individuals, one of whom must have experience in and knowledge of the lay advice sector and one of whom must have IT experience and knowledge relating to 'end-users' experience of internet portals'. Plainly, once enacted, it will required careful thought how practically to integrate the proposals in the current Bill with what we have now learned about constructing a digital court process and the reality of the existing procedural framework and functioning of OCMC on the ground.

Finally, looking at digital court processes in other jurisdictions, notably Canada, the US and Australia, one of the clear lessons is that we must be careful not to be overly ambitious but to proceed cautiously and incrementally, testing the functioning of the system at each stage. This is what has been done and will continue for OCMC. While we must ensure that those who do not wish to use, or cannot use, the online process are not disadvantaged, I have every reason to believe that OCMC will be a success and a great improvement to access to justice for the many tens of thousands of people with small or modest money claims and for those with limited resources.

4

Discovery

To Disclosure and Beyond

Peter Coulson

A previous speaker referred to a case with 159 million emails. There are times, as the Deputy Head of Civil Justice, when I think most of those land in my inbox.

I must have been very bad in a previous life: not only am I doing the first talk after lunch today, but I am talking to you about disclosure. I am not guaranteed to keep you awake. You might be wondering why it was that I agreed to do this at all. Well it was because I was told that, not only was the Master of the Rolls speaking, but two former Masters of the Rolls would also be speaking to you, as a result of which this was going to be the biggest gathering of Masters of the Rolls in one place ever. They live longer these days. So that got me thinking, what is the collective noun for Masters of the Rolls? I've given that some careful thought, and because they have all gone, I can tell you that the best that I have come up with is 'A Dithering'.

Now this conference is to 'mark' the 20th anniversary of the CPR. And I noted the word 'mark', and saw that it was not 'celebrate'. So I thought that I might just pause and actually celebrate the CPR. Obviously, I am slightly biased because I now chair the Civil Procedure Rule Committee (CPRC), which is a hugely enjoyable job and I am privileged to do it. The members of the CPRC are an absolutely fantastic bunch. And I have to say that because quite a few of them are here today.

The CPR get a lot of stick. 'They are not clear enough'; 'they are too long'; 'they are too lawyerly'. I understand all of that; all of those are fair criticisms. We are trying to improve the CPR all the time. We are not always successful. But civil procedure underpins civil litigation in this country, which is a multi-billion pound industry, and is a significant part of the City's contribution to the UK economy. And it is all made possible because we generally have clear rules which are fairly interpreted by judges who take part in active case management throughout the process.

Peter Coulson, *Discovery* In: *The Civil Procedure Rules at 20.* Edited by: Andrew Higgins, Oxford University Press (2020). © the several contributors. DOI: 10.1093/oso/9780198863182.003.0004.

It is all very different to how it was when I first started. One of my very first appearances was in front of a Master of the QB Division (who shall remain nameless), and half way through my opponent's submissions he looked at me and he said, 'You don't need to worry, young man, you're going to win'. So I thought this was a bit surprising (even though my skeleton argument was brilliant), so I said, 'Why is that?' And the Master said, 'His client's called Jeremy. That's enough for me'. I do not think that a rule banning the name Jeremy ever made it into the White Book.

Moving to disclosure, that has always been a procedural problem child, not only for the CPR, but for the Rules of the Supreme Court that went before them. Ever since the photocopier, the potential scope and cost of the disclosure exercise has always been difficult, if not impossible, to control. And yet the basic principle, that each side has to disclose everything relevant, even the documents that might show them in a very bad light, is in my view a critical foundation of the Rule of Law. It underpins the whole concept of a fair trial in this country. It is a vital part of our common law and it is one of the reasons why people trek from around the world to come here to litigate. It is not always the same in other parts of the world, and it is not always the same in some international arbitration, where you can sometimes avoid disclosing documents, even though they might be very damaging.

So how do you emphasise the need for both sides to disclose everything that is relevant, but also ensure that it does not become an exercise that is too expensive and too enormous? Damien, in the first speech this morning, referred to disclosure as being the most important outstanding item for the CPRC to look at. He is right about that. I have a feeling it will be the most important outstanding item for the speaker who fills this slot in 10 years' time or 20 years' time.

We have all attempted to improve it. Sir Rupert Jackson's first reforms, back in 2013 led to the reform of Part 31, and the move away from standard disclosure. The problem is that lawyers are creatures of habit and, for one reason or another, standard disclosure remained the default option. And it is an understandable human impulse: if you have a chance of getting your hands on documents from the other side, then you are going to err on the side of more rather than less, just in case. And I am afraid that is what happened.

So it was thought what was needed was a mandatory pilot, in one specific area of civil business, so we could see if a different approach might work. And, as you know, the area that has been chosen is the Business and Property Courts (B&PC). The pilot was not done on a whim. There was a huge amount of consultation with the B&PC users before the pilot was created and came into force at the start of this year. There were numerous public meetings. It is right to say that not every aspect of the pilot, even as a pilot, was universally popular with those who were going to be using it. So it is always a question of balance.

Now I will not go through every element of the new pilot scheme. But the important things for me are as follows. First, it gets away from standard disclosure—or indeed Model D, as we now have to call it. That is no longer the default option. It will only be ordered where it is the appropriate order to make.

Secondly, there remains the duty, clearly expressed, to disclose known adverse documents, which, as I have said, I believe is critical.

Thirdly, there is an obligation to give what is called initial disclosure, the first run of documents, being the documents that are key to your case, so that somebody can understand not only what your claim is but also its context.

Fourthly, there is an attempt to try and get the parties to agree wherever they can on what sort of disclosure should be ordered, to identify what is the right order for that case, through a document which is called the disclosure review document. And there are five different models—A to E—of the sort of disclosure that may be appropriate. I have referred to Model D which is defined as narrow search-based disclosure with or without narrative documents. So this is an attempt to try and identify the right model for the right case.

Now, of course, the pilot scheme only started in January. There have been one or two cases, but they have been largely about transitional provisions, so it is too early to say how the pilot is going. But from a personal point of view I think it has much to commend it.

In particular, I like the focus on issues at an early stage. My background is the Technology and Construction Court, and it is second nature to us there to identify issues at the start. So I think that is a positive step. I also like the drafting of the pilot generally. The drafting does not have the potential problems (as we heard reference to earlier) of a rule and a practice direction: it is all in one set of fuller rules. In my view, that is a good way to do it.

On that topic, I agree with what Lord Dyson said about duplication in current parts of the CPR. I would like to see that change, but I recognise that it is a huge task because the CPR is already based very much on rules and practice directions.

Finally, I am very pleased to see the back of standard disclosure as a default option. Is it goodbye to *Peruvian Guano*? There is a really exciting lecture topic for somebody. Given that, I think, *Peruvian Guano* was decided before the photocopier had been invented, certainly a proper kind of photocopier, it seems to me that it is high time we waved it goodbye.

There is also the advantage that the pilot scheme is more geared towards electronic disclosure. There is a regular criticism, which I think is valid, of the current Part 31, to the effect that it is very paper-based. This is an attempt to recognise the vast amount of data that is now stored and exchanged electronically. I agree with the speaker who said technical problems can have technical solutions. The mistake I think is to think that disclosure is *all* about technical problems. There are much wider questions, some of which I have indicated. And even if there is a technological solution, who polices the technology? Who identifies the technology as being in accordance with the law? In the future, we might be able to get away with not having a White Book because it is all in the software, but somebody or something is needed to police it, so we can be sure that the software replicates what is in the Rules.

The pilot is going to be properly evaluated, and it is after that that I think we will be able to work out a way forward. Obviously, the evaluation will be a matter for others. But if you wanted my view now, I would say this; if it makes disclosure cheaper, then I think the pilot will be a success. Probably alone amongst your previous speakers, I am the only one who has spent too much of my life doing cost budgeting. You look at somebody's cost budget and the amount for disclosure is always vast—it is a spike, beaten only by expert's reports—and you baulk at the costs. I often used to slash parties' disclosure budgets.

But I do think that this is a part of the CPR where costs come first, second and third in any sensible evaluation. I agree with Lord Dyson when he said that cost remains the one outstanding thing that the CPR has not yet fully grappled with.

The final point to make is about litigants in person. As the Deputy Head of Civil Justice, I spend a lot of time on the reform programme, and the attempts to make the justice system that is open to all, and therefore open to litigants in person. The problem is that there can be a tension between, on the one hand, open and accessible justice and, on the other, the creation of sensible clear rules by which sophisticated litigation of the kind that happens in the Business and Property Courts can be conducted.

And so, for example, in the new pilot, there is a form—the disclosure review document—that involves 10 steps. Take one example. 'Step 4: The parties must discuss and seek to agree the draft list of issues for disclosure and they should consider whether any of the draft issues for disclosure can be removed. For each issue of disclosure that is maintained, the parties should indicate at this point using section 1A of the disclosure review document which model of extended disclosure is sought for each party. Where model C disclosure is contemplated the parties should discuss the request that might apply for the purpose of that disclosure.'

I am guessing that if this pilot is rolled out to the CPR across the board, then we might need to lighten the drafting to make it intelligible to litigants in person. And perhaps to judges too!

5
Transformation from First Principles

Ernest Ryder

Today I want to stand back and address some of the questions that are being asked about why we should modernise courts and tribunals from the perspective of the ordinary user. I have about 500,000 applications per annum; many from people who are vulnerable; most without representation and as a consequence of that we have developed a body of rules and good practice that are very different from their Civil Procedure Rules and Family Procedure Rules equivalents. The Tribunal Procedure Committee rules are headline indications about what we should be seeking to achieve. They are supported by practice statements that are designed to help users rather than repetitive and confusing directions.

May I start with a proposition? From the perspective of safeguarding the rule of law, if the modernisation of justice is to be successful, it should reflect the fundamental aspects of the functions of the judiciary to ensure that our independence is preserved. And that is a concept too rarely spoken about. If we were to allow others to modernise what we do, what would be left of our independent judicial functions and the protections of both our procedures and centuries of the common law? Perhaps the more obvious but most frequently misunderstood point is that any process of change should be rooted in principle, for example, the obligations that the Lord Chief Justice and I have to deliver justice and its administration in accordance with constitutional norms, ethical principles and our different statutory duties. The headline is easy; it is to deliver justice effectively and efficiently. In addition, using more than 5000 judges and members sitting in more than 500 jurisdictions, I have to provide justice that is swift, informal, flexible, specialist or expert and innovative. The dominant principle in relation to modernisation is that we should provide access to justice as an indivisible right without price rationing as the consequence of austerity. And that is where we started in 2014/2015. I said there were two aspects. The second is that we have an obligation as judges to attend to the detail of our users' experience. If access to justice is to mean anything to our users

Ernest Ryder, *Transformation from First Principles* In: *The Civil Procedure Rules at 20.* Edited by: Andrew Higgins, Oxford University Press (2020). © the several contributors. DOI: 10.1093/oso/9780198863182.003.0005.

then our procedures, processes and language should be inclusive of them, not exclusive.

If I return to 2014/2015 Lord Thomas CJ and I agreed with the then Lord Chancellor, Mr Michael Gove MP, that the management of progressive decline, which is what we were then involved in, could no longer be contemplated because we would not be able to continue to deliver effective access to justice. We were acutely aware of the impact of historic under-investment, particularly in estates and IT, but also of the impact of austerity following the financial circumstances of 2008. In plain language, at that point, we could not afford to run our 'Rolls Royce' paper-based system. A system that was failing to deliver for a significant number of users, either because it was unaffordable for them or too slow or complex or unintelligible or frankly, in some respects, all of those things. So we agreed with the Executive (i.e. with the Treasury's direct involvement) 'to put in place a new operating model with a sustainable and affordable infrastructure to deliver better services at lower cost . . .'.

Politicians may have been happy to stop there. John Thomas and I didn't. The agreement has a second critically important component and it is this: ' . . . the purpose is to safeguard the rule of law by improving access to justice'. The principle was overt and must be understood if senior judges are to collaborate with the Executive. So I have put before Parliament, and the Justice Select Committee and delivered to the Lord Chancellor, a strategy and a plan for tribunals in a form that is transparent and which acknowledges my civic accountability for the performance of my duties. I am able to be questioned on what we are doing by those who are researching into it, commenting on it and also by the interest groups who reflect the many users that I have. That is important because trust, respect and confidence in the system also invites trustworthiness of those in office. As judges we have an obligation to demonstrate that to those who need to come to us for justice.

The Administrative Justice Council, with its academic, pro-bono and advice sector panels, is advising me of the steps we should take to measure access to justice and outcomes. We should be prepared to answer the question whether new processes and procedures including digital forms of communication are providing a formal legal system which is accessible, with a fair and effective form of hearing, a legal remedy in accordance with substantive law and access to enforcement.

Let me give you three examples of the need for change.

My users want an online tribunal. They want it for a number of reasons. If you need to use the Employment Tribunal after the Supreme Court decision in the *Unison* case you will have experienced the effect of a 166% increase in single employment claims between the last quarter of 2017 and the last quarter of 2018. If you bring an appeal to the Social Security and Child Support Tribunal for a PIP decision, there is a 73% likelihood you will succeed. That raises a serious question about the quality of primary decision making. In the Special Educational Needs Tribunal, for the academic year 2018 the overturn rate for local government decision making was 87%. And these are vulnerable people often in crisis at the point that they come to us. So if you ask me whether we can do things in a better way for them, the answer is, without doubt, yes, we can. The timeliness, quality, style and language of our process is very important to our users.

One aspect of an online tribunal will include testing asynchronous conversations. This is not for everyone. Paper will persist and probably for a significant number of users but perhaps not for as many as some may think. If you can have your conversation with the judge, doctor and disability member without attending a tribunal building, something which is difficult for a seriously disabled appellant to do, with the fear and stress that goes with that, and you can get an effective reassessment, why wouldn't you want to do that online if the process is not going to prejudice you? We are running a pilot to identify which of the cases, for example of the 73% that are successful, can be identified to be determined online and which need to be determined face to face by a panel.

The same process of evaluation can be applied to virtual hearings or, if you prefer the description: 'fully videoed hearings'. At the moment the pilot can accommodate cases with 7 people in different places at the same time including the judge. If you are determining a claim or an appeal that rests primarily on paper i.e. the circumstantial material is in the form of documents rather than oral evidence, you may find, as the tax tribunal has already discovered, that it is easier to do this in a virtual hearing where the appellant need never attend the tribunal building. It can be faster. It may be clearer. You can upload evidence online as you are going along. You can also reduce the content of application forms and other documents in order to inform the process by using intelligent intuitive online questions.

An underlying project that we have for all of my 14 chambers is the creation of a digital case file that every judge and case officer has access to, to improve case management from the beginning. And why is that important? There is nothing new or remarkable about the creation of digital case files. They are now an industry standard. But if the user has access to a case officer who helps to prepare a digital bundle for the judge out of the digital case file, then it is so much easier to go on to identify issues and case management steps that will improve what both lay users and presenting officers do, with the aim of improving the quality of decision making at the end. We are piloting this in the Immigration and Asylum Tribunal to very good effect. The concept of a case officer as the court's officer who can help the judge under his or her direction has been around since the late 1800s when the then Administration of Justice reforms identified the skills which Deputy Masters and Registrars in the Court of Appeal still use. We are now doing exactly the same in tribunals, in particular to help users who have no legal representation, but in a digital process which is designed to speed up, clarify and improve preparation and process.

Will all this work? No. Some of it will fail and that is in the nature of a pilot. Time and testing will tell. But at the end of the process I want something that is cheaper, quicker, clearer and, I hope, better. That is the essence of judicial leadership. But that is a different lecture for another day. Leadership of the justice system is all about improving the way we safeguard the rule of law. It should never be static: it develops in just the same way that the common law has developed over time. Acting in accordance with our principles will help to ensure that modernisation achieves much more than just efficiency.

6

Interventions in Judicial Review Proceedings

Nathalie Lieven

I have been asked to talk about interventions, but more from a substantive than procedural viewpoint. What I say below is very much taken from my career at the Bar, rather than experience on the Bench. This chapter is not an attempt to set out empirical research, or even achieve academic standards, but merely a reflection on my experiences of interventions in practice. I leave it to the reader to decide whether what I say is borne out by the case law. Although interventions occasionally happen in private law, they are by now very much a feature of judicial review cases. They have become common if not normal in public law cases at the Supreme Court level, sometimes at the Court of Appeal level, rarely but occasionally at the High Court.

Interventions were first provided for in the CPR, so they just about get into this birthday party. But the exponential growth in interventions in public law cases has, I would suggest, got a great deal more to do with the introduction of the Human Rights Act (HRA) than the CPR. Having looked at a number of cases where I either know that there have been interventions, or they have been referred to in the judgments, the expansion of interventions over the last 20 years can in my view be put down to two reasons.

First is the increased consideration by the courts and particularly the higher courts, since the HRA, of the wider policy context of public law decisions. And of course in many human rights cases that wider context relevant to whichever article is critical to the determination.

Secondly, and probably related, is the greater preparedness of UK courts, particularly the Supreme Court, not just listen to submissions based on international law, and occasionally comparative law, but to place weight upon them. Certainly in the Supreme Court it is now quite common to refer to international jurisprudence. When I first came to the Bar, referring to international law was a very peculiar and somewhat exotic thing to do, and generally not much liked by the judiciary. That has changed, and the parties often look to

Nathalie Lieven, *Interventions in Judicial Review Proceedings* In: *The Civil Procedure Rules at 20.* Edited by: Andrew Higgins, Oxford University Press (2020). © the several contributors. DOI: 10.1093/oso/9780198863182.003.0006.

intervenors to bring specialist knowledge of international law and the time to research it, into the proceedings.

The decision whether or not to allow an intervention, and then whether to give any weight to its content is discretionary. There can be no doubt that it has been the Supreme Court which has encouraged interventions in recent years, and Baroness Hale has made clear in writing how useful she finds them. Baroness Hale is of course an academic by background and it will be interesting to see whether the liberal approach to allowing interventions and their role in Supreme Court litigation is maintained after her retirement. Without Baroness Hale and some of the current members of the Supreme Court, the breadth of the discretion is such that we might see less interventions in the future.

I am going to focus very briefly on some of the things that make a successful intervention, and some of the underlying tactics that are used by the parties.

In terms of what makes a successful intervention, the critical thing listening to what Maurice Sunkin has said earlier in the conference, is that we do not really know. There is no empirical evidence. As a barrister one can submit an intervention in the case and not even get a 'shout out' in the judgment. But you may know as an advocate in the case that actually the judges were listening, and there are aspects of the judgment that reflect what you as an intervenor said. Whether you get the shout out depends on the identity of the judge rather than, I suspect, whether the interventions have had any influence on the reasoning. Baroness Hale is assiduous in always thanking intervenors when she has found them useful, but with some other judges the intervenor looking for validation of its efforts has to read between the lines. Therefore I fear that no academic project could establish how influential an intervention was.

It is important to understand that interventions come in very different shapes and sizes, and with different levels of authority. This ranges from Government departments, which intervene in a surprisingly large number of cases, including private law cases where there is a wider public issue, particularly a human rights issue; statutory or official bodies—of which I would put the Equalities and Human Rights Commission, the UN Human Rights Commission, and the Northern Irish Human Rights Commission; and NGOs, which are the most frequent interveners.

The Government, in terms of the effectiveness of interventions, is very different from the others. In my experience in appearing for the Government in interventions, the Government is invariably given permission to intervene, and what it says given great weight, simply on the basis that the Government would not have applied to intervene if it did not think the issue in the case was not of significant importance. The weight given to other interveners varies enormously, self-evidently depending on whether they are really adding anything to the parties' submissions and the level of their expertise.

A critical point about the successfulness of interventions, which is one that is rarely publicly mentioned, is the quality of the barrister and their ability and standing compared to the parties' representatives. I have seen cases where the intervenor's barrister effectively puts the case. I am also confident that the identity of the barrister is a significant factor in whether the court allows oral or only written submissions.

An important procedural point about interventions is that the intervenor is not a party and as such has a much freer hand than the parties. In public law that is particularly important because it means the intervenor is not bound by the annoying facts which the claimant will often bring to the case. Those of you who have litigated know that facts are the bane of any barrister's existence, because they can confuse and obscure what would otherwise be a clean precise point of law. The great advantage for the intervenor is that they can come to court and put what looks like an intellectually objective case, untrammelled by the confusion of real facts. The factual simplicity of an intervention can also be very attractive to the judges, particularly at an appellate level, who may not want to be tied in their judgments to the facts, and do not want the wider principle to be constrained by what may be the unfortunate and inconvenient facts of a particular case.

Of course the other factor of not being a party is that an intervenor, even now under the Criminal Justice and Courts Act, is much less likely to be exposed to a costs risk than is a party. The Criminal Justice Act provisions were specifically brought in by the previous Secretary of State to try to limit and discourage intervenors. As far as I could tell from a Westlaw search, they have wholly failed in that endeavour, because they do not seem to have been used at all yet, certainly not in anger as opposed to by consent. There may be some 'chilling effect', but so far that appears to be limited.

What is very clear from the case law is that the courts want intervenors to add value or to fill the gaps in the parties' cases. So any sensible intervenor will work very closely with the party it's seeking to support to divide up the case in the most effective manner. In a case involving international human rights, the sensible claimant will give the representative of the UN HRC the submissions on international law because they will carry more weight than an individual claimant. The sensible claimant tries to persuade the EHRC to come along and make the submissions on equalities law. And the sensible claimant finds a friendly NGO, and there is a fair bit of intervenor shopping that goes on, who will give the policy input in an objective way. So for example if you do a case about abortion, as I have, you make sure you have BPAS there to put the policy background.

The most obvious area looking at the case law where intervenors bring added value is international law. And that is, I think, for two reasons. First is the identity of the intervenor. The UN, the EHRC, or the Northern Ireland Human Rights Commission bring a specialist expertise (and standing) on international law. Second, the parties will rarely have the expertise or the resources to research the detailed international law position. For both reasons the court will often give more weight to the submissions of those intervenors on international law than they would to a private party.

There are a few cases where the Court has specifically mentioned the role of this category of interveners. In *EM (Eritrea) and Ors v. SSHD* [2014] UKSC 12 the Supreme Court made express reference to the submissions of the UNHRC's submissions on international law. In *Belhaj v. Straws and Ors* [2017] UKSC 3 Lord Sumption referred to the UN Conventions on rendition and unlawful detention, which were the subject matter of the UN Rapporteurs' intervention.

The other important expertise of interveners is where they cover the policy context of the issue. Again, intervenors often come with specialist expertise in particular areas, and the courts then give particular weight to their evidence. In *Yemshaw v. Hounslow LBC* [2011] UKSC 3, concerning psychological abuse and domestic violence, Lady Hale made specific reference to the women's groups who had intervened and the wide range of evidence they had introduced about the role of controlling and coercive behaviour and domestic violence.

Intervenors can sometimes avoid procedural tussles between the parties, perhaps because they are there with the agreement of the court, so the court necessarily wants to hear their evidence. In the Northern Irish abortion case (*Re NIHRC* [2018] UKSC 27) one of the intervenors put in post-decision evidence of shifts in public opinion, which the Appellant would have faced considerable difficulty persuading the Supreme Court to admit. The intervenors just slotted it into their exhibits and then the Appellant referred to it. In practice this was an easy way of bypassing a procedural argument.

The final point I want to make is that interventions are a largely procedural free world. They are—to go back to the morning's session between Lords Neuberger and Dyson—absolutely at one extreme of a discretion to the judges. They allow the judges to take very much a pick and mix approach to submissions and evidence. In the Northern Irish abortion case, there were 10 interventions—some in writing, some orally. It seems unlikely that anyone, other perhaps than judicial assistants, read all or even most of the documents that the intervenors produced. But the evidence was there for the judges to dip into when they wanted material to support their respective positions.

This then supports a theme that has come up a few times in this conference, which is a trend to an increasingly inquisitorial jurisdiction. Through the interventions producing a wide corpus of material before the court, but little focus on it in submissions, the judges can choose what evidence to refer to and what approach to take. Now you may think that is a good thing, and it often is, but it is a move away from a more traditional inter partes and adversarial approach.

7

National Security, Closed Material Procedures, and Fair Trials

Martin Chamberlain

'Closed material' is material placed before a court, but for reasons of public interest not shown to one or more parties. Courts have considered closed material for many years when determining applications for public interest immunity (PII) in criminal and civil proceedings. But the function of a PII application is to determine whether the material in question is properly regarded as immune from disclosure. If the court upholds a PII claim, the consequence is that the material to which it relates becomes inadmissible for all purposes and the court cannot take it into account in reaching its decision on the substance.

Since 1997, however, procedures have developed in which closed material may be admitted in evidence and relied upon by the court or tribunal. These are known as 'closed material procedures' (CMPs), in which the court holds part of the proceedings in a closed session from which one or more parties and their lawyers are excluded. The interests of the excluded party are represented by a security-cleared special advocate.[1] The first CMP introduced in the UK was in the Special Immigration Appeals Commission (SIAC), which hears appeals against certain decisions relating to immigration and nationality taken on grounds of national security and, between 2001 and 2004, heard appeals against the potentially indefinite detention of foreign nationals who could not be deported.[2] From SIAC, CMPs spread to other statutory tribunals whose remit required the hearing of evidence that would harm the public interest if disclosed[3] and to certain statutory appeals in the High Court (for the most part

[1] For a brief history of the use of special advocates in CMPs in the UK, see Martin Chamberlain, 'Special advocates and *amici curiae* in national security proceedings in the United Kingdom' (2018) 68 *University of Toronto Law Journal* 496, 505–507. For a more detailed account, see John Jackson, *Special Advocates in the Adversarial System* (Routledge, 2019).

[2] SIAC was established by the Special Immigration Appeals Commission Act 1997.

[3] For example, the Proscribed Organisations Appeal Commission (which hears appeals against decisions to proscribe organisations under the Terrorism Act 2000) and the Employment Tribunal (when it hears claims involving evidence whose disclosure would be contrary to the public interest, e.g. claims

Martin Chamberlain, *National Security, Closed Material Procedures, and Fair Trials* In: *The Civil Procedure Rules at 20.* Edited by: Andrew Higgins, Oxford University Press (2020). © the several contributors.
DOI: 10.1093/oso/9780198863182.003.0007.

appeals against measures imposed by the Government against those suspected of involvement in terrorism).[4]

The question whether the courts could adopt a CMP without specific statutory authorisation to do so was answered in the negative in *Al Rawi v Security Service*.[5] This was because, as Lord Dyson explained, the right to see the evidence against one is such a fundamental element of the common law right to a fair trial that the court cannot abrogate it in the exercise of its inherent power.[6] Lord Kerr went further, saying that without disclosure of the evidence to all parties, a trial between opposing parties cannot lay claim to the marque of judicial proceedings.[7]

These resounding affirmations of the importance of full disclosure to a fair trial were taken up by opponents of the Bill that became the Justice and Security Act 2013 (the 2013 Act).[8] This and the procedural rules that give effect to it in Part 82 of the CPR created a new CMP, modelled on the earlier variants, applicable in principle in any civil proceedings in the High Court and above in which there is evidence whose disclosure would damage national security.

The 2013 Act was controversial. Section 6(7) requires that the court be 'satisfied that the Secretary of State has, before making the application, considered whether to make, or advise another person to make, a claim for public interest immunity in relation to the material on which the application is based'. It was feared, however, that this safeguard would be too weak to prevent the court from regarding the CMP as preferable to PII in almost all cases; and that the CMP would thus become normalised.

In the six years since the 2013 Act came into force, there is some evidence that the both the executive and the courts have tended to view CMPs as preferable in principle to PII as a means for dealing with cases in which there is relevant material whose disclosure would damage national security. The total number of cases in which the 2013 Act has been used is, however, still relatively small. This may be in part because its use was restricted by that Act to cases where the particular public interest that would be damaged by disclosure is

brought by those who have been refused security clearance, pursuant to rules made under s. 10 of the Employment Tribunals Act 1996).

4 For example, appeals against control orders under the Prevention of Terrorism Act 2005 and CPR Pt 76, terrorism prevention and investigation measures (TPIMs) under the Terrorism Prevention and Investigation Measures Act 2011 and CPR Pt 80 and financial restrictions under the Counter-terrorism Act 2008 and CPR Pt 79.

5 [2012] 1 AC 531.

6 Ibid., [41]–[50].

7 Ibid., [89].

8 See e.g. Martin Chamberlain, 'The Justice and Security Bill' (2012) 31 *Civil Justice Quarterly* 424.

national security. (In most statutory CMPs, the 'public interest' is defined more broadly as including the UK's international relations and the public interest in the prevention and investigation of crime.)[9]

The potential of CMPs to produce procedural unfairness has been commented upon extensively.[10] It is important to be clear, however, that the question whether and to what extent CMPs are fair is not the same as the normative question whether they should be adopted. It is perfectly possible to conclude that in certain contexts other public goods, such as national security, must be balanced against procedural fairness. How to strike an appropriate balance between these two desiderata is a matter on which views differ and is not the topic of this chapter. Before one reaches that normative question, however, it is possible to say something about a prior question which is relevant to but not determinative of it: how and when CMPs are likely to generate procedural unfairness.

In that regard, there are at least two key questions. The first is the extent to which the issues considered in closed are ones on which the excluded party will be disadvantaged by having his interests represented by a special advocate, rather than by his own open lawyers. Special advocates are the security-cleared lawyers who represent the interests of the excluded party in the closed parts of the proceedings. Statutory regimes governing the functions of special advocates differ in certain respects, but certain aspects of those regimes are common, in particular the prohibition on communicating with the excluded party after service of the closed material, save with the permission of the court. The difficulties inherent in the role have been described elsewhere.[11] The extent of these difficulties is, however, likely to be dependent on the precise nature of the issues before the court or tribunal in the CMP.

One factor which can be identified is the extent to which the proceedings involve allegations against the excluded party. Procedural unfairness is likely to be most acute when the issue before the court or tribunal is (for example) whether the excluded party is a danger to national security, or whether there

[9] One problematic consequence of the 2013 Act's narrow definition of 'public interest' as encompassing only national security is that in cases where the public interests that would be damaged by disclosure include national security and (for example) the UK's international relations, only material in the first category can be brought within the CMP. Material falling into the second category must still be the subject of an application for PII. This difficulty, which may lead to parallel regimes for two closely related categories of closed material, was identified in *F v Security Service* [2014] 1 WLR 1699 at [50] (Irwin J).

[10] See e.g. Martin Chamberlain, 'Special Advocates and Procedural Fairness in Closed Proceedings' (2009) 28 *C.J.Q.* 314 and Martin Chamberlain, 'Update on Procedural Fairness in Closed Proceedings' (2009) 28 *C.J.Q.* 448.

[11] See Chamberlain (n. 10).

are reasonable grounds for suspecting that he is. That is often the main issue in appeals against control orders or TPIMs and it is often one of the issues in SIAC proceedings. The evidence relevant to that issue might suggest, for example, that the excluded party attended a terrorist training camp between particular dates. On this, the presence of a special advocate (who is not permitted to communicate with the excluded party once he or she has seen the closed material) is unlikely to attenuate the procedural unfairness to a significant degree unless the allegation (or at least the gist of it) is made openly, even if some or all of the supporting evidence is not.

Often, however, the issues in the proceedings are not concerned with allegations against the excluded party. Take, for example, the issue whether there is a real risk that the excluded party will be mistreated in the country to which he is to be deported (often an important issue in SIAC proceedings). Here, what is required is an analysis, familiar from asylum and humanitarian protection cases outside the national security context, of the safety or otherwise of the country of origin. In these cases, at least where the Government's case is generic rather than dependent on the country's attitude towards the individual in question, there may be little reason to suppose that special advocates are markedly less well-placed than open advocates to probe and test the Government's closed case.

It is not always easy to classify cases into those that involve allegations about the excluded party and those that do not. Civil cases alleging false imprisonment, rendition, and other misconduct by the security agencies against individuals thought to be associated with terrorist groups may involve material on both sides of that line. That will no doubt be one factor borne in mind by courts considering whether and to what extent Article 6 ECHR requires disclosure to the excluded party of the essence of the case against him as an irreducible minimum under the principle in *AF (No. 3) v Secretary of State for the Home Department*[12] (the topic of Hayley Hooper's chapter in this book).

A second key question relevant to fairness is whether there is any realistic alternative to a CMP. Those proposing the Bill that became the 2013 Act said that, without it, the Government would have had to claim PII in respect of the relevant closed material, which could leave it with no evidential basis for its defence. The result, it was said, was that the Government would be forced to settle unmeritorious claims. That argument may be doubted because it has been established for some time that claims where the application of PII deprives the

[12] [2010] 2 AC 269.

defendant of the ability fairly to defend the claim may be struck out on that ground.[13]

One category of case to which opponents of the 2013 Act may have given insufficient attention was that in which, without a CMP, the opportunity to challenge a governmental or judicial decision taken on the basis of sensitive material would be very limited or non-existent. This category was the focus of the Supreme Court's recent decision in *R (Haralambous) v St Albans Crown Court*.[14] There the Supreme Court accepted the submission that the High Court, hearing a claim for judicial review of a warrant issued by a magistrate *ex parte* on the basis of closed material, could hold a CMP even though there was no express statutory authority to do so.

The difficulty faced by the court in *Haralambous* was that, if the magistrate had power to entertain closed material, there would in many cases be no way for the High Court to test whether the magistrate's decision was lawful unless the High Court could itself consider the material in question. If the High Court were precluded from considering closed material, the claimant would in most cases be unable to discharge the burden of showing that the challenged decision was unlawful.[15]

A similar approach had been adopted in *R (AHK) v Secretary of State for the Home Department*.[16] That was a challenge by way of judicial review to a decision to deprive the claimant of nationality. Ouseley J held, in the light of the Supreme Court's decision in *Al Rawi*, that there was no power to entertain closed material. The consequence was that:

> If the SSHD gives evidence that there were good reasons and a sound relevant basis for her decision, having considered the Claimant's representations, which she could not further disclose, it would be impossible for the Court fairly or reasonably to hold that she was wrong in saying that. The Claimant would have no prospect of persuading the Court to the contrary. It is not so much that the case is untriable; it can be tried. It is simply that the evidence means that the Claimant cannot win. So there is no point in it going to trial. Even if it were alleged that an immaterial factor had positively been taken

13 *Carnduff v Rock* [2001] 1 WLR 1786.

14 [2018] AC 236. The author was leading counsel for the Chief Constable of the Hertfordshire Constabulary.

15 *R v Inland Revenue Commissioners ex p. Rossminster* [1980] AC 952. This is the 'presumption of regularity', encapsulated in the maxim *omnia praesumuntur rite et solemniter esse acta donec probetur in contrarium*.

16 [2012] EWHC 1117 (Admin).

> into account, unless its context and significance could be fully appreciated, the Claimant still could not win.[17]

Ouseley J rejected the suggestion that the court should 'assume what it knows to be false, which is that there is no more information relevant to the decision'.

The difficulty identified in *AHK* was remedied by the 2013 Act, s. 15 of which amended the Special Immigration Appeals Act 1997, extending the jurisdiction of SIAC to deal with appeals against the deprivation of nationality. In *Haralambous*, it proved possible to imply a power to entertain closed material, applying by analogy the reasoning in *Bank Mellat v HM Treasury*,[18] in which the Supreme Court had implied into the statutory provisions conferring its own jurisdiction (s. 40 of the Constitutional Reform Act 2005) a power to hold a CMP.

Carnduff v Rock showed that in some private law cases the alternative to a CMP may be worse for the claimant, because the application of PII means the case cannot be tried at all. As Lord Dyson observed in *Al Rawi*,[19] there have been few examples of applications of that principle. In the public law arena, however, there can be no doubt that cases exist in which, because of the presumption of regularity, there would be no effective means of challenge without a CMP. *AHK* and *Haralambous* are examples. A more recent one is *R (Campaign Against Arms Trade) v Secretary of State for International Trade*,[20] a challenge to the decision of the Secretary of State not to suspend licences for the export of arms to Saudi Arabia for possible use in the conflict in Yemen.

The claimant's case depended on showing that the Secretary of State had adopted an irrational and unlawful process for deciding, in accordance with the UK Government's policy, whether there was a clear risk that UK-supplied arms might be used to commit a serious violation of international humanitarian law (IHL). The Government's evidence in response included classified material dealing with compliance by Saudi Arabia with IHL. The claimant consented to a CMP under the 2013 Act. Both the Divisional Court and the Court of Appeal held closed, as well as open, hearings and produced closed, as well as open, judgments. The Court of Appeal, overturning the decision of the Divisional Court, held that the Secretary of State's decision was irrational and unlawful because, having considered the open and closed evidence in its entirety, there had been a failure properly to assess whether IHL had been

[17] Ibid., [58].
[18] [2014] AC 700. The author was special advocate for the Bank.
[19] At [50].
[20] [2019] 1 WLR 5765. The author was leading counsel for the claimant.

breached in the past. The Court of Appeal's judgment is itself under appeal to the Supreme Court.

What matters for present purposes is not the outcome, but the procedure by which it was reached. If no CMP had been available, the Government would undoubtedly have claimed PII in respect of the closed material on which it had based its decision. The PII claim would almost certainly have succeeded: it is easy to understand why assessments of the compliance with IHL of a friendly state such as Saudi Arabia would, if disclosed publicly, tend to damage the UK's national security. If the PII claim had succeeded, the closed material would have become inadmissible. The court would then have been faced with a claim seeking to impugn the Secretary of State's decision-making process without any means of knowing about one important part of that process. It seems likely that, applying the presumption of regularity, the claim would have failed, for the reasons given by Ouseley J in *AHK*.

It is possible to draw some tentative conclusions from this brief analysis. Any assessment of the degree to which CMPs give rise to procedural unfairness must be attentive to two factors. The first is the degree to which the excluded party will be disadvantaged by being represented in the closed session by a special advocate, rather than by an open lawyer. On some issues, particularly those which turn on the assessment of allegations against the excluded party that are not disclosed even in the form of a gist, the disadvantage may be relatively great. On others, such as those which depend on an assessment of the compliance of third countries with international human rights law or IHL standards, it may be relatively less so. The second factor is the alternative to a CMP. There is a category of public law cases in which the challenged decision was properly based on closed material. Here, save where the open material reveals a determinative error, it may be impossible for a claimant to show that the decision was unlawful without holding a CMP. Any assessment of the unfairness caused by the holding of a CMP must take that into account. Such an assessment may be relevant to, but is not determinative of, the separate normative question whether CMPs are to be welcomed generally or in particular categories of case.

8

Civil Justice Reform

Where Next?

Rupert Jackson

I've listened with interest today as the speakers descended from the lofty heights of digital courts and artificial intelligence and the like, to the practical problems of the world as it currently is.

Ten years ago, and it seems like a century ago, I was given the task of overhauling the Civil Procedure Rules in order to promote access to justice, and to control costs. Not an easy task. Indeed, about as difficult as enlivening an audience who have been listening to eight hours of lectures on civil procedure.

As Adrian Zuckerman said in his very pertinent comments this morning, what matters is not only the amount of costs, but also predictability. People need to know what litigation will cost in order to decide whether they can afford to bring a claim, or to defend a claim. And if they don't know, they may be deterred at the outset, and never pursue their claim, or never pursue their defence. I entirely agree with that. I remember Adrian making very similar points over 20 years ago, at one of the seminars held by Lord Woolf in the Access to Justice Enquiry in 1994, I think it was.

Now, in my somewhat difficult task of ten years ago, it seemed to me that there were only two ways of controlling costs in advance: either you have a fixed costs regime, or you have ad hoc budgets for each case. Now fixed costs, at least under our rules, unlike under the German regime, are simply not practicable for high value cases. Therefore I came up with the solution of fixed costs for lower value cases, and costs budgeting for the larger cases. And of course costs and funding are linked together. Third party funders will normally link their funding to a court-approved budget. Costs and funding are linked in many other ways as well. I have looked again at these problems more recently. And following the introduction of fixed costs for most fast track cases, I have proposed extending fixed costs for cases of moderate complexity up to a value of £100,000. But above that, it seems to me that the only way to control costs in advance is by ad hoc budgeting on a case by case basis.

Rupert Jackson, *Civil Justice Reform* In: *The Civil Procedure Rules at 20.* Edited by: Andrew Higgins, Oxford University Press (2020). © the several contributors. DOI: 10.1093/oso/9780198863182.003.0008.

Now as I say, costs and funding are closely linked. If you have greater control over costs in advance, you can then devise methods of funding which are more appropriate. My philosophy in relation to funding is that methods of funding which drive up costs must be stopped, and methods of funding which do not drive up costs must be multiplied. Accordingly, I recommended the ending of recoverable success fees and recoverable After the Event (ATE) premiums, which had a massive effect on driving up costs, not just because of the amount of the success fees and the premiums, but because of the way they distorted incentives. Lord Neuberger this morning referred to the huge costs in *Coventry v Lawrence*, which was a case preceding my reforms, where the success fees and the ATE premiums added a horrendous bill to the paying party. So methods of funding like that had to stop, and they have stopped, with one or two exceptions.

On the positive side, I recommended permitting damages based agreements. Not ideal that lawyers have a financial stake in the damages, but better than nothing if we are going to promote access to justice. There are problems with the DBA regulations at the moment. But with Rachael Mulheron and Nick Bacon's help, they will be overcome, and I'm very pleased to see here today the senior representative of the Ministry of Justice, upon whose desk those recommendations now sit, and I'm sure they will soon lead to implementation. So much for damages based agreements, but I'm pleased to see his jocular assent.

I also regard as important to promote before the event insurance, there has been an increase there. And also to promote third party funding, there has been a great increase there as well. I am not one of those who deplores third party funding, provided that there are proper controls to prevent officious meddling and insufficient capital adequacy and so forth. I think third party funding *promotes* access to justice. Rachael Mulheron said in her submission today that as third party funding expands, and is used for class actions which it normally will be, there is a need for regulation. I have always accepted, indeed urged, that the time will come when third party funding has expanded to the point when self-regulation is no longer sufficient and formal regulation is required. It is for others to decide precisely when that point is reached, but clearly if class actions expand and make increasing demands on third party funding, that is a very strong case for regulation.

So to conclude Mr Chairman, controlling costs in advance, limiting costs to recoverable levels, implementing my recent proposals for extending fixed recoverable costs, revising the DBA Regulations and promoting different methods of funding litigation, provided they do not have the iniquitous consequences of recoverable success fees and recoverable ATE premiums, are all good things. And I leave it to the wisdom of subsequent speakers to explain in much more detail how all of this should be achieved. Thank you.

9

Reflections from Former Masters of the Rolls on Managing Civil Justice

Kate O'Regan[1]

Kate O'Regan (KO'R)

Good morning everybody. I'm Kate O'Regan, the Director of the Bonavero Institute, and it's an enormous pleasure to welcome you all here today. I'd particularly like to welcome Yves Bonavero who is the generous benefactor of the Bonavero Institute. I would also like to welcome our two guests, Lord Neuberger and Lord Dyson, who are both former Masters of the Rolls and very distinguished judges.

The idea of this session is to reflect on what we've learned in the past 20 years of the Civil Procedure Rules (CPR). So I want to take us back a little bit from Sir Terence Etherton's address, to thinking about this set of rules as having been an extraordinary innovation at the time that they were introduced. And one of the innovations was to introduce the idea of an 'overriding objective' of the rules in CPR 1.1, to enable courts to deal with cases justly.[2] The rule then provides a range of principles that the overriding objective intends and requires courts to seek to give effect to the overriding objective when exercising powers conferred upon them by the rules and when interpreting the rules. I'll repeat those principles so that you can recall them.

That the court should ensure that:

- Parties are on an equal footing;
- Expense is saved;

[1] In conversation with Lord Neuberger, former President of the UKSC and Master of the Rolls, and Lord Dyson, Former Justice of the UKSC and Master of the Rolls.

[2] The overriding objective was subsequently amended following the Jackson review of Costs of Civil Litigation to enable the court to deal with cases justly *and at proportionate cost.*

Kate O'Regan, *Reflections from Former Masters of the Rolls on Managing Civil Justice* In: *The Civil Procedure Rules at 20.* Edited by: Andrew Higgins, Oxford University Press (2020). © the several contributors. DOI: 10.1093/oso/9780198863182.003.0009.

- Cases are dealt with in a manner that is proportionate to the amount of money involved, the importance of the case, the complexity of the issues, and the financial position of each of the parties;
- Cases are dealt with expeditiously and fairly;
- Each case is allotted a proportionate share of the court's resources, taking into account the need to allot resources to other cases; and
- Compliance with rules, practice directions and orders is enforced.

I wondered if I could ask both of you whether you feel that this concept of an overriding objective has worked in practice, and whether it has had a significant impact on the interpretation and application of the rules. Perhaps I might start with you Lord Dyson.

Lord John Dyson (JD)

I think that it has had a massive effect on the way that civil procedure is conducted in this country. I don't know whose idea the overriding objective was—it may have been Lord Woolf's, I've never enquired—but I think it was a brilliant idea. It is a motif which runs right through the rules, and there it sets out right at the beginning of the rules what it is, what it means, and I think it has stood the test of time. I think it's absolutely brilliant.

I think it's not without interest that other jurisdictions have followed suit. I know from personal experience that this is happening in Cyprus, where I have been advising the Cypriots. They're very much going down that route. They have also introduced something very similar, only slightly different, in Israel. So I think the overriding objective—we could talk at great length about the details of it—but I think it has had an enormous effect on the way in which judges have approached the task of interpreting and applying the rules, and the way in which the practitioners operate the rules, and I think it has been on the whole a great success.

We can talk about some of the points raised by Damien at the outset. I'll just say this, and leave it to David to continue. I was extremely interested in hearing his checklist of, let's say, successes and—he didn't call them failures, but I think that is what he was driving at. The one thing he didn't mention was costs. I wondered whether, perhaps uncharitably, that is because lawyers have an interest in seeing costs maintained at their current levels. That's very unkind of course. But I think one of the objects of the Woolf reforms—which because it wasn't achieved Sir Rupert Jackson was asked to do *his* work—was to deal with excessive costs. A lot of steps have been taken in that direction. But I think that costs, from my point of view, still remain a real problem.

KO'R

Yes, one of the things that the overriding objective does talk about is dealing with cases in a proportionate manner—not only, it seems, in relation to costs, but one assumes that that is one of the underlying concerns there. What are your thoughts on this, Lord Neuberger?

Lord David Neuberger (DN)

I think that the two words that spring to mind are justice and proportionality. It could be argued that proportionality is part of justice, but I think until the CPR came into force proportionality as a word was little used in connection with procedural rules and the approach to directions. I accept that proportionality was starting to enter our vocabulary and thought-processes, but I entirely agree with John that it was clinched by the overriding objective. One or two judges—certainly in the division that I was in, the chancery division—rather objected to being told that they should deal with cases justly. They thought that it was rather taken for granted. I felt it was rather appropriate, in the first case that I decided on the basis of the overriding objective, that I got the transcript of my judgment, and every reference to the 'overriding objective' was the 'overriding objection'—which I—slightly regretfully—corrected.

But more seriously I agree with John. The truth is that whatever the rules say, you can have judges who are naturally generally good at having a feel for how to deal with cases, and judges who have other strengths, perhaps, but are not necessarily that good at case management. And I think proportionality gives a very good peg on which to hang some difficult decisions. Like any expression, it can be used to hide lack of thought or lack of real concentration on the issues: it is tempting just lazily to shove a decision off on the basis of proportionality, knowing that the Court of Appeal is going to say that it's a case management decision and they're not going to interfere. But nonetheless as a lazy hook it is better than most, and I think it does concentrate one's mind on what is an essential aspect of justice, as the two preceding speeches have emphasised.

KO'R

As a non-UK trained lawyer, one of the things that intrigues me about the objective is whether it has meant that the rules are variably applied, because of the principle of proportionality—so that courts say, for example, 'Well this is a fairly simple case, and in these circumstances this rule should be interpreted to avoid making it particularly complex'—or whether the principle has sustained relatively consistent application of the rules.

JD

Well I think that raises a very interesting and difficult point. It seems to me that so long as decisions of any kind are taken by human beings, you are going to get differences; you are going to find some judges who take a slightly different approach to others. You can make your rules as tight as you want, but you can't completely eliminate the risk of inconsistency of approach. I think that one of the good things that happened in this country was that the judicial college made everybody who sat as a judge undergo some fairly rigorous training.

I remember that the training conducted in my case was by a district judge from Cornwall. I can't remember his name now, but he was absolutely excellent. Of course, he was totally committed to the cause, and he gave us examples of cases—how would you have done it under the old regime and how would you do it now. We were being told all the time, 'Well that's wrong, that's the old way of doing it.' But you can't eliminate the possibility of inconsistency in civil procedure, as in anything else that involves a certain amount of discretion. The rules don't take away discretion.

KO'R

That raises another question. When drafting new rules, there are perhaps two possible approaches—you can adopt rules where you have broad principles and leave substantial discretion to individual decision, or you can adopt rules where you try to stipulate closely what should happen in each different circumstance. It seems to me that the approach in the CPR could often be said to fall into the latter category. I wondered how you found that in practice—the detailed way in which the rules work—and whether you think that this has again been a successful initiative which you would encourage other jurisdictions to follow. Or whether you feel there are certain areas where detailed regulation might perhaps better be avoided and discretion afforded to judges.

DN

There is a pendulum, isn't there? We all know that if we came back in 50 years, 100 years, 200 years, whatever was being done, there would be a move to try and go the other way. There are two different philosophies. One is keep the rules short, general, and easily accessible, and let the judges decide on the facts of the case. The other approach, which is more the way the CPR has gone, is to try and cater for everything—as a result of which you do have more guidance, but you get rules that grow and grow and grow and grow, and people are at risk of losing their way.

I don't believe that there is a right answer. I think that each individual tends to prefer one way or the other. My instinct—ironically as I was Master of the Rolls when the rules were growing and growing—is more the former way: to try and have general guidance. But as John says, the advantage of more and more specific rules is that you get more predictability and more consistency. The disadvantage is that you get more and more rules coming out of your ears.

JD

Well I agree with that. But my instinct is—uncharacteristically, because we tend to agree about most things—I think I would tend slightly in the other direction. I think that inconsistency is a bad thing. The idea that because you turn up before one judge you'll get one answer and you turn up before another a different answer, I find that inherently unsatisfactory. I think that it is unfair and it can in extreme cases lead to parties, who know about the tendencies of particular judges, to forum shopping, and I think that is a particularly bad thing.

There are limits on how far it is right to take it, of course. I'm very interested to hear what Sir Terence Etherton has been telling us about the bright new future—who knows, ultimately all of these decisions will be taken for us by technology, and so you won't need these rules anymore. As I understand it, that is the possible ultimate goal. But, for the moment, it concerns me that we have rules that are just getting longer and longer, and more and more complex. We have practice directions that are getting more and more complex. And that's troublesome. I know this because when I was discussing what we should be doing in Cyprus, we decided there not to have practice directions, but we imported what we thought was useful from the practice directions into the rules.

The problem as I see it at the moment is that you have an enormous amount of duplication as between the rules and the practice directions. The practice directions seem to say—in a rather discursive way, often—what is in the rules. So having to look at one complicated set of instructions in the rules, and another complicated set in the practice directions—it can be a nightmare. I say this, but I should make it clear that I left the Bar before the Woolf reforms came in. I'd ceased to be a circuit judge or first instance judge before the Woolf reforms came in. So I have no first-hand experience of doing this. It is only through looking at it through the eyes of an appellate judge, and of course chairing the Civil Procedure Rule Committee. But I think the rules and the practice directions have got so complicated now. How on earth litigants in person are meant to manage that, I simply do not know.

DN

From my experience, it's only a few litigants in person who appear to be in command of all the rules. But more seriously, John and I normally agree but we diverge here, but only slightly as I absolutely see his point. The trouble is that as the rules get more and more complicated, and cater more and more for every new situation that comes up, the risk is—like with contracts, which run on for pages—you amend some rule without realising the effect on another rule and so on. By trying to cater for everything, in a Borges-like way, you find yourself almost having a set of rules that cover the world. I think there is a happy medium, and that is what one is striving for.

JD

I think so. Because if you have just some very bare principles, then people won't really know where they are, and you'll encourage a lot of litigation about the application of the rules. And one of the consequences of having very detailed rules is that, on the whole, the meaning of the rules is well understood. You don't have to go to court to ask the court to say what should happen in this situation, because it is all legislated for in the rules. So, as David says, it is a question as always it seems to me of striking a balance and finding a happy medium. I'm not at all convinced that we've got it.

KO'R

Well I'm sure that's an ongoing challenge. But to turn to something else—which I think has been a concerning feature of the last 20 years, and one which you jointly commented on in the judgment of *Coventry v. Lawrence*[3]—has been the fact of the sharp decline in funding for civil legal aid and the concomitant increase in the cost of civil litigation.

The question is whether in the absence of a widely accessible civil legal aid system, it is possible to devise a system that protects access to justice. The next session will contemplate whether the new online system is going to address this problem. But leaving aside for a moment the development of the online system, would both of you like to reflect on your anxieties and concerns about access to justice and in a sense the promises that a legal system makes but cannot meet if there is not some way for indigent people to be able to bring cases before courts?

JD

Well I re-read *Coventry v. Lawrence* because I knew you were going to raise this. A trip down memory lane. We didn't say that the then current situation denied access to justice to *all* litigants. It denied access to justice to *some* litigants.

The problem is that a political decision was taken to reduce legal aid. Many people in this room probably would say, 'Isn't it a pity we can't go back to the status quo ante'—but that I don't think is going to happen. There is no indication that that will happen, and so something has got to be put in its place. In *Coventry v. Lawrence*, we had to consider what had been put in its place, which on the facts of that case led to pretty outrageous consequences.

That's the reason why, I think, David you were party to the decision to encourage this being brought to the court. Because, in *Coventry v. Lawrence No. 2*,[4] you were made aware of the horrendous cost consequences of the success fee and the ATE premium on a claim which was worth very little indeed, and

[3] *Coventry v. Lawrence (No. 3)* [2015] UKSC 50.
[4] *Coventry v. Lawrence (No. 2)* [2014] UKSC 46.

the consequences for the Defendant of having to face the risk of having to pay all of that in order to defend the case.

It was a shocking case; it was a very extreme case. The view we took, right or wrongly, was that there will be some very bad cases like this, but you have to look at the thing across the board more broadly. You ask yourself whether—looking at it in that way—this is a system that is acceptable, and we thought that it was. But there were dissents, as you know.

DN

Can I start by going off message, in one sense? I think the worst disgrace is not to do with litigation, but to do with ordinary people being unable to get legal advice on little problems, vital to them—housing, social security, and so on—for which we now depend on lawyers giving up their spare time going to law centres and to the Citizens Advice Bureau. That is a glaring disgrace.

When it comes to litigation, I entirely agree with John—as usual, as he says. I think, picking up what Professor Higgins said, there are two strands to this. One is the Government does have a duty to make money available. The second is that we—the judges, the lawyers, the policy makers, the civil servants even—have a duty to do our absolute best to ensure that the cost of litigation is proportionate. Why *should* the Government be expected to pay out large sums of money in an extreme case like *Coventry v. Lawrence*, to support cases simply for somebody who cannot afford them? The old legal aid approach was that the Government—the Legal Aid Board, the Legal Aid Committee—would support litigation if a person with sufficient funds would have paid for it. We have the answer from Lord Briggs on that: most people making small claims would be advised by any sensible lawyer not to go to court.

So, I approve of online dispute resolution—and anything else like that that can be done—to facilitate what I referred to in my role as Master of the Rolls as quick and dirty litigation. It is better to have those sorts of procedures, even if you may not get the vital document in disclosure, and even if you do not have much cross-examination: at least you are getting access to the courts and you are getting an answer in a proportionate manner. So I think it is a combination of the Government and the legal fraternity.

KO'R

Yes, there have been many attempts to try to find a way forward. And we have seen a lot of innovations that try to address the problem: protective costs orders (PCOs),[5] cost capping orders (CCOs),[6] qualified one way cost shifting (QOCS),[7] the Aarhus Convention for environmental litigation[8] . . .

DN

Damages-based agreements (DBAs)[9] . . .

KO'R

Exactly. Do you think any of these have been particularly important—ones that again you would single out as having addressed the problem particularly effectively?

DN

I think—I can't speak for John, but he's hinted at this—my problem is that I haven't really been at the coalface for a long time. To pontificate about it would be on the basis of hearsay evidence. But John may have more to say.

JD

Well, not much more. I think you'll be hearing from Rupert Jackson later, and he knows far more about the detail than I think either of us do. But it seems to me that these various devices or mechanisms that have been introduced to try to make litigation less expensive are all of them good things. I think in combination they must have had some beneficial effect.

It is in the major commercial litigation where the huge fees are incurred, and I suspect that none of these things have much of an impact there. Fixed costs,

[5] *R (Corner House Research) v. Secretary of State for Trade and Industry* [2005] EWCA Civ 192.

[6] CPR 3.19–3.21.

[7] CPR 44.13–44.17.

[8] The United Nations Economic Commission for Europe (UNECE) Convention on Access to Information, Public Participation in Decision-Making and Access to Justice in Environmental Matters. The Convention was adopted on 25 June 1998 in Aarhus (Denmark) and entered into force on 30 October 2001.

[9] Damages-Based Agreements Regulations 2013.

which is something that was dear to my heart to introduce, does not apply in those very big cases. But in a way those big boys can look after themselves, or that is the argument at any rate.

I should say very quickly that I regarded, and continue to regard, fixed recoverable costs as a very important way forward. It was a great frustration to me when I was Master of the Rolls that I kept asking, 'What about fixed rate costs? Can't we extend it?' And I never got an answer. I was always told that the Government had other priorities.

Professor Adrian Zuckerman, who knew about my frustrations, asked me very sweetly on one occasion whether I would mind if he went and spoke to the Lord Chancellor—who was Michael Gove, it is interesting how we come back to Michael Gove all the time—and tried to persuade him. I said, of course, I wouldn't mind, and I left him to it. And the next thing I heard was that he had persuaded Michael Gove of the need to extend fixed recoverable costs: so his advocacy was far more effective than was mine. But fixed costs are still at a fairly low level. Rupert Jackson has done some excellent work on this, and I know that it has been taken forward. But I do believe that, certainly for the smaller cases, which are the vast bulk as we have heard, fixed recoverable costs—subject to exceptions—really are the way forward.

DN

At the risk of sounding a bit old-fashioned, I must admit to concerns about the fact that we have systems whereby the lawyers have an economic interest, a financial interest, in the outcome of a case. I think it is regrettable that we have gone down that route. I quite accept, having discussed it with Rupert when he and I were working together, that it may be an inevitable consequence of where we are. But I think it is retrograde, and I fear it is something we will come to regret.

JD

It may be of interest to the people in this room to hear that when I spoke on one occasion about this to Michael Gove, when he was Lord Chancellor, he immediately expressed the view that damages based agreements sounds wrong. He didn't like the idea of lawyers having a stake in the outcome of litigation at all.

I thought that was very, very interesting coming from his mouth, and so different from anything that came out of the mouth of his predecessor.

KO'R

So turning to another issue—and in many ways, I suppose, an issue that comes very close to the work of this Institute in relation to human rights. And that is the challenging issue of closed material procedures, a matter which you both had to consider in the *Al Rawi*[10] case.

This obviously again is a field where there are competing considerations at play, where a balance has to be found. Do you have any thoughts on that, looking back—about how one can balance interests of state security with the principles of fairness and the rights of parties to be able to challenge evidence that is being used against them?

JD

I think this issue is very, very difficult. We agreed on this occasion—David was Master of the Rolls, and I gave the lead judgment in the Supreme Court—that these fundamental rights, of access to justice and natural justice and so on, were so fundamental that they couldn't be taken away, or in any way interfered with, by court decision. It was a matter for Parliament. That whole question of in what circumstances courts can push things forward, and in what circumstances it is matter for Parliament, of course is highly topical—with the Reith Lectures.[11] That's a whole other area which we haven't got time to talk about, but which I'm fascinated by, and I'm afraid I disagree with Jonathan Sumption on a lot of what he says there.

We took the view that this is for Parliament. Perhaps surprisingly, Parliament did actually legislate fairly quickly after that. I still think it was right that we left it to Parliament because, as you point out, the question of how you strike a balance between these two interests—in which we all of us have a stake—is very difficult. And it is very difficult to define and describe it in any kind of detailed way in a judgment.

[10] *Al Rawi v. The Security Service* [2011] UKSC 34.

[11] Lord Sumption's Reith lectures, available at https://www.bbc.co.uk/programmes/m00057m8, have since been published as a book: see Jonathan Sumption, *Trials of the State: Law and the Decline of Politics* (Profile Books 2019).

I looked at the statute of the 2013 Act—which I'm sure you are well familiar with, and probably many people in this room are—but I have to confess that I hadn't had any dealings with that statute. I hadn't had a case on it. If I understand the statute correctly, it doesn't actually say anything about how interests are to be balanced: it just seems to promote the security interests. Unless I have misread it, it doesn't say anything about how that should be balanced against the rights of people to fair hearings and fair trials and so on. The trouble is that it is very, very difficult. How do you balance those things? It isn't really an answer to your question. It's just to say that it is incredibly difficult.

DN

John has referred to Jonathan Sumption, and like John I don't agree with everything Jonathan says, although I don't disagree with everything he says either. I think he has the interesting theory, which has considerable force, namely that one of the differences between law and politics is that law laid down by judges involves the application of clear principles whereas democratic government legislation is the result of fudge. That is something of a sort of caricature, although there is a lot in the difference he identifies. I think in a country where the law is largely made by Parliament, and where we have the common law made by judges, there are inevitably difficult questions.

This was a particularly difficult one in *Al Rawi*: should it be up to the courts or Parliament to change the present system in relation to open hearings where both sides are there and represented, and can hear what is going on. In my view, the issue involves an encroachment on such a fundamental principle, namely that each party should be able to know the other side's case before the judge in full, that it could only be decided by the democratically elected legislature, as well as being something of a fudge issue for Parliament to sort out.

It was not for the judges to take up the mantle of interfering with open justice. If they were instructed, in a system where we have a system of parliamentary supremacy, by a democratically accountable Parliament to do it, then the judges could properly do it.

As John says, another of many interesting aspects of that sort of case is that it faces the judge with a problem which is so familiar in judging, that, when carrying out a balancing exercise, the two features that one is trying to balance are completely incommensurate. They are two ships that pass in the night. It isn't as if one party's case is more convincing compared with that of the other: each side has a strong factor that does not relate to the other party's strong point.

How do you carry out the balancing exercise? Parliament had decided that it was not going to go there. So although the judges say, 'We are not going to deal with this', it goes to the legislature, they say, 'Yes, you are', and the judges then have to do the best they can. What happens then, is that (I should imagine—because like John I haven't had to deal with this statute very much at all) the judges develop the law in a common law way of trying to give guidance, building up the law on a case by case basis.

JD

I suppose, being crude about it, the best you can do is to say how much of a risk to security would it be on the one hand, and how damaging would it be to the litigant to be deprived of access to open justice on the other. And if the risk to security—as far as the judge is able to assess it, which is in itself a very difficult question—but in so far as the judge is able to assess it—if the assessment is that it isn't very much, and on the other side the damage or potential damage to the litigant of being deprived of open justice is potentially very great, then that would tend to swing the balance that way. That is fairly obvious stuff. But I don't see how else you could do it.

DN

I agree that that would be the approach. But then you have problems like we had in another case,[12] when I was in the Court of Appeal, where you are told, 'Yes, this information seems extremely insignificant and unimportant if it gets out, but the Americans have supplied the information, and they are saying that if you reveal it, they are not going to give the secret service in this country any more information'. Do you think 'that is a load of old nonsense', or do you think actually it is a very serious possibility? That is the sort of issue that I'm sure Jonathan Sumption would say that judges should not have to decide, but the answer to him is that Parliament has told us we have to.

[12] *R (Binyam Mohamed) v Secretary of State* [2010] EWCA Civ 65.

KO'R

Well, it seems to me that that is a good illustration of how hard it is to be a judge, and how complex the questions are that come before the judiciary. I'd like to thank both of you for your interesting and illuminating insights across the range of the issues that we've traversed. Please would you all join me in thanking Lord Neuberger and Lord Dyson.

PART III
COLLECTIVE REDRESS

10

Taking Stock of the Collective Proceedings Regime in the Competition Appeal Tribunal—A Successful Compromise?

Stephen Wisking and Ruth Allen[1]

Introduction

Competition law claims have long been considered to be particularly suited to collective redress mechanisms and already form a prominent part of the class action landscape in jurisdictions such as the United States and Canada. They have been the subject of detailed attention as part of the extensive policy debate about the introduction and expansion of collective redress at both UK and EU level.

Competition law infringements are a classic example of a legal wrong which can cause loss to a large number of potential claimants. In some cases the individual harm allegedly caused can be material and claims by businesses are now frequently being brought in the UK. This can be on a purely individual basis or within an informal grouping in which a number of claimants represented by the same solicitors bring individual claims together in a single action. However, for consumers and small businesses affected by a competition law infringement the level of individual loss can be relatively small and litigating competition claims is complex and costly, involving extensive expert economic evidence. As a result, some competition claims may not be economically viable as individual claims, even though the aggregate loss arising from the alleged infringement may be substantial. Since a key element of competition law is safeguarding the interests of consumers, there are clear policy reasons for promoting collective redress in this area, particularly where, in the absence of

[1] This chapter is based on a presentation by Stephen Wisking at 'The Civil Procedure Rules At 20' conference on 10 June 2019 at the Bonavero Institute of Human Rights, University of Oxford. The views set out here are the authors' own.

Stephen Wisking and Ruth Allen, *Taking Stock of the Collective Proceedings Regime in the Competition Appeal Tribunal—A Successful Compromise?* In: *The Civil Procedure Rules at 20.* Edited by: Andrew Higgins, Oxford University Press (2020). © the several contributors. DOI: 10.1093/oso/9780198863182.003.0010.

an effective group collective redress mechanism, consumer or small business loss is likely to go uncompensated even where the conduct has been sanctioned through public enforcement by competition authorities. Finally, although policy makers have emphasised the compensatory function of collective redress, class actions undoubtedly also have a deterrent effect, which complements the public competition law enforcement regime.

These considerations led to the introduction of a specific regime in the UK for collective actions seeking damages for loss caused by competition law breaches in 2003. However, this regime was limited in scope to allowing a consumer representative organisation designated by the Secretary of State to bring 'follow-on'[2] damages claims in competition cases on behalf of consumers, on an 'opt-in' basis only.[3] These restrictions proved to be a significant hurdle, with only one claim being brought between 2003 and 2015.[4] However, the regime was significantly broadened in 2015 as part of a wider package of competition litigation reforms. The stated intentions of the reform package were to, first, promote greater use of private actions (in particular by small and medium sized enterprises and consumers) to challenge, and to obtain effective redress for loss caused by, anti-competitive behaviour; and second, to establish the Competition Appeal Tribunal (the 'CAT') as the primary venue for competition claims in the UK.[5]

In framing the competition collective actions regime, the Government sought to balance the aim of enhancing the scope for victims of anti-competitive behaviour to obtain redress against the risk of frivolous or unmeritorious litigation (and the perceived excesses of the US class action system). In particular, there was a fear that class actions could put pressure on defendants to settle regardless of the merits of the claim, or that the only beneficiaries of a successful claim would be lawyers and funders, rather than the claimants. As a result, the regime includes a series of safeguards which seek to strike a balance between facilitating redress for competition law infringements and minimising the risk of vexatious or otherwise unmeritorious class claims being brought.

This chapter examines how that balance has been struck in the collective claims brought under the new regime to date, and whether, four years after the introduction of the regime, it can be considered to be a successful compromise.

[2] 'Follow-on' claims are those based on an infringement decision by the UK Competition and Markets Authority or, at the time of writing, the European Commission. See n 47 regarding the impact of the exit of the UK from the European Union ('Brexit').

[3] ie on behalf of named consumers who had taken active steps to 'opt in' to joining the claim.

[4] *The Consumers' Association v. JJB Sports Plc* (Case No. 1078/7/9/07).

[5] At the time, claimants tended to bring competition claims in the High Court, as a result of various limitations on the CAT's jurisdiction.

It focuses in particular on the two cases in which certification hearings have taken place and judgments have been given—*Gibson v. Pride*[6] and *Merricks v. Mastercard*[7] —and the question of the intensity of the control that the CAT should have over collective actions through the certification process. It also considers the potential implications of the recent Court of Appeal judgment in *Lloyd v. Google*,[8] which some commentators have suggested may encourage claimants to re-consider using the representative action route offered by Rule 19.6 of the Civil Procedure Rules ('CPR'), as an alternative to the competition collective actions regime.[9]

At the time of writing, the determination of the appeal in *Merricks v. Mastercard* by the Supreme Court is pending, following a hearing held on 13 and 14 May 2020. The issues in that appeal are discussed further below, but the decision of the Supreme Court is likely to have a considerable bearing on where the balance lies between facilitating redress and avoiding the risk of unmeritorious class claims, and indeed on the future of collective proceedings in the CAT.

Overview of the competition collective actions regime

Prior to 2003, the options available to a group of unrelated claimants seeking to bring a joint claim for damages for an infringement of competition law were limited to informal claims aggregation by naming multiple claimants on a standard claim form, joint case management of similar cases, or—more formally—bringing the claim as a representative action or pursuant to a Group Litigation Order ('GLO'), under CPR 19. These latter more formal routes were little used in practice,[10] and there was a general consensus that a specific

[6] *Gibson v. Pride Mobility Products Ltd* [2017] CAT 9.

[7] *Merricks v. Mastercard Inc and others* [2017] CAT 16 (CAT judgment); [2019] EWCA Civ 674 (Court of Appeal judgment).

[8] *Lloyd v. Google LLC* [2019] EWCA Civ 1599.

[9] As discussed further below, the representative action route has not been used in a competition law context since the Court of Appeal upheld the decision of the High Court to strike out an attempt by Emerald Supplies to use this form of action to claim damages on behalf of itself and all other direct and indirect purchasers of air cargo services from British Airways allegedly affected by a price-fixing cartel (*Emerald Supplies Ltd and another v. British Airways Plc* [2010] EWCA 1284). *Lloyd v. Google* (n 8) is not a competition case, but it has been suggested that the more permissive approach adopted by the Court of Appeal in that case to the question of whether all members of the class had 'the same interest' in the claim could potentially have some read-across to the competition law context, and may encourage claimants to re-consider using the representative action route in respect of competition claims.

[10] As noted in the previous footnote, no attempt has been made to use the representative action route in a competition case since *Emerald Supplies Ltd. v. British Airways plc*. The list of GLOs maintained by the UK government indicates that only one GLO has ever been issued in a competition case (*Prentice Ltd/Daimler Chrysler UK Ltd Litigation* (30 April 2001, 2001 Folio 398), which ultimately settled before

competition collective actions regime was needed to enable consumers to obtain effective redress for damage suffered as a result of competition law infringements, provided sufficient safeguards were also introduced to prevent vexatious or unmeritorious claims from proceeding.

As briefly described above, a competition law-specific collective procedure was first introduced in the UK with effect from 20 June 2003.[11] This allowed bodies designated by the Secretary of State (in practice limited to the consumer organisation *Which?*) to bring follow-on competition law claims on behalf of consumers in the specialist Competition Appeal Tribunal, on an opt-in basis. However, the regime was widely perceived as a failure: only one claim was ever brought, in relation to overcharging for football shirts,[12] and in that case only 130 claimants opted in (less than one per cent of those estimated to have been affected by the competition law infringement in question). The case ultimately settled, with costs understood to have far outweighed the ultimate settlement. *Which?* subsequently stated that it would not bring another claim so long as the mechanism remained opt-in in nature.[13]

Against this background, a far-reaching overhaul of the competition private actions regime was undertaken in 2015, with a new broader regime for bringing collective competition proceedings in the CAT introduced by the Consumer Rights Act 2015, through amendments to the Competition Act 1998 ('CA98').[14] The new regime allows class actions for both 'follow-on' and 'standalone'[15] claims based on (alleged) competition law infringements to be brought in the CAT, on either an 'opt-in' or an 'opt-out'[16] basis. Claims must be brought by a class representative approved by the CAT,[17] on behalf of a defined

trial) <www.gov.uk/guidance/group-litigation-orders#list-of-all-group-litigation-orders> accessed 16 June 2020.

[11] By way of the former section 47B of the Competition Act 1998.

[12] *The Consumers' Association v. JJB Sports Plc* (Case No. 1078/7/9/07).

[13] 'Class action is one big headache, says Which?', *The Lawyer*, 1 December 2008, <www.thelawyer.com/issues/1-december-2008/class-action-is-one-big-headache-says-which/> accessed 16 June 2020.

[14] This amended the CA98 by introducing new sections 47B–47E and 49A–49B, alongside related new rules 73–97 of the updated CAT Rules 2015 (SI 2015/1648). At the same time, the CAT published an updated Guide to Proceedings, which covers collective actions in section 6. The Guide to Proceedings constitutes a Practice Direction issued by the CAT President pursuant to Rule 115(3) of the CAT Rules 2015.

[15] 'Standalone' claims are those where there is no underlying infringement decision that can be relied upon as binding before the court, meaning that claimants must prove liability as well as causation and quantum.

[16] In an opt-out claim, anyone resident in the UK falling within the definition of the relevant class is automatically included in the claim (and loses their right to bring an individual action), unless they actively choose to 'opt-out'.

[17] Unlike collective actions brought under the previous section 47B CA98, under the new regime the class representative is not limited to designated organisations; it can be either a class member or

class of persons (whether consumers or businesses or, in theory, a combination of the two). The primary intention behind the introduction of the new broader regime was to ensure the full effectiveness of competition law, by enhancing the ability of consumers and small businesses to obtain compensation for competition law infringements.[18]

As discussed in more detail below, a number of safeguards against vexatious or otherwise unmeritorious claims are hardwired into the legislative structure of the collective actions regime. These safeguards were primarily included in response to concerns about the risk of vexatious or otherwise unmeritorious claims and the resulting costs for businesses. However, they also address a broader policy concern that, in the case of opt-out proceedings, the CAT is there to protect the interests of the claimants in whose name the claim is being brought but who have not authorised the proceedings. First, the collective actions regime is limited to claims based on infringements of competition law.[19] It is not possible to roll other causes of action into the collective proceedings. Secondly, only compensatory damages are available (at least in principle);[20] the CAT may not award exemplary damages.[21] Thirdly, it is not possible to have damages based costs agreements for the funding of opt-out claims (although these may be available in opt-in claims).[22] Fourth, the starting point for the assessment of costs is that the successful party should be awarded its costs, payable by the unsuccessful party.[23] Finally—and very importantly—primary control over collective proceedings lies with the CAT through a certification process whereby a class representative seeking to bring collective proceedings must first apply for and obtain a collective

a representative body, subject to authorisation from the CAT. This authorisation process is discussed further below.

[18] This is notably different from the approach taken in the United States, where competition class actions are seen as a tool of policy, sometimes referred to as a 'private attorney general'.

[19] Section 47B(1) CA98.

[20] The Court of Appeal held in *Merricks v. Mastercard* that although assessed on an aggregate compensatory basis there is no requirement for an aggregate damages award made in collective proceedings to be distributed on a compensatory basis to individual claimants ([2019] EWCA Civ 674, [57]–[61]).

[21] Schedule 47C(1) and Schedule 8A, paragraph 36, CA98. In contrast, in the case of proceedings in the High Court seeking damages for a competition law infringement, it is open to the Court to award exemplary damages where the defendant has not been the subject of a fine as a result of public enforcement: *2 Travel v. Cardiff Bus* [2012] CAT 1; *Devenish Nutrition v. Sanofi-Aventis* [2008] EWCA Civ 1086.

[22] Section 47C(8) CA98, although the CAT may order that all or any part of the damages awarded not claimed by the represented claimants within a specified period will instead be paid to the representative in respect of all or part of the costs or expenses that it has incurred, under section 47C(6) CA98.

[23] Rule 104 of the CAT Rules 2015 (n 14).

proceedings order ('CPO') from the CAT before the collective proceedings can commence.

The high-level requirements for a CPO to be granted are that the CAT considers that:

- it is just and reasonable for the proposed class representative to act as the representative in the proceedings;[24] and
- the claims:
    - are brought on behalf of an identifiable class of persons;[25]
    - raise the same, similar or related issues of fact or law; and
    - are suitable to be brought in collective proceedings.[26]

Rule 79(2) of the CAT Rules 2015 contains a non-exclusive list of factors which the Tribunal shall take into account when assessing the suitability of claims to be brought in collective proceedings, including whether collective proceedings are an appropriate means for the fair and efficient resolution of the common issues; the costs and benefits of continuing the collective proceedings; the size and nature of the class; whether the claims are suitable for an aggregate award of damages; and the availability of alternative dispute resolution or redress mechanisms.

In determining whether the claim should proceed on an opt-in or opt-out basis, the CAT must additionally take into account the strength of the claims and the practicality of the claims being brought as opt-in claims, including having regard to the amount of damages that individual class members may recover.[27]

Finally, whether opt-out collective proceedings have been brought or not, the CAT can authorise a settlement reached between the class representative and the defendants such that the terms of settlement bind the entire class.[28]

[24] Section 47B(5) and (8) CA98. A list of factors that the CAT should take into account is set out in Rule 78 of the CAT Rules 2015 (n 14). These include whether the representative would fairly and adequately act in the interests of class members; has no material interest which is in conflict with class members on the issues which are common to them; the ability to pay the defendant's recoverable costs if ordered to do so; its suitability to manage the proceedings; and the representative's plan for the proceedings including governance and consultation processes for the class.

[25] Rule 79(1) of the CAT Rules 2015 (n 14).

[26] Sections 47B(5) and (6) CA98 and rules 79(2) and (3) of the CAT Rules 2015 (n 14).

[27] Rule 79(3) of the 2015 CAT Rules (n 14).

[28] Sections 49A–49B CA98.

CPO applications made to date

The new competition collective actions regime got off to a relatively slow start, but there are signs of increasing momentum. At the time of writing, eight CPO applications have been made to the CAT (all but one on an opt-out basis), relating to five competition law infringements. A brief description of each of these applications is set out below.

These figures may not, at first sight, appear encouraging. However, given the relatively early stage of the regime, its success cannot be judged by the number of applications: it is simply too soon to say. Furthermore, there are a number of reasons why a relatively small number of actions is not surprising. First, as noted above, claims are limited to competition law infringements. As a result the potential pool of claims is necessary limited. Second, the way in which the collective actions regime was implemented with respect to limitation periods has made it difficult to bring collective actions in respect of more historic competition law infringements, which has further reduced the pool of potential claims. Limitation periods in the CAT were aligned with those applicable in the High Court with effect from 1 October 2015 (ie six years from the date the cause of action arose, subject to rules relating to concealment and suspension of the running of the period in certain circumstances),[29] but transitional provisions mean that the previous two-year CAT limitation period applies to claims arising before 1 October 2015.[30] Finally, not all competition law infringements will give rise to claims which will be suitable for collective proceedings.

The CPO applications that have been made to date suggest that collective claims will, as intended, be used in a broad range of cases involving both consumer and business claims, covering a range of alleged competition law infringements (including both anti-competitive agreements and abuse of dominance). Unsurprisingly, collective claims have tended to brought on a follow-on basis, but the *Travelcards* applications made in February 2019 (see the following list) have notably been brought on a standalone basis. All but one of the CPO applications made to date has sought certification to proceed on an opt-out basis; this is unsurprising as in each of those cases the alleged loss suffered by each individual claimant is relatively small.

A brief summary of the factual background and context for each of the CPO applications made to date is set out below.

[29] Part 5 of Schedule 8A, CA98.

[30] Rule 119(2)–(4) of the CAT Rules 2015 (n 14) and *Gibson v. Pride Mobility Products Limited* [2017] CAT9, [110].

- ***Gibson v. Pride (Mobility Scooters)***:[31] This case involved an action brought by Ms. Gibson, the General Secretary of the National Pensioners Convention, on behalf of the purchasers of mobility scooters between 1 February 2010 and 29 February 2012. The claim was brought on an opt-out basis, and it was estimated that the class would comprise between 27,000 and 32,000 UK purchasers. The claim was framed as a follow-on claim based on a Competition and Markets Authority ('CMA') infringement decision, which found that Pride Mobility Products Ltd and eight retailers had suppliers of mobility scooters had engaged in a form of resale price maintenance.[32] The essence of the claim was that class members had overpaid for mobility scooters as a result of the infringement. A CPO application was heard on 12–14 December 2016, during which a number of issues were identified with the scope of the claim and the methodology proposed for estimating individual loss within various sub-classes of claimant (see below). The CAT invited Ms. Gibson to reformulate her claim and amend the proposed methodology, but the claim was ultimately withdrawn.[33]
- ***Merricks v. Mastercard (Retail Purchases)***:[34] This ongoing case involves an opt-out claim for £14 billion brought by Mr. Merricks (the former Chief Ombudsman of the Financial Ombudsman service) against Mastercard, on behalf of approximately 46 million customers who purchased goods and services from businesses in the UK that accepted Mastercard payment cards between May 1992 and June 2008 (even if the purchase in question was not actually made using a Mastercard). The claim purportedly follows on from a European Commission competition infringement decision relating to multi-lateral interchange fees ('MIFs') charged in relation to retail transactions involving the use of a Mastercard.[35] The essence of the claim is that the

[31] *Gibson v. Pride Mobility Products Limited* [2017] CAT9. An opt-out CPO application was lodged on 25 May 2016, and the hearing of the application took place on 12–14 December 2016. The CAT's judgment was handed down on 31 March 2017. The claim was withdrawn by consent on 25 May 2017.

[32] The CMA found that Pride Mobility Products Ltd. and eight retailers had infringed competition law by entering into agreements and concerted practices aimed at prohibiting the online advertising of prices for certain models of Pride mobility scooters below Pride's recommended retail prices.

[33] No statement was made by Ms. Gibson explaining this decision, but it is believed that reformulating the claim as indicated by the CAT would have resulted in a much smaller class of claimants, and the economics of the claim would no longer have made sense.

[34] *Merricks v. Mastercard* (n 7). An opt-out CPO application was lodged on 8 September 2016, and the hearing of the application took place on 18–20 January 2017. The CAT's judgment, refusing certification, was handed down on 21 July 2017. That decision was appealed to the Court of Appeal, which gave judgment on 16 April 2019. The Court of Appeal overturned the decision to refuse certification and remitted the claim to the CAT for reconsideration. That judgment is now the subject of a further appeal to the Supreme Court, which was heard on 13 and 14 May 2020. At the time of writing, judgment is still awaited.

[35] The European Commission decision relied upon in this case relates to intra-EEA fees, while the proposed collective action relates to domestic UK fees. If the collective action brought by Mr. Merricks is ultimately permitted to proceed following determination of the pending appeal by the Supreme Court

MIF overcharge was passed on to consumers in the form of higher prices charged by retailers for goods and services. The CPO application was dismissed by the CAT, but that decision was overturned by the Court of Appeal. An appeal is pending to the Supreme Court.

- ***UK Trucks Claim v. Fiat Chrysler and others/Road Haulage Association v. Man SE and others (Trucks)***:[36] These two cases both involve claims against truck manufacturers following on from the European Commission's 2016 *Trucks* decision,[37] brought on behalf of purchasers of trucks allegedly affected by the infringement. The CPO application made by UK Trucks Claim Ltd has been made on an opt-out basis, whereas the application made by the Road Haulage Association has been made on an opt-in basis. Both applications have been adjourned pending the hearing of the appeal to the Supreme Court in *Merricks v. Mastercard* (save for a funding issue which was relevant to the authorisation of the proposed class representative, discussed further below). At a case management conference held on 12 December 2018 Roth J made clear that the CAT did not consider there to be anything as a matter of law to prevent two competing CPOs from proceeding where either both applications are made on an opt-in basis, or, as in these cases, one is made on an opt-in basis and the other on an opt-out basis.[38] However, it remains to be determined whether both applications will be certified to proceed. A number of larger companies have chosen not to participate in these collective claims and have instead initiated follow-on claims separately, both before the CAT and in the High Court.
- ***Gutmann v. London and South Eastern Railway/Gutmann v. First MTR South Western Trains (Travelcards)***:[39] These two CPO applications have

against the Court of Appeal's judgment overturning CAT's refusal to certify the claim, this is likely to be a key issue in dispute.

[36] *UK Trucks Claim Ltd v. Fiat Chrysler Automobiles NV and others* (opt-out application lodged on 18 May 2018; adjourned pending the outcome of the appeal in *Merricks v. Mastercard* (n 7)) and *Road Haulage Association Ltd v. Man SE and others* (opt-in application lodged on 17 July 2018; adjourned pending the outcome of the appeal in *Merricks v. Mastercard* (n 7)).

[37] Case AT.39824.

[38] Roth J pointed out that the consideration in the CAT Guide to Proceedings 2015 of the question of which class representative is most suitable is limited to the scenario where there are two applications for certification of opt-out proceedings. In such circumstances, if the two opt-out applications are made on behalf of the same or overlapping classes, the CAT would need to decide which could proceed, if either (as illustrated by the two *Forex* applications, discussed below). However, where there are two opt-in proceedings, or one opt-in and one opt-out, Roth J considered that choosing between the two actions is a matter for the individual claimant. See pages 1 and 2 of the transcript of the case management conference (available on the CAT website: <www.catribunal.org.uk/sites/default/files/2019-01/1282-1289_Trucks_Transcript_121218_1.pdf> accessed 16 June 2020).

[39] *Gutmann v. London and South Eastern Railway Ltd* and *Gutmann v. First MTR South Western Trains Ltd and Stagecoach South Western Trains Ltd* (both opt-out applications lodged on 27 February 2019). The applications are being heard jointly, and advance similar claims against three different defendants.

been brought on a standalone basis (ie without relying on any underlying infringement decision by the CMA or the European Commission). Both claims allege abuse of dominance by rail companies, by not making so-called 'boundary fares' readily available for purchase to holders of Transport for London Travelcards (or making passengers aware of the existence of such fares).[40] It is alleged that this has led to approximately 2 million rail travellers unnecessarily paying twice for the part of their journey to or from the outer boundaries of Transport for London's fare zones. The alleged losses are estimated by the class representative to amount to around £93 million. Both applications have been stayed pending the outcome of the appeal to the Supreme Court in *Merricks v. Mastercard.*

- ***Michael O'Higgins FX Class Representative v. Barclays and others/Mr. Phillip Evans v Barclays Bank and others (Forex)*:**[41] These two CPO applications involve claims against a number of banks, following on from the European Commission's settlement decisions announced in May 2019 relating to two foreign exchange rate-fixing cartels known as the 'Essex Express' cartel and the 'Three-Way Banana Split' cartel.[42] The proposed claimants in each application include the main customers of foreign exchange traders referred to the Commission's press release, namely asset managers, pension funds, hedge funds, major companies and other banks, and both applications have been made on an opt-out basis. On 6 March 2020 the CAT held that the two competing applicants must go 'head to head' for the right to represent the potential class in one single substantive hearing (currently listed for March 2021), which will also determine whether a CPO is made at all. In reaching this conclusion, the CAT rejected arguments that the so-called 'carriage dispute' should be heard as a preliminary issue prior to the main certification hearing. A separate follow-on claim relating to the *Forex* decision was also lodged in the High Court in December 2018 by multiple claimants, primarily investment management firms.[43]

[40] A 'boundary fare' is a ticket which covers the portion of a mainline train journey to or from the edge of the outer boundaries of Transport for London's fare zones. For passengers who also have a Transport for London Travelcard (permitting unlimited travel within one or more designated zones), the remainder of their journey will be covered by their Travelcard. Where such a passenger purchases a standard mainline train ticket, it is alleged that they will effectively be paying twice for that portion of their journey.

[41] *Michael O'Higgins FX Class Representative Ltd v. Barclays Bank Plc and others* (opt-out application lodged on 29 July 2019) and *Mr. Phillip Evans v Barclays Bank and others* (opt-out application lodged on 11 December 2019).

[42] Case AT.40135. No public versions of the infringement decisions are available at the time of writing.

[43] *Allianz Global Investors GmbH and others v. Barclays Bank Plc and others* (Claim No. CL-2018-000840).

The approach to the certification process to date

As outlined above, the intention behind requiring all competition collective actions to be certified by the CAT before proceeding to trial was to help strike the appropriate balance between facilitating redress for competition law infringements and minimising the risk of vexatious or otherwise unmeritorious class claims being brought. At the time of writing, only two of the eight CPO applications made to date have reached the certification hearing stage—*Gibson v. Pride* and *Merricks v. Mastercard*—and there remain a number of important unanswered questions about how that balance should be struck. However, it is nonetheless possible to undertake a preliminary assessment of the approach adopted by the CAT and the Court of Appeal to date, and to highlight some of the key issues which have arisen.

Types of claim

The CAT is a tribunal of limited jurisdiction.[44] Claimants are therefore only able to bring claims in the CAT that are specified in the legislation. Under section 47A CA98, claims are limited to claims for damages or an injunction based upon infringements or alleged infringements of UK or EU prohibitions on anti-competitive agreements[45] and/or abuse of dominance.[46] Further to the outcome of the referendum on the UK's membership of the European Union, it remains to be seen whether, following the UK's exit from the EU, section 47A will be amended to remove claims based on a breach of Article 101 or 102 of the Treaty on the Functioning of the European Union ('TFEU') from the CAT's jurisdiction.[47]

The wording of section 47A CA98 allows for a CPO application to be made on a follow-on or standalone basis. However, the CAT has made clear that where a claim involves both follow-on and standalone elements (for example

[44] *Enron Coal Services Limited (In Liquidation) v. English Welsh and Scottish Railway Limited* [2009] EWCA Civ 647.

[45] Chapter I CA98 and Article 101 TFEU.

[46] Chapter II CA98 and Article 102 TFEU.

[47] After the expiry of transitional arrangements due to end on 31 December 2020, new European Commission infringement decisions may not have a binding effect on the UK courts. However, any such change should not affect claims relating to conduct for which the European Commission had jurisdiction before 31 December 2020, whether the decision is adopted before or after that date. Such decisions will remain binding in the UK (Article 95 Withdrawal Agreement) and there is therefore likely to be a significant number of existing and future decisions which will continue to affect the UK and provide a basis for follow-on damages claims.

where it is based on an underlying infringement decision by the CMA or the European Commission but also includes claims for losses beyond the scope of the that infringement decision), this must be clearly acknowledged and any sub-classes of claimant properly identified.

In *Gibson v. Pride*[48] the proposed claimant class included purchasers of new Pride mobility scooters during a specified period, including both models subject to the online price restrictions identified in the underlying infringement decision as well as other models, purchased in physical stores or online. As discussed further below, the methodology for calculating loss suffered by the claimants did not distinguish between the eight retailers identified in the underlying infringement decision and other retailers of Pride mobility scooters. The CAT considered this was incorrect, given that the claim had been framed solely as a follow-on claim, and as such was limited to the boundaries of the infringement identified in the underlying OFT infringement decision. This ultimately proved fatal to the issue of whether there was sufficient commonality of issues between each of the individual claims to certify the claim to proceed by way of collective proceedings.[49]

Establishing sufficient commonality of issues

One of the fundamental requirements which must be met in order for a CPO application to be granted is that the claims raise the same, similar or related issues of fact or law.[50] Establishing such commonality of issues has proved to be a major stumbling block in the two CPO applications heard by the CAT to date, and determining exactly where the bar should be set and what supporting evidence should be required at the certification stage is one of the key issues to be addressed by the Supreme Court in the pending appeal in *Merricks v. Mastercard.*

The CAT has stated that it does not require all significant issues to be deemed 'common issues' for a claim to be considered suitable for a CPO,[51] or for the common issues to predominate over the individual issues. However, there

[48] *Gibson v. Pride Mobility Products Limited* [2017] CAT9.

[49] The CAT invited Ms. Gibson to reformulate her claim and amend the proposed methodology to focus on the effects of agreements that were the subject of the underlying infringement decision, but the claim was ultimately withdrawn.

[50] Section 47B(6) CA98.

[51] *Merricks v. Mastercard Inc and others* [2017] CAT 16, [67].

must still be sufficient commonality of issues to enable the CAT to conclude that the claim is suitable to be brought in collective proceedings.

The claims which have been heard to date indicate that a key battleground at the certification stage will be whether the alleged loss suffered by the claimants can be treated as a 'common issue' and established on a class-wide basis. A related and equally important issue is the extent to which a CPO applicant must be able, at the time of the certification hearing, to show that loss is capable of calculation as a common issue. In the applications to date economic evidence has been adduced proposing a methodology for calculating loss.

As noted above, in *Gibson v. Pride* Ms. Gibson argued that a fair approximation of the estimated individual loss on a common basis could be calculated within the four sub-classes of claimants identified in the CPO application,[52] and relied on an expert economist report setting out a proposed methodology for doing so. However, that methodology did not distinguish between the eight retailers identified in the underlying infringement decision and other retailers of Pride mobility scooters. The CAT considered that this was not the correct approach. It concluded that that alleged losses suffered by the members of the proposed claimant class were in fact so diverse (and, in some cases, outside the scope of the infringement decision on which the follow-on claim was based), that there was insufficient commonality of issues between each of the individual claims to certify the claim to proceed by way of collective proceedings. Ms. Gibson was invited to reformulate her claim and amend the proposed methodology, but she ultimately chose to withdraw her claim.

In *Merricks v. Mastercard*,[53] difficulties arose in determining how to deal with the fact that there was likely to be significant variation in pass-on of the alleged overcharge between different kinds of goods and services and different kinds of retailers. The CAT accepted that damages could, in principle, be calculated on an aggregate basis using a weighted average pass-on percentage. However, it concluded that the methodology proposed by Mr. Merricks for doing so was inadequate, due to a lack of evidence as to the availability of the data that would be required to apply the proposed methodology on a sufficiently sound basis. On this issue the CAT relied on the judgment of the Canadian Supreme Court

[52] Purchasers of new Pride mobility scooters which were subject to the online price advertising restrictions identified in the underlying infringement decision and purchased online; purchasers of new Pride mobility scooters which were subject to the online price advertising restrictions identified in the underlying infringement decision and purchased in physical stores; purchasers of other models of new Pride mobility scooters online; purchasers of other models of new Pride mobility scooters in physical stores.

[53] *Merricks v. Mastercard Inc and others* [2017] CAT 16 (CAT judgment); [2019] EWCA Civ 674 (Court of Appeal judgment).

in *Pro-Sys Consultants v. Microsoft Corporation*,[54] which held that the proposed methodology 'must offer a realistic prospect of establishing loss on a class-wide basis' and 'cannot be purely theoretical or hypothetical, but rather must be grounded in the facts of the particular case in question'. In addition, 'there must be some evidence of the availability of the data to which the methodology is to be applied'.

On appeal, the Court of Appeal approved the CAT's reliance on Canadian jurisprudence on this point. However, it held that the CAT had applied the test in *Pro-Sys Consultants v. Microsoft* too strictly when it required Mr. Merricks to do 'more than simply show that he has an arguable case on the pleadings, as if, for example, he was facing an application to strike out'.[55] The Court of Appeal took the view that the 'realistic prospect of success' test to be applied at the certification stage should not involve conducting a 'mini-trial' (which it considered the CAT had effectively done). In particular, the Court of Appeal held that the CAT had set the bar too high in requiring Mr. Merricks to be able to produce the data required to apply the proposed methodology for assessing the level of pass-on to the represented class of claimants at the time of the certification hearing, rather than simply demonstrating that the necessary data was, or was likely to be, available for use at the trial.[56]

It remains to be seen whether the Supreme Court will uphold the less restrictive approach advocated by the Court of Appeal. However, it is submitted that this approach is at odds with what was intended when the current regime was introduced. The Government's response to the consultation on the reform package which introduced the current competition collective actions regime expressly referred to introducing a 'strict' and 'strong' judicial certification process, including a preliminary merits test, 'so that only meritorious cases are taken forward'.[57] Whilst conducting a 'mini trial' at the certification stage would indeed set the bar too high, it seems that framing the relevant test in the same terms as that applied on a strike out application is equally setting the bar too low.

Moreover, it is also implicit in the legislation and accompanying CAT Rules 2015 that the test to be applied at the certification stage should set a higher threshold than the strike out test. The CAT Rules 2015 include a separate rule dealing with applications to strike out claims made under section 47A,[58] which

[54] *Pro-Sys Consultants Ltd v. Microsoft Corp.* [2013] SCC 57.

[55] *Merricks v. Mastercard Inc and others* [2017] CAT 16, [57]; [2019] EWCA Civ 674, [52]–[54].

[56] *Merricks v. Mastercard Inc and others* [2019] EWCA Civ 674, [44].

[57] *Private Actions in Competition Law: A consultation on options for reform—government response*; see Executive Summary, section 2, and also paragraph 5.55.

[58] Rule 41 of the CAT Rules 2015 (n 14).

applies equally to collective proceedings;[59] if the appropriate test to be applied at the certification stage were intended to be equivalent to the test for striking out, this would be redundant.[60] The need to carry out a preliminary assessment of the strength of the claims at the certification stage—beyond simply establishing whether the claim is arguable—is also further reflected in the express inclusion in Rule 79(3)(a) of the CAT Rules 2015 of the strength of the claims as a relevant factor to be taken into account by the CAT when determining, as part of the certification process, whether collective proceedings should proceed on an opt-in or opt-out basis.

In reaching its conclusion on the appropriate test to be applied at the certification stage, the Court of Appeal noted that section 47B(9) CA98 expressly states that the CAT may vary or revoke a CPO at any time.[61] With that in mind, the Court of Appeal emphasised that 'the making of a CPO does not therefore prevent the CAT from subsequently terminating the proceedings if it subsequently transpires that the proposed representative is unable to access sufficient data to enable the experts' method of calculating the rate of pass-on to be performed'.[62] It referred to this course of action being taken in a number of Canadian cases.

However, this reliance on the ability to revoke a CPO at a later date is arguably not in line with what was intended when the current regime was introduced in 2015. As one of the key safeguards introduced to minimise the risk of vexatious or otherwise unmeritorious class claims, certification was intended to be a one-off preliminary assessment of the merits of a claim. Whilst the legislation does provide for the possibility of variation or revocation of a CPO, this possibility was not intended to be deployed as an ongoing case management tool, such that the status of a claim which was certified to proceed should be subject to ongoing review, with a looming threat of withdrawal of certification at any stage.[63] Moreover, it is submitted that such an approach introduces too

[59] In accordance with Rule 74 of the CAT Rules 2015 (n 14).

[60] Rule 74(1) of the CAT Rules 2015 (n 14) provides that Part 4 of the CAT Rules (relating to claims under section 47A, including Rule 41 relating to strike out applications) applies to collective proceedings in accordance with the provisions of Rule 74. Rule 74(3) specifies certain rules of Part 4 which do not apply to collective proceedings, and Rule 74(4) specifies certain rules of Part 4 which apply subject to specified modifications. Rule 41 is not specified in either of these sub-sections; in other words, it applies in unmodified form to collective actions, and independently of the certification process.

[61] See also Rule 85 of the CAT Rules 2015 (n 14).

[62] *Merricks v. Mastercard Inc and others* [2019] EWCA Civ 674, [53].

[63] Indeed, prior to the Court of Appeal decision granting permission to Mr. Merricks to appeal against the CAT's judgment on certification in *Merricks v. Mastercard*, it was thought that a certification decision could not be appealed, but instead only subject to judicial review, in order to avoid protracted litigation. See paragraph 16 of the CAT's decision refusing permission to appeal ([2017] CAT 21), which refers to a 'deliberate policy' to 'confine the right of appeal in collective proceedings to decisions on the substantive claims and preclude prolonged litigation in the process of approving the use of the collective procedure for the pursuit of those claims'.

great a degree of uncertainty for all parties involved, as well as significant practical difficulties in amending a CPO part way through proceedings. This is a particular concern given the significant costs involved in proceeding with a claim and the almost inevitable requirement to involve third party litigation funders.[64]

Assessment and distribution of damages

Section 47C(2) CA98 provides that the CAT may assess damages on an aggregate basis, without undertaking an assessment of the amount of damages recoverable by each individual claimant in the class. Nonetheless, in *Merricks v. Mastercard* the CAT concluded that the absence of any plausible means of calculating the loss suffered by individual claimants so as to devise an appropriate method of distributing any aggregate award of damages to reflect the loss suffered by individual class members meant that the claims should not be permitted to proceed as collective proceedings. It rejected the proposal put forward by the applicant's economic experts involving an annualised per capita division (which the experts agreed bore no link to actual purchases made by each individual and therefore to actual loss).

However, the Court of Appeal reached a different conclusion on this point. It held that there is no requirement for an aggregate damages award to be distributed on a compensatory basis (ie in a way that would bear some relation to the actual loss of individual class members). Rather, 'the vindication of individual claimants is achieved by the aggregate award itself,'[65] and a 'top-down', class-wide approach of the sort proposed by Mr. Merricks was therefore held to be permissible. At first sight this would appear to be contrary to the fundamental premise of the collective actions regime, namely ensuring compensation for those who have suffered loss as a result of competition law infringement. This intention is very clear from the Government's response to the consultation on

[64] Litigating competition law claims can be very complex and costly, involving extensive economic evidence. Unsurprisingly, third party funding has proven particularly important in the context of opt-out collective actions, where the class representative is exposed to significant costs risks (costs may be awarded to, or against, the class representative, but generally cannot be awarded to or against members of the class, and the use of contingency fees or damages-based agreements are not permitted). All of the CPO applications made at the time of writing are known to have involved third party litigation funding to some extent, although little detail about the arrangements is publicly available, with the exception of the arrangements in *Merricks v. Mastercard*, which were considered in some detail in the CAT's judgment on certification—see below.

[65] *Merricks v. Mastercard Inc and others* [2019] EWCA Civ 674, [61].

the package of reforms which introduced the current regime,[66] and is also reflected in the prohibition on exemplary or treble damages in collective actions. However, the Court of Appeal was persuaded that the power of the CAT to make an aggregate award of damages without undertaking an assessment of the loss suffered and recoverable by each individual claimant would be rendered nugatory if distribution could only be conducted by reference to such individual loss. Moreover, the Court of Appeal concluded that the issue of damages distribution was not relevant to the grant of a CPO.

Whilst there may be some logic in this conclusion it does not necessarily follow that the notion of compensation for loss suffered should be wholly discarded,[67] nor that the question of how any aggregate award of damages should be apportioned between individual claimants at the distribution stage is irrelevant at the certification stage. In *Merricks* the Court of Appeal held that questions relating to distribution should be determined following trial, when the CAT must give directions as to how any damages award should be apportioned between claimants and ensure that the distribution method proposed is fair and reasonable to the interests of all represented persons.[68] It did not deem that there was any need to consider how damages might ultimately be distributed at the certification stage. Whilst this approach clearly has some advantages in terms of simplifying matters at the certification stage, one of the factors which the CAT is required to have regard to pursuant to Rule 79(2) of the CAT Rules 2015 is a cost/benefit analysis of continuing the collective proceedings;[69] if there are anticipated to be significant difficulties with distributing any damages awarded in a manner which is fair and reasonable to the interests of all represented persons, this should be relevant to this analysis. Indeed, Counsel for Mr. Merricks expressly agreed with the CAT President at the certification hearing that 'if it appears at the outset that there is no methodology that can produce fair distribution, and, therefore, proper compensation, then that is something that must be relevant [at the certification stage]'.[70] It remains to be

[66] *Private Actions in Competition Law: A consultation on options for reform—government response* (January 2013). The Executive Summary concludes that 'The Government believes the measures set out in this document have the potential to stimulate growth and innovation by tackling anticompetitive behaviour and to allow businesses and consumers to get a fair deal by obtaining *compensation* for losses they have suffered' (emphasis added).

[67] A regime that created 'pots' of aggregate damages that were not distributed to claimants or which were distributed in an arbitrary fashion would be clearly inconsistent with the original policy intentions behind the introduction of the current regime.

[68] *Merricks v. Mastercard* [2019] EWCA Civ 674, [61], referring to Rules 92 and 93 of the CAT Rules 2015 (n 14). See further paragraphs 6.82–6.83 of the CAT Guide to Proceedings.

[69] Rule 79(2)(b) of the CAT Rules 2015 (n 14).

[70] See lines 18–22 of page 44 of the transcript of Day One of the certification hearing in *Merricks v. Mastercard* (available on the CAT's website at: <www.catribunal.org.uk/sites/default/files/1266_

seen whether this issue will be further addressed by the Supreme Court, but it is submitted that distribution issues should not be treated as wholly irrelevant for the purposes of certification.

With regard to any damages which remain unclaimed in opt-out cases (which in practice may amount to a substantial sum),[71] section 47C(5) CA98 provides that the default position is that damages not claimed within a specified period should be paid to a prescribed charity (currently the Access to Justice Foundation).[72] However, there is an important exception to this general rule: section 47C(6) provides that the CAT may order that all or part of any unclaimed damages is instead to be paid to the class representative in respect of all or part of the costs or expenses incurred by the representative in connection with the proceedings. In *Merricks v. Mastercard* the CAT confirmed that this allows third party funders to be paid from any unclaimed damage (at the CAT's discretion). The CAT reached this conclusion on the basis that the concept of 'costs or expenses' in section 47C(6) CA98 includes a liability to pay the charge of a third party funder.[73] In practice, this approach is likely to be fundamental to the future development of the regime.[74]

Suitability of the proposed class representative

At an early stage in the debate surrounding the introduction of the new collection actions it was suggested that limitations should be maintained in relation to who could be authorised to act as the class representative (for example, restricting the role to designated consumer bodies). However, these proposals were dropped in favour of the CAT exercising supervision and control via authorisation of the class representative as part of the certification process.

Walter_hugh_Transcript__Hearing_1_180117.pdf> accessed 16 June 2020. This exchange is expressly referred to in the Court of Appeal's judgment in *Merricks v. Mastercard* [2019] EWCA Civ 674, [28].

[71] At least some potential claimants are likely to be unaware of the damages award (even if extensively advertised), some may no longer have the relevant evidence required to prove their entitlement to damages (such as receipts), and some will inevitably not perceive it to be 'worth the hassle' to claim, particularly in a consumer claim involving relatively small sums per claimant.

[72] Section 47C(5) and (7) CA98, Rule 93(6) of the CAT Rules 2015 (n 14), and the Legal Services Act 2007 (Prescribed Charity) Order 2008 (SI 2008/2680).

[73] This conclusion was not affected by the Court of Appeal decision overturning the CAT's decision to reject the CPO application.

[74] When the current regime was first introduced in 2015, concerns were raised about a perceived lack of incentives for funders, given the default position that unclaimed damages in an opt-out claim be paid to charity. The approach taken by the CAT in *Merricks v. Mastercard* was unsurprisingly welcomed by third party litigation funders, and the increased legal certainty on this point is likely to contribute to continued growth of the UK funding market.

Rule 78 of the CAT Rules 2015 states that the CAT may authorise an applicant to act as a class representative provided it considers it 'just and reasonable' for the applicant to do so.[75] The CAT enjoys a wide degree of discretion in this regard. In particular, there is no requirement that the applicant be a member of the proposed class of claimants. Objections to the proposed class representative were raised in both of the CPO applications which have been heard by the CAT to date, and have also arisen in the *Trucks* claims (where they were dealt with as a preliminary issue ahead of the main certification hearing, which has been adjourned pending the outcome of the *Merricks* appeal). However, in practice these have not proven to be a significant stumbling block to the grant of a CPO.

In *Gibson v. Pride*, the defendant objected to Ms. Gibson acting as the class representative on general suitability grounds, and also on the basis that she would be unable to pay their recoverable costs if ordered to do so. The CAT rejected these arguments, noting that Ms. Gibson was the General Secretary of the National Pensioners Convention ('NPC') and the majority of the claimants she sought to represent were pensioners. There was no reason to believe that she would be unable to understand the legal advice given to her, or that (in consultation as appropriate with the National Council or Executive Committee of the NPC) she would not be able to take appropriate decisions about the litigation in the interests of the represented class. The fact that the impetus for the collective proceedings came from Ms. Gibson's solicitors was not deemed objectionable. On the issue of payment of recoverable costs, the CAT noted that Ms. Gibson had an after-the-event ('ATE') insurance policy in place (arranged through a third party litigation funder), which covered any liability to pay Pride's costs up to £1.08 million and her own disbursements in the event that the claim was unsuccessful. The CAT took the preliminary view that the issue of ability to pay recoverable costs was therefore not a basis for refusing to authorise Ms. Gibson to act as a class representative at that stage. It indicated that this particular aspect of Pride's objections could be considered further at the renewed application for a CPO (due to issues identified with the methodology proposed for estimating individual loss within various sub-classes of claimant), but the claim was subsequently withdrawn.[76]

In *Merricks v. Mastercard* the objections raised in relation to Mr. Merricks' suitability to act centred on the terms of a funding agreement with Burford Capital, a third party litigation funder that had agreed to make £40 million

[75] Rule 78 of the CAT Rules 2015 (n 14).
[76] Withdrawal Order dated 25 May 2017.

available to fund the claim. The agreement provided that the funder's return in the event that the claim was successful should be paid out of undistributed damages and any costs awarded to Mr. Merricks. The total investment return for the funder was set at the greater of either £135 million or 30 per cent of any undistributed damages up to £1 billion plus 20 per cent of any undistributed damages in excess of £1 billion. The agreement further provided that if the CAT made any 'negative commentary' on the funding arrangements then the funder could terminate the agreement. A £10 million limit was also set in relation to the funder's liability for Mastercard's costs. Mastercard objected to these terms on three grounds:

(i) the funding agreement would not necessarily enable Mr. Merricks to fund the litigation or pay Mastercard's recoverable costs (if so ordered), since it could be terminated by the funder;
(ii) the £10 million limit on the funder's liability for Mastercard's costs was inadequate and did not meet the statutory requirement that Mr. Merricks must be able to pay the defendant's recoverable costs if ordered to do so; and
(iii) the arrangement gave rise to a conflict of interest.

The CAT rejected these objections. On the issue of termination risk, Mastercard had argued that the CAT could not order the total investment return to be paid out of any undistributed damages, on the basis that this did not fall within the statutory definition of 'costs or expenses' in section 47C(6) CA98 (pursuant to which the CAT has the power to order that all or part of unclaimed funds may be paid to the class representative in respect of all or part of the costs it incurred in connection with the proceedings). However, the CAT held that the concept of 'costs or expenses' does include a liability to pay the charge of a third party funder in this context. It agreed with Mastercard that, as drafted, the total investment return specified in the agreement could not be said to be 'incurred' by Mr. Merricks, as it contained no actual obligation on Mr. Merricks to pay the fee. However, at the certification hearing Mr. Merricks agreed to amend the agreement so that it provided that he agreed to pay the total investment return to the funder, limited to the proportion of this determined by the CAT to be payable pursuant to section 47C(6) CA98. The CAT considered that this created a conditional liability on Mr. Merricks to pay the fee, which could then be said to be 'incurred' by him for the purposes of the legislation. The CAT also noted in passing that a similar conditional obligation to pay an uplift or success fee in a CFA would be covered. The funding agreement, as amended, was therefore not rendered ineffective by section 47C(6) CA98 and the termination risk did not arise.

Objections to the suitability of the proposed class representative based on the terms of funding arrangements were also raised in the two *Trucks* collective claims. These were considered by the CAT at a preliminary hearing in June 2019.[77] A number of arguments were put forward as to the nature and adequacy of the funding arrangements relied upon by the Road Haulage Association and UK Trucks Claim Limited: (i) that the arrangements constituted damages-based agreements subject to the statutory regime set out in section 58AA of the Courts and Legal Services Act 1990 ('CLSA'), and as such were unlawful and unenforceable due to non-compliance with the Damages-Based Agreements Regulations 2013; (ii) that the level of committed funding was inadequate to cover the costs likely to be incurred; and (iii) that the level of ATE insurance cover obtained by the applicants was insufficient to ensure repayment of the defendants' recoverable costs in the event that the claims were unsuccessful.

In a judgment handed down on 28 October 2019,[78] the CAT held that the funding arrangements which had been (or would be) put in place by the applicants (as amended both prior to and after the hearing) did not prevent it from authorising the proposed class representatives. Following a detailed review of the legislative history and context of the relevant statutory provisions,[79] the CAT ruled that third party litigation funding arrangements did not amount to 'damages-based agreements' subject to the CLSA regime, on the basis that such arrangements are not 'claims management services'.[80] It considered that litigation funders are engaged in the funding of a claim, not the management of the making of a claim. As a result, it rejected the argument that the arrangements were unlawful and unenforceable due to non-compliance with the Damages-Based Agreements Regulations.

77 As noted above, the main certification hearing for these claims has been adjourned pending the outcome of the appeal to the Supreme Court in *Merricks v. Mastercard*.

78 *UK Trucks Claim Limited v. Fiat Chrysler and others* and *Road Haulage Association v. Man SE and others* [2019] CAT 26.

79 *UK Trucks Claim Limited v. Fiat Chrysler and others* and *Road Haulage Association v. Man SE and others* [2019] CAT 26, [22]–[35].

80 Section 58AA(3)(a) CLSA provides that a damages-based agreement to which the statutory regime applies is an agreement between a person providing advocacy services, litigation services or claims management services, and the recipient of those services, which provides that: (i) the recipient is to make a payment to the person providing the services if the recipient obtains a specified financial benefit in connection with the matter in relation to which the services are provided; and (ii) the amount of that payment is to be determined by reference to the amount of the financial benefit obtained. For these purposes, 'claims management services' are defined by cross-reference to section 4(2) of the Compensation Act 2006. That provides that claims management services include advice or other services in relation to the making of a claim, including the provision of financial services or assistance.

With regard to the issue of whether sufficient funding was in place, the CAT concluded that the total committed funds under the agreements[81] were not insufficient to enable the representatives to pursue the litigation effectively in the interests of the class members. Significantly, the CAT held in this regard that it is not required to determine the likely costs of a CPO applicant to the end of trial and be satisfied that the proposed class representative has secured sufficient funding to cover those costs. Rather, it must simply take into account the estimated costs and arrangements which the applicant has made in that regard, as part of its assessment of whether to authorise them as the class representative. The two key questions which the CAT should consider are limited to: (a) whether the terms of the funding arrangement impair the ability of the class representative to act fairly and adequately in the interests of the class members; and (b) whether adequate funding has been arranged to pursue the litigation effectively in the interests of the class members.[82]

On the related issue of the adequacy of ATE insurance to pay the defendants' recoverable costs in the event that the claim was unsuccessful, the CAT rejected the argument that unless the CAT finds that a CPO applicant will be able to pay all of the defendant's recoverable costs to the end of trial if ordered to do so, it cannot find that it is just and reasonable for that person to act as the class representative. It concluded instead that, where there is no other reason to refuse the authorisation of a proposed class representative, 'the proper approach to such a very high costs case is to determine that the class representative has at the outset the ability to pay a substantial level of adverse costs cover that should be sufficient for at least a significant part of the proceedings'.[83] In reaching this conclusion, the CAT relied in part on the fact that this issue could be revisited as the proceedings advance, with the option of varying or revoking the terms of the CPO accordingly. However, such an approach risks an undesirable degree of uncertainty, and—as discussed above—is arguably at odds with what was intended at the time the current regime was introduced. It remains to be seen how the CAT will approach this issue in practice, and the impact this may have on the willingness of third party funders to support future collective claims (which, as the CAT has acknowledged, is fundamental to enabling claims to be brought).

[81] £27 million in the case of the agreement entered into by the Road Haulage Association and £24 million in the case of the agreement entered into by UK Trucks Claim Limited, including sums reserved for insurance premiums in both cases.

[82] *UK Trucks Claim Limited v. Fiat Chrysler and others* and *Road Haulage Association v. Man SE and others* [2019] CAT 26, [66].

[83] *UK Trucks Claim Limited v. Fiat Chrysler and others* and *Road Haulage Association v. Man SE and others* [2019] CAT 26, [109].

Whilst it is now relatively clear what a proposed class representative needs to show, the suitability of a proposed class representative will no doubt nonetheless remain a contentious issue in future cases. However, objections seem likely to focus on the representative's ability to pay the defendant's costs if the action is unsuccessful and the terms of any funding arrangement, rather than the personal suitability of the representative.

The potential impact of *Lloyd v. Google*

On 2 October 2019 the Court of Appeal handed down its judgment in *Lloyd v. Google*.[84] This is not a competition case; rather, it relates to representative proceedings brought under CPR 19.6 seeking around £3 billion in damages on behalf of four million Apple iPhone users, in respect of alleged breaches of the Data Protection Act 1998.[85] However, subject to the outcome of a pending appeal to the Supreme Court,[86] it has been suggested that the case may 're-open the door' to the use of opt-out representative actions under CPR 19.6 in competition claims, as an alternative to the collective actions regime (which had been widely perceived to be unlikely to be successful following the failed attempt to use CPR19.6 to bring collective proceedings seeking damages arising from the air cargo cartel, in *Emerald Supplies v. British Airways*).[87]

CPR19.6 allows representative proceedings to be brought on behalf of a class of claimants on an opt-out basis where they have 'the same interest' in the claim. The Court of Appeal ruled in *Lloyd v. Google* that permission should be given to serve Google out of the jurisdiction and proceed with the claim, on the basis that the members of the class were readily identifiable and had the same interest: they were all victims of the same alleged wrong (illegal extraction of personal data), during the same period, and had all sustained the same loss, namely the loss of control of data (without needing to prove individual pecuniary loss or distress). The Court considered that it was irrelevant that the claim was being brought on behalf of a large number of claimants, which was defined in a fluid manner. This outcome was in notable contrast to *Emerald Supplies v. British Airways*.[88] In that earlier case the Court of Appeal upheld a

[84] *Lloyd v. Google LLC* [2019] EWCA Civ 1599.
[85] The case arose out of the so-called 'Safari Workaround', which enabled Google to bypass the cookie settings on the Safari browser and place tracking cookies without the individual's knowledge or consent.
[86] Permission to appeal against the Court of Appeal's judgment was granted to Google by the Supreme Court on 11 March 2020.
[87] *Emerald Supplies Ltd and another v. British Airways Plc* [2010] EWCA 1284.
[88] *Emerald Supplies Ltd and another v. British Airways Plc* [2010] EWCA 1284.

decision by the High Court to strike out the claim on the basis that it was not possible to determine the membership of the represented class and that they did not necessarily have the same interest, as defences may be available to some claims and not others (due to the inclusion of both direct and indirect purchases in the same claimant class).[89]

However, it is by no means clear that the more permissive approach adopted by the court in *Lloyd* would be adopted in other contexts, and a key factor in the Court of Appeal's reasoning in *Lloyd* appears to have been the exceptional circumstances of the facts of that case. Notwithstanding *Lloyd*, it therefore seems unlikely that the interests of claimants in a competition case would be considered to be 'the same' such that they could rely on CPR19.6 to bring representative proceedings in the High Court, in particular because damages are unlikely to be the same for each class member.[90] Moreover, the cost/benefit analysis expressly required by Rule 79(2)(b) of the CAT Rules 2015 would seem likely to point towards a different conclusion to that reached in *Lloyd*, where the claim was permitted to proceed despite the conclusion of the first instance judge that, in his view, the main beneficiaries of the claim would be the funders and the lawyers, the litigation would generate significant costs and that the amount recovered by each class member would be modest, and none of the millions of affected individuals had come forward to complain.[91] That said, it is interesting to note the emphasis placed by the Court in *Lloyd* on the fact that failure to allow the representative action to proceed would result in a lack of redress for consumers affected and a lack of sanction on Google for its allegedly illegal conduct.[92]

[89] Ibid., [62]–[65].

[90] In *Lloyd v. Google*, Mr. Lloyd is claiming a uniform amount by way of damages on behalf of each person within the defined class, without seeking to allege or prove any distinctive facts affecting any of them, save that they did not consent to the abstraction of their data. A similar approach seems unlikely to be applicable in a competition law context.

[91] The Court of Appeal confirmed that the first instance judge was justified in taking these matters into account, although it suggested that it 'might have been better to invite argument on the first two matters'. However, it considered that it was nonetheless open to the Court of Appeal to exercise its discretion afresh, due to the first instance judge also taking into account two further matters which the Court of Appeal considered irrelevant to the exercise of the trial judge's discretion, namely: (i) the inability to identify the members of the class (the Court of Appeal considered that the class was identifiable), and (ii) that the members of the class had not authorised the claim (which the Court of Appeal emphasised was not a requirement for bringing a representative action under CPR 19.6). *Lloyd v. Google LLC* [2019] EWCA Civ 1599, [83]–[84].

[92] Giving the unanimous judgment of the Court, Sir Geoffrey Vos C. stated that 'this case, quite properly if the allegations are proved, seeks to call Google to account for its allegedly wholesale and deliberate misuse of personal data without consent, undertaken with a view to commercial profit. It is not disproportionate to pursue such litigation in circumstances where, as was common ground, there will, if the judge were upheld, be no other remedy' (*Lloyd v. Google LLC* [2019] EWCA Civ 1599, [86]). In the competition law context, where a follow-on claim is being made (as has been the case in almost all the CPO applications lodged to date), the issue of sanction has of course already been addressed.

Conclusion

The competition class action regime is still in its early stages although the number of CPO applications is increasing. Only two of the seven CPO applications have been fully determined by the CAT, and judgment in the *Merricks* appeal heard by the Supreme Court in May 2020 is still awaited at the time of writing. In a number of respects the regime has operated as intended, such as the question as to whether the representative is suitable. However, the *Merricks* decision by the Court of Appeal does appear to have lowered the bar for claimants to obtain a CPO which it is submitted was not contemplated during the legislative consultation process. The Supreme Court decision will therefore be highly significant in striking a balance between claimants and defendants. Notwithstanding this uncertainty in the future operation of the regime, CPO applications continue to be brought and it is doubtful the uncertainty is operating as a deterrent.

11

Lord Woolf, Multi-Party Situations, and Limitation Periods

Rachael Mulheron[1]

Introduction

On the twentieth anniversary of the implementation of the Civil Procedure Rules, it is appropriate to reflect that, for all the progress which resulted from the Woolf reforms, one particular recommendation did *not* bear fruit:

> The court should have powers to progress [a] multi-party situation on an 'opt-out' or 'opt-in' basis, whichever contributes best to the effective and efficient disposition of the case.[2]

This statement, made in 1996, occurred almost two decades before *any* such regime came into force in English law—and even then, the regime is on a fairly modest scale. The introduction of an opt-out class action on 1 October 2015, strictly for competition law grievances and for no other type ('the UK Competition Law Class Action'[3]) falls well short of the hopes which Lord Woolf had for the development of a generic collective redress regime (or a 'multi-party situation', as Lord Woolf proposed that it be called).[4] Lord Woolf

[1] The views expressed in this chapter are written in a personal academic capacity, and should not be taken to necessarily represent the views of any entity with which the author is associated, or of which the author is or was a member. The author is grateful to Dr Vincent Smith for helpful discussions during the course of preparing this chapter about the operation of limitation periods under the representative rule.

[2] Lord Woolf, *Access to Justice: Final Report to the Lord Chancellor on the Civil Justice System in England and Wales* (1996), Section IV, ch 17, 'Multi-Party Actions' (hereafter, '*Woolf Final Report*') [46].

[3] The regime is contained primarily in the Competition Act 1998 ('CA 1998'), and with some ancillary provisions in the Enterprise Act 2002. Entitled, 'Private Actions in Competition Law', the regime was contained in Sch 8 of the Consumer Rights Act 2015, and took effect on 1 October 2015. Supporting court rules were inserted into the Competition Appeal Tribunal Rules 2015, SI 2015/1648, Pt 5, rr 73–98 ('CAT Rules').

[4] *Woolf Final Report* (n 2) [18] ('where proceedings will or may require collective treatment to a greater or lesser degree, provision should be made for a multi-party situation (MPS) to be established').

Rachael Mulheron, *Lord Woolf, Multi-Party Situations, and Limitation Periods* In: *The Civil Procedure Rules at 20.* Edited by: Andrew Higgins, Oxford University Press (2020). © the several contributors.
DOI: 10.1093/oso/9780198863182.003.0011.

and his legal team considered that an opt-out regime would offer significant benefits for English civil procedure:

> In some circumstances, it will be appropriate to commence an MPS on an 'opt-out' basis and to establish an 'opt-in' register at a later stage.[5]

The ad hoc nature of how some very substantial group actions had been conducted to that point troubled Lord Woolf, prompting his comment that:

> In the absence of legislative support, courts have had to tackle these problems [associated with group litigation] pragmatically, making decisions on a creative and improvised basis with regard to cut-off dates, on how investigation should be conducted, on whether to process some or all cases in the group and on costs. While many judges have risen to the challenge, they themselves have indicated the need for a clearer framework in which to operate.[6]

Such 'legislative support' can take many forms, of course: an Act of Parliament; a Statutory Instrument; relevant Rules of Court; and Practice Directions. However, Lord Woolf recognised, entirely correctly, that if a 'multi-party situation' was to be implemented, then aspects of it would require primary legislation, and certainly not rules of court, given that some matters of substantive law were involved in the drafting of an opt-out class action. One of those matters—the subject of this chapter—is that of limitation periods. In an important passage in his report, Lord Woolf stated that:

> There is . . . a need for action to be taken in relation to the limitation period and this can only be effective if there are provisions to suspend or freeze the running of the limitation period on certification of the Multi-Party Situation, as in many other jurisdictions, so that further claimants whose claims were not being considered in detail at this stage were not disadvantaged. This will require primary legislation.[7]

Ultimately, provisions about limitation periods were encompassed in the overarching statute by which the Competition Law Class Action was enacted, by virtue of section 47E of the Competition Act 1998.[8]

[5] ibid, [46].
[6] ibid, [13].
[7] ibid, [45].
[8] Entitled, 'Limitation or prescriptive periods for proceedings under section 47A and collective proceedings'.

This chapter analyses some of the drafting issues surrounding the enactment of section 47E. Thus far, this provision has not been the subject of judicial scrutiny. However, this chapter bears testament to the fact that section 47E has been carefully and deliberately drafted, and with a close eye to the experiences of opt-out class actions regimes elsewhere.[9] A few of these aspects are considered in this chapter.

A matter of substantive law

There is both English and overseas judicial opinion which states that limitation periods change the substantive law governing an individual's entitlement to bring proceedings—especially when operative in the class actions context.

In England, Lord Woolf's suggestion that primary legislation would be required has already been noted. In addition, the Civil Justice Council's Comparative Law Committee Collective Redress Working Party concluded, in 2009,[10] that:

> 'some primary legislative intervention will . . . be necessary in order to allow suspension of limitation periods for all absent claimants on the representative claimant filing his pleadings, until a defined event occurs (such as the absent claimant opting out of the class, or the collective action being decertified)',[11] and that 'this is a matter to be taken into account in considering whether the whole regime should be implemented by primary legislation.'[12]

The fact that limitation periods are a matter of substantive law was also intimated by the Law Society in a very early proposal for opt-out reform in England.[13]

[9] This chapter is substantially drawn from a memo drafted by the author to the Department of Business, Innovation and Skills (BIS) in October 2012, in response to requests for information relating to limitation periods as they operated in opt-out and opt-in class action regimes elsewhere. As part of the comparative study, the author made various drafting suggestions for any new UK statutory regime on the basis of lessons learnt from the experiences garnered in various comparative opt-out jurisdictions. The chapter also refers to jurisprudence which is analysed in more detail by the author in: *The Class Action in Common Law Legal Systems: A Comparative Perspective* (Hart, Oxford, 2004) 379–82.

[10] *Improving Access to Justice through Collective Actions: Developing a More Efficient and Effective Procedure for Collective Actions: Final Report* (November 2008).

[11] ibid, p 125, [37], referring to the 'common ground' as between Professor John Sorabji and the author, regarding whether or not primary legislation was required for a class action, as examined in the memos produced by those authors in ibid, App M and N, respectively.

[12] ibid, [39].

[13] Law Society Civil Litigation Committee, *Group Actions Made Easier* (September 1995) [6.12.7].

Judicial opinion in that direction is also evident in class actions case law. In his response to another early law reform proposal for opt-out collective actions, the then-Master of the Rolls, Lord Phillips, noted that:

> [t]o permit representative claims on behalf of unnamed individuals would be to introduce a new concept into English law. I share the view . . . that they are likely to require primary legislation.[14]

In Canada too, in *Pauli v ACE INA Insurance*,[15] Rooke J accepted that limitation periods being suspended by a class action regime would effect the sort of change to substantive law that would lie outside the scope of power of the Alberta Rules of Court Committee (of which he was a member), noting that:

> [t]he only limitation to such case management rules or more formal rules by the Alberta Rules of Court Committee would appear to be substantive provisions relevant to limitations and the like.[16]

Similarly, a number of justices of the South Australian Supreme Court put their opinion in this fashion:

> Class actions require some modification of the rules regarding limitation of actions. The ordinary limitation provisions must be made subject to the right of individual members of a class to establish their claims after the common questions have been determined, notwithstanding that the time for instituting proceedings has expired. Some provision must also be made for members of the class who may have delayed their remedy as the result of the class action but who are disappointed in that expectation, as where an order to proceed as a class action is refused or having been granted, is subsequently rescinded. We have not included these provisions in our draft bill as the parliamentary counsel will doubtless wish to advise the government as to whether such provisions should be included in the Class Actions Bill or in the statutes relating to limitations of actions.[17]

[14] Cited in: Lord Chancellor's Dept, *Representative Claims: Proposed New Procedures: Consultation Response* (April 2002) 4.

[15] [2002] ABQB 715, 322 AR 126, 12 Alta LR (4th) 332, [36].

[16] See too: *Das v George Weston Ltd* [2017] ONSC 4129, [214] ('limitation periods . . . are matters of substantive law'), aff'd: *Das v George Weston Ltd* [2018] ONCA 1053.

[17] Law Reform Committee of South Australia, *Report Relating to Class Actions* (Rep 36, 1977) 10.

Overseas law reform commissions in, for example, Alberta,[18] Manitoba,[19] and federal Canada[20] have expressed a similar view, that the tolling of limitation periods is a matter of substantive law, requiring legislation and not rules of court.

Others made the point that it can be difficult to characterize or to define the difference between substantive and procedural law ('a clear test concerning the difference . . . has never been articulated'), thus rendering rules of court susceptible to being struck down as being *ultra vires* or outside the scope of the powers vested in a rules-making body if they turn out to be matters of substantive law.[21]

In light of these observations, it seemed wise that, for the UK Competition Law Class Action, all of the relevant provisions relating to limitation periods should be contained in overarching or superior legislation.[22] The power to make Tribunal Rules for the CAT[23] probably provides wider scope for the drafters of those rules to deal with substantive law and time periods than the CPR Committee enjoys.[24] However, the reality is that the precise ambit of these provisions, and whether they do permit substantive law matters regarding the suspension and resumption triggers for limitation periods in class actions to be introduced via CAT rules, could be circumvented by reliance on primary legislation. Parliament duly obliged, courtesy of section 47E of the Competition Act 1998.

Tolling (or suspending) the limitation period for all class members

The Ontario Law Reform Commission put it well, when it said that there is an inherent tension between class actions and limitation periods:

> The policies underlying class actions and statutory limitation periods, in effect, serve different masters. A class action procedure is predominantly

[18] Alberta Law Reform Institute, *Class Actions* (Rep No 85, 2000) [484].
[19] Manitoba Law Reform Comm, *Class Proceedings* (Rep No 100, 1999) 38.
[20] Federal Court of Canada, The Rules Committee, *Class Proceedings in the Federal Court of Canada* (DP 2000) 95.
[21] Ontario Law Reform Commission, *Report on Class Actions* (1982) 306.
[22] Recommended per Memo (n 9), Issue #3.
[23] As contained in the Enterprise Act 2002, s 15, and also in Sch 4, Part 2.
[24] Pursuant to the Civil Procedure Act 1997, s 1(1) and Sch 1, r 4.

> a plaintiff's vehicle for redress, while a statutory limitation period is a defendant's shield [against indefinite and interminable litigation].[25]

The whole situation is further complicated by the fact that those who fall within the class description do not need to come forward at the point at which the class suit is filed, but the defendant/s will naturally wish to be informed in a timely fashion as to who is suing the defendant/s, to ensure that documentary and witness evidence is either preserved or acquired. Resolving these tensions is one of the challenges for those drafting a class actions regime.

How tolling operates

In one important respect, Lord Woolf's vision for the statutory implementation of suspended limitation periods did not accord with common class actions jurisprudence on limitation periods. It will be recalled that, in the Woolf Report, it was said that provisions were needed in any opt-out regime 'to suspend or freeze the running of the limitation period *on certification* of the Multi-Party Situation'.[26] However, in reality, the suspension frequently occurs well *prior* to that.

Take the scenario given in Figure 11.1 overpage, where widgets were price-fixed by various defendants the subject of the class actions law suit.

In class action regimes elsewhere which operate on an opt-out basis, the *filing* (or *commencement*) of the class action by the representative claimant will stop the limitation period from running against, not only the representative claimant, but against *all* potential class members who fall within the description of the class, until a defined event occurs. This result—the tolling or suspension of the limitation period for all class members falling within the class description—was achieved by 'judicial creativity' under the US class action rule,[27] whilst in other, more modern, class action regimes, this outcome was not left to judicial-making, but was ensured by statutory drafting.[28]

This tack of suspending the limitation period for all class members who fall within the class description, at the very *commencement* of the suit, was

[25] Ontario LRC, *Report on Class Actions* (1982) 780.

[26] *Woolf Final Report* (n 7) [45] (emphasis added).

[27] Pursuant to rule 23 of the Federal Rules of Civil Procedure, per the decision in *American Pipe and Construction Co v Utah*, 414 US 538, 551–56, 94 S Ct 756 (1974).

[28] e.g. Federal Court of Australia Act 1976, s 33ZE(1); Ontario's Class Proceedings Act, SO 1992, s 28(1).

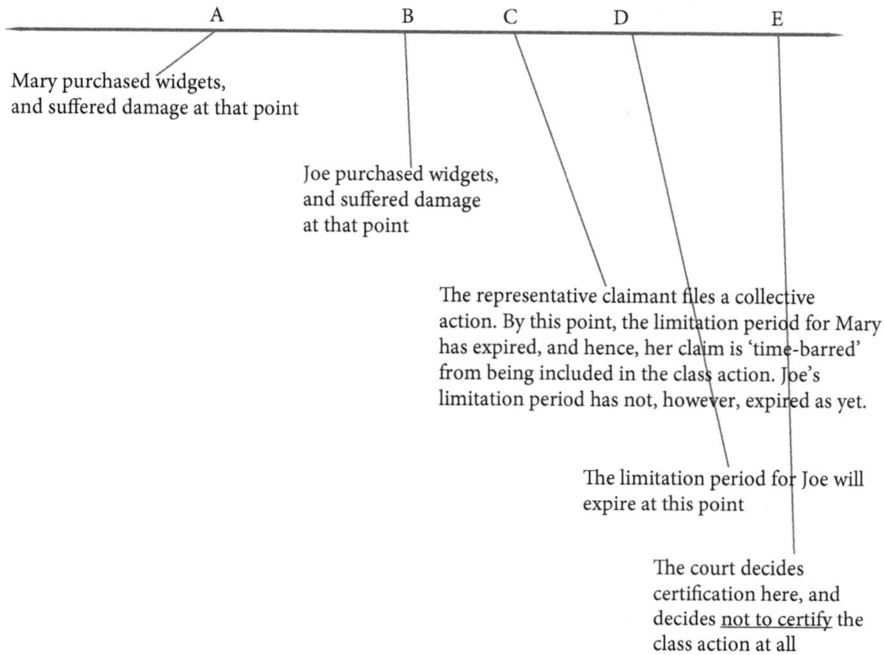

Figure 11.1 The events on a time-line

enacted under the UK Competition Law Class Action in section 47E(4) of the Competition Act 1998. This means that, even without filing any claim themselves, class member Joe will have the benefit of a 'tolled' or suspended limitation period, as soon as the representative claimant files proceedings at Point C. The effect of the legislation is that it shields all 'absent' (i.e. non-filing) class members, including Joe, from having to either file a claim to preserve his rights, or seek agreement from the defendant that the limitation period will not be raised as a defence prior to the expiry of the limitation period at point D.[29]

In practice, it means that notice informing class members of the right to opt-out of a class action will have practical effect in permitting the class member to pursue their claims individually, for otherwise:

> [i]f there were no tolling [of the limitation period], notice would be irrelevant, because the limitation period for absent class members would most

[29] Mulheron, *The Class Action in Common Law Legal Systems: A Comparative Perspective* (Hart Publishing, Oxford, 2004) 377–79.

> likely have expired [by the time that the opt-out notice was received], making the right to pursue a claim separately meaningless.[30]

A provision such as section 47E(4) also precludes the 'needless duplication' of class members, such as Joe, filing individual suits in order to avoid the adverse effects of the running of a limitation period. If Joe is not required to formally indicate his participation in an opt-out class action prior to any determination of the common issues, then why should he be required to file his individual action just to deal with an approaching limitation period? The suspension of limitation periods accords with the economy of litigant and judicial resources that opt-out class actions seek to achieve.[31]

The tolling of limitation periods under an opt-out class action is not contrary to the purposes of limitation statutes either, in the view of the US Supreme Court in *Crown, Cork & Seal Co Inc v Parker*.[32] Statutes of limitation seek to prevent claimants from 'sleeping on their rights'—but if class members fall within the class description, they are not doing so. Furthermore, defendants do receive timely notice of the claims brought against them as the statutes contemplate, as the filing of a class action by the representative claimant, and the class description used in the claim, signify to the defendant/s the probable size and scope of the suit.

Comparison with the representative rule

One motive for Lord Woolf's proposal for the enactment of a multi-party situation in 1996 was the inadequacy of the longstanding representative rule. Back then, the rule was enacted as Order 15, rule 12 of the Rules of the Supreme Court (and since, it has been promulgated as Rule 19.6 of the Civil Procedure Rules).

That rule is generic in nature. In other words, it is not limited by subject matter. And it is certainly true that, as the rule has been judicially interpreted, it has taken on the 'flavour' of a class action from time to time, when sympathetic judges have sought to give the rule some much-needed utility.[33] The very fact

[30] *Vaught v Showa Denko KK*, 107 F 3d 1137, 1147 (5th Cir 1997), revised opinion at 1997 US Lexis 12786. Earlier: *Crown, Cork & Seal Co Inc v Parker*, 462 US 345, 351–54, 103 S Ct 2392 (1983).

[31] This point was made by the Ontario LRC, *Report on Class Actions* (1982) 780.

[32] 462 US 345, 352–53, 103 S Ct 2392 (1983).

[33] As discussed by the author in: 'From Representative Rule to Class Action: Steps rather than Leaps' (2005) 24 *Civil Justice Quarterly* 424.

that there is no generic opt-out class action enacted in English civil procedure, however, puts pressure upon the representative rule to accommodate grievances which are not based upon anti-competitive conduct. Whether the latest attempt to use the representative rule—in *Lloyd v Google LLC*[34]—survives forthcoming Supreme Court scrutiny[35] remains to be seen.

Lord Woolf himself did not possess any great confidence that the representative rule was 'up to the job' of substituting for an opt-out class action. Rather, his Lordship stated that 'the experience here and in comparative jurisdictions is that there are definite limits to the weight the rule can bear'.[36] He concluded that the representative rule was 'not drafted with group actions in mind and . . . has not provided a sufficient answer to the problems they create'.[37] These observations are particularly apposite where limitation periods are concerned. The suspension of limitation periods is one considerable advantage which a statute-based class action provides over the rules-based representative rule in CPR 19.6.

As the law has developed under the representative rule, the filing of a representative action means that the represented class members are also treated as having filed suit themselves—at least where the representative action is validly constituted. This is because they are deemed to be 'parties', even though they may not be named in the writ. This has various ramifications. Three are worth mentioning. First, the Court of Appeal opined, in *Lloyd v Google LLC*, that 'represented claimants could, at least in theory, seek to be joined as parties if they wished to claim additional losses', i.e., additional to the per capita sum being claimed for loss of control of data.[38] Secondly, according to *Moon v Atherton*, the court has power to substitute a represented party for the representative claimant himself, if the representative claimant wishes to discontinue or settle his own individual claim.[39] As a matter of justice, the represented persons should not be 'left out in the cold' (said Lord Denning MR).[40] Consequently, they should not be treated as being in that refrigerator if they are 'parties' to the litigation and the representative claimant settles; as one party can properly be substituted for another. Thirdly, it would always be open to a defendant to run a limitation defence in relation to represented parties who were not actual

[34] [2019] EWCA Civ 1599 (2 Oct 2019), overruling: *Lloyd v Google LLC* [2018] EWHC 2599 (QB) (8 Oct 2018) (Warby J).
[35] Permission to appeal (PTA) has been filed, under reference no: UKSC 2019/0213.
[36] *Woolf Final Report* (n 2) [7].
[37] ibid.
[38] [2019] EWCA Civ 1599, [76].
[39] [1972] 2QB 435 (CA) 442.
[40] ibid.

parties to the litigation and whose limitation period expired prior to the representative action being filed (per *Millharbour Management Ltd v Weston Homes Ltd*[41]).

However, the real problem arises if a court should eventually hold that the requisite and problematical 'same interest' requirement is *not* met by the representative action.[42] The representative action is hence invalid. The limitation period may well have expired by the point of that decision being reached, thus leaving the represented class members statute-barred from filing individual suits. This problem was acutely observed in the leading representative action of *Markt & Co Ltd v Knight Steamship Co Ltd*.[43] The facts are worth recalling. The defendants owned the steamship Knight Commander. In 1904, during the Russo-Japanese war, the ship sailed on a voyage from New York to Japan. Markt & Co Ltd were merchants carrying on business in the United States, and with forty-four other persons or companies, had shipped goods destined for Japan under separate bills of lading. The ship was stopped and searched in Japanese waters by a Russian cruiser; the crew of the Knight Commander were taken on board the cruiser, and the ship itself was sunk by the guns of the cruiser on the ground that she was carrying contraband of war. Both ship and cargo were entirely lost. Claims were made against the Russian Government on behalf of the shipowners and cargo owners, 'but, no final decision having been given, these actions were brought in order to prevent the operation of the Statute of Limitations'.[44] Ultimately, by majority,[45] the action was held to be invalidly constituted. This meant that the *named* plaintiffs in the representative action (which were Markt & Co Ltd and another merchant Sale & Frazar Ltd) could bring personal (not representative) actions, as they had preserved their entitlement to sue by suing within the limitation period. However, with the representative action being invalid, the news was not good for the *represented* parties. In the course of his (dissenting) judgment, Buckley LJ stated that:

> There are here but two writs, and the defendants' complaint is that there are not forty-five. This is an objection which the plaintiffs might easily meet by issuing further numerous writs, but the Statute of Limitations has or may have run since these two writs were issued, and the point of substance is or may be whether these writs should be set aside or limited to the claims of the named

[41] [2011] EWHC 661 (TCC) [22(7)].
[42] Now contained in: CPR 19.6(1).
[43] [1910] 2 KB 1021 (CA).
[44] ibid, 1022.
[45] ibid, Vaughan Williams LJ and Fletcher Moulton LJ, with Buckley LJ dissenting.

> plaintiffs alone, with the result that all the other represented plaintiffs shall become barred by the Statute of Limitations.[46]

In the view of the majority, the claims of the other represented parties were indeed time-barred. That consequence is inevitable, for the representative rule cannot be used to abrogate substantive law. It is merely contained within rules of procedure, and the rules-making committee had no power to (and did not) legislate for any adjustment of limitation periods under CPR 19.6 or its predecessor rules. Hence, if a representative action is treated as not having been validly commenced, then the represented persons are not 'parties' in any sense. They have not filed themselves; and hence, whilst the representative claimants can duly file personal (non-representative) actions, the rest of the class is statute-barred. That was the (valid) concern of Buckley LJ in *Markt*.

That particular problem would not be evident under the UK Competition Law Class Action, by virtue of the enactment of section 47E(4). That is because all the represented persons (including Joe in our example) benefit from a suspended limitation period, 'from the date on which the collective proceedings are commenced'. The clock does not keep ticking, in the event of an invalidly-commenced class action.

Resuming the limitation period for class members

The triggers

Apart from providing for when the limitation period stops running, the 'triggers' which cause the limitation period to start ticking again against the class member are vitally important.

There are plenty of possibilities—and the drafters of the UK Competition Law Class Action were undoubtedly interested that the drafters of the Australian and Canadian regimes differed markedly, when stating what events triggered the limitation period to resume. The Canadian regimes were much more explicit about that, specifying a far greater number of trigger points than does the Australian federal regime.[47] At the time, the author considered that to be a real advantage and benefit of the Canadian legislation—as defendants

[46] ibid, 1043.
[47] 33ZE(2).

should never be in the position of being faced with a 'proceeding without end', because of some ongoing suspension of a limitation period arising under the class action.[48]

Ultimately, section 47E(5) of the Competition Act 1998 provides for *ten* separate triggers upon which a class action under the UK Competition Law regime will resume. It is a most comprehensive provision. Even the more recent of the Canadian regimes, e.g. New Brunswick's, only lists seven resumption triggers.[49]

The two most commonly-occurring resumption triggers occur where either the class member decides to opt-out of the proceedings; or the proceedings are not certified as a class action at all. Dealing with each separately:

Opting out

If a class member such as Joe opts out of the class after the representative claimant achieves certification of the class action, then Joe's limitation period resumes running at that point. That means that if Joe had one month left of his original limitation period when the representative claimant filed suit, and Joe's limitation period was suspended for four months between when the class action was filed by the representative claimant and when Joe decided (after certification) to opt out of it, then Joe has one month from when he opted out in which to file individual proceedings, should he wish to.

This scenario is explicitly dealt with under the UK Competition Law Class Action in section 47E(5)(e)(i) of the Competition Act 1998.

Not certified at all

If the class action is not ultimately certified because one of the certification requirements is absent, and the limitation periods of some class members (or of the representative claimant himself) have expired in the meantime, i.e. between when the collective proceedings were filed and when the certification hearing occurred, then what is the optimal solution?

This scenario is outlined in Figure 11.1—for class member Joe, his limitation period would ordinarily expire at point D, if his limitation period was never suspended whilst the class action was awaiting a certification hearing, but certification was ultimately doomed. However, Joe does not find out until point E (or shortly after that, when notice of the outcome of the certification hearing

[48] Memo (n 9) Issue #1.

[49] Class Proceedings Act 2011 (which came into force in September 2011), s 41(1).

is received by the putative class) that the class action is not certified—by which point Joe's claim is statute-barred, and it is too late to do anything about it.

The problem is that, unless there is suitable legislative drafting, the class members' limitation periods may be taken *never* to have been suspended, because there was *never* a valid class action on foot.

Back when this issue was being considered by the UK drafters, it was of great interest to observe that Canadian provincial regimes differed significantly on the point. The clearest example of drafting on this issue appeared from the Manitoba Class Proceedings Act 2003. This statute provided that a suspended limitation period in a class action resumed running against the member 'when a ruling is made by the court refusing to certify the proceeding as a class proceeding, or that has the effect of excluding the member from the class proceeding or from being considered to have ever been a class member'.[50] In other words, the point was explicitly dealt with on the face of the statute, i.e., that the limitation period was suspended, even if the class action was not ultimately certified. On the other hand, unclear examples of drafting were evident in some other Canadian provincial regimes. Ontario's drafters did not provide a similar provision to Manitoba's, and hence, it was unclear under the Ontario Act as to whether the limitation period for class members was ever suspended simply because a class action had been commenced, if the class action was not ultimately certified—until the Ontario Superior Court of Justice clarified that it was.[51] By contrast, the drafters of British Columbia's Class Proceedings Act 1996 seemed to intend that the limitation period for class members would *not* be suspended at all for class members, if the certification application ended up failing. That Act provided that:

> Subject to subsection (2), any limitation period applicable to a cause of action asserted in a proceeding that is certified as a class proceeding under this Act is suspended in favour of a class member on the commencement of the proceeding and resumes running against the class member when any of the following occurs [including where a class member opts out].[52]

The provision, taken literally, seemed to suggest that, if the proceeding was *not* 'certified as a class proceeding under this Act', then the limitation period was never suspended.

[50] See: s 39(2)(a)(i) and (ii).
[51] *Logan v Ontario (Minister of Health)* (2003), 36 CPC (5th) 176.
[52] See: s 39(1)(a).

Ultimately, the UK drafters adopted the Manitoba approach, by deciding that it would be wise for the Competition Law Class Action to deal explicitly with what should happen in the event that the certification application fails, in order to avoid any uncertainty and satellite litigation of the sort which occurred in Ontario. Section 47E(5)(a) accordingly provides that the limitation period resumes on the date when 'the Tribunal declines to make a collective proceedings order in respect of the collective proceedings'. That is, the limitation period is triggered again for Joe at point E.

Undoubtedly, this was the fairest mode of drafting.[53] It ensures that the limitation period does stop ticking, between the period of filing of the class action and any failed certification hearing—so that the limitation period does not run out for class members (or for the representative claimant) whilst they are waiting for the certification hearing. Otherwise, during that waiting period, class members could feel compelled to file individual proceedings in the CAT merely to preserve their limitation period from expiring, or to seek undertakings from the defendant that a limitation period defence will not be raised against them—all of which would add to the costs and difficulties of the litigation.

Potentially, there may be perceived hardship to the defendant, if the limitation period is suspended at the point of commencement of the action—but then, ultimately, the class action is not certified. In *American Pipe and Construction Co v Utah*,[54] that very argument was raised by the defendant—that it would be 'punished' by the class members' ability to stop time running by grouping under the rubric of a class action which turned out not to be valid, and if the limitation period were suspended until the class action was not certified. However, the US Supreme Court rejected that concern, on the basis that the unfairness to class members would be far more acute, if the limitation *did not* suspend and if they were left in a state of uncertainty as to whether the class action would be certified. In that event, class members would have to protect their interests (by filing suit) in the meantime, to preserve their interests, or risk their claims becoming statute-barred, whilst they were waiting for the certification verdict. Similarly, in *Logan v Ontario (Minister of Health)*,[55] the Ontario Superior Court of Justice supported the suspension of limitation periods until the action was certified or not certified (as the case may be), on the basis that such suspension promoted access to justice, and reduced inefficiencies of multiple suits being filed, both of which were principal goals of a collective action.

[53] As argued in: Memo (n 9) Issue #1, pp 4–5.
[54] 414 US 538, 94 S Ct 756 (1974).
[55] (2003), 36 CPC (5th) 176.

For another thing, in *American Pipe*, the US Supreme Court made the point that a longer suspension of limitation period than the defendant would strictly like was *not* prejudicial to the defendant, because it could use the entirety of the limitation period (actual and suspended) to investigate the claim and to prepare its defence, whether or not the claim was ultimately conducted as a class action or as a series of individual suits (or not at all).

The extended limitation period

In fact, New Brunswick's drafters added an interesting and different provision to their Class Proceedings Act 2011:

> If the running of a limitation period is suspended under this section and the period has less than six months to run when the suspension ends, the limitation period, despite anything in this section, is extended to the day that is six months after the day on which the suspension ends.[56]

Hence, if a limitation period resumed against a class member (or the representative) because one of the triggers in the list occurred, then the limitation period thereafter could not be shorter than six months.

The author suggested the adoption of such a provision for the UK Competition Law Class Action regime,[57] on the basis that it ensured that the class members can get themselves organised and/or be notified that the limitation period has started ticking against them again, without being subject to perhaps a matter of days in which to file proceedings to preserve their right to sue. Just because the CAT declines to certify the class action does not mean that the class members, such as Joe, know about that. Appropriate notice *may* be required, so as to advise the class members such as Joe of the failed certification, and of their entitlement to pursue their individual actions, should they choose.[58]

Ultimately, the New Brunswick precedent was followed (with slightly differing wording) in section 47E(6) of the Competition Act 1998.

[56] See: s 41(3).

[57] Memo (n 9) Issue #1, p 6.

[58] There is no such obligation couched within the Competition Appeal Tribunal Rules. Notice of any collective proceedings order (CPO) must be provided to the class by the representative, per rule 81(1), but a similar provision has not been enacted where a CPO is *declined*. The CAT's *Guide to Proceedings 2015*, [6.12], [6.58], does not refer to the scenario in which a CPO is declined either, but notes that, where a CPO is granted, then the subsequent notice 'is the first formal notice [of the class action] and will be carefully scrutinised by the Tribunal'.

How limitation periods have operated in *opt-in* collective action regimes

As already mentioned, the model implemented under the UK Competition Law Class Action permits the CAT to elect as between the opt-in and the opt-out approach to class formation. The question arises: if the class action is established at certification to be more suitably conducted as an *opt-in*, rather than as an opt-out, class action, when would it be preferable for the limitation period to resume, as against the class members? There are a few options: when the court determines, at the certification hearing, that the class members need to opt-in to form part of the class; or when the relevant period for opting-in expires; or at some other nominated date

Suppose the scenario is as shown in Figure 11.2.

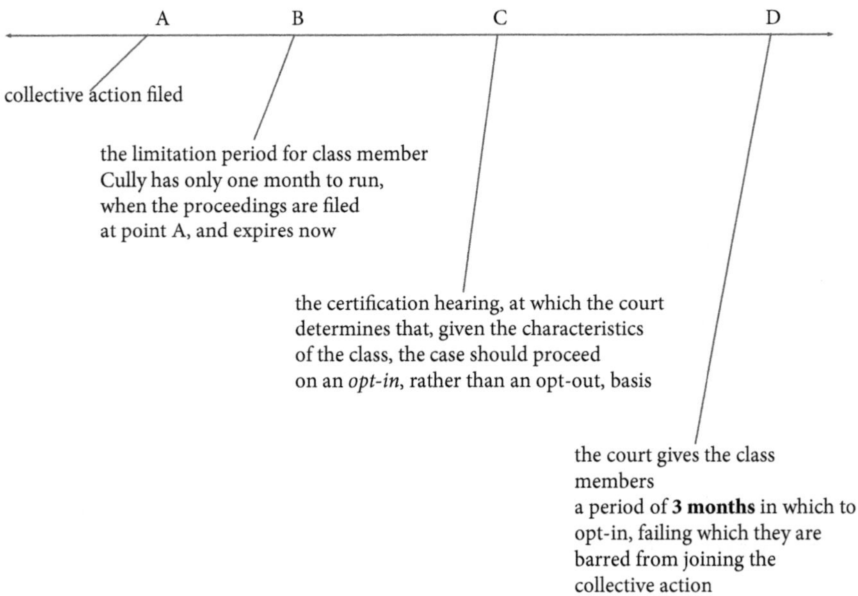

Figure 11.2 Opting-in and limitation periods

In the author's view,[59] the optimal solution in this scenario was three-fold:

- the limitation period is tolled (stopped) at the point of filing of the collective action for all class members, including for Cully, i.e. at Point A;

[59] Memo (n 9) Issue #4.

- the limitation period should resume at the expiry of the period set by the court in which to opt-in (i.e. at Point D); and
- the limitation period should *not* resume at the date of the certification hearing (at Point C).

Hence, in the example in Figure 11.2, Cully would have to opt-in to the class action by Point D, if she wished to be part of that class action. Otherwise, she would have just *one month after Point D* in which to file individual proceedings, if she did not wish to join the opt-in collective action but wished to sue the defendant nevertheless on an individual basis. The limitation period is tolled between Points A and D, but resumes at Point D. (Quite why Cully would wish to file individual proceedings in that month, after Point D, rather than opt-in to the class action prior to Point D, it is perhaps hard to envisage—but litigation can follow many strange and tortuous paths!).

Ultimately, this solution was the one that was enacted for the UK Competition Law Class Action, per section 47E(5)(d):

> Following suspension under subsection (4), the running of the limitation or prescriptive period in respect of the claim resumes on the date on which any of the following occurs: (d) in the case of opt-in collective proceedings, the period within which a person may choose to have the section 47B claim included in the proceedings expires without the person having done so.

There are several reasons as to why this solution to the dilemma is preferable.

First, the CAT must order that the representative claimant 'shall give notice of the collective proceedings order to class members in a form and manner approved by the Tribunal'.[60] To insist upon the resumption of the limitation period immediately upon that certification decision (at point C) may seriously prejudice some class members, who perhaps only have days left of their limitation period. As already adverted to, that period may expire, prior to their realising that the court certified the action on an opt-in basis.

Secondly, the resumption of the limitation period at the end of the opting-in period (at point D) would provide a symmetry with an opt-out collective action, in which class members' time periods do not begin to run until the class

[60] CAT Rules, r 81(1).

member opts out—and the class member has the *entire* opting-out period in which to opt-out (i.e. he can opt-out on the last day of the opting-out period). Hence, it seems unfair to treat a class member under an opt-in class action more harshly than a class member under an opt-out class action.

Thirdly, in response to any concern that class members would get the benefit of a suspension of their limitation periods until point D, even if they ultimately chose not to opt-in to the collective action—thus causing hardship or prejudice to the defendant—it will be recalled[61] that the 'hardship to the defendant' argument was run in the context of *opt-out* class actions in *American Pipe*, but was rebutted by the US Supreme Court. Those rebuttal points would appear to have equal relevance and weight, where the collective action was being conducted on an opt-in basis.

Collectively for these reasons, it was preferable that, given that the UK Competition Law Class Action has been set up such that it is necessary for the court to judicially choose between opt-in and opt-out—and the court *may* decide to certify on an opt-in basis—then the limitation period for class members should resume, *not* at the point of the certification hearing, but at the point of the expiry of the opting-in period.

Conclusion

In his Final Report, Lord Woolf stated that, in the area of multi-party situations:

> more than any other, my examination of the problems does not pretend to present the final answer, but merely to try to be the next step forward in a lively debate within which parties and judges are hammering out better ways of managing the unmanageable.[62]

This statement is as true of limitation periods as of any other design point.

The operation of limitation periods is a complex field. The CAT *Guide to Proceedings 2015* aptly remarks that its content in relation to limitation issues:

> are merely general guidelines, and it is beyond the scope of this Guide to provide definitive advice. Determining whether a particular claim is still in time

[61] See p 148 above.
[62] *Woolf Final Report* (n 2) [6].

can be a complex matter, and potential claimants should seek legal advice at the earliest available opportunity.[63]

The interplay between limitation periods and class action conundrums may take years to resolve under the UK Competition Law Class Action, if experience elsewhere is anything to go by. In Ontario, in *Coulson v Citigroup Global Markets Inc*, Perell J remarked that, even some twenty years after the Ontario statute was implemented, this case 'raises questions in unchartered legal territory of what it means to suspend and then resume the running of a limitation period in the context of a class proceeding'.[64]

Obviously, not everything can be anticipated in the drafting of the class actions regime itself. The UK drafters adopted the 'best practice' solution of clearly providing for what *suspends* the limitation period, and what *triggers the resumption of it*. Many other problems will henceforth be left to imaginative judicial clarification and management, as Lord Woolf himself foreshadowed.

[63] CAT *Guide to Proceedings 2015*, [5.15], commenting upon the preceding advice contained in [5.8]–[5.14].

[64] [2010] ONSC 1596, [4].

PART IV
DISCLOSURE

12

Disclosure

Should We Have Stayed with the RSC?

Charles Hollander

Combining a new set of procedural rules with the abolition of the use of Latin was always going to lead to problems. Thus when you give short notice of your *ex parte* application you now make an *application without notice on notice.* And changing the words can lead to grief too: so when your opportunity to apply for documents *referred* to in affidavits or pleadings was changed to 'documents mentioned in a pleading or witness statement' you can foresee the argument: the draftsman must have intended that by changing the wording, he was changing the test. I have no idea what the difference is between 'documents referred' and 'documents mentioned' but it required a line of cases before the Court of Appeal held the new wording was intended to mean, yes, the same as the old.[1]

The question I pose as the title of this talk is intended to invite consideration of the approach in Hong Kong, where I also practise: the Chief Justice's Working Party received evidence that the CPR was not fulfilling its objective of saving costs, and decided that, given the regulatory risks of a new set of rules, they would do better to stick with the RSC and cherry-pick what they viewed as the best bits of the CPR. They also took the decision not to change the Latin: the abolition of Latin in this jurisdiction was to make the rules more accessible to non-lawyers, but as the evidence they received was that over 99% of the non-lawyers who looked at the rules read them in Chinese, they thought abolishing Latin was of limited value.[2] So I can still apply in Hong Kong for an *ex parte* on notice.

But having posed the question, in reality it is an unfair one to pose. One of the concerns of Lord Woolf was that there was too much discovery and the

[1] *Expandable v Rubin* 2008 EWCA Civ 59.

[2] See generally, Hollander, *Documentary Evidence in Hong Kong* (1st ed, Sweet & Maxwell 2015), 1-005.

Charles Hollander, *Disclosure* In: *The Civil Procedure Rules at 20.* Edited by: Andrew Higgins, Oxford University Press (2020). © the several contributors. DOI: 10.1093/oso/9780198863182.003.0012.

limiting of discovery was a major plank in his reforms. I am not sure whether changing its name to disclosure helped much (although it was quite amusing that one of my competitors had to change the title of their book as a result) but things did not really work out as he had planned. For many years the profession and the judges largely ignored the change in the rules[3] and carried on doing what they had always done on disclosure. But Lord Woolf reported a few years before we had to grapple with electronic disclosure. Electronic disclosure meant that there was far more disclosure than there ever had been in Lord Woolf's time. One can hardly blame him for electronic disclosure. The problem was exacerbated by the fact that by the time any subsequent committee had consulted, reported and drafted, technological advances had made their proposals obsolete, and it is only really since Jackson that the courts have had any form of weaponry (or perhaps 'menu') to deal with the problems.

Hong Kong stayed with *Peruvian Guano* (and continued to call it 'discovery' rather than 'disclosure') but adopted the narrower Woolf test for disclosure merely for pre-action discovery. In truth, discovery plays a less important part in Hong Kong litigation than it does in the UK, there are very few cases with discovery on the scale of major UK litigation, and there is less confidence that the opposing clients will give up damaging documents. So the 'too much discovery' argument does not resonate there as it does here.

In the UK, the cost and scale of disclosure in substantial litigation continues to drive the costs of litigation to utterly disproportionate levels. This is not the place to debate the merits of the new Disclosure Pilot with its emphasis on early (and arguably premature) debate of disclosure issues, but one cannot help thinking that the time has come for radical rather than piecemeal change. All one can say about the Woolf report here is that it made a constructive effort to resolve a real problem but its intended solution became obsolete in the light of subsequent developments in electronic disclosure.

What has been interesting speaking as a commentator who wrote on the RSC, wrote on how I thought the courts would interpret the CPR, and then watched what happened, is how things really did not turn out as Lord Woolf planned. So I just want to show how the Court of Appeal have blown hot and cold in interpreting the CPR.

First, non-party disclosure. This doesn't get a mention in *Access to Justice* and the new CPR 31.17 was simply intended by Lord Woolf to make unnecessary the fiction propagated in *Khanna v Lovell White Durrant*[4] whereby the

[3] As the CA pointed out in *Nichia v Argos* 2007 EWCA Civ 741.
[4] 1995 1WLR 1380.

problem that a *subpoena duces tecum* could historically only be returnable at trial was obviated by nominating an earlier date as the first day of the trial merely so the documents could be obtained in good time. Yet in *American Home Products v Novartis*[5] and *Three Rivers (No 4)*[6] the Court of Appeal used the new wording to expand the jurisdiction beyond anything which had been contemplated by Lord Woolf. A further related decision of the Court of Appeal considering the interplay under the CPR between non-party disclosure and the continuing power to order a *subpoena duces tecum, Tajik Aluminium*,[7] was, despite a very strong court, marred by being premised on a fundamental misunderstanding of the circumstances in which the two parallel powers could be used.[8] Yet, despite that, no one seems to have doubted in the last 15 years that *Tajik Aluminium* represents the law.

The most famous exposition of the 'fresh start' school can be seen in *Smith Kline Beecham v Generics*.[9] There was no express provision for the collateral undertaking under the RSC, but it was well established that it applied when there was disclosure by *compulsion*.[10] So if you disclosed or relied voluntarily (even if you had no practical alternative), it didn't apply. Easy to apply, consistent with ECHR privacy rights, and the *quid pro quo* for compulsory disclosure. *Smith Kline Beecham* decided that because there was now a new express rule, it was impermissible to refer back at all to the old position because the CPR was a fresh start, and amazingly (and surely without appreciating the consequences) abolished the compulsion principle completely. Worse still, this obviously not being the intent of the draftsman, they replaced it with an eccentric construction of the new rules as to when the undertaking should apply which has been criticised even more than the Court of Appeal's famous misstep on legal advice privilege in T*hree Rivers(No 5)*.[11]

But contrast this with the rules on inadvertent disclosure of privileged documents. Here the principles, which were developed by the courts in the 1980s and do not depend on the wording of any rule, have been rightly criticised by Andrew Higgins and others.[12] To hold that you can only get back a privileged document mistakenly disclosed where the receiving solicitor knows or should

[5] 2001 EWCA Civ 165.
[6] 2002 4All ER 881.
[7] 2005 4All ER 1232.
[8] See the discussion in *Documentary Evidence* (13th ed, Sweet & Maxwell 2018),3–26, supported by Cockerill, *The Law and Practice of Compelled Evidence in Civil Proceedings* (2011) paras 4.08–4.10.
[9] 2003 EWCA Civ 1109.
[10] See eg *Derby v Weldon (No 2)* unrep Times, 20 October 1988.
[11] Hollander, 'The Dysfunctional Collateral Undertaking' (2019) CJQ 265.
[12] Higgins, *Legal Professional Privilege for Corporations* (OUP 2014), para 7.137, adopted by Longmore LJ obiter in *Rawlinson & Hunter Trustees SA v Director of the SFO* 2014 EWCA Civ 1129.

reasonably have known he was seeing what he shouldn't, can provide an unjustified windfall to the receiving party. The problem is now more serious than it was, because large scale electronic disclosure creates much greater opportunity for innocent error here. The CPR created an entirely new provision in relation to inadvertent disclosure (there previously being no RSC rule on the subject at all) where for the very first time you had to *apply for leave* under CPR 31.20 to use a document inadvertently disclosed. So—new rule, new structure, a chance to change the old rules where change was richly deserved. And what does the Court of Appeal do? They hold in two cases that there was no intent to change the principles which applied under the old law notwithstanding the new rule and leave requirement: see *Breeze v Stacy*[13] followed in the better-known *Al Fayed v Commissioner of Police for the Metropolis.*[14]

At times one feels almost an element of randomness or fortuity in how the law has developed. Perhaps that is true of the common law at times, but it is more striking when one can trace clearly (i) RSC law; (ii) Woolf proposal; (iii) CPR rule and (iv) interpretation of new rule.

I just want to look at one more area of disclosure where the CPR has, for reasons not anticipated, not worked out quite as planned. Pre-action disclosure under the RSC only applied to cases of personal injuries or death, but has unrestricted scope under the CPR. This was seen by Lord Woolf as an important reform, and indeed it has been adopted under the Hong Kong rules. Consistent with Lord Woolf's favoured 'cards on the table' approach reflected in pre-action protocols and exchange of information prior to commencement of proceedings, pre-action disclosure was intended to provide potential litigants with another route to obtain relevant documents to help them to decide whether they had a case at all, or one worth pursuing. One can see why it was useful in personal injury cases (particularly in the days of legal aid): the patient who comes out of hospital with a gangrenous leg has no way of knowing whether the mishap was due to medical negligence without an opportunity to review the medical notes. Nor here can one fairly complain about the way the jurisdiction has been interpreted by the courts.[15]

But pre-action disclosure has not to my mind been a particular success. First, it is particularly difficult to predict in any given case whether the court will exercise its discretion for or against an order: if the case is relatively strong, why can't the claimant just get on and sue without the documents? If the case

[13] 2000 CP Rep 77.

[14] 2002 EWCA Civ 780.

[15] *Black v Sumitomo* 2002 1WLR 1562.

is relatively weak, the application may be thrown out as too speculative. So it is unusually hard to advise as to prospects of success, and it can be unattractive to encourage the client to kick off hostilities by spending money on such an unpredictable application. Secondly, court and appeal delays have often meant that the documents sought were not obtained within a reasonable time and the claimant has had no option but to take a decision whether to proceed without the documents in order to avoid limitation problems or excessive delay. I was recently instructed on an appeal where the judge had surprisingly discovered a jurisdiction to serve an application for pre-action disclosure out of the jurisdiction.[16] There was a stay on the order pending appeal. Given the delay after the application was made fixing the hearing, then a further delay before judgment was given, then in making an application for leave to appeal,[17] then in getting a hearing date from the Court of Appeal, almost two years passed between date of first application and date of appeal hearing. The claimants simply could not wait that long and ultimately started the action without the documents prior to the appeal. And the third problem is the costs regime. Under CPR 46 r 1 there is a presumption here that the applicant will pay the costs of the respondent. That will usually cover both the costs of the document search and the application, often even if the applicant succeeds in the application.[18] So the first thing that the client has to do is not merely to pay his own lawyers' bill but to write a large cheque to the adversary too: it is hardly surprising this has not proved a popular venture. Nor is it fair or necessary: if proceedings are commenced, the costs of the disclosure exercise will normally be costs in the case. Why should there be a transfer of the costs burden here? However, on this last point let me at least end on a high note: the Court of Appeal very recently adopted a costs proposal for pre-action disclosure I have been advocating for the last 20 years which deals with this particular problem: 'Defendant to have his costs unless a claim form is issued within 90 days of receipt of the documents, in which case costs in case.'[19]

[16] See *ED&F Man Capital Markets LLP v Obex Securities LLC* 2017 EWHC 2965 (Ch). Surely wrong!
[17] The judge had even more surprisingly refused leave to appeal.
[18] *SES Contracting Ltd v UK Coal plc* 2007 EWCA Civ 791.
[19] See *Documentary Evidence*, 13th ed, 1.31, see now *Jofa v Benherst Finance* 2019 EWCA Civ 899 at [38].

13

Proportionality and Search-based Disclosure

Stuart Sime

Introduction

Achieving justice in civil claims at proportionate cost remains a major challenge twenty years after the introduction of the Civil Procedure Rules.[1] In his Final Report[2] Lord Woolf observed that the only way to limit the costs of a case is to limit the amount of work that the lawyer has to do on the case.[3] Modern methods of communication, and the explosion of documentation produced in the digital age, generates an ever increasing amount of work in all types of litigation. With lawyers typically charging on an hourly rate basis, it is far too easy for the work in identifying, categorising, listing, inspecting[4] and analysing[5] documents to push the costs of litigating to disproportionate levels.

A great deal of thought, and a complex array of new rules and pilot schemes, have been introduced in England and Wales since the civil justice reforms of 2013 to tackle the burgeoning cost of disclosure in High Court claims. It will be seen that innovations designed to reduce the complexity of the disclosure process in the High Court have resulted in approaching 20 different disclosure schemes and models, some sharing common features, others taking significantly different approaches. It also produces a position

[1] Civil Procedure Rules 1998 (SI 1998/3132) ('CPR'). The overriding objective of the CPR as originally framed was to deal with cases justly (CPR, r. 1.1(1)). While proportionality was part of the CPR from the beginning (the original r. 1.4(2)(h) required the court to consider whether the likely benefits of taking a particular step justified the costs of taking it), the need to ensure costs are proportionate was formally added to the overriding objective by the Civil Procedure (Amendment) Rules 2013 (SI 2013/262).

[2] *Access to Justice: Final Report* (London: HMSO July 1996) ('Woolf Final Report').

[3] Woolf Final Report, ch. 2, para. 23, adopting a point made by the London Litigation Solicitors' Association.

[4] As required by CPR, Part 31.

[5] To advise the client, and for negotiation and trial purposes. For a senior litigator's insights into the practicalities of conducting the disclosure process, see Mackie, *Discovery in Commercial Litigation in Zuckerman and Cranston Reform of Civil Procedure* (Oxford: OUP 1995) at pp. 143–148.

Stuart Sime, *Proportionality and Search-based Disclosure* In: *The Civil Procedure Rules at 20.* Edited by: Andrew Higgins, Oxford University Press (2020). © the several contributors. DOI: 10.1093/oso/9780198863182.003.0013.

where fast track County Court claims of modest value[6] have been left with disclosure rules that are more demanding than those applying in many High Court claims.

This chapter will consider whether search-based standard disclosure continues to be a proportionate approach, and the knock-on impact on costs in cases where there has been extensive disclosure in the later stages in litigation. It will argue that disclosure in fast track litigation is out of step with the position in the High Court. Some of the important ideas contained in the Business and Property Courts disclosure pilot will be considered. It will argue that the numerous approaches currently provided by the CPR and various Practice Directions need to be replaced by a new 'standard disclosure' test which should apply across both the fast track and the multi-track.[7] It will recommend that the best approach is to revert to a modern version[8] of Lord Woolf's original recommendation that search-based disclosure should be a second stage disclosure process, and confined to cases where it can be justified in accordance with the overriding objective.

A long-standing problem

Pre-CPR discovery obligations[9] were based on the *Peruvian Guano*[10] interpretation of the requirement in the rules to disclose documents 'relating to any matter in question' between the parties in the proceedings. Brett LJ's formulation[11] was that:

> ... every document relates to the matters in question in the action, which not only would be evidence upon any issue, but also which, it is reasonable to suppose, contains information which *may*—not which *must*—either directly or indirectly enable the party [seeking discovery] either to advance his own case or to damage the case of his adversary ... a document can properly be said to contain information which may enable the party [seeking discovery] either to advance his own case or to damage the case of his adversary, if it is a document which may fairly lead him to a train of inquiry, which may have either of these two consequences.

[6] Fast track claims typically have values between £10,000 and £25,000: CPR, r. 26.6.
[7] With any special disclosure rules for specialised cases being kept to the absolute minimum.
[8] Informed by ideas in PD 51U.
[9] In RSC ord. 24, rr. 2 and 3.
[10] *Compagnie Financiere et Commerciale du Pacifique v Peruvian Guano Co.* (1882) 11 QBD 55.
[11] At p. 63. Emphasis in the original.

Lord Woolf has commented that the test laid down by Brett LJ is a sophisticated one, more readily applied to the limited number of documents which were being considered by the courts back in 1881 than to the bulk of documents which had to be considered by parties litigating 100 years later in the mid-1990s.[12] An extensive discovery obligation was affordable in the nineteenth century when many documents were hand-written, and copying was difficult, simply because in most disputes there was a limited volume of written material that might be relevant to the issues in a case. As document reproduction technology advanced in the twentieth century, culminating in the high-speed photocopier,[13] the established *Peruvian Guano* position became increasingly untenable.

In their report in 1993, Heilbron and Hodge commented that the cost of litigation at that time had made it uneconomic to go to court unless the amount in dispute was very large. They concluded that much of the expense was caused by discovery.[14] Heilbron and Hodge felt that the cost of disclosure was mainly a problem in larger value cases. On considering the evidence presented to his review, Lord Woolf disagreed,[15] and concluded that discovery costs were a major problem adversely affecting what we would now call fast track claims as well. It was for this reason that standard disclosure was introduced in fast track cases as well as on the multi-track.[16]

While computing and word processing had been in existence for some time when Lord Woolf delivered his *Final Report* in 1996,[17] the next 14 years saw something like a five-fold increase in annual personal computer sales.[18] Combined with widespread use of mobile devices, the volume of digital documents produced today is massively greater than the position causing so much concern in 1996. Producing a workable disclosure system to cope with the digital revolution is far from straightforward, as is illustrated by the fact there have been three major initiatives[19] in England and Wales since 2010 to regulate the disclosure of e-documents.

[12] *Access to Justice: Interim Report* (London: HMSO July 1995) ('Woolf Interim Report'), ch. 21, para. 16.

[13] Photocopiers were identified as a driver of discovery costs by solicitors who gave evidence to Lord Woolf's review (Woolf Interim report, ch. 21, para. 7).

[14] Heilbron and Hodge, *Civil Justice on Trial—A Case for Change*, Joint Report of the Bar Council and Law Society (1993).

[15] Woolf Interim report, ch. 21, para. 28.

[16] Woolf Interim report, ch. 21, para. 27, and implemented by CPR, r. 31.6.

[17] The Intel 4004 microprocessor was developed in 1971, and the first personal computer is widely regarded as being the Altair 8800 of 1974.

[18] From about 70 million p.a. in 1996 to 350 million p.a. in 2010.

[19] PD 31B on disclosure of electronic documents, menu disclosure introduced as part of the civil justice reforms in 2013, and PD 51U, the disclosure pilot in the Business and Property Courts.

In his *Final Report*[20] Sir Rupert Jackson quoted evidence from a City firm saying: 'in "heavy" commercial litigation, by far the largest costs driver is disclosure. The costs incurred in the disclosure process have significantly increased over recent years, principally because litigants, their advisers and the courts have struggled to grapple with the practical and logistical difficulties involved with e-disclosure.' In the 7th Implementation Lecture Sir Rupert Jackson said that: 'In larger actions where the relevant documents are electronic the problem is multiplied many times over. That problem is accentuated because relatively few solicitors and even fewer barristers really understand how to undertake e-disclosure in an effective way.'[21]

It is not just the largest cases that cause concern. In the 7th Implementation Lecture Sir Rupert Jackson pointed out that even in medium-sized claims where all the documents are in paper form disclosure can be a major exercise which generates disproportionate costs.[22] David Mackie has commented that the volume of documentation produced in a small case in 1995 approximated to the volume of documents in a large case 40 years earlier in about 1955.[23]

There are considerable pressures on legal representatives that push them towards providing wider disclosure. Taking a professional, responsible approach will incline them to full compliance with their disclosure obligations. Lawyers, like other professionals, prefer to gather all the facts before analysing them and reaching a decision or providing advice. You never really know whether something might be relevant until you have seen it. No lawyer wants a client to complain that a case was lost because of a lack of effort on the part of the lawyer, so guarding against complaints leads towards an approach of leaving no stone unturned. Clients also directly contribute to this pressure. Any lawyer suggesting to a client that they will not ask the other side to look for or provide various documents will invariably be quickly disabused by the client. If we are to have an affordable civil justice system the rules need to protect clients from themselves as much as regulating the position between the parties.

[20] Sir Rupert Jackson's *Final Report on Civil Litigation Costs* (December 2009) ('Jackson Final Report'), ch. 27, para. 2.1; Sime and French (eds), *Blackstone's Guide to the Civil Justice Reforms* (Oxford: OUP 2013), para. 8.01.

[21] 7th Implementation Lecture supporting the civil justice reforms 2013, Lord Justice Jackson, *Controlling the Costs of Disclosure* 24 November 2011 (7th Implementation Lecture), para. 2.2. The passage of time has no doubt been accompanied by greater familiarity with e-disclosure, and many commercial solicitors have ensured their fee earners have received training on the requirements of PD 51U.

[22] 7th Implementation Lecture, para. 2.2.

[23] Mackie, *Discovery in Commercial Litigation in Zuckerman and Cranston Reform of Civil Procedure* (Oxford: OUP 1995) at p. 141.

Disclosure wins cases

Evidence given to the Woolf review by the Bar of England and Wales was to the effect that discovery is vital to achieving a just result in civil proceedings. The way it was put by the Bar was that: 'it is not mere anecdote that discovery wins cases'.[24] Judges and practitioners can all no doubt think of cases where interim battles over disclosure may have been made the difference between winning and losing a case. Sometimes this arises where neither side has a full set of documents on the issues in the case, but when the claimant's documents are put together with those from the defendant what was a murky picture of events suddenly comes into full focus. In other cases, disclosure proves pivotal not so much from what is obtained from the other side, but as a result of the judge drawing adverse inferences from a party's repeated failure to provide full disclosure, or some other failing in the obligations imposed by CPR, Part 31.[25]

The question then arises as to whether the number of cases where full disclosure makes an appreciable difference in the just disposal of the case justifies the expense imposed across whole categories of cases in making the searches and subsequent document management involved in standard disclosure and other search-based disclosure requirements.[26]

In 1995 the Head of Litigation at Allen and Overy conducted a survey of 45 solicitors at the firm, covering 86 cases, ranging from smaller cases with a value under £50,000 to cases worth hundreds of millions.[27] The survey asked whether discovery had been useful in the case, and asked for a description of how the significant documents produced in the discovery process had helped in the case. In 17 of the 86 cases (19.8%) discovery made a significant difference. In two of these 17 cases the significant impact was in persuading the firm's own clients to provide documents to prove their own case, which is not the central purpose of disclosure. Most of the rest were cases involving fraud or dishonesty.[28]

[24] Woolf Interim Report, ch. 21, para. 8.

[25] Repeated failure to sign a disclosure statement in *Global Torch Ltd v Apex Global Management (No 2)* [2014] 1 WLR 4495 resulted in the defence being struck out, and a refusal of relief from sanctions.

[26] Evidence cited from the City of London Law Society in the Woolf Interim report, ch. 21, included the comment that an important question was whether the value of discovery, as it was under the RSC, justified its disadvantages.

[27] Mackie, at p. 137.

[28] Mackie, at p. 142. This was a survey of one City firm, and some time ago. As mentioned above, there are also cases where, without any hint of fraud or dishonesty, opposing litigants each have incomplete sets of documents, which sometimes fit almost like a jigsaw when put together. Again, these cases are comparatively unusual.

In 1992 Steyn LJ said:[29] ' "The discovery process adds greatly to the duration and cost of litigation, and . . . contributes to the tyranny of modern litigation". The learned judge commented that the experience of the Commercial Court judges was that usually 95% of the documents contained in the trial bundles were wholly irrelevant and never mentioned by either side. That the vast bulk of disclosed documents end up being redundant is well known to every litigator. David Mackie in 1995 described a typical substantial commercial claim, where discovery might produce 2,000 files of documents. Of these, perhaps 120 would be selected for inclusion in the trial bundles, and of those perhaps 16 would be used extensively in the trial.[30] David Mackie then observed that 'it is very common at the end of a case when judge, counsel and clients have all gone home, for the solicitors on each side to look ruefully at each other and the mounds of unopened files over which they fought so hard in the pre-trial exchanges'. As Sir Rupert Jackson has observed, extensive disclosure 'can also result in a formidable bundle, most of which is never looked at during the trial'.[31]

Traditional English disclosure rules place the emphasis on wide disclosure, thereby making it clear to all litigants that they are obliged to give full disclosure. The advantage of this is that any party who is reluctant to disclose, or who fails to disclose relevant documents, is already in breach of the rules, and should be on the defensive when the other side asks for an order compelling disclosure. The down side is that the starting point is that every litigant has a wide disclosure duty, regardless of whether the case really merits such an investment of resources, and regardless of whether they will seek to conceal useful documents that will promote the just disposal of the dispute. In other words, rather than tailoring more extensive disclosure obligations to the needs of the minority of cases that require it, all parties in all cases have to go to the expense of full disclosure.

It is hard to disagree with Lord Woolf's conclusion that it is desirable to retain some form of disclosure because of its contribution to the just disposal of disputes.[32] The difficulty arises because of the tension between the key concepts in the overriding objective,[33] namely the need to deal with cases justly, but also at proportionate cost. As Lord Woolf went on to say, the benefits of a system of disclosure need to be balanced against the costs to the

[29] Foreword to Matthews and Malek, *Discovery* (London: Sweet and Maxwell 1992).

[30] Mackie, *Discovery in Commercial Litigation in Zuckerman and Cranston Reform of Civil Procedure* (Oxford: OUP 1995) at pp. 140–141.

[31] 7th Implementation Lecture, para. 2.2.

[32] Woolf Final Report, ch. 21, para. 18.

[33] CPR, r. 1.1(1).

parties and the court system,[34] and the waste of resources involved in excessive disclosure.

While finding firm figures on the proportion of claims where disclosure makes a significant difference is difficult, it is perhaps somewhere in the region of 20% of contested cases. These 20% of cases cannot be ignored. To achieve a proportionate and efficient outcome, with resources targeted at the cases where they will do the most good, it is suggested that search-based disclosure should not be required in the majority of cases, but that tailored disclosure orders should be available for the minority of cases that need it.

Underlying purpose of the Woolf reforms

In the twenty-first-century world we have become so fixated with money that we have forgotten the wider aims of Lord Woolf's Access to Justice review. These were:[35]

(a) to improve access to justice and reduce the cost of litigation;
(b) to reduce the complexity of the rules and modernise terminology; and
(c) to remove unnecessary distinctions of practice and procedure.

Obviously, the more expensive it is to litigate a case, the less accessible the justice system becomes for potential litigants. Controlling costs is the main theme of this chapter.

Lord Woolf's conception was for the CPR to be expressed more like a guide than a detailed instruction manual.[36] Obviously, every word in a set of rules of procedure must have a purpose. However, it does not follow that everything needs an exact meaning. Lord Woolf preferred to avoid detailed rules, relying on judges and parties to apply the rules in accordance with the fundamental purpose of the civil justice system as set out in the overriding objective. Statutory force was given to this second aim of Lord Woolf's review by the Civil Procedure Act 1997, s. 2(7). This provides that: 'The Civil Procedure Rule Committee must, when making Civil Procedure Rules, try to make rules which are both simple and simply expressed.'

[34] Caused by greater reading time for judges and longer hearings.
[35] Woolf Interim Report.
[36] Woolf Final Report, ch. 20, paras 10–11.

While the Civil Procedure Rules are expressed in modern language,[37] thereby complying with the second half of para. (b) above, the Civil Procedure Rule Committee abandoned any attempt to keep the rules simple many years ago. Length is not a direct measure of simplicity, but the CPR, Practice Directions and preserved pre-CPR rules have approximately doubled in length from their original form in April 1999, when they covered 545 pages, to their approximately 1,100 pages in 2019.[38] Some Parts of the CPR are virtually unchanged since 1999. Problem areas, such as service, case management, disclosure, offers to settle, costs and appeals,[39] have been radically changed, often by completely replacing the original text.

Being an amalgam of original 1999 text and more recent insertions and replacements, the modern CPR are a mix of simple rules, simply expressed, and rules written in a highly technical way. The modern technical rules are not always a success. Any set of rules that needs to have a Practice Direction dealing with the meaning of words like 'will' and 'must',[40] and which makes different provision for the meanings to be given to these words depending on whether the particular CPR rule was made before or after a stated date, is hard to justify as being simply expressed.

One of the great achievements of the Woolf reforms was the replacement of the former High Court and County Court rules with a unified set of civil procedure rules.[41] The new landscape envisaged by Lord Woolf had a number of elements, one of which was that litigation would be less complex.[42] The single set of rules applying to the High Court and County Court would be simpler than the RSC and CCR, and special rules for specific types of litigation would be reduced to a minimum. Under this heading Lord Woolf said that discovery would be controlled. While in a minority of cases the pre-CPR scale of discovery would be possible, in the

[37] From the introduction of the CPR in April 1999 there was a determination across the judiciary, the legal profession and the Civil Procedure Rule Committee to stop using archaic language when discussing civil procedure. Sime and French (eds), *Blackstone's Civil Practice 2020* (Oxford: OUP 2020) ch. 92 provides modern language equivalents for 73 pre-CPR expressions.

[38] Plant (ed.), *Blackstone's Guide to the Civil Procedure Rules* (London: Blackstone's Press 1999) app. 1, compared with app. 1 in Sime and French (eds), *Blackstone's Civil Practice 2019*. The preserved provisions from the pre-CPR rules have been drastically cut back since 1999 as their provisions have been assimilated into the CPR. Some of the expansion can be explained by the addition of quasi-criminal provisions into the CPR, but these are a small part of the overall increase. Without the quasi-criminal provisions the 2019 version is about 1,015 pages.

[39] CPR, Parts 6, 26, 31, 36, 44–48 and 52 respectively.

[40] PD 2D.

[41] Woolf Final Report, recommendation 72, and implemented by the CPR.

[42] Woolf Final Report, Sect. I, para. 9.

majority of cases there would be a new standard test for more restricted disclosure.

Since 2013 nearly all these ideals have been broken. As will be described below, special rules for different types of case have proliferated. Rather than most cases being governed by standard disclosure, standard disclosure now applies by rule primarily to cases on the fast track, with almost all other categories of case having their own disclosure rules. There has been no clear policy statement on why this has happened. Piecing together what we do know, there appear to be two main motivating forces:

(a) Ensuring costs are kept under control. This was overtly the reason for introducing menu disclosure in multi-track claims in 2013,[43] and explains some of the other developments; and
(b) Segmenting civil procedure to make it easier to computerise court procedures.[44]

The unfortunate outcome is an overly complex system, with special rules applying not just to specialist litigation, but to whole swaths of litigation. Reforms to the rules on disclosure of documents since 2010, made no doubt to achieve these two policy aims, have made disclosure the most complicated and fragmented topic in the CPR. Lawyers with a range of cases need to apply a range of disclosure rules that differ from case to case. A litigant in person may have considerable difficulty in identifying which particular disclosure regime applies to their case.

Lord Woolf's recommendations on disclosure

In his Final Report Lord Woolf identified four categories of documents that might need to be disclosed:[45]

(1) The parties' own documents, which they rely upon in support of their contentions in the proceedings;

[43] What is now CPR, r. 31.5 was introduced as part of the civil justice reforms 2013, and was based on recommendations in the Jackson Final Report, ch. 37.

[44] Goodman, *Her Majesty's Court and Tribunals Service reform programme in The Civil Procedure Rules at 20* conference, Oxford, 10 June 2019.

[45] Woolf Final Report, ch. 12, para. 38.

(2) Adverse documents of which a party is aware and which to a material extent adversely affect his own case or support another party's case;
(3) Documents which do not fall within categories (1) or (2) above, but are part of the 'story' or background, including documents which, though relevant, may not be necessary for the fair disposal of the case;
(4) Train of inquiry documents: these are documents which may lead to a train of inquiry enabling a party to advance his own case or damage that of his opponent.

Lord Woolf recommended that in both fast track and multi-track claims disclosure should be limited to standard disclosure, covering documents in categories (1) and (2) only,[46] and with no duty to search beyond disclosure of documents of which a party is aware.[47] In fast track claims standard disclosure in this form was envisaged as likely to be the final position, as there should have been little scope for subsequent interim skirmishing over disclosure given the time constraints to trial.[48] On the multi-track, non-search-based standard disclosure was seen as being the first stage,[49] with the possibility of an application to a procedural judge for 'extra discovery'.

Dispensing with a search, and limiting standard disclosure to documents of which a party was aware, was possibly the most controversial aspect of the recommendations in Lord Woolf's review. Practitioners pointed to the lack of clarity in what is meant by a party being 'aware' of a document. Further problems were raised over who within a corporate body should be regarded as being 'aware' of documents for this purpose. Suggestions for solutions included organisations appointing a supervising officer whose task would be to identify individuals within the organization who would be likely to be able to identify relevant documents. There was also discussion on the extent to which former employees needed to be asked about the organisation's documents.[50] Lord Woolf perceptively concluded that including a search requirement in standard disclosure would result in disproportionate costs. He preferred to rely on the honesty and integrity of the legal representatives dealing with disclosure, with problems caused by parties not complying, or where there was a need for disclosure going beyond the documents of which a party was aware, being dealt with by applications for disclosure orders.[51]

[46] Woolf Final Report, ch. 12, paras 39 and 40, and recommendations 135 and 136.
[47] Woolf Final Report, ch. 12, paras 41–46, and recommendation 141.
[48] 30 weeks between directions and trial. Implemented in CPR, r. 28.2(4).
[49] Woolf Final Report, recommendation 136.
[50] Woolf Final Report, ch. 12, paras 41–43.
[51] Woolf Final Report, ch. 12, paras 40–46. This concept is used in PD 51U, where initial disclosure covers documents of which a party is aware. Awareness as a test was criticised by the legal profession in 1996 as being too uncertain. Some of the problems raised in 1996, such as whether an organisation is

Implementation and subsequent proliferation of disclosure regimes

As is well known, Lord Woolf's recommendations on disclosure were partially implemented in CPR, Part 31. Categories (1) and (2) from Lord Woolf's disclosure taxonomy were faithfully implemented, albeit in more detail, by CPR, r. 31.6. Until 2013, standard disclosure applied to both fast track and multi-track claims. The CPR departed from Lord Woolf's recommendations by imposing a general search obligation in r. 31.7, which applies at the point when disclosure is initially given. The extent of the search required depends on the circumstances of the case, and should be reasonable and proportionate.[52] Places searched, the time period covered by the search, and the range of digital, etc. devices searched all need to be identified on the disclosure statement forming part of the list of documents.[53]

Since 2013, concern about the escalating cost of disclosure has resulted in a proliferation of schemes for giving disclosure. Currently there are the following disclosure systems in place:

(1) disclosure of documents relied upon, with no duty to search, for small claims track cases;[54]

(2) standard disclosure, with the reasonable search requirement in r. 31.7, which applies to fast track claims, personal injury claims on the multi-track, and other multi-track claims where the court makes a specific order to that effect;[55]

(3) menu disclosure, which applies to multi-track claims other than personal injury claims and claims in the Business and Property Courts of England and Wales.[56] Menu disclosure provides the court with a choice of six types of disclosure order, namely:[57]

    (a) an order dispensing with disclosure;

fixed with being aware of documents known by former employees, have been addressed in the careful definition of the term in PD 51U, para. 2.9.

[52] PD 31A, para. 2.
[53] Form N265.
[54] CPR, r. 27.4(3)(a)(i).
[55] CPR, rr. 31.5(1a) and 31.6.
[56] CPR, r. 31.5, but which does not apply to cases covered by PD 51U. Menu disclosure applies to claims in the pilot for insolvency express trials by virtue of PD 51P, para. 3.3(b).
[57] CPR, r. 31.5(7).

(b) an order that a party disclose the documents on which it relies, and at the same time request any specific disclosure it requires from any other party;
(c) an order that directs, where practicable, that disclosure be given by each party on an issue by issue basis;
(d) an order that each party disclose any documents which it is reasonable to suppose may contain information which enables that party to advance its own case or to damage that of any other party, or which leads to an enquiry which has either of those consequences;[58]
(e) an order that a party give standard disclosure; and
(f) any other order in relation to disclosure that the court considers appropriate;

(4) initial disclosure and extended disclosure under the disclosure pilot for most High Court Business and Property Courts claims.[59] There is no search requirement for initial disclosure.[60] Extended disclosure requires a court order.[61] There are five models for extended disclosure. Models A and B involve no duty to search for documents, so any searches in fact made will be those the party chose to make when it prepared its case. Models C, D and E are search-based disclosure models. Model A is limited to known adverse documents, which is far less than required by standard disclosure. Model D is described as narrow search-based disclosure, with or without narrative documents. Narrative documents[62] are approximately equivalent to Lord Woolf's category (3) documents, which are not part of standard disclosure. Model E is the widest version, and includes train of inquiry documents, Lord Woolf's category (4);
(5) initial disclosure and extended disclosure, limited by PD 63, para. 6.1, for Patents Court claims;[63]
(6) disclosure and inspection of relevant evidence in competition claims must be proportionate, and is only available if ordered by the court on a normal interim application;[64]

[58] Similar to the *Peruvian Guano test* (n 10).
[59] PD 51U.
[60] PD 51U, para. 5.4(1).
[61] PD 51U, para. 8.2. An order for extended disclosure will only be made if it is reasonable and proportionate, with detailed criteria set out in PD 51U, para. 6.4.
[62] By PD 51U, app 1, para 1.11, these are documents which are relevant only to the background or context of material facts or events, and are not directly relevant to the issues in dispute.
[63] PD 51U, para. 1.5.
[64] PD 31C, paras 1.2 and 1.5.

(7) disclosure of documents relied upon together with documents requested by the other side for claims on the shorter trial scheme.[65] There is no duty to search;[66]

(8) disclosure of documents relied upon together with documents actually known to adversely affect or support or which are covered by a practice direction for claims on the flexible trial scheme.[67] There is again no duty to search,[68] but the parties may agree that there should be wider disclosure adopting one of the six forms available in menu disclosure, but in relation to defined issues. It is also possible to have an order for specific disclosure in these cases;[69]

(9) for claims on the capped costs list no disclosure is allowed, as a general rule, beyond core documents served with the parties' statements of case.[70] There is no duty to search;[71]

(10) restrictions on disclosure of mediation evidence.[72]

That it is possible to list 10 different approaches to disclosure that apply in one jurisdiction in this way is astounding. Something has gone horribly wrong here. No rational system of civil justice would have deliberately devised 10 different systems of disclosure for different categories of civil claim, with a further 11 types of disclosure order or models of disclosure as sub-categories. It puts lawyers and clients contemplating litigation in a quandary over what their disclosure obligations will be if the claim is defended, unless they can be certain over which track and specialist rules will apply to the case. Proliferation of procedures flies directly against the statutory requirement that the rules should be simple and simply expressed, and against Lord Woolf's vision of a unified set of rules with no more than limited special rules for special cases. It is as though every working party has been allowed to insert its own take on what might be the best disclosure approach in its own area of responsibility, with no thought for how it fits into the overall system.

[65] PD 57AB, para. 2.42(b).
[66] PD 57AB, para. 2.39.
[67] PD 57AB, para. 3.9(a).
[68] Also PD 57AB, para. 3.9(a).
[69] PD 57AB, para. 3.9(b).
[70] PD 51W, paras 2.9(2) and 2.28. In exceptional circumstances an order can be obtained for further disclosure in the nature of specific disclosure (paras 2.29 and 2.30).
[71] PD 51W, para. 2.27.
[72] CPR, r. 78.26, which may not survive Brexit. See Civil Procedure Rules 1998 (Amendment) (EU Exit) Regulations 2019 (SI 2019/521), reg. 16.

Categories (3), (4), (7), (8) and (9) above apply to High Court claims of various sorts. They all have the potential to have disclosure without a search. What this reveals is that the working parties who put forward the relevant provisions in these cases all realised that a default position of requiring a search, even a reasonable and proportionate search, leads to disproportionate costs.

Position of fast track disclosure within the scheme of English civil procedure

Fast track disclosure remains governed by the original 1999 CPR approach, with standard disclosure based on a reasonable and proportionate search. While the volume of documents that might be expected in a fast track claim will be less extensive than typical High Court claims, the value of a fast track claim will also be far less than the High Court claims that do not necessarily require search-based disclosure. Proportionality applies in the County Court as much as in the High Court. Fast track litigants are often private individuals and small businesses, and can ill-afford unnecessarily expensive procedures. It is high time that fast track disclosure was freed from the automatic requirement for a r. 31.7 search.

A more sensible and proportionate disclosure regime for the fast track would be to adopt a similar position to that provided for initial disclosure by PD 51U on the scope of the documents to be disclosed. That would mean limiting the parties' fast track disclosure obligations to the documents they intend to rely upon, documents required to understand the party's case, and to known adverse documents.[73] There should be no automatic duty to search.[74] Unlike PD 51U, disclosure would continue to take place after directions questionnaires, as in the current CPR, r. 28.3(1). This would also be far more closely aligned with Lord Woolf's recommendations.

This is similar to the scope of initial disclosure in the Business and Property Courts. Provided the PD 51U pilot is deemed to be a success on initial disclosure, in the interests of simplicity and consistency, it is suggested the same approach should be taken across the multi-track as well.

[73] The same as PD 51U, paras 2.8 and 5.1.
[74] The same as PD 51U, para. 5.4(1).

Some features of the Business and Property Courts disclosure pilot

The Business and Property Courts disclosure pilot came into force, with no transitional provisions, on 1 January 2019.[75] In these courts the pilot replaced the general disclosure provisions in the CPR.[76] While many of its features are shared with CPR, Part 31, the timing, procedures, scope and searches required are radically different. There are also subtle differences in terminology.[77] Three aspects of the pilot will be considered here: timing, process and the five disclosure models.

Cases covered by the pilot will predominantly be commercial and chancery claims. Unless proceedings are issued on an urgent basis, there should have been pre-action disclosure of key documents by each of the parties.[78] Under the pilot the parties are required to serve an initial disclosure list of documents with their particulars of claim or defence, together with copies of the listed documents.[79] While there is no duty to search,[80] the initial list of documents is required to include the key documents relied upon or which are necessary to enable the other parties to understand the statement of case.[81] There is also a general duty, from the moment proceedings are commenced, to disclose known adverse documents.[82] As extended disclosure requires a court order,[83] there will be cases where a claimant completes its disclosure obligations with initial disclosure before the issues have finally been defined by the statements of case.[84] Claimants therefore need to ensure they have made sufficient inquiries

[75] PD 51U and Ministry of Justice Update 100. PD 51U comprises a sophisticated set of rules and supporting documents extending to 55 pages. For a full discussion, see *Blackstone's Civil Practice 2020* at paras 50.32–50.82. Having no transitional provisions meant that while existing disclosure orders remained in effect, at case management conferences in the relevant courts from 1 January 2019 it was only possible to make disclosure orders in accordance with the pilot (PD 51U, paras 1.2 and 1.3, and Practice Note Business and Property claims in court, 3 December 2018, para. 10).

[76] PD 51U, para. 1.9, with some minor savings for pre-action and non-party disclosure, etc.

[77] Such as a new definition for 'document' (see *Blackstone's Civil Practice 2020* at para. 50.44), using the concepts of materiality (para. 2.7) and relevance (Model C in para. 8.3) instead of the standard disclosure categories in CPR, r. 31.6, and replacing 'inspection' with 'accompany', 'production', 'provide' and 'provision' (see *Blackstone's Civil Practice 2020* at para. 50.71).

[78] Practice Direction—Pre-action Conduct and Protocols, para. 6(c).

[79] PD 51U, para. 5.1. There are exceptions where initial disclosure is not required, set out in para. 5.3.

[80] PD 51U, para. 5.4.

[81] PD 51U, para. 5.1.

[82] PD 51U, para. 3.1(2). 'Known adverse documents' is defined as documents other than privileged documents of which a party is actually aware containing information which contradicts or materially damages the party's contention or version of events on an issue in dispute (paras 2.8 and 2.9).

[83] PD 51U, para. 8.2.

[84] The supplementary provisions in PD 51U, sect. 5, paras 5.5–5.14 anticipate there might well be subsequent applications for court orders dealing with initial disclosure. Unless para. 5.10 is given an unnatural meaning, none of the further provisions deal with a situation where a party wishes to provide further disclosure of supporting documentation after initial disclosure in the absence of an order for extended disclosure.

to find the documents they will need to rely upon in the period leading up to service of the particulars of claim. Defendants may also find themselves in a difficult position. While they will know the issues raised by the particulars of claim when they need to provide initial disclosure, unless they have been given good notice under the pre-action protocols, they will often have very limited time to find the key documents they need to disclose with their defence.[85]

While the radicalism may not be immediately apparent, where a party intends to seek extended disclosure, the pilot inverts the sequence of work generally followed by lawyers. It requires the parties to define the issues for disclosure first,[86] which are then used as a basis for deciding how extensive a search to conduct.[87] In an ideal world the issues that need to be decided at trial will have been defined by the original statements of case served by the parties. In the real world the way a case has been pleaded often needs to be refined by amendment as the evidence that will be deployed at trial comes to light through searches, inspection of the other side's documents, and subsequent service of factual and expert evidence. What the pilot requires is either a restriction to issues as set out in the original statements of case, which might work against the intention in Lord Woolf's Final Report that statements of case should be less technical,[88] or, something which might be very beneficial, a higher level of analysis by the legal representatives at an earlier stage in the case so that the right issues for disclosure are identified.

The third main feature of the pilot is that it introduces its five extended disclosure models.[89] These are to be welcomed, because the wider the range of possible orders that are available to a court, the more likely it is that the court will be able to find an order that meets the requirements of dealing with a case justly and at proportionate cost. These new models are clearly the product of careful thought. They are not the same as the six disclosure orders on the menu in other multi-track claims.[90] The way things work at present is that for claims on the pilot, it is the five extended disclosure models that are available if the court so orders, whereas for other multi-track claims it is possible for the court to adopt any of the pilot models in addition to the other orders set out in r. 31.5(7). This is because r. 31.5(7)(f) allows the court in a multi-track claim to

[85] Possibly forcing defendants to apply to extend time under CPR, r. 3.1(1)(a) for giving initial disclosure, which in turn may result in initial disclosure being divorced from service of the defence.

[86] PD 51U, sect. 7. Technically, these are not the legal issues in the case, but big picture issues on which extended disclosure might be necessary (*McParland & Partners Ltd v Whitehead* [2020] EWHC 298 (Ch)).

[87] The purpose is to limit costs, PD 51U, para. 2.4.

[88] Woolf Final Report, sect I para. 9 and CPR Part 16.

[89] Set out in PD 51U, para. 8.3.

[90] As listed in CPR, r. 31.5(7).

make any other disclosure order it thinks appropriate. It might be difficult for a non-pilot multi-track claim to assign different pilot models to different disclosure issues, because there will be no identification of disclosure issues, but it could adopt a pilot model to define the scope of disclosure across all issues in the case.

Conclusion: a new 'standard disclosure'

For the reasons mentioned above, in most cases legal representatives for the parties will in any event want to gather together the documents that are likely to have a bearing on the issues in the dispute. These inquiries are in most cases likely to produce a range of documents that support or undermine the client's case. Most legal representatives will reconsider the case in the light of these documents, and may well ask their client to provide further documents that are needed in order to prove or defend the case. That level of work is normal in any type of case.

Given the expense of search-based disclosure, and the limited range of cases where obligatory searches produce significant documents, it is suggested that the documents produced in this way, without any rule or court directed search, should be the new 'standard disclosure' across all categories of case on the fast and multi-tracks. This will remove the time and expense in conducting searches, and drastically reduce the volume of disclosed materials, with knock on costs savings through the subsequent stages of a case through to trial.

How should the scope of disclosure in this form be defined? There are a number of candidates:

(a) The existing CPR, r. 31.6, definition of standard disclosure, simply removing the universal search requirement in r. 31.7. While r. 31.6 technically has five sub-categories, it basically covers the documents a party relies upon and adverse documents;
(b) The formula used in CPR, r. 31.17(3) for non-party disclosure orders. This is not quite the same as standard disclosure, and covers documents which are likely to support the case of one party or adversely affect the case of another party, together with documents that are necessary in order to dispose fairly of the claim;
(c) The documents covered by initial disclosure in PD 51U. These are the key documents relied upon or which are necessary to enable the other parties

to understand the disclosing party's statement of case, and known adverse documents.

In order to promote simplicity across the CPR, it is suggested that a single test should be used across all categories of case proceeding on either the fast track or the multi-track, including specialist cases and cases on the shorter trials, flexible trials and capped costs schemes. The aim should be to get as close as possible to requiring disclosure of the documents that are actually likely to be referred to if the case were to reach trial, so each side has advance access to all the relevant documents in the case, with as little wasted expenditure on unnecessary disclosure as possible.[91] Given the careful work put into PD 51U, it is suggested that the best modern test is that the parties should disclose the documents relied upon or which are necessary to enable the other parties to understand the disclosing party's statement of case, and known adverse documents.[92]

There remain the minority of cases where experience shows fuller disclosure can make a significant difference. It is suggested that disclosure going beyond the new non-search-based standard disclosure should be a second stage in the disclosure process, and only available with a court order.[93]

From the survey conducted by David Mackie,[94] most cases likely to benefit from further disclosure should be easily identifiable, as many will involve allegations of fraud or dishonesty. Given judicial case management applies to most of these cases, obtaining search-based disclosure orders ought not to be that difficult.[95] Other cases where there is no suggestion of misconduct, but which would justify search-based disclosure, such as where one or more of the parties has incomplete documentation after the new 'standard disclosure', would have to be justified at a case management hearing.

It is suggested that where a second stage further disclosure order is made, the fullest range of further disclosure orders, comprising specific disclosure and inspection, the six orders on the menu in multi-track claims and the five PD 51U disclosure models, should be available to the court. Document heavy complex litigation would justify tailored disclosure directions, including

[91] In other words, to get as close as possible to the 16 files actually used at trial out of the 2,000 files referred to by David Mackie in his article on *Discovery in Commercial Litigation*.

[92] This omits the word 'key', which is used in PD 51U, para. 5.1, because it is possible that some lawyers will use that word to excuse not disclosing some of the documents they rely upon on the basis the documents are not 'key'.

[93] Specific disclosure is provided by CPR, r. 31.12, menu options are in r. 31.5(7), and the extended disclosure models are in PD 51U, para. 8.3.

[94] See n 28.

[95] If the case is an obvious one for further disclosure the court could make an order on its own initiative under CPR, r. 3.3.

possibly some or all of the PD 51U processes, such as the disclosure review document and technology assisted reviews, etc.[96]

The starting point for the duty to search would involve seeking a court order, but the expense would be justifiable given that it is the case in hand that gives rise to wider, search-based, disclosure. Even in these cases there may ultimately be a costs saving, because the search-based disclosure order, having been sought in the specific circumstances of the case, should end up being more focused to the issues, locations and categories of documents that will need to be searched for than an open-ended search obligation. The result ought to be a simplified, more certain, and cost effective disclosure system, that is fit for the modern digital world.

[96] PD 51U and notes in the disclosure review document include detailed provisions dealing with electronic documents, de-duplication, password protected documents, methods for excluding documents unlikely to be relevant (DeNISTing), and software tools for prioritising or coding harvested documents. See *Blackstone's Civil Practice 2020* at paras 50.62 and 50.63.

PART V

JUDICIAL REVIEW

14

The Use of Empirically Based Information when Reforming and Evaluating Judicial Review

Maurice Sunkin

Introduction

This chapter traces the availability and use of empirically based evidence relating to judicial review in England and Wales. It considers in particular how such evidence has been used by reformers of judicial review and those concerned to evaluate the effectiveness or otherwise of reforms. My purpose is not to provide a detailed discussion of the empirical evidence itself or to provide an in depth account of the trends in the use of judicial review, although references to such matters will be necessary.[1] I should also make it clear that this chapter concentrates on only one feature of our system, judicial review. There is a rich and varied body of empirically base scholarship concerned with other matters of importance to public lawyers including, for example, research on: the changing constitutional landscape; the development of regulatory practices; how public institutions actually work; the legislative process; and the use and effectiveness of accountability mechanisms across the wider administrative justice landscape.[2]

I focus on judicial review for four main reasons, first because it is the process that is most closely associated with the practical application of the rule of the law in our system. For this reason alone it is important. Second, there are many

[1] For a more detailed recent discussion of the statistical trends see S. Nason, 'Plus ça Change: An Empirical Analysis of Judicial Review in Modern Administrative Law' in Richard Kirkham and Lindsay Stirton (eds), *Executive Decision Making and the Courts* (Hart Publishing, forthcoming). Note that this chapter does not consider the empirical research beyond judicial review, nor does it deal in any depth with the use of empirical data by the courts.

[2] There are now significant literatures on these and related matters relevant to public lawyers. For an excellent overview see: Simon Halliday, 'The Role of Empirical Legal Research in the Study of UK Public Law' in Caroline Hunter and David Cowan (eds), *Integrating Socio-Legal Studies into the Law Curriculum* (Palgrave Macmillan, 2012).

Maurice Sunkin, *The Use of Empirically Based Information when Reforming and Evaluating Judicial Review* In: *The Civil Procedure Rules at 20.* Edited by: Andrew Higgins, Oxford University Press (2020). © the several contributors.
DOI: 10.1093/oso/9780198863182.003.0014.

assumptions about the place of judicial review in our system that we have only recently been able to test against sound empirically based evidence. Third, this area provides an interesting case study of how lawyers and legal reformers have used empirical and statistical data. Finally, this topic highlights the importance of understanding such data, especially when they are used by government to justify restricting access to the courts.

This volume, like the conference upon which it is based, marks the 20th anniversary of the 1999 reforms to the Civil Procedure Rules (CPR). These reforms did not specifically concern the judicial review procedure, which was reformed the following year in the light of the recommendations of the Bowman Committee.[3] I am therefore grateful to the organisers and editors for welcoming this topic as a guest at the anniversary event.

While the CPR did not directly concern judicial review much of the thinking behind the 1999 reforms also informed the later changes to the judicial review procedure. In particular, both sets of reforms encouraged the view that litigation is a last resort, hence the value of ADR and the use of pre-action protocols. They also recognised that court litigation is inevitably affected by what goes on elsewhere and that changes to one aspect of the system may have implications up or downstream.[4] In this sense they accepted that procedural design cannot be treated as a purely technical matter of concern only to litigators, but plays a key role in determining how people behave, how systems operate, where costs lie, and how the quality of the system is experienced and perceived.

This chapter is concerned with how empirically based information has been used when judicial review has been reformed. My starting point, which I expect is now uncontroversial, is that good quality empirically based evidence relating to the use and working of the court system helps us to understand the system and the effects that reforms are likely to have. Such evidence should also assist when evaluating whether reforms have been successful.

To be clear, I am not suggesting that reforms should be driven solely by such things as statistical data, nor do I assume that empirical data will remove controversy or necessarily provide a clear way forward. My working assumption is simply that good quality empirically based evidence should play an important role in the overall reform process. This is particularly important in the context of judicial review. This process is concerned with ensuring that public bodies are legally accountable. If reforms are aimed at restricting access to judicial

[3] *Review of the Crown Office List*, March 2000.

[4] eg the reduction in the availability of legal aid has led to an increase in self-representation with consequences for the incidence and quality of settlements and for how judges handle cases.

review it is constitutionally important to ensure that restrictions are justified, that they are necessary and proportionate. Sound evidence can play a key role here. I will return to this later.

Suffice to say for now that the attitude of lawyers and legal reformers to empirical and statistical data has changed significantly since the early 20th century and the main purpose of this chapter is to trace this change. For convenience the chapter is structured around the following phases: from the 1930s to the early 1960s which was typified by the absence of empirically based evidence and scepticism amongst legal academics regarding the value of such evidence; from the early 1960s to the mid-1980s during which the value of empirical evidence on judicial review emerged; the 1980s to the mid-2000s which saw a significant growth in the available empirical evidence; and finally, the period from the mid-2000s during which empirical and statistical evidence relating to the process took centre stage.

From the 1930s to the early 1960s: the absence of empirically based evidence

I shall start with work of the Hanworth Committee that was established in December 1932 to 'consider the state of business in the Supreme Court, and to report whether greater expedition in the dispatch of business, or greater economy in the administration of justice in that court, is practicable . . .'.[5] For present purposes the most significant of its contributions was the introduction of the leave (now permission) requirement. This has remained the central, and the unique, characteristic of our judicial review procedure.[6]

The committee had been concerned to improve the efficiency of the procedure for seeking the prerogative writs of Certiorari, Mandamus and Prohibition. The procedure for Certiorari and Mandamus usually required the applicant to make an *ex parte* application to the Divisional Court for a rule nisi. Applications for Prohibition, by contrast, were normally made to a judge in Chambers. If the rule nisi was granted the writ would be issued and it was then for the defendant to apply to the Divisional Court to have the writ annulled. The Hanworth committee initially, unanimously, recommended a relatively minor reform whereby applications for Certiorari and Mandamus would be

[5] The Business of Courts Committee, Third and Final Report, 1936 Cmd 5066. Interim reports were issued in 1933: Cmd 4265 and Cmd 4471.

[6] Andrew Le Sueur and Maurice Sunkin, 'Applications for Judicial Review: The Requirement of Leave' (1992) *Public Law* 102–29.

dealt with in the same way as applications for Prohibition, namely by an initial *ex parte* application for a rule nisi to a judge in chambers.[7]

But when this proposal was debated in the House of Lords Lord Atkin objected on the grounds that the proposal conflicted with the requirements of public justice:

> It has always been a matter of considerable moment that in applications . . . which involve a suggestion that there has been some excess of jurisdiction, or some breach of duty on the part of some government official by which the subject has been injured, the proceedings take place in public and that it should be known from the beginning that they should take place in public.[8]

This response also struck a chord with the government which was keen to maintain an open process because this enabled defendants to hear why writs were being sought. The committee was forced to pause for thought: was it possible to arrive at an open procedure that would also save court time? Sir Claude Schuster suggested that a new leave requirement would provide a way forward. Applicants would apply *ex parte* in open court for leave to seek the prerogative writs. If leave was granted there would be a substantive hearing into whether the writs should be issued and writs normally would not be issued before that hearing. Defendants would therefore be able to hear the grounds upon which the applicant sought leave and, because they would no longer have to apply to the Divisional Court to have writs dismissed, there would be efficiency savings for both the defendant and the court. This proposal was ultimately accepted.

Looking back it is striking that this key element of the judicial review procedure was introduced without any significant assessment of empirical or statistical evidence. There are likely to have been several reasons. One is that little if any relevant and useful statistical evidence existed. Although statistics on the courts had been available since 1858 these provided little more than an annual indication of the overall number of cases handled by particular courts[9] and it is unlikely that such statistics would have assisted this aspect of the committee's work.[10] Another factor may well have been that the committee, composed as

[7] First Interim report, para 30.

[8] H.L. Deb, Vol 88 Col 119 (15 June 1933).

[9] As we shall see, in more recent times the reliability and adequacy of the court statistics have in any case been widely criticised, see eg H. Genn, 'Why the Privatisation of Civil Justice is a Rule of Law Issue', 36th FA Mann Lecture at Lincoln's Inn, 19 November 2012, 12. See generally, W. M. Teeder, 'Judicial Review and the Vanishing Trial' unpublished MPhil dissertation, LSE November 2019, especially Ch 2.

[10] In relation to other matters the committee drew on a range of statistical information, eg in relation to the jurisdiction of the County Court, we are told that Sir Claude Schuster 'had the judicial statistics

it was of people with direct expertise of the court system, was content to rely on its knowledge and experience.[11] It was felt sufficient, for instance, to note without reference to any evidence that prerogative writs 'are sometimes applied for on frivolous grounds'[12] and that a decision of the Divisional Court that a *prima facie* case has been established against a public body 'often has the effect of restraining persons from continuing to do acts which are subsequently proved to be unlawful'.[13]

A further broader factor is that there appears to have been no relevant academic empirical research available to the committee. While much public law scholarship was empirical in approach,[14] it was not until the 1960s that academics became interested in undertaking empirical research that specifically focused on judicial review and court reformers started to draw on such work.

Herbert M. Kritzer has contrasted the development of empirical research in the United States with the absence of such work in other English-speaking countries.[15] He says that the major reason for this was associated with the different role of universities and legal education in the United States and these other countries:

> [T]he role of academic institutions in preparing practitioners came much later in England, Canada, and Australia than was true in the U.S[.] which meant that the legal academy outside the United States was a less significant part of university communities. The result was that . . . in the pre-World War II period empirical work was virtually unheard of among legal academics outside the U.S.[16]

at his fingertips'. See Patrick Polden, *A History of the County Court, 1846–1971* (Cambridge Studies in English Legal History, 1999) 145. It may be noted that the Donoughmore committee, which reported a year or so before the establishment of the Hanworth Committee, also did not draw on empirically based data on such matters as the use of the courts to control ministerial powers: *Committee on Ministers Powers Report* 1932, Cmnd 4060.

[11] As well as Lord Hanworth, the Master of the Rolls, the committee comprised senior judges, the President of the Law Society, and the Permanent Secretary to the Lord Chancellor's Department.

[12] First Interim report, para 30.

[13] Final Report, para 9.

[14] Martin Loughlin notes that in the Diceyian empirical tradition the purpose of public law is 'to state what are the laws which form part of the constitution, to arrange them in their order, to explain their meaning, and to exhibit where possible their logical connection', Martin Loughlin, *Public Law and Political Theory* (Clarendon Press, 1992) 183. See also Simon Halliday's observation that public law scholarship is 'unavoidably' concerned 'with constitutional practice in light of the uncodified nature of our constitution'. See Halliday (n 2).

[15] Herbert M. Kritzer, 'The (Nearly) Forgotten Early Empirical Legal Research' in Peter Cane and Herbert M. Kritzer (eds), *The Oxford Handbook of Empirical Legal Research* (OUP, 2010) Ch 36.

[16] Ibid at 882.

In the United States academics were accustomed to seeing law as being concerned with practice and Kritzer stresses the close connections that existed between legal academics and policy makers. He points, for instance, to the work of eminent lawyers such as Felix Frankfurter and William Douglas who were legal academics and senior judges and who both carried out empirical research: 'In contrast, the legal academy in England was not a path into the upper reaches of government office or the senior judiciary.'[17] A further factor, he argues, was the relative isolation of the legal academy in Britain from the social sciences. By contrast 'the university as a center of research in the social sciences and humanities developed strongly in the U.S. in the early twentieth century.'[18]

Even by the late 1950s there was next to no attempt to link discussions of the value of judicial review to evidence relating to such matters as how the system was actually being used, or what, if anything, claimants gained from litigation, or how judicial review impacted upon public bodies. To take Professor S. A. de Smith's groundbreaking book *Judicial Review of Administrative Action*, first published in 1959 as an example.[19] This work was empirical in the sense that it aimed to 'expound the rules comprised in judicial review'.[20] It also rested on some key empirical assumptions, see in particular his famous opening sentence commenting that:

> In the broad context of the administrative process the role of judicial institutions is inevitably sporadic and peripheral.[21]

No empirical evidence is cited to support this, perhaps because de Smith regarded the matter as too obvious for this to be needed. In any case de Smith was clearly sceptical about the value of statistics, noting that:

> The true significance of the part played by judicial institutions in any system of administrative law cannot be evaluated only by reference to the frequency with which their jurisdiction is invoked.[22]

de Smith was, of course, correct to distrust the ability of statistics to fully reflect the importance of judicial review. However, his scepticism was overstated

[17] Ibid.
[18] Ibid.
[19] S. A. de Smith, *Judicial Review of Administrative Action* (Stevens, 1959).
[20] See n 14.
[21] Smith (n 19) 3.
[22] Ibid.

and subsequent developments have shown that statistics and other empirically based evidence can contribute to our understanding of the value and limitations of the procedure.

The 1960s to the 1980s: an emerging awareness of the value of empirical evidence

While the overwhelming view amongst legal academics for much of the 20th century was that empirical investigation of the legal system was at most of marginal interest, by the 1960s there were signs that things were beginning to change. J. A. G. Griffith was particularly influential as one of the very few public lawyers of the period who was enthusiastic about the need for empirical research. His *Central Departments and Local Authorities*, published in 1966, for instance drew on a programme of interviews and other related work to explore the working relationships between central and local government in England and Wales. Griffith was a lawyer who was not constrained by the traditional isolation of doctrinal legal scholarship and positively sought to work with social and political scientists. For this study, for example, his three research officers were by training a sociologist, a political scientist, and an historian who in addition 'all had previous experience in different sections of public administration'.[23] While this cross-disciplinary approach was late in coming, in the 1960s it helped to nurture developments such as the law in context and critical legal studies movements and the wider use of socio-legal methods that has become a central feature of academic legal scholarship.

As is well known during this period there was growing concern about the state of administrative law, leading in May 1969 to the Law Commission recommending the establishment of a Royal Commission, or a similar body, 'which includes members with legal, administrative and political experience', to undertake an urgent inquiry into administrative law.[24] As is also well known the government did not consider the time to be right for such a wide inquiry and instead the Law Commission was charged with the much more specific task to: 'review the existing remedies for the judicial control administrative

[23] J. A. G. Griffith, *Central Departments and Local Authorities*, (George Allen & Unwin Ltd, 1966), Preface. See also his work on Parliament (with Michael Ryle) that was concerned to provide an accurate description of how Parliament works: J. A. G. Griffith and Michael Ryle and M. A. J. Wheeler-Booth, *Parliament: Functions, Practice and Procedures* (Sweet & Maxwell, 1989).

[24] For an account of the developments during this period, see T. T. Arvind and L. Stirton, "The Curious Origins of Judicial Review" (2017) *Law Quarterly Review* 133, 91–117.

acts and omissions with a view to evolving a simpler and more effective procedure'.[25] The Law Commission's work attracted much attention and there was 'a wide response' to their Working Paper and consultation.[26] Significantly in the present context, while there were many criticisms of the legal system and suggested reforms, there appears to have been little if any reference to empirically based evidence on judicial review.[27]

The Law Commission's recommendation led to the introduction in 1977 of the 'new' RSC Order 53 procedure for claiming judicial review which enabled applicants to seek injunctions and declarations as well as the prerogative orders in the same claim.[28] While some had argued in favour of modelling the judicial review procedure on ordinary civil proceedings rather than on the prerogative writ procedure, thereby avoiding the leave requirement, the Law Commission favoured retention of the leave requirement subject to the 'important safeguard for the litigant' that the decision be given by three judges in open court 'especially if the application is to be refused'.[29]

In so recommending the Law Commission acknowledged the value of the first independent study of the work of the Queen's Bench Divisional Court, including judicial review, undertaken by the Legal Research Unit at Bedford College, London under the direction of Louis Blom-Cooper QC and Gavin Drewry with the support of the Social Science Research Council.[30] This appears to have been the first time that reformers of judicial review had benefitted from independent research data.

The Law Commission said that the research data, when read with the official statistics, showed that the leave requirement 'removes at the outset a substantial number of cases'. In the years 1971–75 inclusive the proportion of cases in which leave was refused amounted to a little over one-third of the applications made. The data also showed that since 1947 'a not insignificant number of applications' had been made in person. And because filed affidavits are usually

[25] *Hansard* Vol 306, Cols 189–90.

[26] The organisations and persons who commented on the Law Commission's Working Paper No 40 are listed in Appendix C to the Law Commission's *Report on Remedies in Administrative Law*, Law Com No 73, March 1976.

[27] To take one example, in their report, *Administration under the Law* (JUSTICE, 1971) JUSTICE refers to the 'piecemeal and unsystematic' growth of administrative powers and administrative law (para 10, p 4) and proposes the establishment of a new Administrative Division of the High Court that would be able to 'create a more coherent system' of administrative law (para 26, p 14). However, at no point in the report does there appear to be reference to statistical or empirical evidence concerning such matters as the use of the courts or the effects of court decisions.

[28] The Law Commission, *Report on Remedies in Administrative Law*, Law Com No 73.

[29] Ibid, para 40.

[30] Unfortunately the research was not written up for publication.

read by the court before the hearing, hearings are 'relatively short'. From this the Law Commission observed that:

> A procedure which provides an expeditious method whereby the Court can sift out the cases with no chance of success at relatively little cost to the applicant and no cost to the prospective respondent would seem at first impression worthy of retention.[31]

The Law Commission was also reassured that there was an acceptable risk of arguable cases being filtered from system prematurely because 'only about one-half' of cases granted leave were found to succeed at the substantive hearing.[32] Such considerations, as well as the 'social value' in having a process that enables a person to hear from the court that they have no case, led the Law Commission to recommend retention of the leave requirement.

While the Law Commission indicated the potential value of empirically based evidence and while a small number of empirically inclined researchers were beginning to turn their attention to judicial review this was still a very marginal area of interest and mainstream legal scholarship remained sceptical about the value of statistical evidence. De Smith's fear that the statistics would fail to reveal true qualitative importance of judicial review was one factor here. The dominant theme amongst public lawyers at the time was that the 1960s had seen a revival of judicial review and a beneficial increase in the willingness of the courts to question the activities of public authorities.[33] Such claims may have been justified by the leading decisions of the time and by developments in doctrine, but de Smith's earlier concern that they would not be reflected in the statistics remained. In his 3rd edition, published in 1971 de Smith was able to say that:

> . . . since 1967, there has been a striking increase both in the frequency with which judicial review has been invoked and in the readiness of the courts to intervene.

[31] The Law Commission, *Report on Remedies in Administrative Law*, Law Com No 73, para 38.

[32] Ibid. Some questioned whether decisions after full hearing could tell much about the quality of decisions refused leave on an *ex parte* application.

[33] eg The JUSTICE/All-Souls, *Review of Administrative Law in the United Kingdom Discussion Paper* (April 1981) stated that: 'The courts have been remarkably active in the last 20 years in revitalising judicial review . . . as a result of developments in the late 1960s and in the 1970s judicial review has re-established itself as a powerful controlling force on the activities of public authorities', pp 41–43.

However he cites the *Civil Judicial Statistics* which showed that the number of claims for Certiorari, Prohibition and Mandamus were actually quite small: the number of claims for these writs had increased from 47 in 1966, to 87 in 1968, to 227 in 1971.[34] The number of orders granted during each of these years was: 18 in 1966, 24 in 1968, and 29 in 1977. De Smith observed that:

> These figures suggest, at the very least, that lawyers in 1971 were advising clients more frequently than in 1966 or 1968 that they had an arguable case. And in fact the qualitative record of judicial review is more impressive than the quantitative.[35]

As de Smith suggests, the statistical evidence did little to reinforce the dominant account of judicial review as an area of strikingly growing importance in the overall constitutional system.

The early 1980s to the mid-2000s: the value of empirical evidence is accepted

While de Smith may have been content to assume that the statistics failed to fully reflect the real qualitative importance of judicial review. Others would have viewed matters differently, for example seeing the figures as adding substance to Allan Hutchinson's argument that the dominant 'rhetoric' around the growing stature of judicial review was no more than a 'ruse' and that despite 'all the ballyhoo, the impact of the law on the administrative process is marginal'.[36] Here then we see important potential tensions between the dominant view of the place of the courts on the one hand and the empirical data on the other. Was judicial review as important as some assumed? If there was a gap between the qualitative and quantitative importance of judicial review, what was the nature of this gap and what did it tell us about the real world place of the courts? These were intriguing and important questions and they pointed to the need for more and better empirically based information about judicial review to assist not only practical reform, but also wider understandings of the role of the process

[34] In the 4th edition the editor adds that in 1977 there had been 376 applications for leave to seek the prerogative orders, of which in 29 cases the orders were finally granted: J. M. Evans (ed), de Smith's *Judicial Review of Administrative Action*, 4th ed. (Stevens, 1980) 31.

[35] S. A. de Smith, *Judicial Review of Administrative Action*, 3rd ed. (Stevens, 1973) 28.

[36] Allan C. Hutchinson, 'The Rise and Ruse of Administrative Law' (1985) 48 *Modern Law Review* 293, 294.

in the system. The issue was picked up by Carol Harlow and Richard Rawlings who in 1984 alerted us that:

> Doctrine and case-analysis we possess; research into *who* litigates, how *often*, and in respect of *which* governmental activities, has been singularly lacking.[37]

The first published detailed account of the trends in the use of judicial review, the subject areas litigated, the operation of the leave filter and how matters proceeded through the judicial review process appeared in 1987 (the 1987 study).[38] This was based on the caseload during 1981–86 and drew on published statistics and a study of the court records. Regarding general trends it reported that:

> The [official statistics] show a general increase in the judicial review caseload that continues an upward trend throughout the 1970s. This trend has been with us for so long that it is now almost axiomatic that judicial review is an area of growth, quantitatively as well as qualitatively.[39]

However, there was cause for caution:

> [T]hese figures alone provide a very unreliable basis for concluding that judicial review as a whole is expanding. The basic reason . . . is that the data does not tell us *how* judicial review is being used in particular subject areas, neither does it tell us who is using judicial review and against what agencies.[40] (emphasis in original)

For the first time the study, unlike the official statistics, revealed the subject areas being litigated. In particular, it showed that immigration cases dominated the judicial review caseload to such an extent that the scale of immigration related challenges had been 'masking declines in the use of judicial review beyond the immigration context'.[41] Here then was a warning about the shortcomings of the official statistics at the time and the danger of drawing conclusions regarding the use of judicial review without knowing more about the types of issues that were being litigated. This is something to which I will need to return

[37] Carol Harlow and Richard Rawlings, *Law and Administration* (Weidenfeld and Nicolson, 1984) 257.
[38] M. Sunkin, 'What is Happening to Applications for Judicial Review?' (1987) 50(4) *Modern Law Review* 432–67.
[39] Ibid, 436 (footnotes removed).
[40] Ibid, 436.
[41] Ibid, 442.

because David Cameron's Coalition government based its case for reforming judicial review on a similar failure to distinguish between trends in immigration and non-immigration judicial reviews.

Before moving on it is worth noting in passing that the assumption that resort to judicial review had been growing significantly (and in a manner that had negative effects on public bodies) was also evident in judgments during the period. The best known example is the judgment of Lord Brightman in *Puhlhoffer v Hillingdon LBC*.[42] Here Lord Brightman referred to the 'mass of litigation' under the Housing (Homeless Persons) Act 1977, and said that he was 'troubled at the prolific use of judicial review . . . [to challenge] . . . the performance by local authorities of their functions under the [Act]'. He concluded by expressing 'the hope that there will be a lessening in the number of challenges . . . mounted against local authorities who are endeavouring in extremely circumstances, to perform their duties . . .'.[43]

In fact the 1987 study found that the number of homeless challenges had not come close to the number of immigration cases and paled into insignificance when contrasted with the number of applications to local housing authorities for assistance under the homelessness legislation. For example, in 1985 there were 66 homelessness applications for judicial review, but there were 203,480 applications to local housing authorities for assistance and 93,980 acceptances, leaving over 100,000 unsuccessful applications.[44] The 66 challenges may have appeared 'prolific' to Lord Brightman and perhaps also to some local housing authorities,[45] but when contrasted with the general scale of local authority decision making the numbers of applications reaching the court was tiny. Rather than point to the prolific use of the system the figures actually raised serious questions about why so few cases were being taken to judicial review bearing in mind that at the time this was the only legal remedy available to people who had been refused assistance under the homelessness legislation.

The main point for the moment is that the 1987 study highlighted both the risks of making assumptions about the use and importance of judicial review based on general judicial statistics and the need for more detailed information

[42] [1986] 1 All ER 467.

[43] Ibid, 469, 474.

[44] See n 38, 448.

[45] Later research revealed that judicial review litigation was concentrated on a small number of local authorities, predominantly in the London area: M. Sunkin, K. Calvo, L. Platt and T. Landman, 'Mapping the Use of Judicial Review to Challenge Local Authorities in England and Wales' (2007) *Public Law* 545–67.

about how courts were being used. This message was at least partially recognised when, from 1988, the official statistics identified the number of immigration applications and, for a limited period, the number of homelessness applications.[46]

A more detailed empirical picture of judicial review emerges

Over the next 15 years or so further empirical studies on the use of judicial review and the dynamics and effects of public law litigation were undertaken across the UK.[47] This body of research drew attention to a number of key matters, including: the uncertain nature of the permission stage and in particular the consistent inconsistency of the judges in determining permission applications;[48] the concentration of judicial review litigation especially in London and the South East;[49] the importance of settlement and the factors that encourage and inhibit settlement in judicial review;[50] the effects of judicial review on local authorities and the quality of public services, suggesting that contrary to many impressions, judicial review leads to improvements in the quality of public services.[51] More recent work has examined the effects of judicial review on claimants and highlighted, again contrary to widely held assumptions, the extent to which claimants achieve both non-tangible and tangible benefits from judicial review claims.[52]

[46] Homeless cases were separately identified until 2003. Further improvements to the statistics have subsequently been made, see later in the chapter.

[47] There were parallel projects on the use of judicial review in Scotland: T. Mullen, K. Pick and T. Prosser, *Judicial Review in Scotland* (John Wiley and Sons, 1996); B. Hadfield and E Weaver, 'Trends in Judicial Review in Northern Ireland' (1994) *Public Law* 12–16. A burgeoning literature on the impact of judicial review also emerged, see eg, G. Richardson and M. Sunkin, 'Judicial Review: Questions of Impact' (1996) *Public Law* 79–103; and G. Richardson, 'Impact Studies in the UK' in M. Hertogh and S. Halliday (eds), *Judicial Review and Bureaucratic Impact: International and Interdisciplinary Perspectives* (Cambridge University Press, 2004).

[48] See L. Bridges, G. Meszaros and M. Sunkin, *Judicial Review in Perspective* (Cavendish Publishing, 1995) Ch 8; V. Bondy and M. Sunkin, 'Accessing Judicial Review' (2007) *Public Law* 647–67.

[49] Bridges, Meszaros and Sunkin (n 48). And see especially, the Foreword written by Mr Justice Brooke, then Chairman of the Law Commission. See also S. Nason and M. Sunkin, 'The Regionalisation of Judicial Review: Constitutional Authority, Access to Justice and Specialisation of Legal Services in Public Law' (2013) 76(2) *Modern Law Review* 223–53.

[50] V. Bondy and M. Sunkin, *The Dynamics of Judicial Review Litigation: The Resolution of Public Law Challenges Before Final Hearing* (Public Law Project, 2009); V. Bondy and M. Sunkin, 'Settlement in Judicial Review Proceedings' (2009) *Public Law* 237–59.

[51] L. Platt, K. Calvo and M. Sunkin 'Judicial Review Litigation as an Incentive to Change in Local Authority Public Services in England & Wales' (2010) 20(i) *Journal of Administration Research and Theory* 243–60; M. Sunkin, L. Platt and K. Calvo, 'The Positive Effect of Judicial Review on the Quality of Local Government' (2010) 15(4) *Judicial Review* 337–42.

[52] M. Sunkin, V. Bondy and L. Platt, *The Value and Effects of Judicial Review* (Public Law Project, 2015).

The Bowman Committee

By the late 1990s empirical research on judicial review had become an established area of academic work. It was also now accepted that reformers of court procedures would take account of the best available statistical and empirical evidence.[53] However, as the Bowman Committee discovered, obtaining even basic statistical information about how the judicial review process worked was still no easy matter even for those who were close to the system.[54] In its report the Bowman Committee expressed its frustration as follows:

> In order to ensure that we had a proper factual basis for any decisions we might take, we prepared a list of the statistics we would like from the Crown Office. Our starting point was to ask for an analysis of the applications for permission. What we wanted to see was a table showing the number of applications outstanding at the start of the year, the new applications received in the year, the number of applications disposed of during the year by a decision of the court . . . and the number of applications withdrawn or settled . . . It rapidly became apparent to us that this kind of information was not readily available and was going to be difficult to obtain . . .[55]

Bowman felt obliged to do its own research, in particular to seek to further test whether it would be more efficient to replace the permission requirement with a summary judgment process akin to that in ordinary civil proceedings, bearing in mind that the permission demanded a judge's decision in every claim (save those that had been withdrawn prior to the permission stage) including those that lacked any merit and those that might be withdrawn subsequent to the permission stage. Based on its own study, Bowman recommended, as the Law Commission had done in the 1970s, retaining the permission stage essentially because it filtered a significant proportion of cases and thus 'overall' caused a significant saving of court time.[56]

[53] By this time government departments and policy makers were also being encouraged to draw on empirically based data as part of the push to adopt evidence based decision making, see New Labour's 1999 White Paper, *Modernising Government*; Cabinet Office Performance and Innovation Unit, *Better Policy Delivery and Design: A Discussion Paper* (Cabinet Office, 2001).

[54] Lord Chancellor's Department, *Review of the Crown Office List*, London, 2000 ("Bowman Report"). The review was established to consider how Crown Office procedures, including judicial review, could be adapted to deal with the 'increased workload of the Crown Office' and the potential further increase in workload and delays that were expected following the Human Rights Act 1998. The report led to procedural reforms contained in Part 54 of the CPR, see SI 2000/2092.

[55] Bowman Report, p 10, paras 6–8.

[56] Ibid, p 63, para 11.

While the methods of research adopted by Bowman, as well as the committee's findings were challenged by academics,[57] that the committee sought to base its recommendations on what it considered to be a sound empirical basis was itself significant. It was also important that Bowman, as a priority, called for improvements in the available statistics on the case load and for better management information concerning the Crown Office.[58]

From the mid-2000s: empirical and statistical data take centre stage

My account has traced the improved availability and use of statistical and empirically based evidence relating to judicial review. It has shown a growing academic interest in empirical research in this area, driven in part by an intellectual concern to gain a more informed sense of the place of judicial review in our system.[59] It has also traced the growing use of empirical research and statistically based information by reformers. Since the mid-2000s there has been a further important twist to this account. Over this period governments have driven reforms to legal aid and to the judicial review process that have been directly or indirectly concerned to restrict access to judicial review. And they have sought to justify key elements of these reforms by reference to statistical data.[60] This has placed empirical and statistical information centre stage in discussions concerning the justifications for reform and has meant that it is now difficult to discuss the importance of judicial review without understanding what the empirical and statistical data tells us.

Here my purpose is not to enter into the merits or otherwise of particular reform proposals. Rather my aim is to illustrate how statistically based arguments and empirical research have come to be used by government to justify reforms, and by those who question the need for reform. It goes without saying that where empirically based justifications are used by government it is important that the soundness of the justifications can be assessed. In what

[57] L. Bridges, G. Meszaros and M. Sunkin, 'Regulating the Judicial Review Caseload' (2000) *Public Law* 649–70.

[58] Bowman, pp 116–19.

[59] The empirical study of judicial review in England and Wales was also attracting the interest of political scientists in the US, see eg Susan Sterett, *Creating Constitutionalism? The Politics of Legal Expertise and Administrative Law in England and Wales* (University of Michigan Press, 2000).

[60] For a fuller account of the recent reform programme, see Maurice Sunkin and Varda Bondy, 'The Use and Effects of Judicial Review: Assumptions and the Empirical Evidence' in John Bell, Mark Elliott, Jason N. E. Varuhas and Philip Murray (eds), *Public Law Adjudication in Common Law Systems* (Hart Publishing, 2016)Ch 14.

follows, I try to limit myself to some of the bigger picture issues to highlight the more obvious challenges that statistically based debate presents in this area, including for government.

Much recent attention has understandably focused on the programme of judicial review reform that was launched by David Cameron's Coalition government. However, before turning to this it is worth remembering that the Labour government had earlier flagged up the growth in judicial review as a justification for restricting the availability of legal aid. For example, in its consultation paper, *Legal Aid: Refocusing on Priority Cases*, published in July 2009, the Ministry of Justice said that:[61]

> Figures from Her Majesty's Courts Service show that over the last 15 years the number of applications for permission to bring judicial review has more than doubled, from approximately 3000 to 7000 per year. Over the same period, the proportion of applications where permission was granted has decreased from over 40% to just 20%. A significant number of these failed permission applications will be funded through legal aid, and in some of those cases funding will have been granted using devolved powers.

The consultation went on to say that:

> The Justice Secretary is concerned that limited legal aid resources should not be used to fund hopeless judicial review applications. We are therefore proposing that the delegated power of solicitors to self-grant emergency representation under their existing contracts will be withdrawn for all judicial reviews.[62]

Here we see what has become a regular argument that links the growth in judicial review to an increase in the number of weak claims. In this case, that is then connected to the granting by solicitors of emergency legal aid. The statistics, however, are far too general to establish anything more than possible links between such matters, and certainly the statistics do not establish causal connections between the growth in numbers of applications, the historic decline

[61] The Jackson Report drew on data showing the low rate of success at the permission stage to demonstrate a rather different conclusion, namely the effectiveness of the permission stage as a form of early neutral evaluation: 'The effect of the permission requirement is that approximately 80% of judicial review claims are weeded out in the early stages. Such claims do not have sufficient prospect of success and they are brought to an end at (usually) modest cost.' *Review of Civil Litigation Costs: Final Report*, December 2009, Part 7, Ch 35, p 325, para 2.1.

[62] *Legal Aid: Refocusing on Priority Cases* (July 2009), p 29.

in permission grant rates, and the availability of emergency legal aid. We have already seen why we should be cautious before inferring a growth in judicial review from generalised statistics, and I will return to this in the context of the more recent reform programme. Research has also shown that a variety of factors explain the historic decline in the permission grant rate and that it cannot be assumed that the decline indicates an increase in the proportion of weak claims.[63] Neither of these issues was addressed by the Ministry of Justice. More particularly, empirical research suggests that there was no causal relationship between the number of claims issued and success or failure rates at the permission stage, or between failure rates and the use of devolved powers.[64] In fact, the research shows that the subject areas in which there were the highest rates of refusal of permission were not those in which devolved powers tended to be used. It also shows that the areas with the highest rates of early settlement were likely to be the most urgent, that is to say those where the use of devolved powers was likely to be most common. One further matter stands out from the research, namely that timely settlement was often dependent on the quality of legal representation and the willingness and ability of lawyers on each side to communicate with each other. This being so, it was argued that removal of devolved powers and indeed broader restrictions on legal aid were 'likely to be counterproductive, in so far as they are likely to disrupt the parties' ability to communicate and thereby potentially inhibit the achievement of timely settlement'. In other words, the empirical research indicated not only that the proposed reforms were unjustified by the figures cited, but also that they could undermine the early resolution of disputes and thereby add to the overall costs of litigation. In the event, devolved powers to grant emergency legal aid for judicial review were removed and replaced by a much more limited scheme as from 1 April 2013.[65]

The Prime Minister announces the government's judicial review reform programme

On 19 November 2012, the then Prime Minister, David Cameron, told the CBI that:

[63] See V. Bondy and M. Sunkin, 'Accessing Judicial Review' (2007) *Public Law* 647–67.

[64] Varda Bondy and Maurice Sunkin, 'The Use of Statistics in Proposing Reforms to the Public Funding of Judicial Review Litigation: A Critical View' (2009) *Judicial Review* 372.

[65] In September 2018 the government clarified that such delegated powers remain for urgent homelessness matters. See further.

> [Judicial review] is a massive growth industry in Britain today. Back in 1998 there were four and a half thousand applications for review and that number almost tripled in a decade. Of course some are well-founded . . . But let's face it: so many are completely pointless. Last year, an application was around 5 times more likely to be refused than granted. We urgently needed to get a grip on this. So here's what we're going to do. Reduce the time limit when people can bring cases. Charge more for reviews so people think twice about time-wasting. And instead of giving hopeless cases up to four bites of the cherry to appeal a decision, we will halve that to two.

On 3 September 2013 Chris Grayling MP, the then Minister for Justice and Lord Chancellor, wrote in the *Daily Mail:*

> Of course, the judicial review system is an important way to right wrongs, but it is not a promotional tool for countless Left-wing campaigners. . . . Britain cannot afford to allow a culture of Left-wing-dominated, single-issue activism to hold back our country from investing in infrastructure and new sources of energy and from bringing down the cost of our welfare state.

Here once again we see the government saying that the statistics show judicial review to be a 'massive growth industry' fuelled by weak and abusive claims. Now, however, the highest level in government was pitching that assertion beyond lawyers to the wider public using language indicating that judicial review reform was to be a populist issue aimed at preventing abuse of the system and especially left wing campaigning. As well as massive growth, two further core claims were implied: that judicial review impedes good government and that because judicial review focuses on process, even when claims succeed the substance of decisions do not change. In other words, much judicial review is about technicalities that do not matter and is not worth the cost or the fuss. Each of these claims has been questioned in the light of alternative readings of the statistics and the available research evidence and I will not take space repeating the criticisms here.[66] It is, however, worth making some further general comments regarding the main claim that judicial review has been a 'massive growth industry'.

It is certainly true that the official statistics showed an unprecedented increase in the overall number of applications for judicial review. However, as in the 1980s, this growth is largely attributable to the number of immigration

[66] See further Sunkin and Bondy (n 60).

claims. As in the 1980s, once immigration cases are placed to one side there is no indication of a 'massive increase' in judicial review litigation in non-immigration matters.[67] As the Joint Committee on Human Rights concluded in its inquiry into the implications for access to justice of the government's proposals to reform to judicial review:

> [T]here has been a substantial increase in the number of judicial reviews in recent years, but this has been largely because of the . . . increase in the number of immigration cases being pursued by way of judicial review.
>
> . . . We note that the number of judicial reviews has remained remarkably steady when the increase in the number of immigration judicial reviews is disregarded. . . . We therefore do not consider the Government to have demonstrated by clear evidence that judicial review has 'expanded massively' in recent years as the Lord Chancellor claims, that there are real abuses of the process taking place, or that the current powers of the courts to deal with such abuse are inadequate.[68]

The trends from 2000 to 2018 are shown in the graph in Figure 14.1 which is taken from the Official Statistics. As the graph indicates the numbers of applications for judicial review in non-immigration civil matters have been remarkably consistent over the past two decades at around 2,000 applications annually. More recently the numbers have fallen below this figure.

It is clear beyond doubt that, aside from immigration challenges, there was no 'massive growth' in the numbers of applications for judicial review in the period to which the Prime Minister refers. Given that the immigration cases were separately identified in the statistics this was apparent from the official statistics and we must assume the government will have been aware of this. While the government seemed willing to ride out criticism of their statistical justification for the reform programme there can be little doubt that this significantly weakened the government's case and rallied critics of the reforms.[69]

[67] See further Robert Thomas, 'Mapping Immigration Judicial Review Litigation: An Empirical Legal Analysis (2015) *Public Law* 652; Robert Thomas and Joe Tomlinson, *Immigration Judicial Reviews: An Empirical Study* (Nuffield Foundation, 2019).

[68] 13th Report of Session 2013/14, para [30]. Emphasis in original.

[69] The reforms led to reductions in the time limits for seeking judicial review in planning cases and increased judges' discretion to refuse hear cases certified 'totally without merit'. In 2013 immigration cases were transferred to the Upper Tribunal. In 2014 and 2015 fees for judicial review were increased and new restrictions on remuneration for legal aid claims were introduced. In addition Part 4 of the Criminal Justice and Courts Act 2015 introduced: a duty to refuse permission or relief if 'it appears to the court to be highly likely that the outcome for the applicant would not have been substantially different if the conduct complained of had not occurred' (s 84); new financial disclosure requirements (ss 85–86); and a new duty on the court to award costs against interveners (s 87). Protective costs orders were also placed on a statutory footing (ss 88–89). See *Judicial Review and the Rule of Law: An*

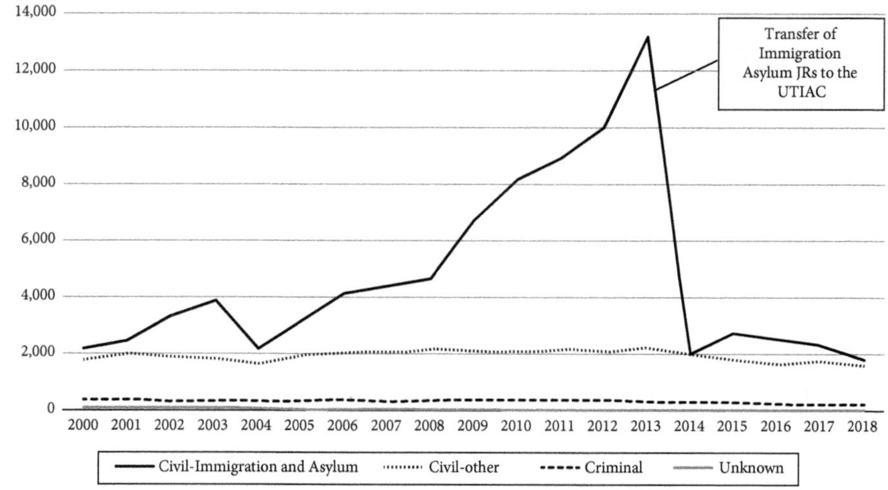

Figure 14.1 Annual Judicial Review Applications, by type; calendar year 2000–2018
(Source: Ministry of Justice)

In fact, rather than pointing to massive growth the official statistics raise important questions about why so little use was, and is, being made of judicial review. Of course there are likely to be a combination of reasons for this. One factor can almost certainly be discounted. It is extremely unlikely that the figures are indicative of the level of legal compliance by public bodies. It would, I think, be unsafe to assume, for instance, that there has been a significant recent improvement in compliance with public law principles, but this could perhaps be tested by empirical research. Other more plausible explanations could be connected to the numbers of potential claims that are settled out of court or resolved by way of other appeal or complaints procedures. The single most likely explanation, however, is likely to be that for most people 'judicial review is simply not available' because of the costs involved and the absence of legal aid. Tom Hickman has described this as 'Public Law's Disgrace'.[70] It means that judicial review is irrelevant to most

Introduction to the Criminal Justice and Courts Act 2015 (Bingham Centre for the Rule of Law, Public Law Project, JUSTICE, October 2015) Part 4.

[70] T. Hickman, 'Public Law's Disgrace' U.K. Constitutional Law Blog (9 Feb 2017) (available at https://ukconstitutionallaw.org/). See also Joe Tomlinson, 'Crowdfunding Public Interest Judicial Reviews: A Risky New Resource and the Case for a Practical Ethics' (2019) *Public Law* 166.

people including when they are most likely to come into contact with pubic administration.[71]

The Public Law Project (PLP), commenting on the government's recent consultation on costs reforms,[72] has rightly argued that this justice gap needs to be fixed: 'but before it can be fixed, it needs to be properly explored and understood'. PLP say that 'the Government needs to undertake such research to better understand the nature of the costs barriers so that sensible, evidence-based policy reform can be effected' and that 'failure to understand and measure the difficulties people face in accessing judicial review will have long term implications for the effectiveness of our constitutional safeguards'.[73] There is clearly a need for empirical research on the barriers facing potential users of judicial review and PLP may be correct that this is work should be done by government. But if government is unwilling academics may be equipped to undertake some useful research if funding can be obtained, which of course cannot be assumed.

Conclusions

This chapter has presented a broad brush picture of the changing availability and use of statistical and empirical data concerning judicial review in England and Wales over the past 90 years or so. This period has seen a significant expansion in empirical research and a general improvement in the available statistical information about the judicial review process. The current official statistics, for example, provide much more information about how the judicial review process is used and how matters proceed through the system than was available say 20 or 30 years ago. Annual figures now show the types of defendants challenged,[74] we can also see the numbers and percentages of cases at each stage of the process so that, for example, it is now possible to know the proportion of initial claims that get to the final hearing stage and also the number and

[71] Sarah Nason, for instance, cites Ahluwalia and Tomlinson who argue that despite the grave risks of unfairness in various stages of the decision to impose benefit sanctions, 'judicial review has largely been an irrelevance': Ahluwalia and Tomlinson, 'Benefit Sanctions, Illegality and Administrative Justice: After Judicial Review?' (2018) 23(4) *Judicial Review* 225, cited by S. Nason (n 1).

[72] https://consult.justice.gov.uk/digital-communications/fixed-recoverable-costs-consultation/.

[73] Sara Lomri, 'The Cost of Access to Justice' (Public Law Project, 20 June 2019), https://publiclawproject.org.uk/blog/the-cost-of-access-to-justice/

[74] During 2018 the Home Office was the department with the largest number of claims lodged against it (1,200); the Ministry of Justice was next largest department challenged (1,100); local authorities were the third largest defendant type with 652 lodged against them.

proportion that are decided for the claimant or the defendant.[75] This is not to say that things are yet perfect. Far from it. Recent experience has shown for example that significant challenges continue to exist in obtaining precise data on the level of costs and the availability of legal aid in judicial review, which makes it difficult to assess the scale of the financial barriers facing claimants.[76] And, as the above discussion indicates, there is still much to learn about how judicial review is accessed as well as about its effects. The recent use by government of statistics has underlined the importance of having access to transparent information about the system as well as the worth of sound, independent empirical research on judicial review. It is true that statistics alone cannot provide an indication of the value judicial review. But equally, it is true that the value of judicial review cannot be assessed without access to sound statistical and empirical information.

[75] The figures are in Excel spreadsheets based on Administrative Court Office (COINS) data: https://www.gov.uk/government/statistics/civil-justice-statistics-quarterly-april-to-june-2019 There is also information on the number of permission claims found to be totally without merit.

[76] Tomlinson (n 70), at p 171.

15

Reforming Judicial Review Costs Rules in an Age of Austerity

Joe Tomlinson and Alison Pickup[1]

Introduction

Recent debates around judicial review reform in the UK have, like much justice policy generally, suffered from a deficient evidence base and this has ultimately hampered the quality of policy. One prominent and significant case in point has been the debate around the costs rules in judicial review. Implicit in almost all views on this subject is that the present costs rules can and do serve as a barrier to accessing judicial review. What is contested is the extent to which the present arrangements do in fact serve as a barrier; many argue that judicial review is widely inaccessible due to the costs rules, while others (including the government) suggest there is no access problem and that the emphasis should be on ensuring judicial review is done at proportionate overall cost for the taxpayer. In a constitutional system where, in practice, the government is both the key designer of and the main 'repeat player' litigant in the judicial review process, it is perhaps unsurprising that much policy breaks in favour of the prevailing government stance.[2] However, we argue in this chapter that the government's responses to Sir Rupert Jackson's landmark review on civil litigation costs—and its recommendations on judicial review—reveal a particularly strong and worrying tendency to proactively disengage with the range of evidence that is available, ignore independent proposals, and insulate its policy preferences from debate. The perverse upshot is that, parallel to an independent review that has sought to

[1] This chapter is based on research for which Ravi Low-Beer provided excellent assistance.

[2] A dynamic observed in various places in the literature, see *e.g.* C. Harlow and R. Rawlings, '"Striking Back" and "Clamping Down": An Alternative Perspective on Judicial Review' in J. Bell et al (eds), *Public Law Adjudication in Common Law Systems: Process and Substance* (Oxford: Hart Publishing, 2016); C. Harlow, 'Administrative Reaction to Judicial Review' [1976] *Public Law* 116; G. Braibant, 'Remarques sur l'efficacité des annulations pour excès de pouvoir' [1961] *E.D.C.E.* 53.

Joe Tomlinson and Alison Pickup, *Reforming Judicial Review Costs Rules in an Age of Austerity* In: *The Civil Procedure Rules at 20.* Edited by: Andrew Higgins, Oxford University Press (2020). © the several contributors.
DOI: 10.1093/oso/9780198863182.003.0015.

improve the accessibility of judicial review for claimants, the rules have been tilted further against them.

This chapter covers three mains areas. First, it offers context for the issues, highlighting the importance of the financial aspects of judicial review, explaining some recent reforms, and outlining the general position on costs in judicial review. It then moves on to consider the first proposals brought forward by Jackson and analyses the government's response to them. The next section offers an analysis of Jackson's—and the Westgate Working Group's—second attempt to generate proposals regarding judicial review costs and the government's latest response. It concludes by offering some comments on what appear to be dim future prospects for reform.

Judicial review costs rules in the context of recent reforms

In the UK, questions of money and finance have become more important in the discussion around judicial review in recent years. In simple terms, there have been two broad, competing narratives. The first narrative is that the cost of bringing a judicial review claim, including the cost of covering a claimant's costs exposure, is a barrier to access to justice, and this impedes the judiciary's ability to uphold the Rule of Law, prevent abuse of power by the executive, and generally produce the 'goods' we hope and understand the judicial review system produces.[3] A second narrative is that the cost of defending judicial review claims—particularly those that are not meritorious—diverts scarce public resources away from defendant public bodies' primary function of governing in the public interest. These two narratives have been put under the spotlight by the general programme of austerity implemented by the UK government from 2010 onwards (including restrictions on legal aid), as well as the reforms undertaken and attempted concerning judicial review specifically.[4]

A number of reforms to judicial review were promoted by the Coalition Government of 2010–2015. Many of them were controversial and many of them were premised on the second narrative of how judicial review consumes scarce government resources. When the UK Government proposed changes to the judicial review system in 2012, the consultation process cited the growing number of 'weak or ill-founded claims' that were taking up 'large amounts of

[3] For discussion, see generally: C.F. Forsyth (ed.), *Judicial Review and the Constitution* (Oxford: Hart Publishing, 2000); C. Harlow and R. Rawlings, *Law and Administration*, 3rd edn (London: Sweet & Maxwell, 2009) 668 *et seq*; S. Nason, *Reconstructing Judicial Review* (Oxford: Hart Publishing, 2016).

[4] Ministry of Justice, *Judicial Review: Proposals for Further Reform* (London: Cm 8703, 2014).

judicial time and costing the court system money'.[5] The reforms to judicial review implemented by the Coalition Government included the following:

- a new court fee payable on application for an oral permission hearing, and a series of increases in the court fees payable in judicial review cases;
- the introduction of changes to legal aid in judicial review cases so that payment to claimant lawyers has become conditional on the grant of permission (with some exceptions);[6]
- the introduction of a lower threshold test ('highly likely' rather than the previous test of inevitability) for when permission or relief can (and in some circumstances, must) be refused on the basis that a defect in procedure would have made no difference to the original outcome;[7]
- the introduction of costs capping orders, which, unlike protective costs orders which they replaced, cannot be granted before permission;[8]
- the introduction of a requirement for judicial review claimants to disclose at the outset information about the financial resources available, or likely to be available to them to meet their litigation liabilities, such information to be considered by the trial judge to determine where costs of the case should fall;[9]
- the introduction of a similar financial disclosure requirement for applicants for costs capping orders;[10] and
- the introduction of new and potentially punitive costs rules for third party interveners.[11]

The impact of these and other changes—along with the associated political rhetoric—has been growing concern about access to judicial review, as well as concerns about the implications of limiting who is able to hold public bodies to account for their actions.[12] Constructing a detailed empirical inquiry into financial barriers to judicial review would be both a worthwhile inquiry and a demanding task—it would have to incorporate consideration of a wide range of issues such as court fees, legal aid, and crowdfunding. The concern of this

[5] Ministry of Justice, 'Judicial Review Consultation—Press Release' (13 December 2012), available at <https://www.gov.uk/government/news/judicial-review-consultation> (accessed 27 March 2018).
[6] Regulation 5A, Civil Legal Aid (Remuneration) Regulations 2013/422, as inserted by the Civil Legal Aid (Remuneration) (Amendment) Regulations 2015/898 reg. 2(3) and subsequently amended.
[7] Section 84, Criminal Justice and Courts Act 2015.
[8] Sections 88–90, Criminal Justice and Courts Act 2015.
[9] Sections 85–86, Criminal Justice and Courts Act 2015 (not yet in force).
[10] Sections 88–89, Criminal Justice and Courts Act 2015.
[11] Section 87, Criminal Justice and Courts Act 2015.
[12] For instance, this was clear in the discussion around the Bach Commission, see The Bach Commission, *The Right to Justice* (London: Fabien Society, 2017).

chapter, however, is specifically with the costs rules. We will therefore, briefly, outline the key cost rules of judicial review in the Administrative Court.[13]

As the level of costs in judicial review is often variable but always significant (a judicial review that goes to a full hearing and runs overall costs of less than £20,000 is rare), how the costs of a judicial review are divided between the parties is an important and controversial issue.[14] Costs rules are complex but the starting point is section 51 of the Senior Courts Act 1981, which provides that costs shall be 'in the discretion of the court'. This discretion is '[s]ubject to the provisions of this or any other enactment and to rules of court'. The main rules to which the court's discretion is subject are contained in the Civil Procedure Rules (CPR) Parts 44–46. CPR 44.2 sets out the general rule in civil litigation that costs will follow the event (*i.e.* loser pays), although the court has a discretion to make a different order as to costs (including to make no order at all). CPR 44.2 requires the court, in exercising its discretion on costs, to have regard to all the circumstances of the case.[15] The rules, like all other parts of the CPR, must be applied and interpreted in accordance with the overriding objective of the CPR, 'to enable[e] the court to deal with cases justly and at proportionate cost'.[16]

The general rule in CPR 44.2 that the loser pays the winner's costs is subject to a range of statutory, procedural, and judge-made modifications. Though there are multiple examples, we will introduce one important and relevant example for the sake of the discussion in this chapter: cost capping orders (CCOs). A consequence of the general rule that costs follow the event, is that the court's discretion as to costs generally falls to be exercised at the end of a case, when the outcome is known. CCOs—and their judge-made predecessors, protective costs orders (PCOs)—represent a departure from the general rule in CPR 44.2(2) since they are sought and made at an early stage in the proceedings. They are also an exception as they confer costs protection on a

[13] Immigration cases, by some distance, represent the majority of judicial reviews in England and Wales. They are heard in the Upper Tribunal (Immigration and Asylum Chamber) and different provision apply. For an overview, see C. Yeo, *Costs in Immigration Cases* (London: Free Movement, 2015).

[14] There is a lack of clear data on the level of costs in each case. A 2007 estimate placed it in the region of £10,000 to £20,000 for a straightforward case, possibly much higher for a more complex matter, see The Public Law Project, *How to Fund a Judicial Review Claim When Public Funding is Not Available* (London: The Public Law Project, 2007), para. 1, which was informed by discussion with practitioners. Further and similar estimates are available in a response to a Ministry of Justice Consultation made available via a Freedom of Information Act 2000 (FOIA) request, see Freedom of Information Act Request No. 171204020.

[15] These circumstances include: the conduct of all the parties (including the reasonableness of the issues pursued, the manner in which the litigation was conducted, and compliance with any relevant pre-action protocol); whether the losing party succeeded on part of its case; and any admissible offer to settle which is drawn to the court's attention.

[16] CPR 1.1.

party regardless of the outcome of the proceedings, therefore limiting the discretion a trial judge has on costs. The rationale for PCOs was considered in the seminal *Corner House* case.[17] It was noted there that the rules of standing have been liberalised to permit judicial review claims to proceed so as to vindicate the Rule of Law and stop the unlawful exercise of public power. However, the Court of Appeal concluded that the liberalisation of standing was sometimes insufficient in cases where there was a public interest in resolving a dispute by litigation which could not reasonably be brought without conferring some form of costs protection on the claimant. The law on PCOs was codified—with some changes—in sections 88–90 of the Criminal Justice and Courts Act 2015, which introduced CCOs for judicial review proceedings in the Administrative Court.[18] The conditions that have to be met before the court can make a CCO are that: permission to apply for judicial review has been granted; the court is satisfied that the proceedings are public interest proceedings; and the court is satisfied that, without a CCO, the applicant would be acting reasonably by withdrawing or ceasing to participate in the proceedings.[19] If a CCO is made, section 89(2) provides that a reciprocal cap must also be imposed, restricting the costs the beneficiary of the order is able to recover.

Another point must be noted in relation to CCOs: claims relating to the environment have special status. Article 9 of the Aarhus Convention[20] confers rights of access to justice on: any person whose request for environmental information has been ignored, refused or inadequately answered;[21] members of the public deemed to have standing to challenge the substantive or procedural legality of decisions, acts or omissions subject to the public participation provisions of Article 6;[22] and members of the public deemed to have standing to challenge other acts or omissions by private persons and public authorities

[17] *R (Corner House Research) v Secretary of State for Trade and Industry* [2005] 1 W.L.R. 2600.

[18] A CCO is defined in section 88(2) as 'an order limiting or removing the liability of a party to judicial review proceedings to pay another party's costs in connection with any stage of the proceedings'.

[19] Proceedings are considered 'public interest proceedings' only if: an issue that is the subject of the proceedings is of general public importance; the public interest requires the issue to be resolved; and the proceedings are likely to provide an appropriate means of resolving it, see: section 88(6)(a) and (7), Criminal Justice and Courts Act 2015. Section 88(8) requires the court to consider a number of matters when determining whether proceedings are 'public interest proceedings'. These include: the number of people likely to be directly affected if relief is granted to the applicant for judicial review; how significant the effect on those people is likely to be; and whether the proceedings involve consideration of a point of law of general public importance. Assuming the relevant statutory conditions for making a CCO are met, section 89(1) sets out a (non-exhaustive) list of matters that the court must take into account when considering whether to make a CCO and what the terms of any order should be.

[20] UNECE Convention on Access to Information, Public Participation in Decision-Making and Access to Justice in Environmental Matters done at Aarhus, Denmark on 25 June 1998 ('Aarhus Convention').

[21] Article 9(1), ibid.

[22] Article 9(2), ibid.

which contravene provisions of national law relating to the environment.[23] By virtue of Article 9(4), the access to justice rights under Article 9 must 'be fair, equitable, timely and not prohibitively expensive'. CPR 45.41–45.44 limit the costs exposure of members of the public bringing certain environmental challenges, in order to meet the 'not prohibitively expensive' criterion. Put simply, this means that the amount of costs that can be recovered from the parties in an Aarhus Convention claim is limited to £5,000 for each claimant[24] and £35,000 for each defendant.[25]

Another important part of the context is the availability of, and limitations on, legal aid for judicial review proceedings. When proposing the drastic cuts to civil legal aid which were later made by the Legal Aid, Sentencing and Punishment of Offenders Act 2012 ('LASPO'), the Government explained that it proposed to retain legal aid for judicial review because of its view that: 'proceedings where the litigant is seeking to hold the state to account by judicial review are important, because these cases are the means by which individual citizens can seek to check the exercise of executive power by appeal to the judiciary. These proceedings therefore represent a crucial way of ensuring that state power is exercised responsibly.'[26] Although some limitations were introduced following that consultation for certain immigration and asylum judicial reviews, in the main, legal aid for judicial review remains available in principle in England and Wales. The particular importance of legal aid in the context of the present discussion is that a grant of legal aid to bring judicial review proceedings attracts costs protection, meaning that a legally aided party will not ordinarily be ordered to pay the successful party's costs if his claim fails.[27] However, there are important limitations on the availability of legal aid which must be

[23] Article 9(3), ibid.

[24] This is provided that the claimant is bringing the case only as an individual and not as, or on behalf of, a business or other legal person, in which case the limit is £10,000.

[25] These limits are subject to a claimant's right to opt out of the costs limits pursuant to CPR 45.43. This is also pursuant to the court's power under CPR 45.44. On an application under CPR 45.44 to vary the size of the costs caps, the court will consider whether the likely costs of the case (including own lawyers' costs, court fees and the potential costs of the other side) 'exceed the financial resources of the claimant', or are 'objectively unreasonable' in light of a number of specified factors, including the financial resources available to the claimant. For these purposes, 'financial resources' are treated as including 'any financial support which any person has provided or is likely to provide to the claimant'. The lack of specific provision for hearings on applications to vary the costs caps to be heard in private was the subject of challenge in the recent case of *R (RSPB) v The Lord Chancellor and the Civil Procedure Rules Committee* [2017] EWHC 2309. Dove J. On 13 December 2017, a Practice Direction was published that stated: 'where the Aarhus Convention costs capping arrangements contained in CPR Part 45.43 apply, any application for variation of the costs cap, where it proceeds to a hearing, will be heard *in private* in the first instance'.

[26] Proposals for the Reform of Legal Aid in England and Wales, Consultation Paper CP12/10, Cm7967, para 4.16.

[27] Section 26, Legal Aid, Sentencing and Punishment of Offenders Act 2012.

taken into account. First, applicants must meet stringent financial eligibility criteria.[28] The disposable income and capital thresholds are set at such a level, and calculated in such a way, as to exclude the vast majority of the working population, or anyone with significant assets.[29] Even for those who are financially eligible, there are areas of the country where it is virtually impossible to find a legal aid provider with the appropriate expertise, particularly given the removal of legal aid from so many substantive areas of law.[30] There are significant disincentives for lawyers to take on any but the strongest cases as they may not be paid at all if permission is refused,[31] and the rates of remuneration are uneconomical.[32] The Administrative Court's statistics show that the number of legal aid certificates for judicial review proceedings has declined dramatically in the last few years.[33]

Against this backdrop, there has been an active debate about the costs rules in judicial review in recent years, no doubt given additional energy and urgency by the reforms of the Coalition Government. There have been a number of broad models floated as the optimum approach. Prominent models have included:

- the general cost-shifting rule as set out in CPR 42.2(a) that the losing party to litigation pays the winner's costs;
- where both parties bear their own costs regardless of the outcome of the case (what has been called 'the US rule');
- one-way costs shifting (OCS), where one party will never be required to pay the other's costs, regardless of the outcome, but costs may be awarded in that party's favour;
- qualified one-way costs shifting (QOCS), where one party will not normally be required to pay the other's costs regardless of the outcome, but where that

[28] Section 21, Legal Aid, Sentencing and Punishment of Offenders Act 2012; the Civil Legal Aid (Financial Resources and Payment for Services) Regulations 2013/480.

[29] D. Hirsch, *Priced out of Justice? Means Testing Legal Aid and Making Ends Meet* (The Law Society: London, 2018); Public Law Project, 'The Gap Between the Legal Aid Means Regulations and Financial Reality' (12 July 2018).

[30] There are, for example, only two providers with a public law contract in the North East (in Newcastle-Upon-Tyne and Stockton-on-Tees, respectively); four in Wales (all of which are in South Wales); two in the East of England (in Luton and Cambridge); and none in Devon or Cornwall. See further J. Wilding, *Droughts and Deserts: A Report on the Immigration Legal Aid Market* (2019).

[31] Regulation 5A, Civil Legal Aid (Remuneration) Regulations 2015/898.

[32] The standard hourly rate for work done under a public law legal aid contract is £71.55, subject to an enhancement of up to 100% where the Legal Aid Agency (LAA) is satisfied the work was done with exceptional competence, skill or expertise; exceptional speed; or that the case involved exceptional circumstances or complexity.

[33] FOIA Request No. 171020004.

general rule is qualified, so that costs may be awarded against the party if certain conditions are met; and

- a system of fixed costs, where the costs that can be recovered from the opponent are fixed by reference to the type of claim and stage reached in the proceedings.

The first attempt

Jackson's review of civil litigation costs is now the major bookmark in the unfolding story of the civil procedure rules.[34] His review was wide in scope and judicial review proceedings were included within it, being subject to the same level of probing analysis as other areas of the civil litigation costs.

The *Preliminary Report*, published in May 2009, closely considered the rationale behind the general costs-shifting rule (*i.e.* loser pays), and the extent to which it was apt to deliver justice in judicial review.[35] Jackson observed that Lord Woolf's *Interim Report on Access to Justice* identified two arguments in favour of retaining the rule: it is fairer that a party who succeeds in litigation should at least recover the major proportion of his own costs from his opponent; and that the rule deters unmeritorious litigation and encourages earlier settlement.[36] He also identified three arguments for abandoning the rule: the rule can deter meritorious claims as, because of the uncertainty of litigation, even the meritorious litigant may be deterred from proceeding by the costs risk; the costs shifting rule favours wealthy litigants over the less wealthy; and once litigation is under way, the costs at stake may be so great that the parties feel impelled to press on. Having balanced the conflicting arguments, Lord Woolf favoured retaining the costs shifting rule. Yet he suggested making it more effective by the courts making more focused costs orders rather than simply awarding the winner all of her costs, and by the court actively managing litigation to try to keep costs proportionate. Reflecting on the experience since the Woolf reforms, Jackson concluded that the 'existing cost shifting regime should not be regarded as a "sacred cow", but on the other hand its complete abolition does not appear to be a realistic option for the foreseeable future'.[37]

[34] For historical context, see J. Sorabji, *English Civil Justice after the Woolf and Jackson Reforms: A Critical Analysis* (Cambridge: Cambridge University Press, 2014).

[35] Lord Justice Jackson, *Review of Civil Litigation Costs: Preliminary Report* (2009), Ch. 46.

[36] Lord Woolf, *Access to Justice: Interim Report to the Lord Chancellor on the Civil Justice System in England and Wales* (Lord Chancellor's Department, 1995), Ch. 25.

[37] Lord Justice Jackson, *Preliminary Report* (2009), p. 476.

The *Preliminary Report* further noted various features of judicial review that impact on the level of costs.[38] These features included the requirement for permission before a judicial review claim can be pursued, streamlined statements of case consisting essentially of the claim form and the acknowledgement of service, the lack (in most cases) of a discovery process, the reliance on written evidence alone in most cases, and the potential for claims to be heard quickly. Jackson concluded that 'principal drivers of costs in "heavy" civil litigation are absent from judicial review proceedings' and that the 'consequence is that the costs of judicial review proceedings, although beyond the means of many litigants, are substantially reduced'.[39] He also noted, however, that '[p]roportionality of costs is more difficult to assess in judicial review claims, because the remedies sought cannot generally be quantified in money terms'.[40] Jackson further questioned whether PCOs provided sufficient access to judicial review to those persons of modest means who were not eligible for legal aid, but would not otherwise be able to cover the costs risk of judicial review litigation. Finally, in relation to environmental judicial review claims, Jackson questioned whether PCOs met the access to justice requirements of the Aarhus Convention, and whether one-way costs shifting might offer a better solution.[41] He also raised the possibility of harmonising the costs rules in environmental judicial review claims and all other judicial reviews.

The *Preliminary Report* was the basis for a wide-ranging discussion of civil litigation costs. What is remarkable, however, is the scant evidence that Jackson had to hand in producing the *Preliminary Report*. In respect of judicial review, he relies on rudimentary government data on how many judicial reviews were brought in the Administrative Court in 2007 and 2008, and there is reference to data on the rate of success at permission hearings. Beyond that, reference is made to only anecdotal evidence, such as discussions with judges and practitioners in Toronto. Yet, multiple empirical claims about the nature of judicial review litigation are made, *e.g.*: 'the principal drivers of costs in "heavy" civil litigation are absent from judicial review proceedings'; '[t]he formulation of the grounds of claim for judicial review ordinarily is, or at least should be, quite concise'; '[t]he effect of the permission requirement is that approximately 80% of judicial review claims are weeded out in the early stages. Such claims do not have sufficient prospect of success and they are brought to an end at (usually) modest cost.' To be clear, this is not to criticise Jackson and nor is to

[38] Ibid, Ch. 35.
[39] Ibid, p. 326.
[40] Ibid, p. 325.
[41] Ibid, p. 330–331.

directly challenge the accuracy of these observations. Instead, it is to highlight the clear absence of evidence underpinning the starting point for this significant review exercise. Against the backdrop of a deficient baseline of evidence, the *Preliminary Report*'s consideration of judicial review concluded by inviting engagement from stakeholders.

Responding to Jackson's call for views, Michael Fordham QC and Jessica Boyd called for a system of OCS.[42] Under such a system, the default position would be that a claimant's costs are recoverable from the defendant public authority if the claimant wins (as is the case at present), but the defendant public authority's costs are not recoverable from the claimant if the claimant loses (reversing the current presumption). This would mean that, other than in special categories of case ('at-risk cases'), or unless there is unreasonable conduct in the course of litigation, the claimant would not have to bear the defendant's or an interested party's costs. The rationale offered for this argument was that judicial review is a constitutional protection, which operates in the public interest to hold public authorities to the Rule of Law, and that the general costs-shifting rule acts as a deterrent to claims being brought. This meant that the present rule itself was not in the public interest, given judicial review's constitutional function and that the permission stage serves to weed out poor cases.

Fordham and Boyd further addressed the reasons given by Lord Woolf for retaining the costs-shifting rule, namely that it is fairer that the successful party recover at least some of their costs (which Fordham and Boyd labelled 'the fairness rationale'), it deters unmeritorious litigation ('the deterrence rationale'), and it encourages earlier settlement ('the settlement rationale'). Each of these rationales, it was argued, failed to justify the general costs-shifting rule in the special context of judicial review. In relation to the fairness rationale, Fordham and Boyd argued that the public law scrutiny engendered by judicial review was itself in the public interest, so that it was fair for the state to absorb the cost (by analogy with an ombudsman investigation, a public inquiry or an inquest, none of which are considered to represent an unfair burden for the state to shoulder). Similarly, the settlement rationale did not militate towards the costs-shifting rule in the context of judicial review, because it will always be open to a public body to reconsider its position (in which case the possibility of settlement is limited), and the court will not permit a purely academic claim to proceed. In relation to the deterrence rationale, it was argued first, that the permission stage served to weed out unmeritorious judicial review claims, and second, that the threat of an adverse costs order deterred meritorious claims as

[42] M. Fordham QC and Jessica Boyd, 'Rethinking Costs in Judicial Review' [2009] *Judicial Review* 306.

well as unmeritorious ones, and, given the role of the permission stage, was unnecessary and so disproportionate.

Fordham and Boyd also pointed to shortcomings in the PCO regime, as laid out in *Corner House*, before suggesting that 'the costs rule that best suits, and acknowledges, the nature and purpose of public law proceedings' is OCS.[43] Finally, Fordham and Boyd referred to the need for costs rules that ensured that Aarhus Convention claims were not prohibitively expensive, and argued that whatever solution would be reached for environmental cases, there was an obvious case for applying it to judicial review in general also.

Opposition to Fordham and Boyd came in a response by James Maurici who observed that OCS could not come at a worse time for the UK's recession-hit public authorities, and noted the pressure on the court list that would arise if the deterrent effect of the general costs-shifting rule resulted in more claims and a judge had in every case to determine at permission whether a case would be 'at risk'.[44] Maurici highlights various points in his argument of the lack of a clear evidence base. For instance, when discussing if defendant public authorities actually recover a significant amount of costs when they are ordered at the end of an unsuccessful judicial review: '[w]hat the exact position is in this regard is not known. Anecdotally I would suggest that public bodies do make real efforts to, and have some success in, recovering costs pursuant to orders made in their favour.'[45] Maurici also references some basic general data on the volume of judicial reviews. This leaves Maurici able to make only ball-park claims about the effects of cost rules, however he still accepts 'there is no question that the present rules act as a deterrent. The only question is whether it is right that they should.'[46]

Jackson's *Final Report*, published in December 2009, concluded that QOCS is 'the right way forward'.[47] He suggested six reasons for this. First, it is the simplest and most obvious way to comply with the UK's obligations under the Aarhus Convention in respect of environmental judicial review cases. Second, it is undesirable to have different costs rules for environmental judicial review and other judicial review cases. Third, the permission requirement is an effective filter to weed out unmeritorious cases, therefore two-way costs shifting is not generally necessary to deter frivolous claims. Fourth, it is not in the public interest that potential claimants should be deterred from bringing properly

43 Ibid, p. 309.
44 J. Maurici, 'Rethinking Costs in Judicial Review—A Response' [2009] *Judicial Review* 388.
45 Ibid, p. 388.
46 Ibid, p. 390.
47 Lord Justice Jackson, *Review of Civil Litigation Costs: Final Report* (2009), Ch. 30.

arguable judicial review proceedings by the very considerable financial risks involved. Fifth, OCS in judicial review cases has proved satisfactory in Canada. Sixth, the PCO regime is not effective to protect claimants against excessive costs liability as it is expensive to operate and uncertain in its outcome because, in many instances, the PCO decision comes too late in the proceedings to be of value.[48] In these reasons, we see Jackson accepting many constitutionalist preferences: there is emphasis on access to justice and how the costs rules may act as a barrier in that respect.

Following from this conclusion was the 'more difficult question' of how a 'rule should be formulated, in order to sift out cases where claimants do not merit costs protection'.[49] Jackson ultimately suggested the following rule:

> Costs ordered against the claimant in any claim for personal injuries, clinical negligence or judicial review shall not exceed the amount (if any) which is a reasonable one for him to pay having regard to all the circumstances including:

(a) the financial resources of all the parties to the proceedings, and
(b) their conduct in connection with the dispute to which the proceedings relate.[50]

This is a rule which mirrors the statutory costs protection available to legally aided claimants,[51] and would put non-legally aided claimants in a stronger position than the current principle. As a result, Jackson suggested that, in order to 'strike the right balance as between claimant and defendant in judicial review proceedings', claimants should no longer be able to recover a success fee in claims funded by a conditional fee agreement,[52] and that any success fee must in future be a private matter solely between the claimant and the claimant's solicitor.[53]

The Government response to Jackson's recommendations was published in March 2011.[54] The paper announced that Jackson's proposal for QOCS

[48] Ibid.
[49] Ibid.
[50] Ibid.
[51] Section 26, Legal Aid, Sentencing and Punishment of Offenders Act 2012.
[52] Conditional fee agreements are sometimes referred to as 'no win no fee agreements'. They are agreements between claimants and their lawyers in which the lawyers agree to act in a case on the basis that they will only be paid if the case is successful.
[53] Lord Justice Jackson, *Review of Civil Litigation Costs: Final Report* (2009), Ch. 30.
[54] 'Reforming Civil Litigation Funding and Costs in England and Wales—Implementation of Lord Justice Jackson's Recommendations: The Government Response' (2011, Cm 8041).

had been accepted—but for the time being only in relation to Personal Injury cases[55]—while a decision had been taken to end defendants' liability for success fees in all conditional fee agreement cases.[56] The result was that the balance between judicial review claimants and defendants shifted in favour of the defendant, as the ending of defendants' liability for success fees under conditional fee agreements meant that claimants had to pay any success fees themselves.

The second attempt

In November 2016, Jackson announced that he had been commissioned by the Lord Chief Justice and the Master of the Rolls to carry out a further review of civil litigation costs to consider proposals for extending the use of fixed recoverable costs. As part of this continuation, a working group was set up under the chairmanship of Martin Westgate QC.[57] The group was charged with 'work[ing] up the detail of a model based on the current regime for Aarhus claims that could be applicable to judicial review claims more generally'.[58] This was an attempt to find another solution to the accessibility issues identified in the first report. Perhaps the extension of a regime already applicable to some judicial reviews (environmental cases) could serve as a more palatable policy.

The Westgate Report was published together with Jackson's *Supplementary Report* in July 2017.[59] It identified two problems with the Aarhus scheme from the claimant's perspective; that the £5,000 costs limit on claimants was too high and that the £35,000 costs limit on defendants was too low. As a flexible approach to those costs limits would add uncertainty (which itself could be a chilling factor on claims), a majority of the group expressed a preference for QOCS, rather than a version of the Aarhus model. That said, the Group agreed that a version of the Aarhus model would be an advance for general judicial review claimants on the current position. The group concluded unanimously that the caps should not apply to legally aided claims, so that legally aided claimants should retain *de facto* costs protection. By a majority, it was agreed

[55] The Government said it was 'not persuaded' the case for extending QOCS beyond personal injury 'has been made out at this stage' and it would 'examine the experience of QOCS in personal injury claims before considering whether it should be extended further'.

[56] This included judicial reviews, even though Jackson's recommendation that success fees should not be payable by defendants in judicial review cases was expressly justified by the introduction of qualified one-way costs shifting to achieve 'balance'.

[57] Alison Pickup was a member of this working group.

[58] Lord Justice Jackson, *Review of Civil Litigation Costs: Supplemental Report, Fixed Recoverable Costs* (2017), Appendix 16.

[59] Ibid.

that caps should be capable of being varied on application, with such application being made before permission and (subject to one exception) decided at the same time as permission.[60]

Jackson's *Supplementary Report* again emphasised judicial review's constitutional role and the importance of ensuring access to judicial review.[61] He concluded that, even though many judicial review cases fall into a standard pattern, costs are too variable to permit the introduction of a grid of fixed recoverable costs. Jackson further concluded that CCOs are of little practical value, because the procedure for obtaining such orders is too cumbersome and too expensive, the criteria for granting CCOs are unacceptably wide so that the outcome of any application must be uncertain, and will not be known until too late in the litigation process. It was suggested that there was merit in extending the Aarhus Rules, suitably amended, to all judicial review claims. The fact that most judicial review cases fall into a standard pattern was said to make it possible to set default figures as caps, even though it is not practicable to draw up a grid of fixed recoverable costs. On the Westgate Report, Jackson observed that it 'neatly identifies the issues and the conflicting views within the profession'.[62] He accepted the 'general thrust of that report, although not all its specific recommendations'.[63] He recorded the view of government lawyers, expressed at a meeting with him on 19 April 2017, that 'that there is no access to justice problem which needs to be addressed. The CCO regime together with the current Aarhus Rules for environmental cases provide sufficient protection for impecunious claimants in JR.'[64] Despite this opposition, Jackson recommended that 'if QOCS in JR is not acceptable, the Aarhus Rules should be extended to all [judicial review] claims'.[65] This, it was said, is necessary in order to increase access to justice and to promote the public interest, while accepting that 'it is both tiresome and expensive for hard pressed public authorities to face (as they do) . . . a stream of unmeritorious claims . . . and a much smaller number of meritorious claims'.[66]

[60] The exception relates to the situation where a defendant or interested party lodges evidence or other material that significantly increases the work required to be done on behalf of the claimant beyond that which was reasonably anticipated at the permission stage. A majority of the group also considered that in that situation, the claimant should be able to apply post-permission to increase the cap on the costs recoverable from the defendant.

[61] Lord Justice Jackson, *Review of Civil Litigation Costs: Supplemental Report, Fixed Recoverable Costs* (2017).

[62] Ibid, p.129.

[63] Ibid.

[64] Ibid, p.128.

[65] Ibid, p.129.

[66] Ibid.

In 2019, the Ministry of Justice produced a consultation paper setting out, amongst other proposals, what it intends to do in respect of Jackson's latest recommendations concerning judicial review.[67] First, it is important to note that the response is premised on a clear government view that it does not consider there to be an access to justice issue in respect of non-Aarhus judicial reviews (echoing the view expressed to Jackson by government lawyers during preparation of the Supplemental Report). In starting from this point, they begin from a substantially different assumption than that of Jackson. There are, essentially, three noteworthy elements of the proposals. First, there is the rejection of the latest recommendation on costs rules on the basis that '[e]xtending cost capping increases the risk of less meritorious JRs coming forward with increased costs to the government and other public-sector defendants'. Second, there is the planned implementation of the recommendation that there should be costs budgeting for 'heavier' judicial reviews over £100k. Third, there is a suggestion that there will be a future proposal to introduce fixed costs in respect of immigration judicial review in the Upper Tribunal (Immigration and Asylum Chamber).[68]

In essence, this new response to Jackson is another attempt to cherry-pick recommendations and a straightforward failure to engage with two tranches of independent proposals, even when a considered reformulation of those proposals has taken place. Sir Rupert Jackson's review took eight months to complete, took in over 140 responses, and involved public debate and engagement. The Government offered no evidence for the position it adopted against Jackson's proposals save for a meeting where government lawyers put forward reservations about reform. When asked to produce the record of this meeting, there was none.[69]

Conclusion

After repeated attempts, undertaken by way of an independent review by a senior judge, to formulate recommendations which improve the accessibility of

[67] Ministry of Justice, *Extending Fixed Recoverable Costs in Civil Cases: Implementing Sir Rupert Jackson's proposals* (28 March 2019).

[68] For a fuller analysis of the proposals than we are able to provide in this chapter, see Public Law Project, 'Submission to the Ministry of Justice's consultation 'Extending Fixed Recoverable Costs in Civil Cases: Implementing Sir Rupert Jackson's Proposals' (2019).

[69] The exact response was: '[a]t the meeting handwritten notes were taken, rather than there being actual minutes (of which none were taken). These notes summarised the key points of the meeting, however due to the meeting being around two years ago, the handwritten notes cannot be located, despite a thorough search having been carried out', see M. Fouzder, 'MoJ can't find key Jackson costs note' (*The Law Society Gazette*, 15 July 2019).

judicial review for claimants, the position of claimants has, if anything, worsened. Over a sustained period of time, the Ministry of Justice has demonstrated a determination to actively disengage with the prospect of reforming the judicial review costs rules. In this respect, Jackson has for the most part found himself speaking at a policy brick wall. This situation is a product of the underlying constitutional and institutional arrangements that create a dynamic where the government is both key designer of and the main 'repeat player' party in the judicial review process. Under such arrangements, proper policy engagement presupposes a virtuous government which is open to acting in a way which may be against immediate self-interest and political preferences (*i.e.* to reduce costs and delay) in the pursuit of good government. When that supposition falls away, so do the foundations of progress. At present, the prospects for reform appear dim.

PART VI

COSTS AND FUNDING

16

The Overriding Principles of Affordable and Expeditious Adjudication

Rabeea Assy

Introduction

Law enforcement lies at the foundation of any legal system governed by the rule of law. Rights have little value for their holders if they are not adequately enforced.[1] Without a robust and accessible system of resolving disputes according to public, stable, and pre-established rules, communities will find it difficult to escape the state of nature, maintain social order, and justify the state's monopoly over the use of force.[2] Courts do not maintain social order merely by resolving disputes peacefully. Rather, they declare legal rights and grant remedies that can be enforced with the help of state agencies and, when needed, by using force.[3] Convenient access to courts is therefore a critical requirement of the

[1] Jeremy Bentham observed that the function of procedural law is to apply the correct substantive law to the true facts of the case. This, he insisted, is the *only* defensible function of procedural law. See *The Works of Jeremy Bentham*, ed J Bowring (William Tait, Edinburgh 1838–43) vol 2 at 5–6: 'For in jurisprudence, the laws termed adjective, can no more exist without the laws termed substantive, than in grammar a noun termed adjective, can present a distinct idea without the help of a noun of the substantive class, conjoined with it. As in fact every act by which a course of procedure is commenced has for its end or object, the bringing about the execution of some law of the substantive class, so, in point of utility, it may be said that the course of procedure ought to have in every instance, for its main and primary end at least, the accomplishment of the will manifested in the body of substantive laws. For this is not only a use of it, but the only use for it. . . . Of the adjective branch of the law, the only defensible object, or say end in view, is the maximization of the execution and effect given to the substantive branch of the law'; see also vol 6 at 7: 'The *adjective* branch of law, or *law of procedure*, and therein the *law of evidence*, has everywhere for its object, at least ought to have, the giving effect throughout to the several regulations and arrangements of which the *substantive branch* or *main body* of the law is composed' (emphasis in original).

[2] See FA Hayek, *The Road to Serfdom* (Chicago University Press 1944) 85–6: 'Stripped of all technicalities [the rule of law] means that government in all its actions is bound by rules fixed and announced beforehand—rules which make it possible to foresee with fair certainty how the authority will use its coercive powers in given circumstances, and to plan one's individual affairs on the basis of this knowledge.' See also L Fuller, *The Morality of Law*, 2nd ed, (Yale University Press 1969).

[3] See, eg, D Luban, *Lawyers and Justice: An Ethical Study* (Princeton University Press 1988); S Issacharoff, *Civil Procedure*, 3rd ed (Foundation Press 2012); K Scott, 'Two Models of the Civil Process' (1975) 27 *Stanford Law Review* 937.

Rabeea Assy, *The Overriding Principles of Affordable and Expeditious Adjudication* In: *The Civil Procedure Rules at 20.* Edited by: Andrew Higgins, Oxford University Press (2020). © the several contributors.
DOI: 10.1093/oso/9780198863182.003.0016.

rule of law.[4] It is necessary also to maintain a social environment sufficiently conducive to economic prosperity and welfare.[5] Individuals can lead autonomous lives, make short- and long-term plans, pursue their own desires and careers, or otherwise develop as autonomous agents, only if they can know with reasonable certainty what the legal consequences of their actions are.[6]

Inevitably, however, law enforcement is time consuming and requires financial resources from litigants and legal system alike. The more accurate we want court judgments to be, the more thorough and complex the process has to be. Pursuing high levels of accuracy is therefore likely to render the process expensive and lengthy, sometimes disproportionately to the value of the case. Such a process, however, is no less harmful to the rule of law than an erroneous judgment, because it is likely to deter litigants from pursuing rights enforcement in the first place.

The tension between the pursuit of accurate outcomes and the need to save resources has been a corrupting force in the design of many legal systems, including the English system. Indeed, as Jeremy Bentham put it:

> When the whole body of the Law has for its object the greatest happiness of the greatest number, the whole of the adjective branch taken together may be said to have two specific ends: the one *positive*, maximizing the execution and effect given to the substantive branch; the other *negative*, minimizing the evil, the hardship in various shapes necessary to the accomplishment of the main specified end. Between these two pursuits the conflict is all pervading and perpetual. Whatsoever arrangement is taken for the attainment of the one

[4] J Raz, 'The Rule of Law and its Virtue' (1977) 93 *Law Quarterly Review* 195, 217: 'The courts should be easily accessible. Given the central position of the courts in ensuring the rule of law . . . it is obvious that their accessibility is of paramount importance. Long delays, excessive costs, etc, may effectively turn the most enlightened law to a dead letter and frustrate one's ability effectively to guide oneself by the law.'

[5] See, eg, Lord Neuberger, 'Justice in an Age of Austerity', Tom Sargant Memorial Lecture, 15 October 2013, para 5: 'The defence of the realm from abroad and maintaining the rule of law at home are the two sole traditional duties of a government. More importantly, they are fundamental. If we are not free from invasion, or the rule of law breaks down, then social security, health, and education become valueless, or at any rate very severely devalued.' (Available at: https://2bquk8cdew6192tsu41lay8t-wpengine.netdna-ssl.com/wp-content/uploads/2015/02/Justice-in-an-age-of-austerity-Lord-Neuberger.pdf).

[6] See, eg, F Michelman, 'Formal and Associational Aims in Procedural Due Process' in R Pennock and J Chapman (eds), *Nomos: Due Process*, vol 18 (New York University Press 1977) 126, 129: 'According to [a positivistic and libertarian] model, all allowable impairments of our immediate freedom are clearly set out in general rules emanating from a legislative sovereign whose rule-enactments can be seen as somehow embodying our more fundamental and comprehensive consent. The rules thus have a double aspect. By their very effect of staking out the limits of each person's guaranteed freedom, they also stake out zones of autonomy wherein each is protected from exposure to unpredictable, arbitrary or discretionary interferences by others. In this model, the only, but necessary, job of judges is to make sure that the rules are applied as enacted.' See also R Assy, *Injustice in Person: The Right to Self-Representation* (Oxford University Press 2015) ch 7.

end, it can scarcely avoid being in a greater or less degree obstructive to the attainment of the other end.[7] (emphasis in original)

Compromise is therefore required. Balancing and prioritising are inevitable. Furthermore, there is no one-size-fits-all point of balance between the competing imperatives of justice, namely: accurate judgments, reasonable costs, and reasonable duration. The optimal point of balance may depend on various cultural, social, or legal conditions; it may also vary within a single jurisdiction, depending on the type of case in question, its importance to the parties, the presence of a special public interest, and so on.[8]

Nevertheless, while the precise balance can differ from one context to another, the overriding principles of both grand design and ad hoc management must be clear and sharp, and capable of being consistently applied by judges. Such clarity of principle is urgently needed also because it is easier to agree on a vague and general principle that the pursuit of accurate judgments must be restricted by considerations of resources, than to agree on the degree to which we are prepared to forsake accuracy in favour of quick and inexpensive resolutions.

The traditional approach against which the Civil Procedure Rules 1998 (CPR) was conceived is that the duty to arrive at correct outcomes is the ultimate duty of court, to which considerations of time and cost are secondary. Such a 'justice on the merits' approach that permits the pursuit of accurate judgments regardless of the cost or duration of litigation is no longer sustainable. It cannot be justified merely by pointing to the old days of 'forms of action' where the slightest technical defect could have nullified the whole process, causing great injustice and immense waste.[9] The need to depart from rigid formalism should not necessarily lead to rigid 'substantialism' (so to speak), that is, policies preferring substance over form at all time and at any cost. Legal systems must recognise that justice is multi-dimensional. That is, cost and

[7] *The Works of Jeremy Bentham* (n 1) vol 2 at 8.

[8] While this chapter focuses on the need to make additional sacrifices in the pursuit of accuracy to promote expedition and affordability, sacrifices in accuracy have been defended also to promote other values, such as judicial integrity, human dignity, bodily integrity, good name, personal autonomy, political legitimacy, and social acceptability; see discussion in Rabeea Assy, 'Taking Seriously Accuracy, Expedition, and Integrity in Adjudication' in Rabeea Assy and Andrew Higgins (eds), *Principles, Procedure, and Justice: Essays in Honour of Adrian Zuckerman* (Oxford University Press 2020). On the relationship between procedure, culture, and tradition, see H Patrick Glenn, *Legal Traditions of the World*, 3rd edn (Oxford University Press 2007).

[9] For a concise description of forms of action, see F Maitland, *Equity: Also the Forms of Action at Common Law* (Cambridge University Press 1910). On the rigidness of this system, see WB Odgers, 'Changes in Procedure and in the Law of Evidence' in *A Century of Law Reform* (Macmillan and Co 1901) 203.

time should be no longer be treated as unfortunate side-effects in the course of achieving justice on the merits; they must be treated as intrinsic components of the definition of justice, just as accuracy of outcome is. The fundamental right of access to justice must be taken to mean access to an effective and convenient system of adjudication that provides an appropriate balance between the three imperatives of justice in the legal process: a correct judgment, within a reasonable time, and at a reasonable cost.[10]

Arriving at this conclusion is just a starting point. For legal systems to meet the needs of its users, they must take the multi-dimensional nature of justice seriously and be ready to embrace its far-reaching implications. This chapter argues that it is now time to pursue affordable and timely resolution of conflicts more ambitiously than before. To this end, it argues that affordability and timeliness should be treated as overriding principles both in the design of procedural systems and in the management of cases by courts. This can have far-reaching implications not only for judicial discretion on case management, procedural default, or time limits, but also for procedural design as a whole.

Affordability and timeliness as overriding principles

Statement of principles

Rule 1 of the CPR employs a principle of proportionality as part of its definition of what a just process is.[11] Under this principle, courts are required to allocate resources to cases in proportion to the value of the case, its importance, its complexity, and the financial positions of the parties. However, these criteria are open-ended and potentially conflicting, rendering such a proportionality test all but meaningless.[12] The absence of a clear and coherent principle leaves judges with no concrete guidance on how to determine proportionality,

[10] The most passionate articulator of this approach has been Adrian Zuckerman: A Zuckerman, 'Justice in Crisis: Comparative Dimensions of Civil Procedure' in A Zuckerman (ed), *Civil Justice in Crisis* (Oxford University Press 1999) 3; A Zuckerman, 'Quality and Economy in Civil Procedure The Case for Commuting Correct Judgments for Timely Judgments' (1994) 14 *Oxford Journal of Legal Studies* 353; A Zuckerman, *Civil Procedure: Principles of Practice*, 3rd edn (Sweet & Maxwell 2013) esp chs 1, 2, and 11.

[11] The Australian state of Victoria has followed suit and incorporated a similar principle in its procedural code; Civil Procedure Act 2010 (Victoria, Australia) sections 7, 24, 25.

[12] For a useful analysis of the proportionality requirement, see A Higgins and A Zuckerman, 'Lord Justice Brigg's "SWOT" Analysis Underlines English Law's Troubled Relationship with Proportionate Costs' (2017) 36 *Civil Justice Quarterly* 1.

which is likely to produce inconsistency and unpredictability—in other words, a judge-dependent style of implementation. Moreover, the current definition of proportionality does not rule out a scenario in which the resources allocated are beyond the reach of either or both litigants, since the financial means of the parties constitutes just one consideration among others.

In order for the conceptualisation of cost and time as *dimensions* of justice—or as components of the *definition* of justice—to mean anything more than a plea for eliminating waste, the proportionality test should be replaced by tests for affordability and expedition. When affordability and expedition are prioritised as overriding objectives that can be pursued independently of accurate judgment, courts will be expected to ensure that litigation remains within the financial reach of litigants and that it concludes within a short time. This means that the court must avoid unaffordable spending or lengthy litigation even when these might otherwise be justified by the features of the case in question, such as its value, complexity, importance, etc. Rather than ask how much time or money a given case deserves based on the features of the case itself, the court should focus instead mainly on the financial and temporal resources available to the parties, and aspire to achieve the most accurate result within these constraints.

Possible implications for costs

A strong commitment to affordability may require us to challenge the toxic combination of unrestricted hourly fees and cost-shifting. As is well known, this combination has substantially increased cost liability, sometimes beyond the amount at stake, thus creating a chilling effect and intimidating litigants from bringing their meritorious claims forward.[13] Prioritising affordability

[13] See, eg, G Cookson, *Unintended Consequences: The Cost of the Government's Legal Aid Reforms* (A Report for the Law Society of England and Wales, November 2011) [1.5], estimating the financial cost of the unintended consequences of the legal aid cuts to be at least £139 million per annum, rendering the government savings less than half those predicted (available at: <http://www. kcl.ac.uk/campuslife/student/news/stories/UnintendedConsequences-FinalReport.pdf>). See also *Access to Justice and Legal Needs: Legal Australia-Wide Survey* (Law and Justice Foundation of NSW, August 2012) at xvi, finding that in all the jurisdictions surveyed, legal problems often have considerable adverse impacts on a broad range of life circumstances, including health, financial, and social circumstances: over half of the respondents with legal problems (55%) in Australia as a whole had a 'substantial' legal problem that had a 'severe' or 'moderate' impact on their everyday life. The most common adverse consequences resulting from the legal problems experienced by Australian LAW Survey respondents were income loss or financial strain (29%), followed by stress-related illness (20%) and physical ill health (19%); relationship breakdown (10%) and moving home (5%) were also evident (available at: <http://www.lawfoundation.net.au/ljf/site/templates/LAW_AUS/$file/ LAW_Survey_Australia.pdf>).

enables us to reconsider both the cost-shifting rule and lawyers' freedom to charge as they like—such as by regulating legal fees or limiting recoverable costs to fixed and relatively low tariffs, as in Germany.[14] Such modifications may become legitimate even if they risk lowering the quality of legal representation and, as a result, reducing the legal system's ability to achieve an accurate outcome.

Moreover, the cost shifting rule has an expressive dimension that may impact the social meaning of litigation and access to court. Whether a prevailing litigant should be able to recover her costs from the opponent (generally the English rule), or whether each litigant must bear her own costs irrespective of the outcome (generally the American rule), have been typically assessed by comparing their direct effects on access to justice: which rule better encourages litigants with meritorious claims, deters those with frivolous ones, and enables those with limited financial means to bring their claims forward. But more can be said about these rules if we focus on their attitude towards access to justice, independently of their direct consequences.

Each such rule can be said to make a different statement on what access to justice means. Arguably, the cost-shifting rule applies a tort law logic that treats the losing party as a wrongdoer liable for damages—the wrongdoing being going to court and losing. This expresses a value judgment: an adverse outcome delegitimises commencing proceedings. Furthermore, the social meaning of losing in court is presumably different when the law attaches a negative financial consequence to it, potentially lending it a negative connotation of blame and disapproval. By contrast, the American rule legitimises losing in court by treating it as an irrelevant factor in allocating costs, which correspondingly acknowledges and respects people's capacity to engage in genuine disputes whatever the outcome. Here, making costs orders only against litigants who bring frivolous claims can convey disapproval of *that* behaviour.

Possible implications for the right to legal representation

Prioritising affordability could trigger a discussion of the limits of the right to legal representation. Under the proposed new framework, it becomes legitimate to wonder whether this right could be restricted in appropriate

[14] See, eg, P Murray and R Stürner, *German Civil Justice* (Carolina Academic Press 2004) 112–23, 239–45, 626–8; G Wagner, 'Litigation Costs and their Recovery: The German Experience' (2009) 28 *Civil Justice Quarterly* 367; B Hess and R Heubner, 'Cost and Fee Allocation in German Civil Procedure' in M Reimann (ed), *Cost and Fee Allocation in Civil Procedure* (Springer 2012) 151.

circumstances where this helps to achieve a cheaper and quicker outcome, or to eliminate inequalities between parties. Although the right to legal representation has been recognised as an important procedural safeguard and as an integral part of the right to fair trial,[15] there can be circumstances that justify subjecting this right to some restrictions. In some countries, for example, legal representation is prohibited in small claims court.[16]

In the same vein, it may be time to challenge the present scope of professional monopoly and adopt a more liberal scheme of lay representation, to the extent that doing so could enhance competition in the market for legal services and reduce the cost of legal services, including those provided by lawyers. The typical justifications for lawyer monopoly are customer protection and public interest. In return for monopoly, lawyers are expected to satisfy professional and ethical standards. Threats to the monopoly are therefore resisted for fear of a race to the bottom and of undermining the adjudication process and the values served by a law-enforcing court. While self-interest and self-preservation are likely to play a role in reinforcing the profession's monopoly, the high commitment to accurate law-enforcement provides the necessary rhetoric.

However, the principle of affordability requires assessment of the monopoly also by its impact on affordability. High representation fees undermine the rule of law and, when unaffordable, also create inequality that undermine the court's ability to deliver accurate judgments to all. While this can be partially addressed through improved price transparency, fee regulation, cost capping, legal aid or legal insurance, there is no reason to adhere to the dichotomy of representation as either in person or through lawyers. A more diverse and competitive market where non-lawyers can provide representation services should be explored. Such a market may exert down-pressure on lawyers' fees[17], and can lead to new solutions for litigants who cannot afford lawyers or whose cases are not economically attractive to lawyers. Not all areas of law require comprehensive knowledge of the law, so in certain types of cases trained and experienced non-lawyers may be able to deliver a reasonable service, even if lawyers could do better.

[15] See *Airey v Ireland* (1979) 2 EHRR 305; *Golder v UK* (1975) 1 EHRR 524.

[16] See, eg, California Code of Civil Procedure s 116.530; Revised Code of Washington s 12.40.080; Nebraska Revised Statute 25-2803; Magistrates Court Act 1991 s 38(4) (South Australia); Victorian Civil and Administrative Tribunal Act 1998 s 78. In England and Wales, however, legal representation is permitted as a matter of right; see in general CPR Pt 27.

[17] This was the effect of reforms allowing non-lawyers to do conveyances; see S Domberger and A Sherr, 'The Impact of Competition on Pricing and Quality of Legal Services' (1989) 9 *International Review of Law and Economics* 41.

This is not such a radical idea as may appear at first sight. Some de-monopolisation of the legal profession has been implemented in a number of places, including in England and Wales. For example, certain out-of-court activities can be performed by non-lawyers, such as the provision of legal advice (which is generally prohibited in the US), or conveyancing (buying and selling real estate property).[18] Furthermore, English courts have developed the instrument of a 'McKenzie Friend', which started as permission granted for self-representing litigants to have a supportive friend or relative in the courtroom, but has been extended to include permission to address the court. While still unregulated, a market of fee-charging lay assistances has developed notwithstanding the hesitance demonstrated by English courts in granting permissions to fee-charging lay assistants.[19]

Lay participation in the representation market is becoming popular in additional jurisdictions. The liberalisation of litigation-related activities is becoming increasingly topical in the US through discussion of 'unbundled services',[20] and the Washington Supreme Court's certification scheme of 'Limited License Legal Technicians', who may assist litigants in family disputes by completing paper work and navigating the system.[21] In Ontario Canada, the Law Society has started to train and license paralegals with power to represent in small-claims or specific administrative boards and tribunals.[22]

Even in civil law systems, where mandatory legal representation is widespread,[23] some jurisdictions have endorsed the idea of lay participation. In Sweden, for example, the Code of Judicial Procedure (*rättegångsbalken*)

[18] Ibid; *Conveyancing Services Market* (CERO COMP/2006/D3/003 Study for the European Commission 2007) available at: http://ec.europa.eu/competition/sectors/professional_services/studies/csm_study_complete.pdf.

[19] *Fee-Charging McKenzie Friends* (Legal Services Consumer Panel, April 2014) available online at: http://www.legalservicesconsumerpanel.org.uk/publications/research_and_reports/documents/2014%2004%2017%20MKF_Final.pdf; *Practice Guidance: McKenzie Friends* (Civil and Family Court) [2012] 2 FLR 962 available online at: http://www.judiciary.gov.uk/wp-content/uploads/JCO/Documents/Guidance/mckenzie-friends-practice-guidance-july-2010.pdf; R Moorhead, 'Access or Aggravation? Litigants in Person, McKenzie Friends and Lay Representation' (2003) 22 *Civil Justice Quarterly* 133.

[20] J. Charn, 'Legal Services for All: Is the Profession Ready' (2009) 42 *Loyola of Los Angeles Law Review* 1021.

[21] https://www.wsba.org/for-legal-professionals/join-the-legal-profession-in-wa/limited-license-legal-technicians; R. Zorza and D. Udell, 'New Roles for Non-Lawyers to Increase Access to Justice' (2014) 41 *Fordham Urban Law Journal* 1259.

[22] *Report to the Attorney General of Ontario: Pursuant to Section 63.1 of the Law Society Act* (Law Society of Upper Canada, 2012) available at: http://lawsocietygazette.ca/wp-content/uploads/2012/07/Paralegal-5-year-Review.pdf.

[23] For a comparative and theoretical analyses of the right to self-representation and the duty to be represented by lawyers, see Rabeea Assy, *Injustice in Person: The Right to Self-Representation* (Oxford University Press 2015).

empowers courts to permit non-lawyers to represent in court, even on a fee-charging basis.[24]

* * *

To be sure, the proposals mentioned above in relation to costs and lay representation merely express initial thoughts that can be contemplated under a conceptual framework that treats affordability and expedition as imperatives of justice in adjudication. Such a framework paves the path for implementing bold and unorthodox measures that go beyond modest exercises of eliminating unnecessary waste through case management. Any such measure, however, may be fraught with risks and disadvantages that require careful and detailed assessment of their own merits. For example, any discussion of the liberalisation of legal representation must pay attention to such questions as: whether a system of certification should be applied, and if so, what code of conduct lay assistants should follow; how consumers can be protected, and whether an insurance market could develop; the type of cases in which lay representation can be permitted; and the role of judicial supervision over the activities of lay representatives.

Accurate judgments and the measurability bias

While accuracy of judgments is usually the ultimate aspiration of judges, the truth is that accuracy is an unnatural term in this context. This is because the truthfulness of judgments delivered by courts is neither measurable nor verifiable, especially in relation to factual findings, which can only be ascertained as a matter of probability.[25] Questions of law and interpretation, too, are often uncertain, and disagreements about them can be prevalent and intense.[26]

[24] However, various incentives are created to encourage litigants to choose lawyers (eligibility for legal aid or legal insurance is, for instance, reserved for lawyers). See *rättegångsbalken* (1942:740) ch 12 ss 1, 2, 5, and 22; for administrative proceedings, see *förvaltningsprocesslagen* (1971:291) s 48. See also Statens offentliga utredningar 1926:31 pp. 198–210 (especially pp. 209–10), Statens offentliga utredningar 1938:44 pp. 19–21, proposition 1931:80 pp. 101–2, proposition 1942:5 pp. 369 and 478, Ekelöf, Edelstam & Pauli, Rättegång – andra häftet (Norstedts Juridik: 2015) pp. 81–4, Ekelöf, Edelstam, Heuman & Pauli, Rättegång – första häftet (Wolters Kluwer: 2016) pp. 217–22 and Wejedal, Rätten till biträde (Juridiska institutionens skriftserie, Handelshögskolan vid Göteborgs universitet: 2017) pp. 922–6.

[25] See K Popper, *The Logic of Scientific Discovery* (Routledge edition 2002); LJ Cohen, *The Probable and the Provable* (Oxford University Press 1977).

[26] See discussion of Hart and Fuller's views on whether legal rules have a clear 'core', or whether uncertainties are typical only of the 'fringes' of rules, in F Schauer, *Thinking Like a Lawyer* (Harvard University Press 2009) 151–8.

Thus, we can measure neither the level of accuracy that current procedures achieve, nor the loss of accuracy that policies pursuing fast and affordable litigation enable (if at all). These variables are uncertain and unquantifiable, which is further complicated by the fact that the adjudication process is sometimes expected to serve additional objectives—beyond the mere application of substantive law—that are themselves imprecise and therefore immeasurable (eg integrity or good faith).[27] This creates fertile ground for controversy regarding the extent to which a given process delivers, and on what promises.

Unlike outcome accuracy, the cost and duration of litigation are generally measurable. This renders the principles of affordability and expedition attractive and easy to use, and policies promoting them easier to assess and control. But there is more to this than meets the eye. Difficulties may arise if we adopt broad definitions of cost and time that incorporate such factors as the social and economic cost of erroneous judgments for the litigants and other relevant non-parties, or the detrimental impact of continuous uncertainty pending final resolution. For instance, a mistaken decision to shut down a factory or a decision that establishes a misguided rule of law may affect many more people than just the direct litigants. Litigation also creates additional, indirect costs for litigants who must delay certain decisions or purchases until a case has been decided (eg family members, investors who want to purchase a property whose ownership is disputed, children in a divorce case, etc).

For affordability to be reasonably measurable, we must use a narrow interpretation of the cost and time factors. The cost factor should be limited to the direct costs incurred by parties in carrying out the actual court proceedings (mainly court fees and fees for lawyers and experts). Likewise, the time factor should be limited to the length of the actual court proceedings. However, even under such narrow definitions, controversies may still arise regarding what counts as affordable or timely, and from whose perspective: the claimant's? the defendant's? the average person's (whoever they may be)?

More fundamentally, one might object by arguing that the fact that a factor is easier to measure does not necessarily make it a more desirable or appropriate measure. The ranking of scientific journals, for instance, has been criticised precisely on the ground that impact factor does not fully capture academic novelty and contribution.[28] The seduction of quantification has been resisted in several contexts. Arguably, numbers cannot capture the intangible value of,

[27] See Assy (n 8).

[28] See, eg, R Perry, 'The Relative Value of American Law Reviews: A Critical Appraisal of Ranking Methods' (2006) 11 *Virginia Journal of Law and Technology* 1.

say, human rights or intellectual development, and their seemingly objective nature is a fallacy used to disguise agendas and subjective beliefs.[29]

In approaching this criticism, however, it is important to remind ourselves of what cost and time stand for. Whether or not the frequency of citation serves as an adequate proxy for assessing academic contribution, the length of and the expenses incurred during litigation are not proxies or indicators for measuring other objectives. They are themselves criteria for measuring the quality of the process. If cost and time are dimensions of justice, then the numbers do matter, and the costs and the time spent on any given proceeding become criteria for measuring the quality of such a process. There can be no doubt that expensive and lengthy proceedings are bad in and of themselves and should be avoided; no intangible value lies in them. The pressing question concerns the price—in terms of accuracy—that we are willing to pay to avoid them.

Nevertheless, measurability gives rise to two serious problems which are important to note. The first is how to strike a balance between immeasurable (accurate judgments) and measurable parameters (time/cost), which poses a potential problem of incommensurability.[30] The second problem is how to avoid the temptation and convenience of focusing on the measurable (cost/time) at the expense of the immeasurable (accuracy). Excessive focus on what is measurable may blind us to the value of the immeasurable. In other words, measurability creates a practical bias and temptation for focusing disproportionately on convenient and easy to use numbers.[31]

Curiously, current legal systems have traditionally avoided the potential risk of preferring the measurable to the immeasurable, tending to focus more on accuracy than on affordability and expedition. But this is changing. Ongoing attempts to optimise the administration of courts require that judges be responsible for managing their own cases. Concerns have arisen, however, that during this process, judges have become less worried about resolving disputes

[29] See, eg, Sally Merry, *The Seductions of Quantification: Measuring Human Rights, Gender Violence, and Sex Trafficking* (University of Chicago Press 2016).

[30] For a general discussion of incommensurability and for possible techniques to address it, see R Chang (ed), *Incommensurability, Incomparability, and Practical Reason* (Harvard University Press 1977); D Luban, 'Incommensurable Values, Rational Choice, and Moral Absolutes' (1990) 38 *Cleveland State Law Review* 65; J Waldron, 'Fake Incommensurability: A Response to Professor Schauer' (1993) 45 *Hastings Law Journal* 813; F Urbina, 'Incommensurability and Balancing' (2015) 35 *Oxford Journal of Legal Studies* 575.

[31] On a potential bias in favour of measurable factors, see discussion in M Nussbaum, 'The Costs of Tragedy: Some Moral Limits of the Cost-Benefit Analysis' (2000) 29 *Journal of Legal Studies* 1005; F Ackerman and L Heinzerling, 'Pricing the Priceless: Cost-benefit Analysis of Environmental Protection' (2002) 150 *University of Pennsylvania Law Review* 1553; H Richardson, *Practical Reasoning about Final Ends* (Cambridge University Press 1994); L Caviola et al, 'The Evaluability Bias in Charitable Giving: Saving Administration Costs or Saving Lives?' (2014) 9 *Judgment and Decision Making* 303.

correctly than they are about how their dockets look and how to speed through cases as quickly as possible.

The upshot of this discussion is that defining justice in a multi-dimensional fashion raises several questions and challenges that require detailed assessment and exploration. Nevertheless, the re-conceptualisation of time and cost as dimensions of justice can serve an expressive function, conveying a clear message that courts should prioritise timeliness and affordability more vigorously than they do currently.

Conclusion

This chapter has argued that it is self-defeating to pursue law enforcement through an exaggerated commitment to judgment accuracy, because this is likely to result in lengthy and expensive litigation that will deter many from seeking enforcement in the first place. Lengthy and expensive litigation can distort justice also by subjecting the process to economic inequalities and by forcing the parties to make substantial sacrifices in terms of resources. Delayed or expensive judgments are as unjust as wrong judgments. Law enforcement is therefore not served by a high commitment to accurate judgments. Terminating the uncertainty concerning the legal rights of the litigants through affordable and expeditious resolution has value that is independent of outcome accuracy; it simply enables people to move on with their lives. This realisation can trigger discussion of ambitious schemes for achieving quick and cheap litigation, with far reaching implications for both procedural design and judicial case management.

17

The Long Struggle for Fixed Cost Reform

John Sorabji

Introduction

Litigation cost and effective funding remain today, as they were at the time of the tenth anniversary of the Civil Procedure Rules (CPR), matters of considerable concern.[1] By November 2008, concerns over the continuing high level of litigation costs had prompted the then Master of the Rolls, Sir Anthony Clarke, to appoint Sir Rupert Jackson to conduct a fundamental review of civil litigation cost (the Jackson cost review). That review reported in May and December 2009, and made detailed recommendations for the reform of both civil procedure and the law governing litigation funding; one particular aspect of the latter, conditional fee agreements, having been identified as a significant cause of the CPR's failure to control litigation cost.[2] The vast majority of its recommendations were implemented in 2012 by the Legal Aid, Sentencing and Punishment of Offenders Act (the 2012 Act), which effected the Jackson cost review's litigation funding reforms, and by largescale amendments to the CPR.[3]

One significant aspect of the review that was not implemented was the recommendation that a fixed recoverable cost regime be introduced i.e., that while litigation costs would remain recoverable as between party and party, with the losing party indemnifying the winning party in respect of the costs they have incurred in bringing or defending a claim, the level of indemnification would be limited to a fixed amount, the level of which would be prescribed in advance within the CPR.[4] A similar recommendation had previously been made

[1] J. Sorabji and R. Musgrove, 'Litigation, Cost, Funding and the Future' in D. Dwyer (ed), *The Civil Procedure Rules Ten Years On* (OUP, 2009). The title for the present chapter owes a debt to Edson Sunderland's famous paper on the difficulty in achieving civil procedural reform: E. Sunderland, *The English Struggle for Procedural Reform* (1925–26) (29) *Harvard Law Review* 725.

[2] R. Jackson, *Review of Civil Litigation Costs: Preliminary Report* (TSO) (May 2009, Vols. I & II); R. Jackson, *Review of Civil Litigation Costs: Final Report* (TSO) (December 2009).

[3] For an outline of the reforms to the CPR as implemented in 2013 see, S. Sime and D. French, *Blackstone's Guide to The Civil Justice Reforms 2013* (OUP, 2013). For a discussion of the Jackson reforms see R. Jackson and S. Clark, *The Reform of Civil Justice* (Sweet & Maxwell, 2018).

[4] R. Jackson (December 2009) chapters 15–17.

John Sorabji, *The Long Struggle for Fixed Cost Reform* In: *The Civil Procedure Rules at 20.* Edited by: Andrew Higgins, Oxford University Press (2020). © the several contributors. DOI: 10.1093/oso/9780198863182.003.0017.

by Lord Woolf in the Access to Justice Review.[5] It too had not been introduced when the CPR was brought into effect in 1999. In November 2016, three years after the majority of the Jackson costs reforms were introduced, the question of fixed recoverable costs was considered for a third time, as Sir Rupert Jackson was commissioned to revisit his 2009 recommendation.[6] That review, the Fixed Recoverable Costs Review, concluded in July 2017, with further recommendations being made as to how a fixed recoverable costs regime ought to be implemented.[7] Shortly after the Jackson Fixed Costs Review commenced, in January 2017, the government conducted its own subject-specific fixed costs review in the area of clinical negligence (the clinical negligence review).[8] The government published its response in February 2018, which recommended the establishment of a working group to devise a grid of fixed costs, while it awaiting the outcome of further work on Jackson's recommendations.[9] After some considerable delay, in March to June 2019 the government consulted on the Jackson Fixed Costs Review's recommendations.[10]

While the government has not, as yet, issued its response to the responses to its Jackson consultation paper, the expectation is that fixed recoverable costs will now be introduced in one form or another. That that is likely to be the case is apparent from government's response to the clinical negligence review. It accepted Sir Rupert Jackson's recommendation from his fixed recoverable cost review that the Civil Justice Council (the CJC) establish a working party to develop a workable process for the application of recoverable fixed costs in such cases. The CJC's working party reported in October 2019. It offered some positive encouragement that the implementation of fixed recoverable costs had moved a step closer, as it demonstrated a degree of agreement on the approach to take to such a regime by claimant and defendant representatives. It

[5] H. Woolf, *Access to Justice: Final Report to the Lord Chancellor on the Civil Justice System in England and Wales* (HMSO) (1996) chapters 2, 4, 7.16ff.

[6] Senior Judiciary Announces Review of Fixed Recoverable Costs (11 November 2016) <https://www.judiciary.uk/announcements/senior-judiciary-announces-review-of-fixed-recoverable-costs/>.

[7] R. Jackson, *Review of Civil Litigation Costs: Supplemental Report Fixed Recoverable Costs* (Judicial Office, July 2017) <https://www.judiciary.uk/wp-content/uploads/2017/07/fixed-recoverable-costs-supplemental-report-online-3.pdf>.

[8] Department of Health, *Introducing Fixed Recoverable Costs for Lower Value Clinical Negligence Claims: a Consultation* (January 2017) <https://assets.publishing.service.gov.uk/government/uploads/system/uploads/attachment_data/file/586641/FRC_consultation.pdf>.

[9] Department of Health, *Consultation on Introducing Fixed Recoverable Costs in Lower Value Clinical Negligence Claims: the Summary of Consultation Responses* (February 2018) <https://assets.publishing.service.gov.uk/government/uploads/system/uploads/attachment_data/file/681387/2018_FRC_Consultation_response_.pdf>.

[10] Ministry of Justice, *Extending Fixed Recoverable Costs in Civil Cases: Implementing Sir Rupert Jackson's Proposals* (28 March 2019) <https://consult.justice.gov.uk/digital-communications/fixed-recoverable-costs-consultation/supporting_documents/fixedrecoverablecostsconsultationpaper.pdf>.

did, however, also negatively conclude that agreement on the level at which recoverability should be set could not be reached. It was thus for the government to consult on the level of clinical negligence recoverable costs.[11] It is possible that the possibility and extent of any such consultation may be dealt with in the government's response to its March 2019 consultation on the Jackson fixed recoverable cost review.

Twenty years after the Woolf reforms were implemented, it appears that the English civil justice system is moving slowly towards its incorporation of one significant and previously unimplemented aspect of Lord Woolf's vision. If this is correct and fixed recoverable costs are finally introduced then, in addition to promoting litigation at proportionate cost, the foundation may have been laid to increase access to litigation funding. In particular, the basis for expanding the availability of legal expenses insurance (LEI) as a viable widely available form of litigation funding may have been put in place. With the effective evisceration of civil legal aid by the 2012 Act, such a development may go some way to redress the adverse effect on access to justice that created.[12] More ambitiously, it may form the foundation for a potential successor to the civil legal aid scheme, should there be no political will to revitalise it, that is capable of providing greater access to justice than it did at its greatest extent. As the CPR reaches its twentieth anniversary, it may well—as was the case at its tenth anniversary—about to see 'the funding of civil litigation . . . in the throes of a revolution'.[13] The cause of that in 2009 was the early stages of the development of third party litigation funding. The cause of a revolution in funding now may well be the expansion of LEI as a final consequence of both the Woolf and Jackson reforms. In order to consider these issues, this chapter first outlines the history of the English civil justice's struggle to introduce fixed recoverable costs. It then considers the nature of LEI, before turning to how its expansion may be facilitated by fixed recoverable costs and then how that might effect

[11] Civil Justice Council, *Fixed Recoverable Costs In Lower Value Clinical Negligence Claims* (October 2019) <https://www.judiciary.uk/wp-content/uploads/2019/10/Fixed-recoverable-costs-in-lower-value-clinical-negligence-claims-report-141019.pdf>.

[12] For an outline of the problems caused by the reduction in civil legal aid see, for instance, House of Commons, Justice Select Committee, *Eighth Report—Impact of Changes to Civil Legal Aid under Part 1 of the Legal Aid, Sentencing and Punishment of Offenders Act 2012* (4 March 2015) <https://publications.parliament.uk/pa/cm201415/cmselect/cmjust/311/31102.htm>; The Bach Commission on Access to Justice, Interim Report (November 2016) <https://www.fabians.org.uk/wp-content/uploads/2016/11/Access-to-Justice_final_web.pdf> and Final Report (September 2017) <https://fabians.org.uk/wp-content/uploads/2017/09/Bach-Commission_Right-to-Justice-Report-WEB-2.pdf>; N. Byrom, 'Cuts to Civil Legal Aid and the Identity Crisis in Lawyering: Lessons from the Experience of England and Wales' in A. Flynn and J. Hodgson, *Access to Justice and Legal Aid* (Routledge, 2017);

[13] M. Zander cited in J. Sorabji and R. Musgrove (2009) at 234.

wider access to justice than has previously been achieved by either civil procedural reform or litigation funding reform.

Fixed recoverable costs

There are currently three trans-substantive costs regimes operative in England, and three discrete ones. The trans-substantive ones apply on the small claims, fast and multi-tracks. The latter, discrete, ones apply to three types of pre-action procedure, to claims brought in the Intellectual Property and Enterprise Court (IPEC) small claims track, and, in a very limited extent, to debt enforcement claims brought in the County Court by Commissioners of Her Majesty's Revenue and Customs.[14] On the small claims track, for claims up to £10,000 there is a no-costs-shifting regime subject to limited low value recoverability of administrative costs,[15] unless in exceptional circumstances one party is held to have acted unreasonably.[16] On the fast track, for claims from £10,000 to £25,000 there is a fixed recoverable costs regime operative. That scheme is however limited to trial costs; it does not render the entire costs of the proceedings fixed in terms of recoverability.[17] Finally, the multi-track, for claims above £25,000, full costs shifting is operative. The general approach to costs-shifting i.e., that the loser pays a proportion of the winning party's litigation costs through an application of the indemnity principle, in English civil procedure is thus tripartite: for small claims, there is no costs-shifting and each party generally bears their own costs; limited fixed recoverability on the fast track; and full costs-shifting on the multi-track. In addition to this, discrete fixed recoverability arises in respect of three specific types of pre-action procedures which operate outside the scope of the Rules of Court, the aim of which is to increase pre-action settlement.[18] Those procedures are set out in the Road Traffic Accident and Employer and Public Liability Protocols (the RTA Protocol and the EL/PL Protocol), and the Pre-Action Protocol for Resolution of Package Travel Claims, with the fixed cost regime set out in CPR Pt 45. The IPEC small claims procedure, the aim of which is to provide a proportionate process for

[14] Recoverability for such debt enforcement claims is limited to recoverability of the issue fee, the amount of which depends on the value of the debt claim, see CPR r.45.34.

[15] For instance, recoverability of the costs of issuing proceedings, a low level fixed recoverability for lawyers' or experts' fees and witness expenses, see CPR PD27 para.7.

[16] The £10,000 limit is a generally applicable one, exceptions do apply to, for instance, personal injury claims where the limit is £1,000, see CPR r.27.1(2), r.27.14.

For instance, personal injury claims.

[17] CPR Pt 45.

[18] See the RTA and EL/PL Protocols.

love value intellectual property claims also operates a fixed recoverable cost regime.[19]

The generally applicable tripartite structure was recommended by the Woolf Reforms and was introduced in the CPR in 1999.[20] It has remained broadly unchanged since then, except for one increase in the small claims limit from £5,000 to the current limit, which took place in 2013.[21] The discrete mechanisms came later i.e., policy decisions aimed at diverting certain claims from the civil courts by encouraging pre-issue settlement in the case of the pre-action protocols,[22] and the Jackson Cost Reforms in the case of the IPEC small claims process.[23] The general structure may have been introduced following the Woolf reforms, but it was not their intention. While the small claims and multi tracks were introduced as intended, the fast track was intended to have a full fixed recoverable costs regime. There were to be fixed costs as between solicitor and client, although that could be varied by agreement. There were to be fixed recoverable costs capped at £2,500, with an additional capped fixed recoverable cost for an advocates trial fee. Costs also would be payable by reference to the stage at which litigation had reached i.e., there would be staged payments.[24] The level at which the costs were set was to be subject to annual review, with a general triennial review of civil costs carried out by a committee of the CJC.[25] In essence, the model proposed was that which Zuckerman had recommended in his evidence to the Woolf Inquiry, which was itself based on his examination of the fixed recoverable costs regime applicable in Germany.[26] While the Woolf reforms were generally accepted, and introduced, the recommendation that a fully fixed costs regime, with annual and triennial reviews, should be introduced on the fast track was not. There were, at least, two reasons for this.

First, the general outcry from the legal profession against such a scheme. As Sunderland, one of the drafters of the US Federal Rules in the 1930s and who wrote about the, in his words, long struggle for procedural reform in England

[19] CPR Pt 45, section IV.

[20] H. Woolf (1996) Section I, para.3.

[21] Civil Procedure (Amendment) Rules 2013 (SI 2013/262) art.9.

[22] See G. Vos (ed), *Civil Procedure 2019* (Thomson Reuters, 2019) Vol. 1 at C13A--005, for the background to the introduction of, as it puts it, these forms of 'civil diversion'.

[23] A detailed history of the creation of this fixed recoverable costs regime is set out in Mr. Justice Arnold, *Intellectual Property Litigation: Implementation of the Jackson Report's Recommendations* (Seventeenth Lecture in the Jackson Implementation Programme) (12 February 2013) <https://www.judiciary.uk/wp-content/uploads/JCO/Documents/Speeches/justice-arnold-speech-implementation-programme-lecture-17.pdf>

[24] H. Woolf (1996) chapter 4.24.

[25] H. Woolf (1996) recommendations 21–31.

[26] H. Woolf, *Access to Justice: Interim Report to the Lord Chancellor on the Civil Justice System in England and Wales* (HMSO) (1995), Annex V; H. Woolf (1996) chapter 4.14-15; J. Peysner, 'A Blot on the Landscape' in D. Dwyer (2009) at 164–166.

in the mid-to-late 19th century, procedural reform was something that always came in the teeth of staunch opposition from lawyers.[27] Such opposition was the primary response to the Woolf Report's initial suggestion, in its Interim Report,[28] that a fixed recoverable cost regime be introduced on the new fast track. As Peysner put it, it was 'not an exaggeration to say that these ideas [one of which was the introduction of fixed recoverable costs] were met with a storm of protest by the legal profession . . . .'[29] The basis of the opposition was both self-interested and principled. It was that lawyers would not be able to work at the level of remuneration provided by the fixed level of recoverability, and that as a consequence the proposal ought not to be pursued. As Woolf noted in the Interim Woolf Report, this was implicit in such arguments raised against fixed recoverability,

> In their generally positive submission in writing to me, APIL vigorously argued against any form of cost capping. Their arguments, which were advanced on the basis of a general understanding of what I was likely to recommend, would apply equally to fixed costs. It was, however, not appreciated that I accept that exceptionally complex cases would not be appropriate for disposal on the fast track. Nonetheless, it is implicit in APIL's arguments that it would be impracticable to expect their members to work within the range of costs that I have in mind.[30]

Fixing costs would thus inevitably lead to lawyers to reduce the amount of work done to ensure that it remained economically viable for them. While such opposition could be set aside as special pleading on the part of the profession looking to protect its income and profits, the opposition was advanced on a more principled basis. There were two limbs to this, first that such a consequence would be contrary to the civil process's aim of securing justice on the substantive merits; and secondly, it was inequitable.

The first criticism was, in the present context, a particular example of a general complaint against the Woolf reforms that they were intended to reduce

[27] E. Sunderland (1925–1926).

[28] H. Woolf (1995) chapter 7 and see chapter 7 para.1, 'It [the fast track] will be designed so that the costs of the procedure can be known in advance and the litigant's maximum liability for costs, even if he is unsuccessful, can be anticipated with certainty.' That was to be achieved through the application of fixed recoverable costs, see ibid at chapter 7 paras.16–20. APIL is the Association of Personal Injury Lawyers.

[29] J. Peysner, 'England and Wales—Woolf for Slow Learners' in C. Hodges, S. Vogenauer and M. Tulibacka, *The Costs and Funding of Civil Litigation—A Comparative Perspective* (CH Beck & Hart Publishing, 2010) at 314.

[30] H. Woolf (1995) chapter 7, para.23.

the quality of justice by limiting access to process by reference to the cost and time. A utilitarian calculus was to be applied to civil procedure, which would explicitly link the amount of process, time and hence cost that could be expended on litigation to the value, complexity and importance of the claim. The lower the value and importance of the claim the less process litigants were to be capable of accessing. This was opposed on the basis that the Woolf reforms, rather than seeking to improve access to justice, would in fact increase access to less justice, as Hancyz described it in the context of comparable reforms in Canada.[31] Two consequences would thus flow from this reform. Either it would reduce the quality of access to justice, as lawyers would expend less time and effort on litigating claims to keep their costs within the recoverability levels, or it would reduce access to justice in its entirety as lawyers excited the market for certain classes of claim[32] i.e., those that fell within the fast track limits. Fixing recoverable costs was thus inimical to the achievement of justice on the merits and accordingly was wrong in principle. Woolf rejected these arguments in two ways. From an overarching perspective they were rejected as matching the level of process to the value, complexity and importance of the dispute was part of fundamental shift in the philosophy of litigation; the complaint raised was only valid if securing justice on the merits was the aim of procedure, the reforms rejected that aim. Reducing the quality of justice was thus intentional. The reforms were meant to reduce access to process, through rendering process proportionate to the value, importance etc. of claims. Fixing costs was not additional to that, but a necessary consequence, as well as an integral part of the new focus on proportionality in procedure. As such the criticism missed its mark and was to be rejected.[33]

The second criticism focused on the effect that a fixed recoverable cost regime would have on the principle of equality of arms. Again this argument was advanced by APIL.[34] It was this: defendants, who tended to be wealthier than claimants, or insurance-backed, would be placed in a stronger position due to their greater wealth. They would be able to incur greater irrecoverable costs in delaying the proper prosecution of claims. The consequence of that would be to reduce or exhaust a claimant's resources as, due to the defendant-caused delays and associated procedural applications by claimants aimed at requiring

[31] C. Hanycz, 'More Access to Less Justice: Efficiency, Proportionality and Costs in Canadian Civil Justice Reform' (2008) 27 *CJQ* 98

[32] H. Woolf (1995) chapter 7.23.

[33] See J. Sorabji, *English Civil Justice after Woolf and Jackson* (CUP, 2014) at 188–197; D. de Saulles, *Reforming Civil Procedure—The Hardest Path* (Hart Publishing, 2019).

[34] H. Woolf (1996) chapter 7.16ff; J. Pesyner in D. Dwyer (2009) at 163.

defendants to act, they would incur costs over and above the fixed recoverable cost limit. This would mean they would either have to under-settle claims as they were priced out of the justice system. Alternatively, they would either have to withdraw their claims, or ironically given the reforms were intended to increase access to justice, not pursue them in the first place due to the advance knowledge of the level of likely irrecoverable costs of litigating. One other alternative presenting itself: to litigate but know that a percentage of potential damages would have to be paid by claimants to their lawyers to cover costs over and above the fixed recoverable costs.[35] Each of these points, which identified the introduction of a form of structural inequality into the civil justice system called for detailed consideration. These concerns were, however, rejected on the basis that the introduction of a limited and fixed standard procedure for fast track claims and robust and active court case management, which took the control of the pre-trial process out of the hands of the parties, would eliminate the possibility of defendants engaging in a litigation strategy aimed at reducing access to justice in the way suggested. The court would thus be responsible for ensuring that fixed recoverability did not become a source of procedural inequality.[36] It was also expected that should defendants adopt such tactics, there was no reason why, as on the small claims track and in the no-cost shifting regime in Employment Tribunals, the court could not go outside the fixed cost regime where a party had acting unreasonably in the conduct of litigation.[37] The expectation was, however, that through the introduction of a streamlined fast track procedure and robust management, lawyers would alter their behaviour and would as a consequence focus their work levels, and hence billing, to levels appropriate to the nature and value of the claim. Rather than exit the market, the expectation was that lawyers would ensure that the work they did in the course of litigation would be properly limited to the level of fixed recoverable costs, which would themselves provide a 'realistic and fair reward for litigating such cases'.[38]

[35] H. Woolf (1996) chapter 2.26, 'APIL's concern is that fixed recoverable costs will diminish the amount of costs recovered by claimants on their behalf from defendants because the cost of litigating an individual case may be in excess of the fixed recoverable costs if those are not fixed at a realistic level. If that were to happen, clients would have to meet the extra out of their damages, in addition to the success fee, or solicitors would be pressured to do the work for less. APIL has said that in those circumstances, either clients would cease to use conditional fee agreements or experienced personal injury lawyers would no longer be able to undertake the work. Either outcome would reduce access to justice.' And see ibid at chapter 4.4.

[36] H. Woolf (1996) chapter 2.30, 4.10.

[37] H. Woolf (1996) chapter 2.30, noting the potential for cost and other sanctions to be imposed on parties engaging in such conduct. This point would be emphasised in the Jackson Costs Review, see R. Jackson (December 2009) at 147.

[38] H. Woolf (1996) chapter 2.27.

In the event, a full fixed recoverable costs regime was not introduced for a more mundane reason: agreement could not be reached on what level to fix the costs.[39] It foundered on practicalities. As Peysner summarises it, two approaches were adopted to try to develop an agreed scale of fixed costs. One approach, taken by Goriely, started from first principles. It worked out what work needed to be done and attempted to cost it. The other, by Peysner and Armstrong, analysed actual case files to then try to devise reasonable costs for each stage of the proposed fast track. Consensus could not be reached, and it was thought best to wait until the CPR had been in operation before an attempt was made to work out such a scheme.[40] At best, and using a third model based on an historical analysis of insurers' costs databases i.e., on costs incurred prior to any cost reductions effected by the Woolf reforms, an agreement was brokered by the CJC after the CPR was introduced to develop fixed costs for road traffic accident disputes that settled following amendments to the Senior Courts Act 1981 made in 2003, and later the introduction of fixed recoverability in a limited number of pre-action processes.[41]

There the matter rested. Apart from limited fixed recoverable costs being introduced for advocacy work done on the fast track and the introduction of fixed recoverability for a limited number of pre-action processes, the central aim of introducing a generic fixed recoverability scheme on the fast track was shelved following the CPR's introduction in 1999. The silence was occasionally breached by a member of the senior judiciary, such as Lord Dyson MR who while deputy Head of Civil Justice between 2003 and 2006 regretted that this aspect of the reforms had not been introduced.[42] Such comments bore no fruit.

[39] J. Peynser in D. Dwyer (2009) at 164.

[40] See R. Jackson (May 2009) Vol. 1 at 203.

[41] See *Butt v Nizami* [2006] EWHC 159 (QB) for an account of the former, and the RTA Protocol and CPR Pt 45, for the latter.

[42] See Lord Dyson MR, *The Challenges Facing Civil Justice Today*, (Leeds Law Society, 26 May 2016) (copy on file with author). And see, M. Fouzder, 'Dyson: Extending Fixed Costs Is the Way Forward' *Law Gazette*, 6 June 2016, <https://www.lawgazette.co.uk/law/dyson-extending-fixed-costs-is-the-way-forward/5055647.article>. Lord Dyson MR had already expressed the same view the previous year, when he stated that it was time that the government accepted the principle that fixed recoverable costs be introduced, see Lord Dyson MR, *Confronting Costs Management, Harbour Litigation Lecture* (May 2015), 'Sir Rupert has repeated his plea for an extension of the fixed recoverable costs regime to all fast-track cases as well as to the smaller multi-track cases. I take this opportunity to support him on this. I have been urging it publicly for a considerable period of time. There has been no public response from the Department. I do not know whether there are any objections in principle to it. So far as I am aware, there are none. I can see that, if the proposal were accepted in principle, there would be battles over the levels at which the fees were set and as to the cut-off point for fixed fees in multi-track cases. I can also see that there would have to be a provision for disapplying the regime in exceptional circumstances. But in my view, the time has come for the Department to say that it accepts in principle that the fixed costs regime should be extended. At a stroke, this reform would surely reduce disputes about costs and also reduce the cost of a large swathe of civil litigation more generally.' <https://www.judiciary.uk/wp-content/uploads/2015/05/speech-dyson-lj-confronting-costs-management.pdf>.

Consideration of fixed recoverable costs did not recommence until the Jackson Costs Review. Jackson noted that a full fixed recoverable costs regime was viewed by Woolf as an essential feature of his reforms, and that it had not been implemented. More significantly, Jackson noted that the area on which implementation had foundered in 1999, the absence of appropriate data on which to devise a grid of fixed costs, was no longer an issue: the data was now available.[43] Once more a full fixed recoverable costs regime for the fast track was recommended; Jackson intended to finally bring about this missing aspect of the Woolf reforms.[44] It was, however, noted to be too early to recommend the introduction of fixed recoverability on lower value multi-track cases; that conclusion was, however, to be kept under review.[45] Again, however, the recommendation was not acted upon, agreement could not be reached on the level of fixed costs. Following work by Sir Rupert Jackson and the CJC to develop an effective fixed costs grid, the limit of the proposals focused on personal injury claims.[46] A related development, which had been pursued in the Patents County Court, also saw the introduction of a fixed recoverable costs regime for what would become its IPEC small claims procedure.[47] Piecemeal steps were thus taken. Again, there matters rested, until 2016, when a combination of increasing acceptance of fixed costs as an alternative to costs management and budgeting by the legal profession,[48] the fact that the extant limited fixed cost regimes worked effectively and satisfactorily,[49] and continuing dissatisfaction with the level of litigation costs by the government and judiciary, led to Sir Rupert Jackson being appointed to reconsider the question of fixed recoverable costs.[50] The focus of the reconsideration was not the principle of fixed costs. It

[43] R. Jackson (May 2009) Vol. 1 at 203ff.

[44] R. Jackson (December 2009) chapter 6.

[45] R. Jackson (December 2009) at 172–174.

[46] R. Jackson (December 2009) at 538–539, and chapter 15 generally.

[47] See R. Jackson, *The Reform of Civil Litigation* (Thomson Reuters, 2016) at 178.

[48] It is perhaps ironic that the acceptance of fixed costs by the profession was the introduction of Jackson's recommendation to introduce costs budgeting. Fixed costs were finally perceived to be attractive as, perhaps, the lesser of two evils; a point noted in R. Jackson, *Fixed Costs—The Time Has Come, IPA Annual Lecture*, (28 January 2016) at 4, 'My impression is that the profession is now more willing to accept fixed costs than it was in the past. This is for two main reasons. First, such a regime would dispense with the need for costs budgeting, which not everyone enjoys.' <https://www.judiciary.uk/wp-content/uploads/2016/01/fixedcostslecture-1.pdf>.

[49] Ibid, '. . . experience of the fixed costs regimes introduced in recent years has been satisfactory for both practitioners and litigants'.

[50] See the joint statement of the Lord Chancellor, Lord Chief Justice and Senior President of Tribunals cited in R. Jackson (July 2017) at 12 'More needs to be done to control the costs of civil cases so they are proportionate to the case, and legal costs are more certain from the start. Building on earlier reforms, we will look at options to extend fixed recoverable costs much more widely, so the costs of going to court will be clearer and more appropriate. Our aim is that losing parties should not be hit with disproportionately high legal costs, and people will be able to make more informed decisions on whether to take or defend legal action'.

remained the question of the level at which they should be set. As noted above, this review took place against the background of an independent government consultation by the Department of Health, which was looking at extending the scope of fixed costs for personal injury cases more widely across clinical negligence cases.[51] The outcome of the second Jackson Review was the proposal that a general fixed costs regime should be introduced for fast track claims up to £25,000. It was also to be supplemented by the introduction of a new procedural case track for claims above £25,000 and up to £100,000 i.e., fixed costs for lower value multi-track claims would be introduced by way of taking them out of the multi-track and placing them in a procedural case track.[52] There was no dispute over the question of principle in respect of either the fast track proposal or that of extending fixed costs to the lower end of the multi-track. In 2019 the government accepted both recommendations, albeit it rejected the idea of introducing a new case track to achieve the second of the two proposals.[53] To the extent that questions of principle could have been said to have limited the development of fixed costs, as Lord Dyson MR believed in 2015,[54] this was now set to rest. As it was post-Woolf, the issue remained that of the level at which fixed costs should be set. The expectation is, however, that that question will not now prove as insurmountable as it was post-Woolf. The government has made clear its intention to introduce the Jackson recommendations, including his proposals for the levels at which fixed costs are to be set subject to the views of respondents to its 2019 fixed cost consultation, and use evidence obtained following their introduction to expand fixed recoverable costs further than the fast and lower reaches of the multi-track.[55] As of October 2019, it would appear that twenty years after the CPR was introduced without Woolf's recommendation of generic fixed cost recoverability on the fast track, their introduction is on the verge of taking place. If that expectation is finally realised, it may not only promote further proportionality and predictability in litigation costs, as both Woolf and Jackson expected, but it may have a broader benefit. It may not only increase access to justice, as anticipated, by reducing litigation cost, but it may help its achievement by promoting the growth of an under-used form of litigation funding: LEI.

[51] Department of Health (2017).

[52] R. Jackson (July 2017) at 137.

[53] Ministry of Justice (28 March 2019) at 7. Between 2017 and 2019 further piecemeal developments had taken place, as fixed recoverable costs were extended to package travel holiday claims via the Pre-action Protocol for resolution of package travel claims and CPR Pt 45.

[54] Lord Dyson MR (July 2015).

[55] Ministry of Justice (28 March 2019) at 41. To that end, the Ministry promoted the introduction of a fixed (or capped) costs pilot scheme for multi-track claims within the Business and Property Courts. The pilot commenced in January 2019, see CPR PD51W.

The Future—access to justice—the intersection of fixed recoverable costs and legal expenses insurance

LEI is an established form of litigation funding. It comes in two varieties: before-the-event insurance (BTE), which is purchased before a cause of action has accrued, and after-the-event insurance (ATE), which is purchased after a cause of action accrues. The former typically is an aspect of car insurance or home insurance.[56] The latter is typically a complement to conditional fee agreements.[57] The former is also typically cheaper than the latter.[58] Both forms are used, to varying degrees, in many jurisdictions across the world.[59] It is, for instance, widely used across Europe. In Sweden, Finland, and Germany, for example, it is the predominant means by which litigation is funded.[60] In the former two countries, LEI covers 97% of the population and 75% of the population respectively.[61] In the latter, it has been a key element of litigation funding since the development of social welfare provision from the late 19th century, and accounts for over a third of all litigation funding.[62] In other jurisdictions it has been and is being heavily promoted by governments as a viable alternative to, and replacement for, state-funded civil legal aid. As McKillop and McCamus put it, public policy in Canada now approaches the promotion of LEI, and specifically BTE insurance, on the basis that it is not just an 'important tool for helping Canadians access legal assistance' but more significantly, that the aim is 'for 75% of middle income Canadians to have legal insurance by 2030'.[63]

In England and Wales BTE insurance has, historically, been of limited utility due to, as Clark and Jackson note, its not being generally been widely taken up or, if taken up, used.[64] There are many factors which have contributed to that

[56] Civil Justice Council, *The Law and Practicalities of Before-The-Event (BTE) Insurance—An Information Study* (November 2017) <https://www.judiciary.uk/wp-content/uploads/2017/11/cjc-bte-report.pdf>; S. Clark and R. Jackson, *The Reform of Civil Justice* (Sweet & Maxwell) (2018) at 75.

[57] *PM Law Ltd v Motorplus Ltd* [2016] EWHC 193 (QB) at [6].

[58] S. Clark and R. Jackson (2018) at 75.

[59] See the National Reports annexed to J. Sorabji, *The Crisis of Legal Aid and Alternative Solutions—General Report* (International Association of Procedural Law, Seoul, October 2014) <https://www.ufrgs.br/caar/wp-content/uploads/2014/10/Session-3.2.pdf>

[60] L. Follett, *Access to Justice—Rights or Rations? Comparing European Legal Aid Systems in the Context of a Shrinking Budgetary Environment*, Plymouth Law Review (2008) 1 at 18.

[61] G. Hadfield and J. Heine, 'Life in the Law-Thick World: Legal Resources for Ordinary Americans' in S. Estreicher and J. Radice, *Beyond Elite Law—Access to Civil Justice in America* (CUP, 2014) at 47.

[62] J. Peysner, *Access to Justice—A Critical Analysis of Recoverable Conditional Fees and No-Win No-Fee Funding* (Palgrave Macmillan, 2014) at 13; B. Hess and R. Hubner, 'Germany—National Report' in C. Hodges, S. Vogenauer and M. Tulibacka (2010) at 348–349; P. Murray and R. Sturner, *German Civil Justice* (Carolina Academic Press, 2004) at 123–127.

[63] See D. McKillop and J. McCamus, Canada National Report at 39 in J. Sorabji (2014), citing Canadian Bar Association, *Report of the Canadian Bar Association's Access to Justice Committee, Reaching Equal Justice: An Invitation to Envision and Act* (November 2013) at 103

[64] S. Clark and R. Jackson (2018) at 75; CJC (2017) at xiii and Section G.

result. First, reasonably broad civil legal aid coverage for civil disputes from the introduction of the Legal Aid and Assistance Act 1949. Secondly, as McKillop and McCamus point out, individuals generally speaking do not expect to become involved in litigation. Consequently, they do not 'expect to incur legal costs'.[65] Given that, there is no real awareness of the possibility or the need to take out BTE insurance, or if there is such an awareness, no real belief that such a step is necessary. As the CJC concluded,

> BTE Insurance is perceived to have a 'transparency issue', particularly among consumers, in that BTE is invariably sold to the consumer market together with some other insurance product, either as an 'add-on' or as part of a bundled product. This means that many who have BTE may have little or no awareness of that fact or, if they are aware in general terms that they have such cover, of its precise scope and extent. Individuals who are covered as part of a policy taken out by a family member may be particularly unlikely to be aware of such cover.[66]

It is reasonable to assume that this is compounded by the fact that significant parts of society are, for various reasons, less likely to perceive they have suffered a harm that could attract legal liability or if they do perceive the fact they have suffered such a harm are less likely to believe taking legal action will be of utility, hence they are even less likely to consider taking out such insurance.[67] Thirdly, as van Loggerenberg and Haupt suggest in the context of LEI's limited take-up in South Africa, failure by the legal profession to promote LEI actively can also undermine the development of an healthy BTE market.[68] That BTE policies in England typically seek to limit the insured's ability to choose a lawyer to act for them i.e., they have an adverse impact on the legal profession's ability to obtain work unless an individual lawyer or law firm is pre-selected by an insurance company to carry out work under its BTE policy, has done nothing to engender any real support for such policies by the profession.[69] Finally, and arguably most significantly as it has a direct impact on the ability

[65] D. McKillop and J. McCamus (2014) at 55.

[66] CJC (2017) at 134.

[67] For a discussion see, G. Hadfield and J. Heine (2014); J. Peysner (2014) at 157. Also see C. Hodges, *Delivering Dispute Resolution—A Holistic Review of Models in England and Wales* (Hart Publishing, 2019) at 140, 'Motor and household insurers successfully sold before-the-event (BTE) legal expenses insurance (LEI) widely, but very few people realises that they had cover. It appeared that rates of BTE penetration rise with income.'

[68] D. van Loggerenberg SC and F Haupt, 'South Africa—National Report' in J. Sorabji (2014) at 119.

[69] C. Hodges (2019) at 140, 'Consumer Focus highlighted that one reason why BTE LEI was not popular with lawyers was the rule that clients should be able to choose their own lawyer . . .'.

and willingness of insurance companies to provide BTE policies, the unpredictability of litigation costs has had a negative impact on its development as a viable and widely available source of litigation funding.[70] As Peysner has cogently argued, the link between cost predictability or unpredictability and the development of BTE insurance is evident by comparing its ready availability in Germany, where its fixed predictable costs recoverability has been in place since the end of the 19th century when BTE insurance began to develop, and the comparable lack of development in the market in England, where historically there was no predictability in terms of costs recoverability.[71]

In principle steps could be taken to overcome the first three issues that have been identified as undermining the general uptake of BTE in England. While not a positive step to increase uptake, it has been government policy in England since the 1990s to reduce the availability of civil legal aid. Coverage has been steadily reduced from, as Hodges has noted, '52% in the late 1990s, 41% in 2001 (after the removal of personal injury claims from scope), and 29% in 2007'.[72] One unintended consequence of the reduction in availability of legal aid is thus to place England in a broadly comparable position to that which it was in prior to 1949 and which Germany was in prior to the introduction of its social welfare reforms at the end of the 19th century. Notwithstanding the development of various forms of contingency funding and third party funding, a significant proportion of society is without the means to effectively bring or defend civil claims. Secondly, the promotion of public legal education could go some way to ameliorate lack of uptake and lack of promotion by the legal profession, although this would perhaps be limited in scope to individuals who already suspected they had a claim or who were already considering litigating. Its impact may be limited, and call for further action, which is considered below. Lack of promotion by the profession could also be overcome by restricting the ability of BTE providers to limit the ability of their insureds to choose their own legal representative.

Such steps would however be of limited effect without the introduction of a more predictable litigation cost regime. The key issue for the expansion of BTE is whether it is a viable product for insurers to market. In jurisdictions where there is fixed recoverability, the link between the two is patent in Germany, the model for the promotion of fixed recoverable costs in England since Woolf.

[70] J. Peysner, 'Costs in Personal Injury Cases—Searching for Predictable Costs' (2002) 2 *J.P.I. Law* 166.

[71] B. Hess and R. Hubner (2010) at 349. R. Lewis, 'Litigation Costs and Before-the-event Insurance: The Key to Access to Justice?' (2011) 74 *MLR* 272 at 278 also making the link between unpredictability and the lack of LEI uptake in England.

[72] C. Hodges (2019) at 139, citing S. Hynes and J. Robins, *The Justice Gap* (LSAG, 2009).

This link was borne out by insurance company representatives on the CJC working party that investigated BTE. While other working group members were doubtful of the impact of fixed recoverability on BTE, those involved in the industry itself were more certain of the link between the two and the impact that the former would have on the latter. As the CJC Report noted,

> Presently, the amount of adverse costs is unknown; but if FRC are introduced, that will be quantifiable, depending upon the level of claim (and counterclaim, if any). That enhanced certainty will be attractive to BTE insurers. The insurance representatives on the Working Group predicted that this may have an impact, by either raising the limit of BTE cover per policy, or reducing the premium for the same level of BTE cover.[73]

The same positive response to the possibility of fixed recoverability was also noted by sir Rupert Jackson in his Fixed Costs Review.[74] Either potential consequence of increasing cost predictability would increase the utility and availability of BTE policies and their potential impact on civil litigation funding. Without increased predictability, it is difficult to see how BTE could develop further even if the other issues that could be said to have limited its growth could be dealt with effectively. As Peysner put it, the condition precedent to BTE's growth was the introduction of predictability, of fixed recoverable costs. As he put it,

> the basic problem is that you can't inject BTE insurance into an environment where costs remain uncertain.[75]

Assuming that fixed recoverable costs are finally introduced it is likely that a necessary condition for BTE's expansion will finally be in place in England. On its own that is unlikely to be sufficient to promote its development to the stage where it replicates the role it plays in Scandinavia or Germany. As was noted by Lord Browne-Wilkinson at the time Lord Woolf was recommending the introduction of fixed recoverability based on the work carried out by Zuckerman

[73] CJC (2017) at 147.

[74] S. Clark and R. Jackson (2018) at 76.

[75] J. Peysner cited in J. Robins, 'Legal Insurance—Will Britain Buy It', The Guardian, 28 May 2010 <https://www.theguardian.com/law/2010/may/28/legal-insurance-uk-germany>'. A point noted by Sir Terence Etherton MR in a consideration of possible developments in civil justice post-Jackson, Sir T. Etherton MR, *Civil Justice after Jackson* (19 March 2018) at [9] <https://www.judiciary.uk/announcements/speech-by-sir-terence-etherton-mr-civil-justice-after-jackson/>; and see Sir T. Etherton MR, *LawWorks Annual Pro Bono Awards Lecture 2016* (5 December 2016) at [15] <https://www.judiciary.uk/wp-content/uploads/2016/12/law-works-lecture-mr-20161205.pdf>.

on the German fixed costs system, there are significant structural and cultural differences between the English and German civil justice systems. Those differences include, for instance, greater case management by the German judiciary than is the case even today in England; an absence of disclosure in Germany; differences in trial management e.g., in German witnesses are examined by the judge rather than by parties; and, that there is greater cost-subsidisation by lawyers concerning the work they do.[76] There is likely to be a need to move to a more German style of civil justice system, either by design or as a consequence of the introduction of fixed recoverable costs, in order to fully realise the benefits of their introduction, as well as to realise the potential benefit to the promotion of BTE insurance.

If we assume such obstacles can be overcome, the question raised earlier about increasing uptake of BTE remains, i.e., to increase its uptake for individuals who either do not believe they will need to litigate or who, because they are socially marginalised, are unable or unwilling to take out such insurance. The problem of ensuring individuals take out insurance policies to cover risks they do not believe are those which they are reasonable subject to is well-known in many areas. It underpinned, for instance, the arguments in favour of introducing mandatory health cover via what is generally known as Obamacare in the United States.[77] Its relevance to BTE insurance for litigation costs was acknowledged by the CJC in its investigation of the area. It noted that there were 'particular challenges' in making such cover 'available to those individuals who are in the lower socio-economic demographic'.[78] Whether those problems were financial or otherwise, fixed recoverability and the greater availability of BTE policies are unlikely to remedy them, as Hodges has correctly noted.[79] One possibility that could remedy both of these obstacles to wider uptake is one suggested by Choudhry, Trebilcock and James in respect of BTE provision in Canada. Their argument is straightforward. It is the same one that underpins Obamacare. It is that the state should establish mandatory public BTE insurance. By making it mandatory, they note that the risk pool would be sufficiently diverse to render such a scheme viable. This would be supported by

[76] Lord Browne-Wilkinson, 'The UK Access to Justice Report: A Sheep in Woolf's Clothing' [1999] 28 *Western Australian Law Review* 180.

[77] See S. Brill, *America's Bitter Pill* (Random House, 2015). ; and see S. Butler, *Assuring Affordable Healthcare for All Americans*, The Heritage Lectures 218 (Heritage Foundation) at 6.

[78] CJC (2017) at [xii]. A point also noted by S. Choudhry et al, 'Growing Legal Aid in Ontario into the Middle Class: A Proposal for Public Legal Expenses Insurance' in M. Trebilcock et al, *Middle Income Access to Justice* (University of Toronto Press, 2012) at 396, noting that in Germany where BTE is optional, its uptake correlates to income i.e., the lower the income the less likely it is that an individual will have taken out LEI.

[79] C. Hodges (2019) at 167.

fixed recoverability, which would also promote its viability by providing predictability in terms of cost risk.[80]

Such a scheme would overcome the first problem i.e., of individuals failing to take out insurance because they believed they would never need to use it. It would also help overcome any socio-economic barriers to uptake. As it would be mandatory, cover could be secured through contributions being paid for either by the state e.g., for those in receipt of universal credit (or other forms of social welfare provision) or in full-time education, or employers for those in employment. Such a mandatory scheme would not preclude individuals who wanted to secure additional provision for themselves doing so by taking out their own optional BTE cover. This is a possibility that has not yet been considered to any real degree in England, not least because the promotion of BTE has been hamstrung by the lack of predictability in litigation costs. If Clark and Jackson are correct, and the evidence from other jurisdictions suggest that this is likely to be the case, that the 'predictability and certainty of a FRC (fixed recoverable costs regime) enables BTE insurers to make informed decisions about their likely risk and potential exposure to adverse costs when funding litigation',[81] it is likely that the state should be in a position to also be able to do so. The introduction of fixed recoverability, first promoted by Woolf in the 1990s and then by Jackson in 2009, if finally carried out may not only now have the benefit of reducing litigation cost, and in that way helping to secure greater access to justice; more importantly, it may also help promote the greater availability of private BTE insurance, whilst also laying the foundation for a fundamental restructuring of the civil legal aid system as a universal,[82] mandatory social insurance-based BTE system. If that is correct, the most significant, and unintended, consequence of both the Woolf and Jackson reforms may then be the introduction of a reform to litigation funding that will do more to secure equal access to justice than the procedural reforms to the justice system that they explicitly focused on.

[80] S. Choudhry et al (2012).

[81] S. Clark and R. Jackson (2018) at 76.

[82] It is worth noting that the civil legal aid scheme at no stage was universal in terms of scope or provision.

PART VII

NATIONAL SECURITY

18

A Core Irreducible Minimum? The Operation of the *AF (No. 3)*

Duty in the Closed Material Procedure

Hayley J. Hooper[1]

When we think about fairness in legal proceedings two categories of guarantee spring immediately to mind. The first is that legal proceedings will be public. To that end the cliché that 'publicity is the very soul of justice'[2] is often deployed in support of the principle that justice will be conducted in a public forum. The second guarantee is that each party to the proceedings will have equal access to all the relevant materials which pertain to any legal dispute, including the substance of accusations against them. We call these (extremely broad and multifaceted) principles 'open justice' and 'equality of arms'. However, litigation concerning national security inevitably calls for a compromise as complete fidelity to the principles of public hearings and equality of arms are unlikely to be possible in any given case.

The closed material procedure (CMP) was created to allow legal challenges to national security measures in civil legal proceedings. Critics of the CMP highlight that it departs significantly from both principles, normally to the detriment of the non-government litigants.[3] It was first instigated in the context of immigration litigation[4] and was subsequently expanded to parole hearings,[5] post 9/11 'preventive justice' measures,[6] and finally, to all civil proceedings by

[1] Thanks to Menelaos Markakis, Joanna Bell, and the Editors for helpful comments. Errors and omissions are mine alone.

[2] J. Bentham, 'Draught of a New Plan for the Organization of the Judicial Establishment in France' in J. Bowring (ed), *The Works of Jeremy Bentham*, 11 vols (Tait 1843) 316.

[3] An exception permitting 'reversed closed evidence' was permitted in *W (Algeria) v Home Secretary* [2012] UKSC 8; [2012] 2 AC 115 to protect the identity of a witness on behalf of the non-government party from serious reprisals. See H.J. Hooper, 'The Lesser of Two Evils' (2012) 3 *LQR* 511.

[4] Special Immigration Appeals Commission Act 1997.

[5] *Roberts v Parole Board* [2005] UKHL 45.

[6] L. Zedner, 'Preventive Justice or Pre-Punishment: The Case of Control Orders' (2007) 60 *Current Legal Problems* 174, 174.

Hayley J. Hooper, *A Core Irreducible Minimum? The Operation of the AF (No. 3)* In: *The Civil Procedure Rules at 20.* Edited by: Andrew Higgins, Oxford University Press (2020). © the several contributors.
DOI: 10.1093/oso/9780198863182.003.0018.

virtue of the Justice and Security Act 2013. At first, the CMP permitted hearings based entirely upon 'closed' or 'secret' evidence.[7] This understandably prompted widespread criticisms from lawyers,[8] non-governmental organisations,[9] and parliamentary committees.[10]

The House of Lords decision in *Home Secretary v AF (No. 3)*[11] stands out as a landmark attempt to increase the fairness of CMPs in the context of preventive counter-terrorism sanctions. The ruling directly applied the Strasbourg case of *A and Others v United Kingdom*.[12] The House of Lords held by 9–0 that persons subject to a control order which engaged the civil limb of Art 6(1) ECHR were entitled, according to Lord Hope, to a 'core irreducible minimum' of the allegations against them in order to effectively instruct the Special Advocate appointed to represent them in closed proceedings.[13] No longer would CMPs in this context be fair if conducted entirely using closed evidence.

However, as the province of the CMP expanded, the application of the *AF (No. 3)* duty (as it came to be known) did not keep pace. This chapter argues that judicial treatment of the present application of the duty is inconsistent. The case law is problematic for three core reasons. First, the jurisprudence of the European Court of Human Rights (ECtHR) delineates between which subject matters attract enhanced procedural protection according to the scope of Arts 5(4) and 6(1) ECHR. Circumstances falling outside of these Articles receive lesser procedural protections under the European Convention on Human Rights (ECHR). As a result, the most severe penalties do not always receive the most stringent procedural protections. Secondly, in cases where Art 6(1) ECHR is clearly engaged, the courts have resorted to excessive contextualisation resulting in the non-application of the *AF (No. 3)* duty. Thirdly and finally, the English courts have been unwilling to use the common law to provide protection equivalent to the *AF (No. 3)* rule in cases where Art 6(1) ECHR is not engaged. The solution in

[7] *Home Secretary v MB* [2007] QB 415.

[8] A. McCulloch QC *et al*, 'Justice and Security Green Paper: Response to Consultation from Special Advocates' (16 December 2011) available at <http://consultation.cabinetoffice.gov.uk/justiceandsecurity/wpcontent/uploads/2012/09_Special%20Advocates.pdf>.

[9] Joint Committee on Human Rights, *Counter-Terrorism Policy and Human Rights (19th Report): 28 days, intercept and post-charge questioning* (2006–2007, HL 157/HC 790) [210].

[10] Amnesty International, *Left in the Dark: The Use of Secret Evidence in the United Kingdom* (Amnesty International Publications 2012), 30–31. Joint Committee on Human Rights, *Counter-Terrorism Policy and Human Rights (19th Report): 28 days, intercept and post-charge questioning* (2006–2007, HL 157/HC 790) [210]. Liberty, 'Unsafe, Unfair: TPIMs are fundamentally unsafe—they must go' available at <https://www.liberty-human-rights.org.uk/human-rights/terrorism/control-orders/index.php>.

[11] *Home Secretary v AF (No. 3)* [2009] UKHL 28.

[12] *A and Others v United Kingdom* [2009] ECHR 301.

[13] Ibid [220].

fairness terms would be to extend the *AF (No. 3)* rule to all CMPs engaging Art 6(1) ECHR. Where Art 6 ECHR is not engaged in a CMP the common law should supply equivalent protection.

Analysis proceeds in four stages. Section one sets out the legal background to the creation of the CMP. Section two analyses the House of Lords ruling in *AF (No. 3)* and the lukewarm judicial reception of the ECtHR ruling *A v United Kingdom* that occurred therein. Section three examines the subsequent treatment of the *AF (No. 3)* rule in the context of preventive terrorism orders and national security immigration proceedings. Finally, section four examines the scope of the duty in the context of wider civil proceedings, including under the Justice and Security Act 2013 (JSA 2013).

Closed material procedures: creation and background

The closed material procedure (CMP) was first introduced in the United Kingdom by the Special Immigration Appeal Commission Act 1997[14] in direct response to the ECtHR ruling in *Chahal v United Kingdom*.[15] The essence of a CMP is as follows: The procedure divides a hearing into 'open' and 'closed' sessions and empowers a court to issue 'open' and 'closed' judgments. During 'open' hearings, litigation proceeds as normal and the non-government litigant is represented by his or her own counsel. In a 'closed' hearing the litigant is represented by a Special Advocate: a court appointed lawyer, subject to security vetting by the government. Neither the litigant nor his legal counsel can access the 'closed' proceedings, evidence, or judgments. Only rarely, and at the discretion of the court, can they communicate with the Special Advocate after he has seen the 'closed' evidence.

Before the *Chahal* ruling deportations on national security grounds were not subject to any proceedings before courts or tribunals. National security immigration appeals involved a non-statutory process, in which the Secretary of State consulted with an advisory panel of security experts, entirely in secret. This procedure was sometimes mockingly referred to as the 'council of three wise men'.[16] There was no legal duty upon the Secretary of State to accept the recommendations of the expert panel. The ECtHR held that this process

[14] The Special Immigration Appeals Commission (Procedure) Rules 2003 (SI 1034/2003).

[15] *Chahal v United Kingdom* [1996] ECHR 54.

[16] House of Commons Constitutional Affairs Committee, 'The Operation of the Special Immigration Appeals Commission (SIAC) and the Use of Special Advocates, Vol II Evidence (7th Report), (2004–2005, HC 323-II) [5].

lacked the 'substantial measure of procedural justice'[17] which the Convention required for immigration measures to comply with Arts 5(4) and 13 ECHR.

In the course of the *Chahal* ruling the ECtHR cited an amicus briefing by Amnesty International which favourably presented the Canadian system of security certification hearings as a human-rights compliant alternative to the council of three wise men. This Canadian mechanism was presented a viable means of satisfying the fair trial requirements in Arts 6(1) and 5(4) ECHR. The ECtHR accepted this assessment.[18] Crucially, however, the ECtHR did not take account of the consequences of the prohibition on the Special Advocate from communicating with the claimant save with judicial discretion.[19] The Court's summary over-simplified the Canadian position,[20] and failed to realise that the endorsement 'unintentionally provoked a 'race to the bottom' by the British [government] . . . marked by an executive led security agenda [and] the lowest legally acceptable threshold of due process'.[21] The British government responded to *Chahal* by establishing a specific tribunal for national security immigration cases: The Special Immigration Appeals Commission (SIAC). Both SIAC and the CMP were established using the Special Immigration Appeals Commission 1997 Act (SIAC Act 1997).

At first, judicial review under a CMP could be conducted entirely upon the basis of closed evidence, given that there was no positive duty of disclosure in any of the relevant civil procedure rules pertaining to CMPs. The reticence to disclose national security information is often justified according to the 'mosaic theory'. This is a foundational concept in intelligence gathering which states that '[d]isparate items of information, though individually of limited or no utility, can take on added significance when combined with other items of information'.[22] It is a system of informational analysis for both those involved in intelligence gathering, and for judges in judicial review. It remains a feature of public administration: the British government recognises the mosaic theory

[17] *Chahal* (n 15) Judge Jambrek [2].

[18] Ibid [144].

[19] Immigration and Refugee Protection Act 1976, s. 85.4(2). In Harkat v Canada (Citizenship and Immigration) [2014] SCC 37 the Canadian Supreme Court reaffirmed the constitutionality of the Special Advocate system, holding at 8 (McLachlin C.J.) that: 'The communications restrictions imposed on special advocates do not render the scheme unconstitutional. They are not absolute and can be lifted with judicial authorization, subject to conditions deemed appropriate by the designated judge.'

[20] Rt Hon. Lord Phillips, 'Is Secret Justice no Justice at All? The Use of Closed Material' (King's College, London, 30 September 2013).

[21] D. Jenkins, 'There and Back: The Strange Journey of Special Advocates and Comparative Law Methodology' (2011) 42 *Columbia Human Rights Law Review* 279, 281.

[22] D.E. Pozen, 'The Mosaic Theory, National Security, and the Freedom of Information Act' (2005) 115(3) *The Yale Law Journal* 628, 628.

as a basis for restricting disclosures in the context of freedom of information legislation.[23]

In *W (Algeria)* the Supreme Court recognised the relevance of the mosaic theory in litigation. It is relevant when seemingly innocuous evidence is disclosed from 'closed' to 'open' proceedings and can then be pieced together to form part of a wider matrix of facts which puts national security at risk. The Supreme Court described the issue faced by the executive in the following terms: 'the Secretary of State may then find herself in possession of information which might . . . suggest the existence of a . . . risk to national security. Viewed in the context of . . . other pieces of information, it form[s] part of a jigsaw or mosaic.'[24] This explains why notwithstanding the ruling in *AF (No. 3)* the Civil Procedure Rules do not contain a positive duty of disclosure to ensure fairness. Instead, they still contain a negative duty to prevent disclosures which may damage national security.[25]

Both the government approach to classification and the disjuncture between open and closed proceedings has attracted trenchant criticisms. Dinah Rose QC explained that open and closed procedures differ to the extent that 'case that an appellant thinks they are meeting may not be simply different in extent but wholly different in kind from the case they are actually meeting.'[26] Over-classification was also highlighted as a pervasive problem. One lawyer glibly remarked that 'national security is such an elastic concept that if someone . . . sneeze[d] in the Horn of Africa, the government would argue that it couldn't be disclosed on grounds of national security'.[27]

A and Others v United Kingdom[28] was the first significant milestone for procedural fairness under the CMP. Before this case the House of Lords had ruled that CMPs were generally compatible Art 6(1) ECHR in *Home Secretary v*

[23] Information Commissioner's Office 'International relations, defence, national security or public safety (regulation 12(5)(a)) Environmental Information Regulations' (11 July 2012) available at: https://ico.org.uk/media/for-organisations/documents/1633/eir_international_relations_defence_national_security_public_safety.pdf.

[24] *W (Algeria) v Home Secretary* [2012] UKSC 8; [2012] 2 All ER 699, Lord Brown [11]. The 'mosaic theory' was also relied upon to successfully resist disclosure relating to the subject matter of an arms contract in *Ms X v the Department of Enterprise, Trade & Employment* [2002] IEIC 17.

[25] *K, A, B v Ministry of Defence* [2017] EWHC 830 (Admin) [8]–[9]. CPR 80.24(2)(c) (TPIMs), CPR 79.25(2)(c) (asset-freezing), CPR 76.28(2)(c) (control orders). The SIAC rules have a slightly different formulation. SIAC Rules 2003, Rule 37(3)(c) requires the Secretary of State 'to the extent that it is possible to do so without disclosing information contrary to the public interest, [to provide a] a statement of the material in a form which can be served on the appellant'.

[26] Joint Committee on Human Rights, *The Justice and Security Green Paper (24th Report)* (2010–2012, HL Paper 286/HC 1777) Dinah Rose QC, uncorrected transcript of oral evidence (24 January 2012).

[27] G. Peirce, meeting of Amnesty International (3 August 2011) in Amnesty International, *Left in the Dark: The Use of Secret Evidence in the United Kingdom* (Amnesty International Publications 2012) 15.

[28] *A and Others* (n 12).

MB.[29] However, *A and Others* concerned the compatibility of SIAC hearings with Art 5(4) ECHR. The applicants were foreign national terrorist suspects detained after the House of Lords ruling in *Belmarsh*.[30] In *A and Others* the Grand Chamber concluded that a CMP can be rendered compatible with Art 5(4) ECHR if the claimant 'was provided with sufficient information about the allegations against him to enable him to give effective instructions to the special advocate'.[31] This was the principle, but the standard was not immutable: the Court recognised that the question of sufficient disclosure 'must be decided on a case-by-case basis'.[32] The judgment provided an example of 'sufficient information', in respect of an allegation that several of the detainees had attended a terrorist training camp. To ensure a fair trial per Art 5(4) ECHR an allegation of this nature would need to be disclosed along with the 'stated location between stated dates' of the training camp.[33] Such disclosure would make it 'possible for the applicant to provide the special advocate with exonerating evidence, for example of an alibi or of an alternative explanation for his presence there'.[34] Beyond this no more explicit guidance is given as to how to satisfy procedural obligations.

Home Secretary v AF (No. 3): a lukewarm reception for a baseline rule

However, the categorical test in *A and Others* received a lukewarm reception in the then House of Lords. The ruling in *AF (No. 3)* may have been unanimous, but four of the nine justices expressed significant misgivings about the potential impact of the rule on national security. The context of the ruling was the regime of control orders established by the Prevention of Terrorism Act 2005 (PTA 2005)[35] in the wake of the House of Lords decision in *Belmarsh* that the indefinite detention of foreign nationals but not domestic terrorism suspects was in violation of the Convention. The PTA 2005 created two categories of control order, derogating and non-derogating. Derogating control orders were designed to impose powers which represented a deprivation of liberty contrary to Art 5 ECHR. However, this power was never used. Non-derogating control

29 *Home Secretary v MB* [2007] UKHL 46.
30 *A v Home Secretary (No. 1)* 'Belmarsh' [2004] UKHL 56.
31 *A and Others* (n 12) [220].
32 Ibid.
33 Ibid.
34 Ibid.
35 CPR Part 76.

orders merely represented a restriction upon liberty and did not engage Art 5 ECHR. The litigants in *AF (No. 3)* were all subject to non-derogating control orders. Such control orders permitted various restrictions on suspects. These included: electronic tagging, curfew, telephone reporting to a private security company, compulsory daily attendance at police stations, restrictions on visitors, requirements to seek permission for and notify the Home Office of pre-arranged meetings, prohibitions on meeting certain associates, the requirement to permit random police entry and search of controlees' property, restrictions on communications (both electronic, and with named individuals in the UK and overseas), restrictions to a specific geographical area or physical relocation, financial restrictions, restrictions on education and training, among others. The PTA 2005 did not contain an exhaustive list. Over the life of the control orders regime fifty-two persons were made subject to orders.

The *AF (No. 3)* case was not the first House of Lords ruling concerning the fairness of closed evidence in control orders. The compatibility of the CMP with Art 6(1) ECHR in this context was first litigated in *Home Secretary v MB*.[36] The issue in *MB* was deceptively simple to state: could judicial review of a non-derogating control order using a CMP ever be fair if conducted entirely using closed evidence? The lead speech, delivered by Baroness Hale, has been aptly characterised as 'enigmatic'.[37] She explained that 'the ingredients of a fair trial vary according to the subject matter and nature of the proceedings'.[38] Whilst acknowledging that the executive was prone to over-claim the need for secrecy in terrorism trials,[39] the CMP in MB's case appeared to have been conducted in a manner compatible with Art 6(1) ECHR. However, Lady Hale conceded that a CMP using substantially closed evidence may create unfairness in other circumstances.[40] Her speech became a source of significant legal uncertainty.

The other aspect of the *MB* decision which attracted criticism was the aspect which came to be known as the 'makes no difference' principle. The essence of this rule was that where the closed evidence against a controlee was so compelling that disclosure would not facilitate a meaningful challenge, then neither Art 6(1) ECHR nor the common law would require disclosure.

[36] *Home Secretary v MB* [2007] UKHL 46.

[37] P. Birkinshaw, 'Terrorism, Secrecy, and Human Rights' in K.S. Ziegler and P.M. Huber (eds), *Current Problems in the Protection of Human Rights: Perspectives from Germany and the UK* (Hart Publishing 2013) 249.

[38] *Home Secretary v MB*, [2007] UKHL 46, Baroness Hale [57].

[39] Ibid; *Home Secretary v MB* (n 38) Baroness Hale [66]. See also S. Turner and S.J. Schulhofer, *The Secrecy Problem in Terrorism Trials* (Liberty and National Security Project, Brennan Centre for Justice and NYU School of Law, 2005). : 'over-classification is a constant pitfall and that executive branch officials tend to exaggerate the need to keep information secret' 3.

[40] *Home Secretary v MB* (n 37) Baroness Hale [77].

As stated above, four of the nine justices in *AF (No. 3)* were explicitly reluctant to reverse the ambiguous holding in *MB*. They also indicated limited support for the continuation of the 'makes no difference principle' in some shape or form. In *AF (No. 3)* their Lordships held that *A and Others* made the 'makes no difference' principle unlawful in the context of control orders which engaged the civil limb of Art 6 ECHR. Lord Hope stated that where Art 6(1) was engaged litigants were entitled to a 'core irreducible minimum'[41] of the information to facilitate a fair trial. In the leading speech Lord Philips explained that '[w]here . . . the open material consists purely of general assertions and the case . . . is based solely or to a decisive degree on closed materials the requirements of a fair trial will not be satisfied'.[42] Nevertheless, in his view the 'makes no difference' principle could have continued to be applied in the context of control orders 'without significant risk of producing unjust results'.[43]

Lord Brown was also eager to stress the limitations of the rule in *A and Others* in practice, stating that it 'does not require the disclosure of the witness's identity or even their evidence, whatever difficulties that may pose for the suspect. What is required is rather the substance of the essential allegation founding the Secretary of State's reasonable suspicion.'[44] The practice of providing a summary of allegations came to be known as 'gisting' or providing a 'gist' of allegations. The term originated from parole board hearings.[45]

Lords Brown and Carswell were also reticent about the principle of a categorical minimum core of disclosure. Lord Carswell supported the House of Lords' approach in *MB* despite accepting that the ECtHR ruling was binding.[46] Lord Brown, the former president of the Security Services Tribunal,[47] was of the view that the *A v United Kingdom* ruling did not reflect the reality in which the English courts must operate because securing effective disclosure 'sometimes will be impossible and national security will thereby be put at risk'.[48] Although, he agreed that '[p]lainly there now *is* a rigid principle'.[49]

Lord Hoffmann was the most forthright, declaring that 'I think that the decision of the ECtHR was wrong and that it may well destroy the system of control orders which is a significant part of this country's defences against terrorism.'[50]

41 *AF (No. 3)* (n 11) Lord Hope [81].
42 Ibid Lord Phillips [59].
43 Ibid Lord Philips [62].
44 Ibid [120].
45 *R v Home Secretary, ex parte Doody* [1994] 1 AC 531, Lord Mustill, 560 G.
46 *AF (No. 3)* (n 11) Lord Carswell [107].
47 The Security Services Tribunal was the forerunner to the Investigatory Powers Tribunal. It was established by s. 5 of the Security Services Act 1989.
48 *AF (No. 3)* (n 11) Lord Brown [116], emphasis in the original.
49 Ibid Lord Brown [119].
50 Ibid Lord Hoffmann [70].

Such dicta brings to mind Lord Atkin's reproach that 'when face to face with claims involving the liberty of the subject, judges show themselves more executive-minded than the executive'.[51] Subsequently, the *AF (No. 3)* duty was also extended to asset-freezing measures[52] and financial restrictions[53] which engaged Art 6(1) ECHR.[54] The consequences of being subject to asset-freezing measures have been consistently likened to the effects of a control order. Lord Brown described the measures as capable of creating 'prisoners of the state'.[55] It is unclear whether the House of Lords ruling in *AF (No. 3)* really meant a 'core irreducible minimum' of disclosure of allegations or relevant material is necessary to achieve fairness in every litigation where a CMP is used. Or, if the case in fact stands for a narrower proposition, namely, that a 'core irreducible minimum' of information to assist the special advocate is required to be furnished with such a minimum if the following three criteria are met. First, the legal proceedings must require a CMP, Art 5(4) or Art 6(1) ECHR must be engaged, and thirdly, the non-government party must be seeking review of his or her detention or another form of severe restriction on his or her liberty. The impact of this ambiguity can be felt in the subsequent development of the case law.

Subsequent applications of the *AF (No. 3)* rule

Despite the extension to judicial review proceedings involving sanctions considered analogous to control orders Lord Rodger's declaration that 'Strasbourg has spoken, the case is closed'[56] did not mark the end of argument about the application of the *AF (No. 3)* duty. Far from it. Attempts by the executive to restrict the application of the *AF (No. 3)* duty continued on three main fronts. First, in the immediate context of control orders, new orders were made without the restrictions which engaged Art 6(1).[57] Secondly, argument continued over the application of the *AF (No. 3)* duty to the full universe of SIAC proceedings,[58] Employment tribunal proceedings,[59] and judicial review of police warrants

[51] *Liversidge v Anderson* [1942] AC 206, Lord Atkin.

[52] CPR Part 79 (Proceedings under the Terrorist Asset-Freezing, etc Act 2010).

[53] CPR Part 79 (Proceedings under the Counter-Terrorism Act 2008).

[54] *Gulam Mastafa v H.M. Treasury* [2012] EWHC 3578 (Admin); *Bank Mellat v HM Treasury* [2010] EWCA Civ 483.

[55] *Mohammed Jabar Ahmed v HM Treasury* [2010] UKSC 2 (*Ahmed No. 1)* [60] and Case T-85/09 *Yassin Abdullah Kadi v Commission (No. 2)* [2010] ECR 00000 (30 September 2010) [192].

[56] *AF (No. 3)* (n 11) Lord Rodger [98].

[57] *Secretary of State for the Home Department v BC* [2009] EWHC 2927 (Admin) 'Control Orders Lite'.

[58] *W (Algeria) v Home Secretary* [2010] EWCA Civ 898.

[59] *Home Office (Appellant) v Tariq (Respondent), Home Office (Respondent) v Tariq (Appellant)* [2011] UKSC 35.

unconcerned with national security.[60] Thirdly, with the advent of the Justice and Security Act 2013 which extended the availability of the CMP across all civil proceedings, debate turned to whether the *AF (No. 3)* duty applied to all types of proceedings which engaged the civil limb of Art 6 ECHR. The discussion below argues that the exceptions carved out by courts are both unpredictable and incoherent.

The consequences of the ruling in *Home Secretary v AF (No. 3)*: control orders and terrorism prevention and investigation measures

The immediate reaction to the House of Lords' ruling was (understandably) one of confusion. In *Home Secretary v AS*[61] Collins J noted that 'the balance between the need for national security and a fair hearing has since *AF* come . . . down in favour of a fair hearing'.[62] However, the concept of a 'core, irreducible minimum' was immediately called into question. After *AF (No. 3)* was handed down the Home Secretary conducted an 'urgent review' of all live control orders.[63] Two controlees involved in the litigation had their control orders discontinued because the Home Office was unwilling to authorise further disclosure in compliance with the new standard.[64]

The executive responded to the ruling in *AF (No. 3)* by attempting to create a category of controls orders which did not contain restrictions capable of engaging the civil limb of Art 6(1) ECHR. In two subsequent cases the executive unsuccessfully argued that the obligations imposed as part of control orders did not engage Art 6(1) ECHR, and as such, were not subject to the *AF (No. 3)* rule. In *BB and BC* (known as 'control orders lite')[65] the Home Secretary argued that the absence of the obligation requiring random searches of the controlee's home removed the measures from the purview of Art 6(1) ECHR.[66] But Collins J ruled that the *AF (No. 3)* duty continued to apply to control orders because '[t]he nature of the proceedings in these cases does in my view engage Article 6 because the control orders, as I have said,

60 *R (Haralambous) v Crown Court of St Albans and Another* [2018] UKSC 1.
61 *Home Secretary v AS* [2009] EWHC 2564 (Admin).
62 Ibid [19].
63 *Home Secretary v AM* [2009] EWHC 3053 (Admin) [30].
64 'AF', 'AN', and 'AE' were released from their control orders. A. Jones, 'Terror Suspect Freed from Control Order' *Guardian* (London, 7 September 2009) available at: <www.theguardian.com/uk/2009/sep/07/control-order-terror-law-lords-johnson>.
65 'Control Orders Lite' (n 57).
66 Ibid: 'the basis of the concession was . . . that the search and seizure would constitute a trespass' [9].

are intended to, and do, restrict the rights of the individuals who are subjected to them.'[67]

Many questions about the application of the rule remained, however. For example, in *AS* Collins J noted that the 'distinction . . . drawn between the allegations and the evidence relied on to support those allegations . . . may . . . not be easy to apply' because 'what amounts to an allegation and what amounts to evidence to support an allegation may depend on the width of the allegation.'[68] In the same case, however, Collins J also rejected Lord Hope's absolute formulation of a 'core irreducible minimum', reemphasising that disclosure continued to be limited by considerations of national security. He emphasised that courts 'cannot order disclosure of material . . . which would compromise national security or would be contrary to the public interest.'[69] Despite this limitation Collins J attached no purchase to the 'makes no difference' principle, declaring that: 'the cogency of the undisclosed material is irrelevant. Even if the judge reasonably considers that there can be no answer to the material, it needs to be disclosed.'[70]

In *BM*[71] there was a further attempt to restrict the *AF (No. 3)* duty in the context of control orders. BM appealed against his proposed forced relocation from London to Leicester. The Administrative Court held that preventing BM from residing in his own home engaged civil rights for the purposes of Art 6(1) ECHR.[72] For Mitting J the important point was that BM's civil right to occupy his home was infringed 'on its face'.[73] This was enough to secure the application of the rule.

Although control orders were repealed and replaced by the Terrorism Prevention and Investigation Measures Act 2011 (TPIMA 2011),[74] debate continued about both the application of the *AF (No. 3)* rule and the 'makes no difference' principle. Both the Liberal Democrats and the Conservatives had made electoral pledges during their 2010 campaigns to reform or scrap the control orders regime.[75] However, the 2011 Home Office *Review of Counter-Terrorism and Security Powers* revealed that, despite criticism of

[67] Ibid [40].
[68] *AS* (n 62) [8].
[69] Ibid [17].
[70] Ibid [12].
[71] *Home Secretary v BM* [2009] EWHC 1572 [4].
[72] Ibid [22].
[73] Ibid [7].
[74] CPR Part 76.
[75] N. Clegg, *Change that Works for You: Liberal Democrat General Election Manifesto 2010: Building a Fairer Britain* (Liberal Democrat Publications, 2010) 94 and Conservative Party, *An Invitation to Join the Government of Britain: Conservative Manifesto 2010* (Conservative Research Department 2010) 79.

the existing control orders regime, both the police and security services felt that there was a need to provide a mechanism of *control* for some individuals where surveillance alone was insufficient to mitigate the threat posed by such persons.[76] The Review explained that because some individuals fell through the cracks in terms of eligibility for deportation or criminal prosecution, there was still a need for a 'system which will protect the public but will be less intrusive [but] more clearly and tightly defined [than control orders]'.[77] The initial TPIMA 2011 created terrorism prevention and investigation measures (TPIMs). The main difference between these orders were the abolition of the relocation power which was previously widely used and struck down by judges on several occasions, and a supposed greater nexus with the possibility of criminal prosecution.[78] However, the relocation power was reintroduced by Part 2 of the Counter-Terrorism and Security Act 2015.

In relation to TPIMs the executive continued their attempts to restrict the application of the *AF (No. 3)* rule on three fronts. First, amendments attempting to acknowledge the rule explicitly in the TPIMA 2011 were defeated in Parliament. Secondly in *BM* (discussed above) the government attempted once again to rely upon the 'makes no difference' principle.[79] Finally, the government sought to argue that the *AF (No. 3)* should not apply to a claim for abuse of process in the context of the imposition of a TPIM.[80]

During this period debate continued in the course of other judgments as to the ability of Special Advocates to mitigate unfairness in CMPs. In *AHK and Others v Home Secretary* Ouseley J suggested that the unfairness of CMPs may have been somewhat overstated by the Special Advocates,[81] echoing the dicta of Lord Dyson in *Al Rawi* which indicated that the views expressed by Special Advocates to the Joint Committee on Human Rights 'may not sufficiently take account of specific statutory protections' available in different contexts.[82] It also became clear that in the context of TPIMS the application of the duty was a flexible one. In *BM* the Administrative

[76] Home Office, *Review of Counter-Terrorism and Security Powers* (Cm 8004, 2011) 38 [13].

[77] Ibid 41 [23].

[78] O. Bowcott, 'UK terror suspects sent into internal exile under control orders' *Guardian* (London, 26 March 2012). A. Travis, 'Scrap worst aspects of control orders now, says former DPP Lord Macdonald' *Guardian* (London, 8 February 2011).

[79] *Home Secretary v BM* [2012] EWHC 714 (Admin).

[80] *Home Secretary v CC and CF* [2012] EWHC 2837 (Admin).

[81] *AHK and Others v Home Secretary* [2012] EWHC 1117 (Admin) [78].

[82] *Al Rawi v Security Services* [2011] UKSC 34 Lord Dyson [37].

Court held that whilst *AF (No. 3)* applied to TPIMs, the level of disclosure should be tailored to the 'nature of the allegation' made against the suspect. Moreover, Collins J noted that how the rule would be applied 'will depend on the facts of that case'.[83]

Two litigants also successfully argued that the *AF (No. 3)* rule applied to their abuse of process claim. CC and CF claimed to have been subject to *unlawful* arrest and detention in Somaliland, followed by *unlawful* deportation. They claimed that had these unlawful events not occurred they would not have been in the jurisdiction to face control order or TPIM proceedings.[84] The substance of their conjoined claim was that the British Security Services (MI5) had been complicit in their detention at Hargeisa Prison in Somaliland between January and March 2011 where both men had been subject to documented mistreatment. This mistreatment was within the knowledge of the British authorities.

At first instance CC and CF were denied *AF (No. 3)* disclosure because they were 'well aware of the case they wish to advance in relation to abuse of process'.[85] This decision was reversed by the Court of Appeal, who held that *AF (No. 3)* disclosure was applicable. This was because a TPIM was capable of restricting 'the liberty of the appellants'. The claim for abuse of process in this context was 'a potentially dispositive form of attempted resistance to proceedings in which the appellants did not choose to engage'.[86] Therefore, the Court of Appeal held that *AF (No. 3)* disclosure was required in order to satisfy wider public confidence in the justice system.[87]

At this juncture two things are clear. First, the interpretation of *AF (No. 3)* rule does not point to a 'core, irreducible minimum' in the manner suggested by Lord Hope. Instead, the application of the *AF (No. 3)* rule varies not only according to the information at hand (which is to be expected) but also according to the severity of the allegation against the suspect and the measures imposed. Secondly, the concept of a 'restriction on liberty' seems to be the animus for the rule in contexts of a dispute engaging the civil limb of Art 6 ECHR. However, subsequent case law demonstrates that neither the perception of severity nor the presence of a restriction on liberty is a predictable guide to the application of the duty.

83 *BM* [2012] (n 79) [22].
84 *Home Secretary v CC and CF* [2012] EWHC 2837 (Admin) [77]–[79].
85 Ibid [85].
86 *Mohamed Ahmed Mohamed and CF v Home Secretary* [2014] EWCA Civ 559 [18].
87 Ibid [19].

Procedural fairness in the Special Immigration Appeals Commission

Unlike other statutes making use of the CMP, the proceedings under the SIAC Act 1997 are generally not concerned with making determinations which engage appellants' civil rights or obligations. Therefore, *Home Secretary v MB* remains the leading case on procedural fairness in SIAC.[88] This is so even though the subject matter of appeals before SIAC involve some of the most serious sanctions a state can inflict upon a litigant, including deprivation of citizenship, and deportation. To put the severity of these measures in their broader context it is worth noting that Supreme Court of the United States described the power to revoke citizenship as 'a form of punishment more primitive than torture'.[89]

However, the procedural requirements of SIAC are influenced by substantive human rights law. Immigration measures are considered by the ECtHR as powers that are beyond the scope of Art 6(1) ECHR due to their distinctly public law character.[90] According to Strasbourg, the removal of aliens and the exclusion of non-nationals from state territory form part of a 'hard core of public-authority prerogatives'[91] to which the right to a fair trial does not apply. Similarly, in *AF (No. 3)* Lord Brown explained that there was 'all the difference in the world' between SIAC procedures and control orders because SIAC cases 'concerned the expulsion of undesirable aliens' meaning that 'the process in those cases was beyond the reach of article 6'.[92]

Moreover, the English courts have been unwilling to use the common law to fill the vacuum left by European human rights law.[93] In *W (Algeria)* Sir David Keene stated that in SIAC proceedings: 'there will be instances where there is obvious unfairness to an appellant, but it is an unfairness which Parliament has patently intended'.[94] The exclusion of both Art 6(1) ECHR and common law 'fair trial' rights from the proceedings leaves a vacuum in available protection. Despite this, the Court of Appeal held that the use of the CMP and Special Advocates before SIAC was 'as fair as could reasonably be achieved'.[95]

[88] *Trop v Dulles* (1958) 356 U.S., at 101–102, 78 S.Ct., at 598.
[89] *Ferrazzini v Italy* (2002) 34 EHRR 45 [29].
[90] *Maaouia v France* (2001) 33 EHRR 1037 [41].
[91] *Ferrazzini* (n 89) [29].
[92] Ibid [113]. See also M. Chamberlain, 'Update on Procedural Fairness in Closed Proceedings' (2009) 28(4) *Civil Justice Quarterly* 448–453, 453.
[93] *W (Algeria) v Secretary of State for the Home Department* [2010] EWCA Civ 898.
[94] Ibid [52].
[95] *A v Secretary of State for the Home Department* [2004] 1 Q.B. 335, Lord Woolf C.J. [57].

However, there are two categories of case which result in the application of the *AF (No. 3)* rule or broadly equivalent protection in SIAC. One is paradoxical, the other can involve an accident of birth. Following the decision in *A and Others v United Kingdom*[96] those held in immigration detention for national security reasons can rely upon a minimum disclosure of allegations because such detention engages Art 5(4) ECHR. They are entitled to a gist of allegations in relation to bail applications or conditions, but not (in principle) in relation to the 'core' national security case necessitating their removal. It is not clear this information falls into discrete categories.

The second category of procedural advantage occurs when the appellant is a citizen of a European Union Member State. ZZ was a dual Algerian and French national who had been excluded from the United Kingdom for national security reasons. In the first SIAC proceeding it was found that 'little of the case against' ZZ had been disclosed, and he was unaware of 'the critical issues'.[97] In a reference for a preliminary ruling the Grand Chamber of the Court of Justice held that ZZ could rely upon Art 47 of the EU Charter of Fundamental Rights. This was similar to Art 6(1) ECHR, save that it was broader in scope and applied to immigration proceedings. As such ZZ was entitled to 'the essence of those grounds in a manner which takes due account of the necessary confidentiality of the evidence'.[98] This duty is similar in nature to *AF (No. 3)* disclosure rule.

The Court of Appeal subsequently held that the ZZ must be informed of the 'essence of the grounds' for his refusal of entry, and further that 'the confidential nature of the evidence could not be used as a justification for non-disclosure to this standard'.[99] The result of *ZZ* is that where the SIAC proceedings concern an EU citizen, *Home Secretary v MB*[100] is no longer the determining authority on disclosure and procedural fairness.[101] Non-EU nationals are only entitled to proceedings which comply with Art 8 ECHR. The procedural requirements of Art 8 ECHR in the context of national security are much weaker than Arts 6 and 5(4) ECHR insofar as they only require the CMP to provide 'guarantees against arbitrariness'.[102] Where a litigant is born, as opposed to what is at stake for them, determines the level of procedural protection a litigant receives. This anomaly will disappear, however, if Brexit proceeds. The EU Charter of

96 *AF (No. 3)* (n 11) Lord Brown [113].
97 *ZZ v Secretary of State for the Home Department* [2013] WLR (D) 218 [30].
98 Ibid [69].
99 *ZZ v Home Secretary* [2014] EWCA Civ 7) [26] emphasis added.
100 *MB* (n 38)
101 *ZZ v Home Secretary* (n 99) [36].
102 *IR (Sri Lanka) v Home Secretary* [2011] EWCA Civ 704 [13]. See also *Al-Nashif v Bulgaria*.

Fundamental Rights will not be part of retained EU law, but aspects of the EU Court's Charter jurisprudence may remain legally relevant after exit day.[103]

The application of *AF (No. 3)* in wider civil proceedings

Post-9/11 the volume of national security litigation has steadily increased. The subsequent approach to applying the *AF (No. 3)* rule in cases engaging Art 6(1) ECHR going forward has been referred to as a 'spectrum . . . which is context and case specific'.[104] In *Al Rawi v Security Services* the government asked the Supreme Court to institute a CMP at common law in the context of a damages claim against the security services for their alleged involvement in extraordinary rendition and torture. The Supreme Court refused this application on the basis that it would contradict the fundamental principles of fairness at common law. Lord Dyson explained that 'open justice is not a mere procedural rule. It is a fundamental common law principle. [A] closed material procedure involves a departure from both the open justice and the natural justice principles.'[105] The Supreme Court held that such fundamental incursions into core principles could only be undertaken by Parliament.[106] This ruling catalysed the enactment of the JSA 2013.[107] A report from the Ministry of Justice on the operation of the JSA 2013 during its first five years of enactment remains overdue at the time of writing.[108]

Section 6(1) of the JSA 2013 states that a court may declare that an application for a CMP can be made on two conditions. Condition one is that one of the parties to the proceedings would be required to disclose 'sensitive material', defined exclusively as material related to national security.[109] The second condition is that a declaration is in the 'interests of the fair and effective administration of justice'.[110] Thereafter, a CMP can be authorised without the need to disclose the whole universe of sensitive material to the judge.[111] A declaration

[103] European Union (Withdrawal) Act 2018, ss. 5(4), 6(7). For an illuminating discussion see M. Markakis, 'Brexit and the EU Charter of Fundamental Rights' [2019] *Public Law* 82, 90–95.

[104] *K, A & B v Secretary of State for Defence* [2017] EWHC 830 (Admin) at [12] and [14].

[105] *Al Rawi* (n 82) Lord Dyson [11]–[14]. See P.P. Craig, *Administrative Law*, 8th edn (OUP, 2016) Chs. 12–13.

[106] *Al Rawi* (n 82).

[107] CPR Part 82 'Closed Material Procedure'. See also The Civil Procedure (Amendment No. 5) Rules 2013, SI 1571/2013.

[108] Justice and Security Act 2013: Written question—135211 (13 April 2018) Mr Kenneth Clarke.

[109] Justice and Security Act 2013, s. 6(11).

[110] Justice and Security Act 2013, s. 6(5). For a good overview of the mechanics of s. 6 see L. Graham, 'Statutory Secret Trials: The Judicial Approach to Closed Material Procedures Under the Justice and Security Act 2013' (2019) *Civil Justice Quarterly* 189.

[111] *R (Sarkani and Others) v Foreign Secretary* [2014] EWHC 2359 (Admin).

can however be reviewed and revoked if it no longer is in the 'interests of the fair and effective administration of justice'.[112] According to section 6 any party to the litigation holding sensitive information can apply for a CMP. However, in practice this will usually be the government. After a CMP is authorised, the applicability of *AF (No. 3)* disclosure is considered separately.

The legacy of *Tariq v Home Secretary*

Authority on the application for the *AF (No. 3)* to wider civil proceedings stems from the Supreme Court ruling in *Tariq*,[113] handed down before the enactment of the JSA 2013. The central question in *Tariq* was whether a CMP was available in the context of an Employment Tribunal, and if so, whether the *AF (No. 3)* rule applied to tribunal proceedings. Tariq, an immigration officer, had his security clearance withdrawn because his brother and cousin had been arrested as part of a major counter-terrorism policing operation. Tariq's brother was released without charge, but his cousin was later convicted of conspiracy to murder. After losing an internal security vetting appeal, Tariq took his case to the Employment Appeals tribunal alleging racial and religious discrimination.

The Employment Tribunals Act 1996 contained the statutory power to facilitate a CMP.[114] The Supreme Court chose to assume that employment tribunal proceedings fell within the scope of the right to a fair trial in Art 6(1) ECHR. However, on the question of *AF (No. 3)* type disclosure (referred to as 'A-type disclosure'), the majority rejected Tariq's claim that the House of Lords ruling in *AF (No. 3)* had established a rigid rule that the 'core irreducible minimum' must apply whenever Art 6(1) ECHR was engaged.

Lord Brown gave the clearest statement of the majority's reasons for declining to apply the *AF (No. 3)* rule. The first reason was ECtHR case law demonstrated the Convention did not require disclosure in the context of security clearance appeals or legal proceedings concerning covert surveillance. The second reason was simply that Tariq's claim, despite falling within the scope of Art 6 ECHR, was not important enough to require the government to risk national security by affording him a minimum level of procedural protection.

[112] Justice and Security Act 2013, ss. 7(2) and 6(5).

[113] *Secretary of State for the Home Department (Appellant) v Tariq (Respondent), Secretary of State for the Home Department (Respondent) v Tariq (Appellant)* [2011] UKSC 35.

[114] Employment Tribunals Act 1998, s. 7 and The Employment Tribunals (Constitution and Rules of Procedure) Regulations 2004 (SI 2004/1861).

In respect of the first reason the relevant Strasbourg authorities cited were *Leander v Sweden*[115] and *Kennedy v United Kingdom.*[116] The majority held that *Leander* was factually analogous to Tariq's case. Mr Leander had been refused security clearance to work in a naval museum within a restricted military security zone. This was due to his suspected past involvement with communist politics. Leander petitioned Strasbourg for a declaration that the Swedish authority's refusal to disclose information pertaining to the refusal of security clearance breached his Convention rights. Leander's Art 6 ECHR claim was declared inadmissible. In respect of the Art 8 ECHR claim, the ECtHR held that given that the decision concerned national security, the refusal of the Swedish authorities was lawful.[117] The Court was satisfied that presence of a national policy structuring administrative discretion in this context of security vetting was a sufficient procedural safeguard.[118] However, there is a key distinction between Leander and Tariq's situation: unlike Leander, Mr Tariq was already in post when his security clearance was withdrawn. He incurred a concrete loss, as opposed to the frustration of a mere aspiration for employment. Analogous reasoning from the common law suggest a higher level of procedural protection is appropriate in the context of the loss of an existing licence or right, as opposed to a mere application to be considered.[119]

The extent of procedural protection required by Art 6(1) ECHR in the context of the Investigatory Powers Tribunal (IPT) was considered by Strasbourg in *Kennedy v United Kingdom.*[120] The IPT oversees complaints against the intelligence services related to covert surveillance. Almost all hearings are conducted in private, and the tribunal has near-absolute 'neither confirm nor deny' (NCND) policy in respect of the conduct of investigations to protect the confidentiality and effectiveness of surveillance operations. The ruling in *Kennedy* and its application to *Tariq* was summarised succinctly by Lord Mance: '[a]s to article 6, the Court in *Kennedy* found it unnecessary to decide whether this article applies to proceedings concerning . . . surveillance, because it concluded that, assuming it does, the IPT's rules of procedure complied with the requirements of article 6(1)'[121] without further disclosure.

The notion that Tariq's claim was insufficiently important to attract *AF (No. 3)* disclosure was explained by Lord Brown. He held that, notwithstanding

[115] *Leander v Sweden* [1987] ECHR 4.
[116] *Kennedy v United Kingdom* (Application No. 26839/05) (unreported) 18 May 2010.
[117] *Leander* (n 115) [66].
[118] Ibid [55]–[56].
[119] *McInnes v Onslow-Fane and Another* [1978] 1 W.L.R. 1520.
[120] *Kennedy* (n 116).
[121] *Tariq* (n 113) Lord Mance [34].

the fact that *A v United Kingdom* established a 'rigid principle', the principle was only applicable in the context of immigration detention. This was so because detention of this nature involved a deprivation of liberty engaging Art 5(4) ECHR. The *AF (No. 3)* rule was, however, also applicable to control orders 'because of the striking similarities between the two situations'.[122] However, this did not mean that the *AF (No 3)* rule should apply to Tariq's case because 'a monetary claim for discrimination' despite also being within the purview of Art 6 ECHR was in a different category to immigration detention and control orders. Tariq had not suffered the same detriment as either detainees or controlees. Lady Hale, who indicated agreement with Lord Brown in *Tariq* explained extra-judicially that the House of Lords in *AF (No. 3)* has essentially extended the 'minimum core' rule to control orders as a prophylactic measure: 'Although *A v United Kingdom* was concerned with detention, and the control order cases were not, the House of Lords . . . considered it inevitable that Strasbourg would take the same view of the procedural requirements for confirming control orders.'[123]

Proceedings under the Justice and Security Act 2013 and beyond

In *Tariq* the Supreme Court created the following principle: *AF (No. 3)* disclosure would only be available if the instant case satisfied two conditions. The first was that it engaged the civil limb of Art 6 ECHR, and the second was that the measure challenged concerned 'severe restrictions on personal liberty'.[124] This 'liberty rule' is an unsatisfactory benchmark. The effect of its application has been the complete exclusion of Justice and Security Act 2013 proceedings from its purview.

First of all, the judicial classification of what sorts of measures amount to a 'severe restriction on liberty' has been internally incoherent. Whilst there is no doubt that control orders meet this threshold, other cases that *prima facie* severely restrict liberty have not been accorded the same treatment. As discussed above, terrorist asset-freezing measures administered by the Treasury fell within the purview of Art 6 and were deemed sufficiently severe to attract *AF (No. 3)* disclosure.[125] However, in *Maftah* and *Khaled*[126] a parallel regime

[122] Ibid Lord Brown [88].
[123] Baroness Hale of Richmond, 'Argentoratum Locutum: Is the Supreme Court Really Supreme?' The 2011 Nottingham Human Rights Lecture, University of Nottingham (1 December 2011).
[124] *Tariq* (n 113) Lord Mance [81].
[125] *Gulam Mastafa* (n 54).
[126] *Foreign Secretary v E Maftah and A Khaled* [2011] EWCA Civ 350.

administered directly by the United Nations Security Council to which the Foreign and Commonwealth Office nominated the appellants was held not to be determinative of 'civil rights and obligations' within the meaning of Art 6(1) ECHR. The legal source of the regime, as opposed to its effect, meant that *AF (No. 3)* disclosure was unavailable. Moreover, there was no reference to the language of 'severe restriction on liberty' but the UN freezing orders nonetheless amounted to 'a targeted assault by the state on an individual's privacy, reputation and property'.[127] For this reason, the common law was deemed to be able to provide a guarantee of disclosure equivalent in nature to the *AF (No. 3)* rule.

An Iranian bank excluded from the UK financial services market was also entitled to benefit from the *AF (No. 3)* rule in the context of their challenge to a freezing order issued under the Counter Terrorism Act 2008.[128] In so ordering the Court of Appeal concluded that both Art 6(1) ECHR and the *AF (No. 3)* applied to the Bank's situation. In so doing, the Court of Appeal did not undertake any comparison with control orders, nor did they refer to a 'severe restriction of liberty' of any kind being necessary for the application of the rule. However, in *Haralambous* the Supreme Court refused *AF (No. 3)* disclosure in the context of a CMP instituted to facilitate judicial review of a warrant for search and seizure made using intelligence from a confidential police informant. Lord Mance held that a person claiming a 'proprietary, possessory or other interest' in relation to the subject matter of the warrant was not entitled to disclosure.[129]

The concept of a severe restriction upon liberty was reaffirmed as the requisite criterion for disclosure in *AZ v Home Secretary*.[130] In this case the Court of Appeal held the *AF (No. 3)* rule was inapplicable to a CMP in the context of judicial review of the legality to refuse a travel document under the Refugee Convention on national security grounds. Burnett LJ, writing for a unanimous bench, held such a refusal 'is not comparable with [the] severe restrictions on liberty'[131] imposed by a control order or an asset-freezing measure.

From the above cases, we can see that the 'liberty principle' has no fixed internal content, and no fixed place in determining when *AF (No. 3)* disclosure is necessary to render a CMP procedurally fair. Some matters which seem to place strong restrictions upon liberty (such as denial of permission to travel) do not attract protection, whereas others such as asset-freezing regimes are

[127] Ibid [26].
[128] CPR Part 79.
[129] *Haralambous* (n 60) [65].
[130] *AZ v Home Secretary* [2017] EWCA Civ 35.
[131] Ibid [17].

protected by the rule. If we broaden the terminology of 'severe restriction on liberty' to include interference with property, we are no further forward in terms of legal certainty. Exclusion from the UK financial markets (essentially a restraint upon economic freedom) attracts protection, but the forced entry into property and its potential seizure does not.

The current scope of the rule is under-inclusive insofar as it ignores the strong interest in providing open justice in cases concerning alleged public wrongs. One of the key problems with confining disclosure to cases involving severe restrictions upon liberty (or perhaps property) is that it implicitly imbeds an assumption that such cases are the most important litigations which will take place under CMP. This is not necessarily so. In *UNISON* Lord Reed explained that individual litigations often have consequences far beyond their own facts: 'the idea that bringing a claim before a court . . . is a purely private activity, and . . . that such claims provide no broader social benefit [is] demonstrably untenable'.[132] Judicial review challenges to government policy may not directly concern the right to liberty or property, but they can still concern issues central to the public interest.

Campaign Against Arms Trade v Secretary of State for International Trade (*CAAT*)[133] is one such example. In *CAAT* the appellants successfully argued that the Secretary of State's decision-making process in relation to granting arms export licences to Saudi Arabia was unlawful for reason of procedural irrationality.[134] The litigation was initiated in the wake of concerns that Saudi Arabia was complicit in serious violations of international human rights law in the context of the civil war in Yemen. In the Administrative Court *AF (No. 3)* disclosure was ruled to be inapplicable to the case when permission for a CMP was granted, however. An action reviewing the lawfulness of the British government's continued permission of arms sales in the context of civil war which has killed an estimated 56,000 people[135] is central to the public interest. The *CAAT* litigation revealed that the British government's decision-making procedure was irrational. Viewed in this light, the decision to refuse *AF (No. 3)* disclosure looks increasingly untenable.

There has been no extension of *AF (No. 3)* disclosure to damages claims under the JSA 2013. This is due to the fact that damages actions occur *ex post facto* and are not direct challenges to severe restrictions on liberty. However,

132 *Unison v Lord Chancellor* [2017] UKSC 51, Lord Reed [67].

133 *Campaign Against Arms Trade v Secretary of State for International Trade* [2019] EWCA Civ 1020.

134 *Associated Provincial Picture Houses v Wednesbury Corporation* [1948] KB 223.

135 P. Cockburn, 'The Yemen War Death Toll is Five Times Higher than We Think' *The Independent* (26 October 2018).

several claims for misconduct in public office allege unlawful detention and other serious human rights violations.

In *Khaled (No. 1)* the claimant brought an action seeking damages for misfeasance in public office against MI5, MI6, the Home Secretary, and the Foreign Secretary.[136] Khaled and others alleged that the defendant intelligence services (overseen by the Secretaries of State) passed questions to Libyan security forces who were detaining him. That information was then passed to the UN Security Council and Khaled's financial assets were frozen under counter-terrorism Resolutions.[137] The claimant alleged that this conduct amounted to misfeasance because the information was obtained in a context where he suffered treatment amounting to torture or inhuman or degrading treatment.

Khaled's lawyer argued that the *AF (No. 3)* rule should apply to the CMP in his case because the conduct giving rise to his damages claim amounted to a 'significant incursion in liberty'[138] that was as severe if not greater than a control order. This argument was rejected. Irwin J held that the rule was inapplicable because the instant case was 'not a case where loss of liberty, detention or incursion on the Claimant's Article 8 rights is in prospect'.[139] In other words, where such conduct is in the past *AF (No. 3)* disclosure is inapplicable. A similar decision was reached in *HTF, ZMS v Ministry of Defence*[140] in which the claimants sought damages for ill-treatment at the hands of the UK armed forces during their detention in Iraq. Once again, the Court held that *AF (No. 3)* was inapplicable because the case 'involve[d] no current risk' to the litigants. Instead, it was a 'a claim for financial compensation for historic events'. Damages claims were 'some way removed from the kind of case in which *AF (No 3)* disclosure has typically been required'.[141] This conclusion was reached notwithstanding that a central plank of the case involved an allegation that the claimants were captured by an unknown UK Special Forces unit. The claimants were not provided with any 'gist' regarding the identity of the Special Forces unit, or the possible extend of their involvement.[142] This invariably makes any claim difficult to advance in open proceedings. Moreover, given the recent concerns about the general lack of accountability for Special Forces missions[143] such a ruling does not bolster public confidence in the justice system.

136 *Khaled v Security Services and Others (No. 1)* [2016] EWHC 1727 (QB).
137 UNSCR 1267 (15 October 1999), UN Doc S/RES/1267.
138 *Khaled v Security Services* (n 136) [16].
139 Ibid [34].
140 *HTF, ZMS v Ministry of Defence* [2018] EWHC 1623 (QB).
141 Ibid [36].
142 Ibid [32].
143 P. Rogers, 'Accountability in Shadow War' Oxford Research Group blog (30 March 2016) Available at <https://www.oxfordresearchgroup.org.uk/uk-special-forces-accountability-in-shadow-war >.

It also makes procedural fairness under the CMP something of a temporal lottery under the 'liberty principle'. Given the circumstances of the detention in *Khaled* and *HTF* it is unlikely that they would have access to lawyers, let alone the resources for judicial review. Had they been in the UK and subject to a control order, *AF (No. 3)* disclosure would have been automatic, even though the infringement of rights would have been less severe.

Conclusion: a core irreducible minimum?

When we step back, the application of the *AF (No. 3)* rule in the context of CMPs looks like an ill-sewn patchwork. There is no doubt that CMPs have become a fixed aspect of civil procedure. Their presence is both necessary for the protection of national security, and to allow some species of claims to proceed which would otherwise be incontestable.[144] The present state of the law shows that the minimum threshold of disclosure envisaged by some of the judges in *AF (No. 3)* is neither core, nor irreducible. Extending the *AF (No. 3)* duty to all situations where Art 6(1) ECHR is engaged and providing equivalent common law protection where Arts 6(1) and 5(4) ECHR are not engaged is the most desirable approach to procedural fairness in the context of the CMP.

There is also the prospect that satisfying the duty in the context of a procedure which is undoubtedly 'elaborate and unusual'[145] will be a burdensome exercise. We have already seen that in some situations, it will leave the government with a hard choice: to meet the standards of the duty and jeopardize national security (which may include relationships with foreign intelligence) or to abandon the contested measure or settle a litigation to avoid doing so. Protecting national security and upholding the rule of law invariably involves such hard decisions.

However, many categories of case will require the balancing of the rule of law against other public interests. Even if we accept this conclusion (which the common law does to some degree), it is not clear that the most important rights and interests in litigation are being accurately identified. Where *AF (No. 3)* disclosure is permitted it can make a material difference to fairness in the context of a CMP, which are governed by an effectively standardised set of procedural rules. It helps to edge non-government litigants further along a spectrum towards the twin goals of open justice and equality of arms.

[144] *Carnduff v Rock* [2001] 1 WLR 1786.
[145] *W (Algeria) v Home Secretary* [2010] EWCA Civ 898, Sir David Keene [15].

The original aim of the CMP was to provide for a 'substantial measure of procedural justice' in immigration proceedings complicated by security sensitive information. Within the context of Art 6 ECHR the approach to contextualisation by the English courts has also been excessive and unprincipled. The current judicial approach to the application of the *AF (No. 3)* principle masks dangerous assumptions about the relative importance of substantive human rights. Even though '[t]here is no support for . . . a hierarchy in the Convention or EU jurisprudence'[146] refusing to institute the *AF (No. 3)* rule in all cases engaging Art 6(1) ECHR implicitly supports the idea that claims about rights such as liberty require a 'fairer' procedure than claims about equality, property, privacy, or the legality of police activity. Lord Kerr's partial dissent in *Tariq* illuminates this issue. He stated that: '[the] eligibility criteria for inclusion in this privileged group are not clear . . . It seems to me that there is no principled basis on which to draw a distinction between the essence of the right to a fair trial based on the nature of the claim that is made.'[147] There seems to be no principled reason as to why some trials should be fairer than others.

[146] *AZ* (n 130) [28].
[147] *Tariq* (n 113) Lord Kerr [134].

PART VIII
TECHNOLOGY

19
Reform of Civil Justice

Richard Goodman

In September 2016, the then Lord Chief Justice and Lord Chancellor, together with the Senior President of Tribunals, set out their joint vision for a reformed, modernised justice system, one that would combine its 'respected traditions with the enabling power of technology'.

They said: '[Our] vision is to modernise and upgrade our justice system so that it works even better for everyone, from judges and legal professionals, to witnesses, litigants and the vulnerable victims of crime. When they have to engage with the system, we want everyone to have available to them the finest justice system in the world.'

For too many years, getting access to our justice system—and to the judges which make it the envy of the global community—has been harder than anyone could want. Arcane processes have made the system ever more difficult to administer, and ever more complex to access. A heavy reliance on paper-based processes and physical interactions has prevailed even for resolving simple matters. This has made the system confusing, costly and inefficient even for those who work within it. Worse, for members of the public—often at the most challenging times of their lives—the system can feel inaccessible, bewildering and even intimidating.

Four years on, change is happening. HM Courts & Tribunals Service (HMCTS)—working closely with the wider judiciary, legal professionals and users of our wider justice system—is now opening up the justice system and making this vision of reform a reality. Civil justice is a pioneer in the effort.

The HMCTS reform programme

The reform programme is a huge endeavour. The Government has committed more than £1 billion of investment to make the system easier to use and more efficient to run across every jurisdiction.[1] As with any transformation of this

[1] A more detailed overview of what this means across jurisdictions is available here: https://assets.

Richard Goodman, *Reform of Civil Justice* In: *The Civil Procedure Rules at 20.* Edited by: Andrew Higgins, Oxford University Press (2020). © the several contributors. DOI: 10.1093/oso/9780198863182.003.0019.

scale, the programme operates within a strict budgetary and governance structure, reporting to the Lord Chancellor, the Lord Chief Justice and the Senior President of Tribunals through an independently chaired Board.[2] The judiciary are a key part of these governance arrangements.

The programme is expected to deliver measurable improvements to the experience of the public,[3] as well as administrative savings over its lifetime. The business case for the investment is refreshed every 18 months or so to assess performance[4] and to release the next tranche of funding, part of which has come from the sale of underused HMCTS buildings.

Modernising the civil courts was, and continues to be, an essential part of what is unquestionably the most ambitious change of its kind anywhere in the world.

The goals of civil reform

The court and tribunal system should be a leveller, a mechanism by which everyone can enforce their rights against another party. Even if never used, the knowledge that there can be ready recourse to the courts to resolve a dispute is fundamental to an effective justice system. Reliable, accessible civil courts underpin the socio-economic relationships which allow trade to flourish and which provide for most disputes to be settled outside of court. This much is well-understood.

Less well-understood is that such a system cannot be built by high quality, independent judges alone (internationally pre-eminent in that respect as we are) or even in partnership with the high quality legal services sector we enjoy. It depends significantly on having a system which is practical, straightforward to use, and which enables people from all walks of life to seek justice. It is telling that developing countries, when making tough decisions about where to invest in infrastructure, see the merits of putting money into making civil courts

publishing.service.gov.uk/government/uploads/system/uploads/attachment_data/file/775594/Public_Accounts_Committee_Recommendation_2_31_Jan_2019.pdf

[2] The governance arrangements for HMCTS are set out in a framework document at https://www.gov.uk/government/publications/hm-courts-and-tribunals-service-framework-document

[3] The programme will be independently evaluated to this effect. The overarching approach to evaluation in the programme is set out here: https://assets.publishing.service.gov.uk/government/uploads/system/uploads/attachment_data/file/775588/Public_Accounts_Committee_Recommendation_4_31_Jan_2019pdf.pdf

[4] Regular updates, including videos of how new services work, are published here: https://www.gov.uk/guidance/hmcts-reform-update-civil

accessible. Such changes are central to overall economic and business confidence.[5] Complexity should not put people off from pursuing justice. Simplicity and intelligibility matter.

The approach of the reform programme is to put the needs of the public at the centre of how the courts system operates. It involves re-designing how court processes and procedures work in order to build them around these needs. This is not simply a digitisation of paper forms, still less an administrative cost-cutting exercise. It involves testing again and again new digital ways of working with real members of the public to establish what works best. It involves changing incrementally to avoid the risky 'big bangs' familiar to many reforms. And it only ever involves *more* ways to access the system. Contrary to some myths, the unrepresented public will still be able to engage with the courts by post, and in person.

In practice, the reforms mean building new, intuitive ways for the public—and their representatives—to structure, submit and manage claims online. They mean new ways—digital and otherwise—to enable parties to settle disputes fairly and speedily where appropriate. They mean giving judges and litigants more, and better, choices about how work can be managed, with the opportunity to make greater use of video (and cut travel) as well as online decision-making. They mean 'push' notifications of what is happening in a case and what needs to happen next. They mean new digital tools to give greater certainty about when cases will be heard. Critically, at every turn it will involve simpler processes for those seeking swifter and more straightforward routes to justice—and the development of end-to-end online courts for increasing numbers of civil disputes.

In doing so, reform aims to retain and enhance our country's world-class position as the trusted jurisdiction of choice for international disputes, and also build public trust in that our civil justice system can work more effectively for the large number of people and small businesses whose smaller claims require redress and resolution.

The case for civil reform

That our civil system of justice needs reform is beyond all reasonable doubt. Countless reviews and studies have highlighted significant weaknesses of a

[5] https://www.doingbusiness.org/en/data/exploretopics/enforcing-contracts/good-practices#Introducing

system that has long been highly reliant on complex, paper-based processes and crippling costs.

Lord (then Lord Justice) Briggs tackled this challenge head-on in his important review of the civil courts in 2015 and 2016.[6] He described it as 'a truly shocking state of affairs' that only wealthy litigants or those eligible for legal aid and other means of free legal representation could access the civil courts effectively. 'Most ordinary people and small businesses,' he said, 'struggle to benefit from the strengths of our civil justice system.'

From an administrative view, the system has long failed to keep pace with user-focused, digital systems adopted by most other commercial and public sector businesses and services. Even today, it is not uncommon to witness dedicated HMCTS staff work in the shadow of enormous piles of paper reminiscent of office life in the 1970s rather than the 21st century.

Such inefficient systems are not just more costly and slower than digital information processes, they are also more prone to error and loss, and, vitally, provide next to no means to shape a service around the needs of those who use it. Instantly emitted digital orders should be the norm, but even decent basics become prohibitively challenging to deliver where there is insufficient digital infrastructure. In a system where there is no means of centrally tracking phone calls or the progress of cases even establishing where a case is at has become a significant administrative burden. More than half the people who call HMCTS do so to get an update on a case or to find out what happens next.[7]

Our approach to reform

Bold change takes time. It requires careful work to ensure that new arrangements have the confidence of those who use and need them. 'Big bang' transformational programmes in the public and private sectors that try to introduce change too quickly have faced considerable challenges.

So, our reform programme, while bold in its ambition, is deliberately incremental in its application enabling us to pilot and iterate change on the back of real-world evidence and practice. It is based, to use the jargon, on an agile

[6] https://www.judiciary.uk/wp-content/uploads/2016/07/civil-courts-structure-review-final-report-jul-16-final-1.pdf

[7] Pg. 12, paragraph 55: This is included in our as yet unpublished response to the Justice Select Committee, whom we are reliant on publishing—HMCTS can provide the link when published. If the publication of this chapter precedes the publication of our response, this reference will need to be removed.

methodology which creates the building blocks to establish wider systems and assembles them in different ways depending on the need at hand. This approach also allows us to be constantly testing our services with their users, and improving them on the back of user behaviour and feedback.

This demands the need to collect data routinely and accurately. This is a vital resource that has been missing in much of the court system for far too long.[8] It allows us to measure the success of any activity and to help shape the HMCTS of the future. It is a strong endorsement of the first reformed service in the civil jurisdiction that it has consistently delivered a service that has satisfied 90% of its users. But this is the first time courts have sought to routinely collect data of this sort.

The development of our online civil money claims (OCMC) service reflects this approach—and provides an example of how the wider of the reform programme is being delivered.

Civil money claims

Civil money claims account for more than four-fifths of the 1.6 million claims issued in the civil courts each year—with the vast majority (83%) uncontested. Yet the system has long been characterised by cumbersome processes for making and then managing a claim; slow administrative responsiveness; and—even with a basic online system (Money Claims Online or MCOL) for claims under £100,000 introduced in 2002—a process that is difficult to navigate for litigants not legally represented.

Our goal was, and is, therefore to reform the whole process as we bring access to it online, creating an end-to-end digital court for the management and resolution of all civil money claims to make the process quicker and easier to access for parties, particularly for those without legal representation, and more efficient to determine and administer.

Drawing on the invaluable work of Briggs LJ, we undertook a considerable amount of work with those who need and use the system most—legal professionals, the advice sector, academics and public users—to establish the best way forward to deliver this goal over time. Collaboration with the judiciary has been vital and we are indebted to the Civil Procedure Rules Committee (CPRC) chaired by LJ Coulson and its CPRC sub-committee chaired by Birss J in helping to shape, guide and lead this vital work.

[8] https://www.gov.uk/government/news/hmcts-publishes-response-to-report-on-use-of-data

The first phase of the project was to develop an easy-to-use online platform to enable litigants in person to make a claim of up to £10,000 online. To this effect, our first early 'private beta' pilot was launched in August 2017 after extensive user testing. This had limited functions and users and was used to trial a working money claims service while, at the same time, making further changes as a result of user feedback.

The online service

In March 2018, our pilot online civil money claims service[9] was made generally available to litigants in person for claims up to £10,000 across England and Wales—and, by the end of last year, had received more than 110,000 claims.

This service enables people and small businesses to make single claims online. Their claim is sent automatically to the defendant. Critically, the service allows users to provide a narrative of events they believe are relevant to their dispute, and facilitates the creation of a structured timeline which helps litigant capture the key statements of fact on which their claim (or defence) relies. This same process also allows them to specify key evidence on which they rely, without having to submit large digital bundles of material from the outset. While this is not yet at the stage of bespoke case-generation by case-type (as outlined in the Briggs review), it is a critical step towards helping litigants frame their case effectively. Later in 2020 the service will expand to enable the upload of documents which can later form a comprehensive digital bundle.

This facilitated early structuring of claims helps all those involved to engage with the case more effectively. The defendant has an opportunity to make an offer, and an online settlement tool allows parties to settle a case without any third-party involvement. More than 340 cases have been settled online in this way. The quickest case has been completed—from the moment of the initial claim to the claim being paid—in 1hr and 58 minutes. This allows those cases—where the parties decide to settle—to be put to bed quickly and efficaciously.

But it also helps drive resolution of cases that are not so straightforwardly settled. The new service is not just about making the system for claiming money more straightforward. It is also more straightforward to *defend* claims. On a recent sampling exercise, the number of defendants who engage with the

[9] Available here: https://www.gov.uk/make-money-claim

claim against them is around *twice*[10] as high in the new service as in the previous service. As well as being further evidence that digital working can help increase overall engagement with the justice system, this means that defendants are more often making active choices about the cases in which they are involved. The net result is fewer people deciding only to engage with the claimant at the point where a bailiff has arrived to enforce a judgment. This means less re-opening of cases, and is further evidence that designing the process better can reduce overall cost while *also* improving the accessibility of the system.

It is particularly encouraging that the new service is helping disadvantaged and vulnerable groups of people. 'I am 71 years old,' wrote one user to us, 'and not quite computer friendly, but I think it is a very good web site and quite easy to use.' Users overall rate the service well. About nine out of ten say they are satisfied or highly satisfied with the new service[11]—though the user feedback about where we can improve has enabled further iterative changes to improve the experience. We read every comment, and are pleased that it is increasingly common for users to describe the service as 'simple and effective'. 'I really can't stress,' added one, 'how well it worked, and the claim I issued on Monday was settled on Thursday.'

This digital service is supported by national telephone assistance, which for the first time now provides additional help and support to those using the new service. This will be bolstered with an online webchat facility when it moves into HMCTS's new national Courts and Tribunals Service Centre (CTSC) in Stoke in July this year. A more focused face-to-face support for those needing additional digital assistance is already available in locations across the country. This is a huge step forward for those who have the greatest challenges getting access to the system.

Further recent additions

By the end of 2019 we had implemented three significant additional features to what remains a pilot online civil money claims service. Gradually it is moving towards becoming the end-to-end system we seek.

[10] HMCTS written evidence to Justice Select Committee March 2019: http://data.parliament.uk/writtenevidence/committeeevidence.svc/evidencedocument/justice-committee/hmcts-court-and-tribunal-reforms/written/97827.html

[11] Available here: This is included in our as yet unpublished response to the Justice Select Committee, whom we are reliant on publishing—HMCTS can provide the link when published. If the publication of this chapter precedes the publication of our response, this reference will need to be removed.

Since September last year, parties to a case have been able to provide hearing requirements via directions questionnaires online for defended cases up to £1,000 and now available to all cases. This is significantly improving the time it takes for a case to be listed for hearing. By asking better questions, more simply, more quickly, and with less human intervention we have cut the time it takes to get a case ready for listing at a local court from an average of 59 days to four days. We will make this feature available to all OCMC cases shortly.

At the same time, we have introduced a feature to promote mediation for lower-value claims. In defended cases up to £300 (and now increased to £500) parties are now required to opt out of mediation rather than opting in, helping people to resolve disputes quickly and in a more proportionate way. Two-thirds of those entering mediation via this process are now settling, and we will be actively working with the CPRC sub-committee and others on the development of this pilot and its evaluation.

In parallel, a pilot is also underway to enable legal advisers to give directions at eight pilot courts for defended cases up to £300. The orders are reviewed and approved by District Judges. These arrangements are intended to free up judicial time, allowing cases to be dealt with more speedily on the digital file alone. The pilot has now been extended this to an additional eleven courts, making nineteen in total. Again, a full evaluation of this work will take place before widespread application.

In the same eight courts, we began to trial a process that, for the first time, introduced paperless working in the county court for the judiciary and administrative staff. Judges have been able to allocate cases and draw orders within the digital platform for defended cases up to £1,000. The monetary ceiling has now been increased to £10,000 and the trial has been expanded to the nineteen courts that the legal adviser pilot is taking place.

Wider civil reforms

There are wider reforms underway to the civil courts too alongside the OCMC . Aside from civil money claims, we are prioritising the delivery of a digital service for Unspecified cases ie. claims filed for an unfixed amount of money. These cases, which often relate to personal injury, form a significant proportion of the remainder of civil claims. A pilot enabling ten legal firms to issue claims digitally was introduced in 2017 and despite expanding this pilot following the covid outbreak, the remainder of the process remains paper based for users.

We will be taking the learning from the OCMC service when developing the digital service for Unspecified Claims. We expect the digital service to provide users with a more efficient service for progressing their cases providing the ability to issue, respond and provide hearing information online; to upload documents online in preparation for hearing; and review the progress of their case online. The service will be rolled out to legal professionals first and we will continue to iterate and improve the service based on user feedback.
At the other end of the spectrum from the lowest-value claims, we are expanding the use of CE-File into the Court of Appeal Civil Division, other High Court jurisdictions not already using CE-File, all Upper Tribunal Chambers and the Employment Appeal Tribunal, including where this work is done outside of London. CE-File is an online digital case management system for use by judiciary and staff, that also offers an external facing E-Filing service for parties, to issue and file documents, pay court fees and review and track their case(s) online.

This will reduce the reliance on paper an create digital working practices. In doing so it should also reduce the frustration some users experience chasing for updates about the progress of their case. We will continue to develop this system for the Court of Appeal Civil Division, Administrative Court, Upper Tribunal Chambers and the Employment Appeal Tribunal over the course of 2020, with deployment into these areas around Easter 2021.

In addition, following successful pilots in the North-East and North-West, we have introduced a further ten Warrant of Control Support Centres across England and Wales to centralise and standardise our service. These centres have helped us engage debtors early with the aim of providing support and resolving the warrant as soon as possible, reducing the need for a bailiff to visit the debtor at their home address.

Next steps

The OCMC pilot will continue to run until the end of next year and will continue to be improved following user feedback. The system we have developed for lawyers to engage digitally in the new services—'MyHMCTS', which is now available in divorce and probate cases—will also follow in due course in the civil jurisdiction, with the service being adapted as needed for unspecified and higher value claims.

Piece-by-piece, these are the building blocks of a digital system of civil justice which is increasingly open to all and progressively easier to run. Based on continuous, rigorous testing it is creating a way of doing justice which is truly built around the needs of those who use it.

There is still a long way to travel before we can say the work is complete. But we have made considerable progress already in helping to open up a process that has been inaccessible for too many, for too long. This globally pioneering work will help us secure the reputation we have earned for outstanding justice into the 21st century.

20

Artificial Intelligence in the Administration of Justice

Adrian Zuckerman

Introduction

Computer-driven systems are increasingly used for decision making in both public administration and in private enterprise. There is a growing body of evidence that before long artificial intelligence (AI) will be able to perform many human activities that are incapable of automation. That is, activities that call for decision making in a variety of circumstances impossible to predict in advance, such as driving cars, or making medical diagnosis. Machine learning is in its infancy and it is not possible to predict to what extent it would be able to replicate human activities such as constructing legal arguments or providing legal representation in litigation. But it is becoming clearer by the day that AI is going to have a considerable role in dispute resolution. Disputes arising from transactions on internet sites such as eBay and Amazon are already handled by computers. Since machine learning is developing at a fast and accelerating pace, we can expect AI systems to compete for legal work within years.

The legal profession has been exploiting the potential of digital technology for some time, in areas such as documentary disclosure in heavy commercial cases, for instance. Digital technology has now reached the court too. The traditional paper-based court process is giving way to digital process. Rather than issue proceedings in paper form, proceedings may be issued digitally online and may be similarly defended.[1] Documentary evidence may be uploaded digitally. On its part, the court will soon be able to manage claims digitally.

Digitisation is seen as a way of providing better government by promoting better policy outcomes, better services and increasing transparency in public

[1] See the use of CE-File: CPR PD510 and https://www.gov.uk/guidance/ce-file-system-information-and-support-advice (accessed 9 March 2019).

Adrian Zuckerman, *Artificial Intelligence in the Administration of Justice* In: *The Civil Procedure Rules at 20.* Edited by: Andrew Higgins, Oxford University Press (2020). © the several contributors.
DOI: 10.1093/oso/9780198863182.003.0020.

services.[2] Today, vehicle and TV licensing is managed by online apps; delivery of welfare benefits is partly automated with algorithmic calculation of benefits; NHS records are digitised.

Tasks that were the preserve of highly trained professionals are increasingly performed by machines. These include medical diagnoses,[3] flying aeroplanes, deciding mortgage applications and assisting in the choice of employees, as well as driving cars. These are tasks which require not only familiarity with data, but also call for contextualised judgment in an infinite combination of circumstances. We are steadily moving beyond the traditional human-controlled, software-powered, computers. The driverless car, for instance, is operated by an AI system which makes instant judgments in multiple situations impossible to anticipate or to program in advance.

The performance of such skills rests on machine learning, on algorithms that continually evolve new ways of achieving a stated objective. Machine learning (ML) refers to 'a set of methods that can automatically detect patterns in data, and then use the uncovered patterns to predict future data, or to perform other kinds of decision making under uncertainty (such as planning how to collect more data)'.[4] ML systems are able to adapt to new circumstances and to detect and extrapolate patterns using statistical models.[5] Such systems can effectively perform a specific task without using explicit instructions, relying instead on patterns and inferences. The use of such systems has given rise to all sorts of problems to do with transparency of, and accountability for, machine generated outcomes, which governments are now confronting.[6]

Closer to home, automation is being introduced in administrative justice with the aim of reducing error rate and encouraging the involvement of applicants.[7] The courts have been slow in taking advantage of computer technology and are only now beginning to see digitisation of paper work, something that lawyers have been doing in their offices for years.

[2] C Harlow and R Rawlings, *Proceduralism and Automation: Challenges to the Values of Administrative Law* in E Fisher, J King and A Young (eds), *The Foundations and Future of Public Law (in honour of Paul Craig)* (OUP, 2019). And see OECD, *The E-Government Imperative* and *E-Government for Better Government* (2003).

[3] W Nicholson Price II, *Artificial Intelligence in the Medical System: Four Roles for Potential Transformation*, Public Law and Legal Theory Research Papers Series, no. 631, May 2019

[4] Kevin P Murphy, *Machine Learning: A Probabilistic Perspective* (MIT Press, 2012) 1.

[5] Stuart Russell and Peter Norvig, *Artificial Intelligence: A Modern Approach*, 3rd ed (Pearson, 2009) 2.

[6] Australian Government, *Automated Assistance in Administrative Decision-Making: Better Practice Guide* (Commonwealth of Australia, 2007). And see Aaron M Bornstein, 'Is Artificial Intelligence Permanently Inscrutable?' *Nautilus* (1 September 2016); Melissa Perry, 'iDecide: Administrative Decision-Making in the Digital World' (2017) 91 *ALJ* 29.

[7] Eva Micheler and Anna Whaley, 'Regulatory Technology: Replacing Law with Computer Code' (2018) LSE Law, Society and Economy Working Papers 14/2018, available online.

A bolder use of digital technology is contemplated for the proposed Online Court. The main objective of this proposal is to offer access to court to the many litigants who cannot afford to pay for legal representation. This digital system is meant to enable unrepresented persons who have no knowledge of the law to produce a coherent legal position and conduct litigation. It is hoped that the Online Court will alleviate the acute problems created by the rapidly increasing number of litigants in person, who disrupt the courts' efforts to effectively manage cases.

The procedure was proposed by Lord Justice Briggs in his report *Civil Courts Structure Review: Final Report 2016.*[8] It consists of three stages: (1) an automated online triage stage designed to help litigants without lawyers articulate their claim in a form which the court can resolve, and to upload their key documents and evidence; (2) a conciliation stage, handled by a Case Officer; and (3) a determination stage, where disputes that cannot be settled are determined by a Judge, by whichever of a face to face trial, video or telephone hearing or determination on the documents is the most appropriate.

Stage 1 triage is the most significant from a technological point of view, the key to the success of the scheme, and the only aspect relevant to our discussion. It is meant to guide litigants through an analysis of their grievance in such a way as to produce a document capable of being understood both by opponents and by the court. Lord Justice Briggs provided an example.[9] Suppose that A has a dispute with B, a builder, relating to works carried out at her house. After entering the online court (OC) Portal, A would be asked to identify the object of her complaint by reference to a series of tick-boxes which might include her bank, her holiday company, her next-door neighbour and her builder. Having ticked 'Builder' the software would present new questions designed to elicit the essential nature of the dispute, for example whether it was about the quality of the work, the amount charged or delays in completion. Ticking (or clicking) the appropriate box would reveal further successive pages, including a page requiring A to identify B and provide B's contact details, to state whether the building works were covered by an agreement and, if in writing, requiring A to attach any electronic copy, or scan or photograph, so that the central document required by the court for determination of the dispute would be lodged electronically from the outset. Further automated pages would question A as to the details of the dispute, in much the same way as a high street solicitor might do when taking instructions from a client.

8 Civil Courts Structure Review: Final Report, The Online Court 36, [6.4].
9 Civil Courts Structure Review: Interim Report, The Online Court 77, [6.8].

The outcome of this process would be a computer-generated document (on screen) broadly approximating to particulars of claim, which A would be invited to approve or amend, and certify as true. The system would then deliver that document and any accompanying evidence electronically to B, or request B to go online by sending B a letter or a text to his mobile phone. The software would then automatically take B through an investigatory process in broadly the same way, so as to generate the electronic approximation of a defence. This online service may assist some lay persons to present a legal case, but only in the limited range of situations programmed into the software. Compared with what AI can do, this is a rather primitive system; it is comparable to equipping a driverless car with software that can only react to situations programmed into the computer in advance but not to others.

As in any other industry, computer technology is likely to see increasing penetration into legal services. The process is bound to be gradual, driven by economic considerations and influenced by the experience gained in other fields.[10] The better AI performs in improving profitability, the greater will be incentives to adapt and develop AI systems for ever more ambitious ends.

The incentive of cost savings is illustrated by the use of AI in disclosure. The disclosure rules were developed at a time when documents were hand written and therefore expensive to produce and to store. Today documents are electronically generated and archived at virtually no cost. While in the past commercial litigation might have involved documents running into hundreds or a few thousands, today electronic communications may run to hundreds of thousands or even millions. The old practices are wholly unsuited to this new reality, not least because the traditional way of managing disclosure could now consume large numbers of billable hours and exorbitant cost.

Digital documentation requires a digital approach to the disclosure process. To begin with simple technology was used, such as identifying documents by searching for key words.[11] This method of search saved some cost but could not identify relevant documents outside its key word remit. As a result, a considerable amount of man-hour would still need to be invested to see whether anything relevant was missed. It did not take long before more sophisticated technology was developed capable of identifying relevant documents, whether or not key words were used, and with greater reliability of outcomes. The rules now contemplate employment of software driven analytical tools.[12]

[10] Richard E Susskind, *The End of Lawyers? Rethinking the Nature of Legal Services* (OUP, 2008).
[11] CPR 31B PD 25.
[12] CPR 51U PD 9.6.

Disclosure is not the only area of legal practice where AI is being used. It is also used in transactional practice, to scan voluminous documentation to identify any unusual, unexpected, or disadvantageous contractual causes.[13] The technology may be in its infancy, but it is not going to take long before machine learning is harnessed to develop more independent systems. As a final example, it is worth mentioning the use of AI by the Serious Fraud Office to identify documents covered by legal professional privilege. To do so the AI system had to apply a concept rather than limit itself to key words.[14]

Had the legal profession been unwilling to develop digital systems to streamline legal services and cutting down labour-intensive costly practices, they would not have been able to resist client pressure forever. Many corporate clients use AI to run their own business operations and are unlikely to tolerate legal practices which consume many lawyer-hours when they believe that the tasks in question can be done more cheaply by machines.

The use of digital technology is continually expanding. The Online Court scheme mentioned above is being replicated in the tribunals, dealing with matters such as bail applications, tax appeals and employment litigation.[15] Digital means would be available to persons appealing decisions to submit to the appeal tribunal an online appeal, including their materials and evidence, to engage in dispute resolution efforts, to follow the progress of their case, and engage in continuous online resolution to the pint of final determination. If these initiatives proved successful, there would be pressure to expand such facilities to other areas of litigation, including high value claims.

Once established, Online Court procedures are unlikely to remain static. Better and more ambitious systems may well become available. Suppose a system developed, which unlike the proposed Online Court, was not limited by a pre-programmed decision-tree method of reasoning, but could independently research a legal topic and articulate a legal position. The option of upgrading to the new system may become tempting, especially if it was shown that it would facilitate wider access to justice and at lower cost. For litigants of limited means AI would be preferable to navigating litigation by themselves.

[13] Joe Dysart, *AI Removes the Drudgery from Legal Due Diligence*, Communications of the ACM, January 2019, https://cacm.acm.org/news/233886-ai-removes-the-drudgery-from-legal-due-diligence/fulltext, accessed 23 May 2019; Lauri Donahue, 'A Primer on Using Artificial Intelligence in the Legal Profession' *Harvard Journal of Law & Technology*, January 2018, https://jolt.law.harvard.edu/digest/a-primer-on-using-artificial-intelligence-in-the-legal-profession, accessed 23 May 2019

[14] Danny Shaw, *A digital game or a powerful weapon against boardroom crime?*, BBC News, September 2018, https://www.bbc.co.uk/news/uk-45399995, accessed 23 May 2019

[15] Report of Senior President of Tribunals, *The Modernisation of Tribunals—Innovation Plan for 2019/2020.*

And, in the course of time, even better resourced litigants may reckon that AI pleadings represent good value for money.

As already mentioned, machine learning is employed in the disclosure process. In this context it known in England as predictive coding.[16] It involves training computers to learn how to discriminate between relevant and irrelevant documents. The training takes the form of an initial selection by lawyers of sample of relevant documents, which the computer analyses for common features and grades them according to the degree of relevance. The results are reviewed by lawyers. Where lawyers have overruled an AI outcome, the information is fed back into the algorithm so that it can adjust its definitions and learn from its mistakes. The process is repeated between three and four times until optimal results are achieved.

Perhaps of greater significance in the present context is the fact that by means of computer technology it is now possible to assess the probability of legal outcomes in contested cases with a fair degree of probability. Again, it is not suggested that a machine that can determine degrees of relevance or predict the outcome of litigation has the required skills for providing comprehensive advocacy. Existing systems cannot articulate arguments or provide explanations for outcomes. But efforts are underway to develop machine systems that not only produce an outcome but also explain the inferences drawn by machines in terms understood by humans. The systems are known as explainable AI or XAI.[17]

While I consider the implications of AI replacing lawyers in advocacy and adjudication, it should be noted that intermediate positions are also possible. AI may augment lawyers tasks in advocacy and adjudication. Lawyers and judges may choose to employ AI systems to analyse precedents, review literature and suggest outcomes while maintaining the final say.

AI lawyers

AI use in legal services is bound to increase gradually. To start with, AI use would probably be limited to simple low value claims or used only by those

[16] *Pyrrho Investments Ltd and another v MWB Property Ltd and others* [2016] EWHC 256 (Ch).

[17] An XAI program has been developed at the Defence Advanced Research Projects Agency in the US that 'will have the ability to explain their rationale, characterise their strengths and weaknesses, and convey an understanding of how they will behave in the future.': D. Gunning, 'Explainable Artificial Intelligence (XAI)' (Defense Advanced Research Projects Agency Project Information) at https://www.darpa.mil/program/explainable-artificial-intelligence (last accessed 16 August 2018). J.A. Kroll et al, 'Accountable Algorithms' (2017) 165 *University of Pennsylvania Law Review* 633.

who cannot afford lawyers. But as AI systems improved, and it is in the nature of such systems to continually get better, they would likely be employed for increasingly more serious tasks and their use may prove financially tempting even for those who can afford lawyers, gradually restricting the scope for human legal practice. The process is bound to be incremental, consisting of small steps at a time, unlikely to be seen as revolutionary or threatening at any particular stage. Little by little AI could reach a level of penetration where AI systems have become a workable alternative to lawyer services.[18] It is therefore appropriate to consider how the legal profession would fare against a background where litigation services, including advocacy, can be handled by AI systems.

One of the most visible effects of such developments would be a shrinking of the legal profession.[19] The public at large may not lament the loss of lawyers' jobs, given that their services are beyond the reach of a majority of the population. But their decline may represent a serious loss of potential judicial talent, and this may well harm the public interest. Since judges in common law systems are appointed from the ranks of practitioners, the pool for judicial appointments would slowly contract as more lawyers cease practising. For a profession to thrive and progressively develop the quality of its output, it requires continual recruitment at entry level. The entry level of practice is important because it provides the cadre from which the more talented and skilful emerge. For instance, one cannot expect the emergence of outstanding brain surgeons capable of performing complicated or delicate operations, unless there is a sufficiently large number of newly qualified surgeons who develop experience in performing many routine operations. Since only a small proportion of the beginners would develop the highest skills, the larger the number of entrants, the more likely it is that some outstanding talent would emerge.[20]

[18] John O. McGinnis and Russell G. Pearce, 'The Great Disruption: How Machine Intelligence Will Transform the Role of Lawyers in the Delivery of Legal Services' 82 *Fordham L Rev* 3041.

[19] It seems that this process is already underway with large firms restricting recruitment. 'Legal services sector forecasts 201702025' The Law Society, August 2018, 14, https://www.lawsociety.org.uk/support-services/research-trends/legal-services-sector-forecasts/, accessed 24 May 2019; Jane Croft, 'More than 100,000 legal roles to become automated' *Financial Times*, March 2016, https://www.ft.com/content/c8ef3f62-ea9c-11e5-888e-2eadd5fbc4a4, accessed 24 May 2019.

[20] Malcolm Gladwell, *Outliers: The Story of Success* (Penguin Books, 2008), puts forward the '10,000-Hour Rule', claiming that the key to achieving world-class expertise in any skill is, to a large extent, a matter of practising the correct way, for a total of around 10,000 hours, though the authors of the original study this was based on have disputed Gladwell's usage. K. Anders Ericsson, 'Training history, deliberate practise and elite sports performance: an analysis in response to Tucker and Collins review—what makes champions?' (2012) 47 *Br J Sports Med* bjsports–2012–091767. doi:10.1136/bjsports-2012-091767. ISSN 0306-3674. PMID 23111333.

The importance of size for the development of high professional expertise or qualitative standards may perhaps be less important than it seems; there seems to be a surplus of lawyers in the market, yet lawyers with specific specialist skills are in short supply. But there is another aspect of the correlation between quantity and quality that should be of concern: competition. Competition contributes to qualitative improvement in most fields of human endeavour. We may therefore assume that the smaller quantitatively profession is, the less competition is likely to take place and that, therefore, the slower qualitative advances would be. There is therefore reason to suppose that once the use of AI becomes widespread in legal representation, the profession will diminish both quantitatively and qualitatively.[21] Since lawyers have an important social function of acting as a buffer between the individual and the state or other powerful actors, the shrinking of this buffer will leave many defenceless against authorities and the rich.

It is possible to imagine a time when AI systems would be able to provide a fully articulated justification for a particular conclusion or explain how the conclusion was reached. If so, it is possible to assume that AI systems would be capable of learning to produce pleadings. Could AI then be employed to provide legal representation? The answer could be obtained empirically. A panel of experts would be presented with briefs written by AI and by lawyers without being told which is which. The panel would be asked to rank the briefs on the basis of the quality and persuasiveness. If it turns out that AI briefs are as good as, or better than, the average human brief (HI), then AI representation become a possible alternative to HI representation.[22]

If AI competence was satisfactory, we would expect litigants to employ AI rather than HI representation for a number of reasons. First, because, it may be assumed, it would be considerably cheaper than human lawyers, and the cost would be fixed in advance. Affordability and cost predictability would be critical for clients of modest means, who are unable to pay for lawyers. Such clients may well employ computer representation even if they thought it inferior to lawyers because it would be better than no expert assistance at all. Secondly, AI would guarantee a good level of legal expertise whereas at present professional

[21] Even as things stand, competition is not wholly efficient, nor does it fully serve the public interest. See D. L. Rhode, *In the Interests of Justice: Reforming the Legal Profession* (Oxford University Press, 2003), 3–8; A. Boon, J. Flood, and J. Webb, 'Postmodern professions? The fragmentation of legal education and the legal profession' (2005) 32 *J of Law and Society* 473–492.

[22] Eugene Volokh, 'Chief Justice Robots' (2019) 68 *Duke Law Journal* 1145–1146 <https://scholarship.law.duke.edu/dlj/vol68/iss6/2>.

services are variable and clients are in no position to assess the standard of the service they actually receive.

It might be objected that AI lacks the human or personal touch required for effective representation. The retort, by way of analogy to medical practice, would probably be: if a computer performs medical diagnoses reliably enough, it's intelligent enough to be a good diagnostician and we should therefore use it notwithstanding that no human doctor is involved. The same could be said about legal representation: if an AI system articulates a sound reasoned argument it would make sense to use it notwithstanding that it was done by a machine.

AI judges

If a good proportion of legal work were done by AI systems, a point may be reached where it might be asked: If AI representation has been found to be satisfactory, would there be any sense in insisting that adjudication should always be carried out by judges rather AI machines? The answer would depend on whether AI could do as good a job as human judges. Again, an empirical test may help provide the answer. We could test the performance of AI judges by the same method proposed for comparing the output of AI lawyers with that of human lawyers. That is to say, we could put before a panel of experts AI and human judgments for blind assessment of their quality. If it turned out that computers could deliver reasonable adjudication of disputes, the Government may be tempted by the saving in cost to expand the jurisdiction of the Online Court and employ machines rather than humans for at least some tasks of dispute resolution. The economic argument would be bolstered if, as seems likely, judges expanded the use of AI systems to research legal issues, analyse evidence and the like. For it could then be argued that given that AI systems are in any event used in adjudication, judges could be replaced by machines with no loss of quality.

The use of AI in adjudication would have certain advantages over human judges: machines are able to avoid mistakes of reasoning and unconscious bias. Unconscious bias in adjudication is both widespread and virtually impossible to overcome.[23] Machine processing power is superior; machines can scan and analyse vast amounts of data and therefore ensure greater

[23] A. Zuckerman, 'No justice without lawyers—the myth of an inquisitorial solution' (2014) 33 *Law Quarterly Review* 355, 361. Machine systems that learnt their skills from human activity can replicate and embed in their function human bias. However, it is practically possible to eliminate bias from machine system, whereas it is impossible to do so from human judgment. Danielle Keats Citron,

compatibility with principle and precedent. Accordingly, AI adjudication would have far greater capacity to analyse and synthesise than humans. Machines would be capable of depths of reasoning which are beyond the reach of individuals or even teams of expert lawyers. AI would have instant access to the entire body of legal sources: legislation in all its varieties, databases of all decisions that have ever been made in all the courts and tribunals, and to the entire body of books and learned articles that have ever been written. Legal research that might take humans hundreds of hours could be done much more comprehensively and in minutes by machines, and at a fraction of the present cost. AI adjudication could reach levels of consistency unimaginable today.

As against AI adjudication it may be said that an important aspect of adjudication is the human touch, consisting of fellow feeling, empathy, and compassion. Computers, it might be said, know nothing of the human touch since they use only mathematical algorithms. Attractive though this argument is at first sight it may be overstated. The great majority of cases are determined by a straightforward application of the law to the facts, without appeal to the extra dimension of the human touch. Second, there are signs that human judges already defer to machines, as in the case of assessing the risk of reoffending.

Besides, it is not necessarily safe to assume machines cannot acquire something resembling the human touch. The human touch comes into adjudication in a variety of ways. Most prominently, it comes into play in the exercise of judicial discretion. However, discretion is not restraint-free, it does not offer judges complete freedom to decide as the whim takes them. Judicial discretion must be exercised judicially; ie within the limitations of established principles.[24] AI can learn these principles and operate within their bounds just as it learns every other aspect of human legal reasoning.[25] AI may well be better at operating the principles of adjudication advocated by Professor Ronald Dworkin, which involve the integration into legal thinking of widely held moral and political

'Technological Due Process' (2007) 85 *Washington University Law Review* 1262, https://heinonline.org/HOL/LandingPage?handle=hein.journals/walq85&div=38&id=&page=&t=1558668547>

[24] Ronald Dworkin, '*Judicial discretion.*' in R Bellamy, Ed, *The Rule of Law and the Separation of Powers* (Routledge, 2017), Ch 7

[25] Machines using unsupervised learning systems can pick up patterns such as equitable considerations. N. Kasabov, 'Evolving fuzzy neural networks for supervised/unsupervised online knowledge-based learning' (2001) 31 *IEEE Transactions on Systems, Man, and Cybernetics, Part B (Cybernetics)* 902–918.

principles.[26] The Herculean task imagined by Dworkin is more likely to be successfully undertaken by computers than by humans.

But let us assume that even if AI adjudication systems were able to exercise judicial discretion as humans do, we would still want to retain a human override to allow for a human touch in some special unforeseeable circumstances. This could be done while at the same time using AI for some judicial tasks. We could train machines to flag cases which require complex exercise of discretion or consideration of important policies of welfare or of social morality, so they could be reviewed by human judges. We might even be able to train AI to flag cases where the result is unexpected or of a kind not encountered before so that it may be reviewed with a human touch. We should therefore be able to devise AI systems that can leave room for human input in borderline cases, or in wholly novel situations or in evolving fields, such as legal aspects of AI.

AI appeal

Let us now assume that AI adjudication has become an acceptable method for the resolution of civil proceedings in at least some cases. This raises the question whether any room is left for AI review of AI decisions at first instance. It is to be assumed that any AI system used for first instance adjudication would be the best available at the time, and that it will continually improve by means of machine learning. There would therefore be no point in a further level of AI review since it will employ the same algorithm. And, if a better algorithm for adjudication was developed, it would replace any existing system employed at first instance.

Appeal from AI to human instance

Since we have excluded an AI appeal the next question is whether we should retain a human appeal system so that judges could review AI decisions at first instance. The advantage of a human appeal would be that a panel of specialised and experienced legal experts would have the last word regarding AI decisions. In this way we would retain the advantage of a tribunal consisting of panels of three or more judges, reaching decisions after thorough discussion from

[26] For an illuminating discussion see B Sheppard, '*Warming Up to Inscrutability: How Technology Could Challenge Our Concept of Law* (2018) 68 *U Tor LJ* 36, 59 *et seq*.

different angles and with different personal experiences. More importantly, such an arrangement would retain the dominance of humans in the application of the law and its development.

But maintaining human dominance is not going to be easy in a world where some adjudication is delivered by machines. Machine processing superiority calls into question the usefulness of human review of AI adjudication. Where AI judgments would be based on a far larger database than humans can absorb, it is difficult to see how humans could meaningfully review AI decisions. Suppose an appeal is made against an otherwise well-founded AI judgment at first instance, which took account of all the relevant legislation, precedents, and academic commentary, and gave due weight to all the considerations that need to be taken into account. On what grounds might a human appeal court reverse such an AI judgment? Might not human reasoning be more likely to induce error rather than correct mistakes?

Appellate review is meant to correct mistakes, such as misinterpretation of legislation or of precedent, or correct errors caused by unfounded factual conclusion. However, such mistakes would be unlikely where AI is employed, at any rate after some initial practice.

AI: adversarial process and legitimacy

Assuming that AI systems became the standard form of adjudication at first instance, we now need to consider the impact that such development would have on the adversarial process. I take the adversarial process to mean that each party to a dispute has a right to present its arguments and evidence, and is provided with an opportunity to respond to, and challenge, the opponent's arguments and evidence. Once the parties have had their say, it is for the court to reach a decision on the basis of the arguments and evidence that parties have presented. Court litigation is essentially a tri-partite institution: claimant, defendant, and an adjudicator.

Suppose AI provides legal representation before an AI court. The claimant's AI machine would receive input from the claimant: the claimant's account of the relevant events giving rise to the claim, the claimant's witness accounts or expert opinions and the like. Let us assume that the claimant's AI (CAI) has examined all the background legal data (legislation, precedents, etc) and has concluded that if the claimant's allegations remain unchallenged the result would be a decision in the claimant's favour. The defendant's AI system (DAI) would perform a similar exercise on the basis of the data provided by the defendant and may conclude that the defendant would prevail.

However, at the point at which the claimant's and defendant's respective AI systems have access to all the materials that the claimant and defendant have provided, they are bound to agree what the outcome would be, assuming that both systems employ the same algorithms and have equal processing power. It is also assumed that the court would be using the same AI system. This assumption reflects the present set up, in the sense that lawyers invoke the same rules, principles, and arguments that would persuade judges who follow the same rules of reasoning on issues and fact and law. Put differently, legal arguments are deployed against a background of a shared normative environment; the same legislative sources, the same general principles, cultural precepts, reasoning processes, and the like.

Once the CAI and DAI have processed the entire body of data submitted by all the parties, in the context of all available legal material, the machines are bound to reach the same conclusion and for the same reasons. This will make redundant any further resort to the court AI system, which, as postulated, employs the same algorithms and has access to the same data. There would therefore be no need to employ different systems because machines would collapse the entire adversarial system into one computer operation. The whole adversarial process which now consists of various steps taken at various time intervals, would become an almost instantaneous process.

Such mutation of the adversarial process would lead to far reaching consequences. The first victim would be disappearance of the court as a physical presence, as a place where disputants go to seek justice. The concept of a day in court will no longer signify an opportunity to go before a judge occupying a place in space and time who pays attention and shows respect to parties and witnesses. There simply would be no day in court. Yet, the day in court is of itself a source of satisfaction which inspires a sense of justice even in those who come out of the legal process with empty hands. For it is an acknowledgement of the humanity and autonomy of the losing party and of his or her as deserving of respect and concern.

An inevitable consequence of the loss of the day in court would be the decline of publicity. A legal process that takes place inside a machine is invisible. Yet, transparency of judicial process is one of the cornerstones of the administration of justice, whose motto has been: 'justice must not only be done but must also be seen to be done'. As Lord Diplock put it, 'the way that courts behave cannot be hidden from the public ear and eye this provides a safeguard against judicial arbitrariness or idiosyncrasy and maintains the public confidence in the administration of justice'.[27] Transparency reduces the scope for ill-informed and malicious criticism of the court, contributes to the determination of truth by encouraging people to come forward with information and by discouraging falsehood. By bringing into the open moral, social, and legal issues, the open trial promotes public debate that is so important to the democratic shaping of moral and legal rules, and the public understanding of the justice system. Lastly, the sight of effective and fair proceedings enhances public confidence in the administration of justice and thereby promotes respect for the law and its institutions.

The rule of law and court authority are underpinned by legitimacy. Legitimacy is the acceptance by the public that legal institutions have a right to demand compliance. The rule of law cannot be maintained by brute force, it relies on wide and instinctive acceptance of legal authority. Compliance with the law is less due to fear of sanction and far more to the widespread belief amongst the population that legal institutions are entitled to dictate our conduct. Public acceptance of court authority is influenced by the confidence that the community has in its moral, as well as its legal, authority. Judges are trusted to do justice because they feel and think like us, share our moral outlook and social consciousness, and adhere to the same values. It is hard to see how machines, which have no consciousness, can generate this kind of public trust. Under a system where adjudication is performed by inanimate machines in the invisible ether, the legitimacy of the court would decline and the rule of law would no longer be sustainable as it is today. Machine justice may have many advantages in terms of economy, consistency, and speed but the legitimacy deficit is a real threat to social wellbeing.

[27] *A-G v Leveller Magazine Ltd* [1979] AC 440 at 450, [1979] 1 All ER 745 at 750, HL. See also *Home Office v Harman* [1982] 1 All ER 532 at 303, (HL). The ECtHR regards the public character of court proceedings as important for the protection of litigants from the abuse of procedural rights which, in conditions of secrecy, may go unchecked: *Axen v Germany* A/72, (1983) 6 E.H.R.R. 195 at [25] (ECtHR). See S. Goldstein, *The Utility of the Comparative Perspective in Understanding, Analysing and Reforming Procedural Law* (University of Oxford, The Institute of European and Comparative Law, Oxford, 1999).

Name Index

For the benefit of digital users, indexed terms that span two pages (e.g., 52–53) may, on occasion, appear on only one of those pages.

General Index

Tables and figures are indicated by *t* and *f* following the page number

For the benefit of digital users, indexed terms that span two pages (e.g., 52–53) may, on occasion, appear on only one of those pages.